MYSTERY AND DETECTIVE FICTION IN THE LIBRARY OF CONGRESS CLASSIFICATION SCHEME

Some Books by MICHAEL BURGESS / ROBERT REGINALD

MYSTERY AND DETECTIVE FICTION

IN THE LIBRARY OF CONGRESS CLASSIFICATION SCHEME

EVA SORRELL &

MICHAEL BURGESS

THE BORGO PRESS

MMXI

Borgo Cataloging Guides
ISSN 0891-9615
Number Two

MYSTERY AND DETECTIVE FICTION

SECOND EDITION

Published by Wildside Press LLC

www.wildsidebooks.com

DEDICATION

(of Eva Sorrell):

In loving memory of my Dad,
Richard Allan.

(of Michael Burgess):

To the Memory of **Vivian C. Prince** (1908-2004), who first taught me cataloging at USC;

and

For **Buckley Barrett**,
and the good days we shared at ole Cal State.

CONTENTS

INTRODUCTION TO
THE SECOND EDITION

This cataloging manual provides a guide to the cataloging of criminous literature (*i.e.*, mystery and detective fiction, spy stories, and suspense novels, with peripheral coverage of horror, gothic, and macabre literature) in the Library of Congress classification scheme, including subject headings, classification numbers, author main entries and literature numbers, and the main entries and class numbers of artists, motion pictures, radio programs, television programs, and comics associated with the field.

The list of authors was originally derived partly from *Crime Fiction, 1749-1980: A Comprehensive Bibliography*, by Allen J. Hubin; *Mystery Index*, by Steven Olderr; the mystery collection of the John M. Pfau Library, California State University, San Bernardino; Ruth Winfeldt's Scene of the Crime bookstore; plus research; and has now been supplemented through CD-ROMs extending Hubin's database through 2000 (Locus Press), plus additional research by Eva Sorrell.

We have concentrated on those authors apt to be found in the modern collection of mystery literature, most of them active in the last two decades; fewer writers of horror fiction are included than those working exclusively in detective fiction. Also listed are mainstream authors who have written one or two books in the genre. Those authors not included are generally obscure even within the field; most also lack literature numbers.

We presume here some general familiarity on the reader's

part with cataloging theory and practice, and with the LC classification scheme in particular, although we have made an effort to explain general principles and specific applications more fully for the neophyte or fan. The science of cataloging may be compared to the practice of law, in that it uses a set of logical rules, plus a series of precedents interpreting those rules, to determine how specific books may be classed. As with the law, cataloging has many quirks, inconsistencies, and exceptions, and may be applied differently by different practitioners; nonetheless, behind these rules and practices there is an established, logical body of thought that is intended to work in a certain fashion and to do certain things. We have tried to provide here some basis for understanding how LC classifies literature, so that even the beginner may gain some insight into what those little numbers on the spine of a book actually mean.

The release in 1978 of the Second Edition of the *Anglo-American Cataloging Rules* (popularly known as AACR2) forced librarians everywhere to reconsider how they would catalog and classify literature of all kinds. Most academic institutions that used LC classification decided to adopt the new rules, and to class the work of creative writers with the national literatures and time periods to which they belonged. However, literature numbers created by the Library of Congress itself were only applied to the cataloging of new works (and their authors) as they were deposited in that institution's collection; so that even today there remain many older writers who have not yet been assigned valid literature numbers by LC's catalogers (since the older materials in the collection were not retroactively reclassed)—and who may never receive such numbers.

Consequently, many academic libraries began assigning their own numbers, creating conflicts in the assignments that were rectified only in local collections. Our revised cataloging manual has only accepted literature numbers generated by the Library of Congress itself.

One must recognize, however, that even LC has occasionally

created internal contradictions and conflicts in the way that it has handled a particular writer's fiction, and that such anomalies are not easily resolved. We've done the best we can here to rectify LC usage wherever possible. We have tried to maintain the principle that one author has one literature number, unless that individual has created works originally in more than one language (for example, Vladimir Nabokov).

This new edition substantially expands the database of the original, 1987 version, increasing the number of authors covered from roughly 6,500 to 15,062, as well as adding 602 call numbers to writers listed in the First Edition that previously had none, and making numerous corrections or changes to the author main entries. Similarly, the section on Mystery Motion Pictures has increased from 17 entries to 109, a new section on Mystery Radio Programs has been added, and the Television and Comic Book sections have grown by tremendous amounts. Every chapter has been reviewed, revised, and added to.

* * * * * * *

I (Michael) couldn't have completed the original edition without the backing of the late Arthur E. Nelson, formerly Library Director at California State University, San Bernardino, and Marty Bloomberg, Associate Library Director Emeritus, who supported my requests for release time, graciously allowed me the use of the facilities, and were always interested in "talking shop."

I (Eva) want to thank Michael for all of his help and support —from cataloging questions to work on this book and many things in between.

Our joint thanks also to Johnnie Ann Ralph, Emerita Dean of Library at CSUSB, and César Caballero, our present Dean, who consistently and enthusiastically supported our research efforts. Finally, our blessings to our long-suffering spouses, Mary and Chad, for allowing us to play with this book—when perhaps we should have been doing something else!

Eva Sorrell,
Principal Cataloger;
Michael Burgess,
Librarian Emeritus;

John M. Pfau Library,
California State University,
San Bernardino
11 November 2011

1-1. SUBJECT HEADINGS
INTRODUCTION

This section includes Library of Congress subject headings in use through 2011. Also listed are the standard subdivisions that have actually been used by LC; these may seem repetitious to the casual observer, but we have included them anyway to provide the researcher with some indication where the major scholarly activity in the field is taking place.

Most of the entries require little explanation. Books about fictitious characters customarily receive two headings: the first includes the name of the character plus description appellation [*e.g.*, "Tarzan (Fictitious character)"]; the second reflects the name of the writer (*e.g.*, "Burroughs, Edgar Rice, 1875-1950—Characters—Tarzan"). Such books are classed under the author's literature number as criticism.

Books about the work of a specific writer use the main entry of the writer as established under AACR2, plus the standard subdivision, "Criticism and interpretation." A biography or autobiography generally has as its subject the name of the author, without further subdivision. There are, of course, many other standard subdivisions which may be applied to authors, some of which may be found below under the sample entries for Agatha Christie and Sir Arthur Conan Doyle.

Library of Congress Subject Headings have historically included headings that indicate what a work *is* rather than what it is *about* (*e.g.*, "Horror tales"). It has not been easy to differentiate in the catalog which headings represent that form/genre and which headings are for works about that form/genre.

In 2007, LC began a project to develop genre/forms terms on a discipline-by-discipline basis. As *Library of Congress Genre/ Form Terms (LCGFT)* are approved, new authority records are issued using X55 tags for the terms and cross-references (155, 455, 555). These are placed in the 655 tag of the bibliographic record. LC has not developed fiction terms yet. Recognizing that it will likely be years before all disciplines are completed, LC has determined that it is appropriate for libraries to code genre/form headings as such rather than as topical headings. LCSH headings that can be applied as genre/form headings in addition to being used as topical headings are marked with an asterisk.

We have used pre-AACR2 filing rules in this section only because the breakdowns of subdivisions are easier to follow with this arrangement. Completists should note that current rules actually require filing these headings on a strict, word-by-word basis, thus intermingling national subheadings (*e.g.*, "Detective and mystery stories, American") with the subdivisions under the heading, "Detective and mystery stories."

1-2. MYSTERY SUBJECT HEADINGS

Action and adventure films. *
  —Asia—Catalogs.
  —Asia—History.
  —Asia—History and criticism.
  —Catalogs.
  —China—Hong Kong—Catalogs.
  —China—Hong Kong—History.
  —China—Hong Kong—History and criticism.
  —Handbooks, manuals, etc.
  —History and criticism.
  —History and criticism—Juvenile literature.
  —India—History.
  —India—History and criticism.
  —Italy—History—20th century.
  —Philippines—History and criticism.
  —Political aspects—United States.
  —Social aspects—United States.
  —United States—History and criticism.
Action and adventure television programs. *
  —Great Britain—History and criticism.
  —Turkey—History and criticism
  —United States—Catalogs.
  —United States—History and criticism.
Adventure and adventurers in literature.
  —Congresses.

—Exhibitions.
—Periodicals.
Adventure films—see: Action and adventure films.
Adventure stories. *
    —Authorship.
    —Authorship—Juvenile literature.
    —Bibliography.
    —Book reviews.
    —Comic books, strips, etc.
    —Comic books, strips, etc.—Juvenile literature.
    —Comic books, strips, etc.—Periodicals.
    —Dictionaries—German.
    —Fiction.
    —History and criticism.
    —History and criticism—Congresses.
    —History and criticism—Periodicals.
    —History and criticism—Theory, etc
    —Illustrations.
    —Juvenile fiction.
    —Juvenile literature.
    —Periodicals.
    —Periodicals—Publishing—France—History—20th
century.
    —Sound recordings.
    —Themes, motives.
    —Translations into German.
    —Translations into Russian.
    —Translations into Russian—Bibliography.
Adventure stories, Afrikaans. *
Adventure stories, American. *
    —Bibliography.
    —Bibliography—Catalogs.
    —Bibliography—Handbooks, manuals, etc.
    —Databases.
    —Dictionaries.
    —Encyclopedias.

—Examinations—Study guides.

—Film adaptations.

—History and criticism.

—History and criticism—Handbooks, manuals, etc.

—History and criticism—Juvenile literature.

—History and criticism—Sources.

—Illustrations.

—Islamic influences.

—Juvenile fiction.

—Periodicals.

—Periodicals—Collectors and collecting.

—Periodicals—Indexes.

—Stories, plots, etc.

—Study and teaching.

—Television adaptations.

—Translations into Danish.

—Translations into French.

—Translations into German.

Adventure stories, Australian. *

—History and criticism.

Adventure stories, Canadian. *

—Bibliography.

—Drama.

—History and criticism.

Adventure stories, English. *

—Adaptations.

—Appreciation—France.

—Appreciation—Germany.

—Appreciation—Sweden.

—Bibliography.

—Bibliography—Exhibitions.

—Bibliography—Handbooks, manuals, etc.

—Bio-bibliography.

—Dictionaries.

—Encyclopedias.

—Examinations—Study guides.

—Film adaptations.
—Handbooks, manuals, etc.
—History and criticism.
—History and criticism—Congresses.
—History and criticism—Handbooks, manuals, etc.
—History and criticism—Juvenile literature.
—History and criticism—Theory, etc.
—Illustrations.
—Televisions adaptations.
—Translations from French—History and criticism.
Adventure stories, French. *
—History and criticism.
—History and criticism—Congresses.
—Translations into English.
Adventure stories, French-Canadian. *
Adventure stories, Galician. *
Adventure stories, German. *
—History and criticism.
Adventure stories, Greek. *
—History and criticism.
Adventure stories, Japanese. *
—History and criticism.
Adventure stories, Latin. *
—History and criticism.
Adventure stories, Russian. *
—20th century—History and criticism.
Adventure stories, Scottish. *
Adventure stories, South African (English)
Adventure stories, Spanish. *
Adventure stories, Spanish—History.
Adventure stories, Spanish—History and criticism.
Adventure stories, Swiss. *
Black mask.
—Indexes.
Bond, James (Fictitious character)
—Bibliography.

—Comic books, strips, etc.

—Congresses.

—Dictionaries.

—Drama.

—Encyclopedias.

—Fiction.

—Juvenile fiction.

—Juvenile literature.

—Maps.

—Miscellanea.

—Parodies, imitations, etc.

—Pictorial works.

—Songs and music.

Brigands and robbers—China—Fiction.

Brigands and robbers—China—Pearl Delta River—Fiction.

Brigands and robbers—Comic books, strips, etc.—Juvenile fiction.

Brigands and robbers—Equator—Fiction.

Brigands and robbers—England—19th century—Fiction.

Brigands and robbers—England—Fiction.

Brigands and robbers— Fiction.

Brigands and robbers—India—Fiction.

Brigands and robbers—Italy—Sardinia—Fiction.

Brigands and robbers—Italy—Sicily—Fiction.

Brigands and robbers—Juvenile fiction.

Brigands and robbers—Juvenile literature.

Brigands and robbers—Juvenile poetry.

Brigands and robbers—Mexico—Fiction.

Brigands and robbers—Mexico—History—19th century—Fiction.

Brigands and robbers—Spain—History—19th century—Fiction.

Brigands and robbers in literature.

Charlie Chan films. *

—Catalogs.

—Drama.

—Encyclopedias.
—History and criticism.
Christie, Agatha, 1890-1976.
    —Adaptations—Handbooks, manuals, etc.
    —Bibliography.
    —Characters.
    —Characters—Dictionaries.
    —Characters—Handbooks, manuals, etc.
    —Characters—Hercule Poirot.
    —Characters—Jane Marple.
    —Criticism and interpretation.
    —Criticism and interpretation—Congresses.
    —Dramatic works.
    —Encyclopedias.
    —Fiction.
    —Film adaptations.
    —Film adaptations—Handbooks, manuals, etc.
    —Friends and associates.
    —Handbooks, manuals, etc.
    —Homes and haunts—England—Devon.
    —Homes and haunts—England—Guidebooks.
    —Illustrations.
    —Juvenile literature.
    —Language.
    —Marriage.
    —Miscellanea.
    —Notebooks, sketchbooks, etc.
    —Parodies, imitations, etc.
    —Quotations.
    —Settings.
    —Settings—Guidebooks.
    —Settings—Maps.
    —Songs and music.
    —Stage history.
    —Stories, plots, etc.—Handbooks, manuals, etc.
    —Themes, motives.

—Translations into Slovenian—History and criticism.
—Travel—Iraq.
—Travel—Middle East.
—Travel—Syria.
Classification—Books—Detective and mystery stories.
Code and cipher stories. *
—History and criticism.
Code and cipher stories, American. *
Code and cipher stories, Japanese. *
Crime—Fiction.
Crime—Fiction—Bibliography.
Crime—Fiction—Comic books, strips, etc.
Crime—Fiction—History and criticism.
Crime—Fiction—Periodicals.
Crime and criminals in literature—see: Crime in literature.
Crime and criminals in mass media—see: Crime in mass media.
Crime in literature.
—Bibliography.
—Bibliography—Exhibitions.
—Congresses.
—Dictionaries.
—Encyclopedias.
—Handbooks, manuals, etc.
—Indexes.
—Juvenile literature.
—Study and teaching (Higher)
Crime in mass media.
—Congresses.
—History—19th century.
—History—20th century.
—Juvenile literature.
—Periodicals.
—United States—Case studies.
Crime on television.
—Congresses.

—Encyclopedias.
—Germany.
—History and criticism.
—Social aspects.
Dast magazine—Indexes.
Detective and mystery comic books, strips, etc. *
—History and criticism.
—Juvenile literature.
—Periodicals.
Detective and mystery films. *
—Argentina—Dictionaries—Spanish.
—Catalogs.
—Dictionaries.
—Egypt—Drama.
—Encyclopedias.
—Exhibitions.
—France—History and criticism.
—Germany—History and criticism.
—Great Britain—History and criticism.
—History and criticism.
—History and criticism—Congresses.
—History and criticism—Indexes.
—Italy—Catalogs.
—Italy—History and criticism.
—Italy—Periodicals.
—Mexico—History and criticism.
—Miscellanea.
—Parodies, imitations, etc.
—Reviews.
—Southwestern States—History and criticism.
—Spain—Barcelona—History and criticism.
—Spain—History and criticism.
—Sweden—History and criticism.
—United States—History and criticism.
—United States—History and criticism—Juvenile
literature.

—United States—Plots, themes, etc.
Detective and mystery plays. *
    —Authorship.
    —Bibliography.
    —Dictionaries.
    —History and criticism.
    —Parodies, imitations, etc.—Drama.
    —Stories, plots, etc.
Detective and mystery plays, American. *
    —History and criticism.
Detective and mystery plays, Canadian. *
Detective and mystery plays, English. *
    —Encyclopedias.
    —History and criticism.
    —Stories, plots, etc.
Detective and mystery plays, Russian. *
Detective and mystery radio programs. *
    —Europe, French-speaking.
    —France.
    —Germany—Catalogs.
    —United States.
    —United States—Authorship.
    —United States—Catalogs.
Detective and mystery stories. *
    —19th century—Periodicals.
    —20th century—History and criticism.
    —20th century—Periodicals.
    —Authorship.
    —Authorship—Bibliography.
    —Authorship—Handbooks, manuals, etc.
    —Authorship—Juvenile literature.
    —Authorship—Marketing—Periodicals.
    —Authorship—Periodicals.
    —Authorship—Sex differences.
    —Authorship—Vocational guidance.
    —Awards.

—Bibliography.
—Bibliography—Catalogs.
—Bibliography—Exhibitions.
—Bibliography—Methodology.
—Bibliography—Periodicals.
—Bio-bibliography.
—Bio-bibliography—Dictionaries—French.
—Bio-bibliography—Dictionaries—German.
—Book reviews.
—Book reviews—Periodicals.
—Collectors and collecting—Periodicals—Indexes.
—Congresses.
—Developing countries—History and criticism.
—Dictionaries.
—Dictionaries—French.
—Dictionaries—German.
—Dictionaries—Italian.
—Encyclopedias.
—Film adaptations.
—First editions—Bibliography.
—History and criticism.
—History and criticism—Bibliography.
—History and criticism—Bibliography—Catalogs.
—History and criticism—Congresses.
—History and criticism—Data processing.
—History and criticism—Indexes.
—History and criticism—Periodicals.
—History and criticism—Periodicals—Indexes.
—History and criticism—Theory, etc.
—Illustrations.
—Juvenile fiction.
—Juvenile literature.
—Juvenile software.
—Juvenile sound recordings.
—Literary collections.
—Miscellanea.

—Miscellanea—Periodicals.
—Parodies, imitations, etc.
—Periodicals.
—Periodicals—History.
—Periodicals—Indexes.
—Problems, exercises, etc.
—Psychological aspects.
—Publishing.
—Publishing—France—History—20th century.
—Publishing—France—Paris—History.
—Publishing—Switzerland—Geneva—History.
—Reference books—Bibliography.
—Research.
—Social aspects.
—Software.
—Stories, plots, etc.
—Study and teaching.
—Study and teaching (Elementary)
—Technique.
—Technique—Bibliography.
—Technique—Drama.
—Technique—Humor.
—Television adaptations.
—Themes, motives.
—Translations into Chinese.
—Translations into Danish.
—Translations into English.
—Translations into English—Bibliography.
—Translations into Finnish—Bibliography.
—Translations into French—Bio-bibliography.
—Translations into German.
—Translations into Hungarian.
—Translations into Japanese—History and criticism.
—Translations into Korean.
—Translations into Korean—Periodicals.
—Translations into Russian.

—Translations into Spanish.
—Translations into Swedish.
—Translations into Turkish—History and criticism.
—Women authors—Bio-bibliography.
Detective and mystery stories, Afrikaans. *
—Bibliography.
Detective and mystery stories, American. *
—Appreciation.
—Bibliography.
—Bibliography—Periodicals.
—Bio-bibliography.
—Bio-bibliography—Dictionaries.
—Bio-bibliography—Periodicals.
—Book reviews.
—Chronology.
—Dictionaries.
—Encyclopedias.
—Examinations, questions, etc.
—Examinations—Study guides.
—Film adaptations.
—Handbooks, manuals, etc.
—History and criticism.
—History and criticism—Bibliography.
—History and criticism—Congresses.
—History and criticism—Guidebooks.
—History and criticism—Handbooks, manuals, etc.
—History and criticism—Juvenile literature.
—History and criticism—Periodicals.
—History and criticism—Periodicals—Indexes.
—History and criticism—Study and teaching (Higher)
—History and criticism—Theory, etc.
—Indexes.
—Juvenile fiction.
—Maps.
—Miscellanea.
—Periodicals.

—Periodicals—Indexes.
—Sources.
—Southern States—History and criticism.
—Southwestern States—History and criticism.
—Stories, plots, etc.
—Study and teaching.
—Television adaptations.
—Translations into French—Bibliography
—Translations into French—Dictionaries.
—Translations into German.
—Translations into Italian.
—Translations into Japanese—History and criticism.
—Translations into Norwegian.
—Translations into Spanish.
—Translations into Swedish.
—Washington (D.C.)—Miscellanea.
—Women authors—History and criticism.
Detective and mystery stories, Argentine. *
—Adaptations.
—History and criticism.
—History and criticism—Congresses.
Detective and mystery stories, Australian. *
—Bibliography.
—First editions—Bibliography.
—History and criticism.
Detective and mystery stories, Austrian. *
—Translations into English.
Detective and mystery stories, Belarusian. *
Detective and mystery stories, Belgian (French) *
—History and criticism.
Detective and mystery stories, Bengali. *
—Comic books, strips, etc.
—History and criticism.
—Translations into English.
Detective and mystery stories, Brazilian. *
Detective and mystery stories, Bulgarian. *

—History and criticism.
Detective and mystery stories, Burmese. *
    —Periodicals.
Detective and mystery stories, Canadian. *
    —Bibliography.
    —Bio-bibliography.
    —History and criticism.
    —Juvenile fiction.
    —Stories, plots, etc.
Detective and mystery stories, Caribbean (French) *
    —History and criticism.
Detective and mystery stories, Catalan. *
    —History and criticism.
Detective and mystery stories, Chilean. *
Detective and mystery stories, Chinese. *
    —Translations into English.
Detective and mystery stories, Columbian. *
    —History and criticism.
Detective and mystery stories, Commonwealth (English) *
    —History and criticism.
Detective and mystery stories, Croatian. *
Detective and mystery stories, Cuban. *
    —History and criticism.
Detective and mystery stories, Czech. *
Detective and mystery stories, Danish. *
    —Bibliography.
    —History and criticism.
Detective and mystery stories, Dominican. *
Detective and mystery stories, Dutch. *
    —History and criticism.
Detective and mystery stories, English. *
    —Adaptations.
    —Appreciation.
    —Appreciation—Japan.
    —Appreciation—Societies, etc.
    —Appreciation—Societies, etc.—History—20th

century—Sources.
—Appreciation—United States.
—Bibliography.
—Bibliography—Catalogs.
—Bibliography—Indexes.
—Bio-bibliography.
—Bio-bibliography—Dictionaries.
—Bio-bibliography—Periodicals.
—Book reviews.
—Chronology.
—Dictionaries.
—Encyclopedias.
—Examinations, questions, etc.
—Film adaptations.
—Handbooks, manuals, etc.
—History and criticism.
—History and criticism—Bibliography.
—History and criticism—Bibliography—Indexes.
—History and criticism—Congresses.
—History and criticism—Guidebooks.
—History and criticism—Juvenile literature.
—History and criticism—Periodicals.
—History and criticism—Periodicals—Indexes.
—History and criticism—Theory, etc.
—Illustrations.
—Illustrations—Catalogs.
—Indexes.
—Library resources.
—Miscellanea.
—Parodies, imitations, etc.
—Periodicals.
—Periodicals—Indexes.
—Scottish authors.
—Societies, etc.
—Sources.
—Stories, plots, etc.

—Stories, plots, etc.—Handbooks, manuals, etc.
—Television adaptations.
—Translations into Danish—Bibliography.
—Translations into French—Bibliography.
—Translations into French—History and criticism.
—Translations into German.
—Translations into Irish.
—Translations into Italian.
—Translations into Japanese—History and criticism.
—Translations into Norwegian.
—Translations into Portuguese.
—Translations into Russian.
—Translations into Swedish.
—Translations into Swedish—Bibliography.
—Women authors.
—Women authors—History and criticism.
Detective and mystery stories, Finnish. *
—Bibliography.
—History and criticism.
Detective and mystery stories, French. *
—Bibliography.
—Bibliography—Exhibitions.
—Bio-bibliography.
—French-speaking countries—History and criticism.
—History and criticism.
—History and criticism—20th century.
—Illustrations—Catalogs.
—Influence.
—Publishing—History—20th century.
—Translations into English.
—Translations into Japanese—History and criticism.
Detective and mystery stories, French-Canadian. *
—Bibliography.
Detective and mystery stories, Frisian. *
Detective and mystery stories, German. *
—Bibliography.

—Bio-bibliography.
—Germany (East)—Bibliography.
—Germany (East)—History and criticism.
—Germany (West)—History and criticism.
—History and criticism.
—History and criticism—Bibliography.
—History and criticism—Congresses.
—Translations into English.
—Translations into Hebrew.
—Translations into Japanese—History and criticism.
Detective and mystery stories, Greek. *
Detective and mystery stories, Greek (Modern) *
Detective and mystery stories, Hebrew. *
Detective and mystery stories, Hindi. *
—History and criticism.
Detective and mystery stories, Hungarian. *
—History and criticism.
Detective and mystery stories, Icelandic. *
—History and criticism.
Detective and mystery stories, Indic (English) *
Detective and mystery stories, Israeli. *
Detective and mystery stories, Italian. *
—20th century—History and criticism—Congresses.
—21st century—History and criticism—Congresses.
—Bibliography.
—History and criticism.
—History and criticism—Congresses.
—Italy—Turin—History and criticism.
—Publishing—History—20th century.
Detective and mystery stories, Japanese. *
—Authorship.
—Comic books, strips, etc.
—Dictionaries—Japanese.
—Exhibitions.
—History and criticism.
—Periodicals.

—Periodicals—Indexes.
—Stories, plots, etc.
—Translations into Chinese.
—Translations into English.
—Translations into English—History and criticism.
—Yearbooks.
Detective and mystery stories, Kannada. *
Detective and mystery stories, Korean. *
—History and criticism.
—Periodicals.
Detective and mystery stories, Latin American. *
—Bio-bibliography—Dictionaries.
—History and criticism.
—History and criticism—Dictionaries.
—Translations into English.
Detective and mystery stories, Latvian. *
Detective and mystery stories, Lithuanian. *
Detective and mystery stories, Marathi. *
Detective and mystery stories, Mexican. *
—History and criticism.
Detective and mystery stories, New Zealand. *
—History and criticism.
Detective and mystery stories, Norwegian. *
—History and criticism.
—Translations into Danish.
Detective and mystery stories, Pacific Island (English) *
—Themes, motives.
Detective and mystery stories, Polish. *
—Translations into Ukrainian.
Detective and mystery stories, Portuguese. *
—History and criticism.
Detective and mystery stories, Romanian. *
—History and criticism.
Detective and mystery stories, Russian. *
—Bibliography.
—Bio-bibliography.

—History and criticism.
—Periodicals.
—Translations into English.
—Translations into German.
Detective and mystery stories, Sanskrit. *
Detective and mystery stories, Scandinavian. *
—Bio-bibliography—Dictionaries—French.
Detective and mystery stories, Scottish. *
Detective and mystery stories, South African (English) *
—Bibliography.
Detective and mystery stories, Spanish. *
—History and criticism.
Detective and mystery stories, Spanish American. *
—History and criticism.
—Translations into English.
Detective and mystery stories, Swedish. *
—Bibliography.
—History and criticism.
—Translations into English.
Detective and mystery stories, Swiss. *
—Bibliography.
—History and criticism.
Detective and mystery stories, Tamil. *
Detective and mystery stories, Turkish. *
—Translations into English.
Detective and mystery stories, Ukrainian. *
Detective and mystery stories, Venezuelan. *
Detective and mystery stories, Vietnamese. *
Detective and mystery television programs. *
—Comic books, strips, etc.
—Encyclopedias.
—France—History and criticism.
—France—History and criticism—Congresses.
—Germany
—Germany—History and criticism.
—Germany (West)

—Great Britain.
—Great Britain—History and criticism.
—History and criticism.
—Sweden—History and criticism.
—United States.
—United States—20th century—History and criticism.
—United States—Encyclopedias.
—United States—History and criticism.
—United States—History and criticism—Congresses.
—United States—Miscellanea.
Detectives in art.
Detectives in literature.
—Bibliography.
—Bibliography—Indexes.
—Congresses.
—Dictionaries.
—Miscellanea.
—Periodicals.
—Pictorial works.
Detectives in mass media.
—Congresses.
—Dictionaries.
—Handbooks, manuals, etc.
—History.
—Miscellanea.
—United States.
Doyle, Arthur Conan, Sir, 1859-1930.
—Adaptations.
—Allusions.
—Appreciation—Denmark—Bibliography.
—Appreciation—Europe, German-speaking—Bibliography.
—Appreciation—France.
—Appreciation—Japan.
—Appreciation—Scandinavia.

—Authorship.
—Bibliography.
—Bibliography—Catalogs.
—Bibliography—Exhibitions.
—Bibliography—Indexes.
—Characters.
—Characters—Dictionaries.
—Characters—John H. Watson.
—Characters—Maps.
—Characters—Men.
—Characters—Sherlock Holmes.
—Characters—Sherlock Holmes—Bibliography.
—Characters—Sherlock Holmes—Bibliography—
Catalogs.
—Characters—Sherlock Holmes—Dictionaries.
—Characters—Sherlock Holmes—Encyclopedias.
—Characters—Sherlock Holmes—Handbooks,
manuals, etc.
—Characters—Sherlock Holmes—Indexes.
—Characters—Sherlock Holmes—Library resources.
—Characters—Sherlock Holmes—Maps.
—Characters—Sherlock Holmes—Miscellanea.
—Characters—Sherlock Holmes—Periodicals.
—Characters—Sherlock Holmes—Periodicals—
Indexes.
—Characters—Sherlock Holmes—Pictorial works.
—Characters—Sherlock Holmes—Societies, etc.
—Chronology.
—Correspondence.
—Criticism and interpretation.
—Film adaptations.
—First editions—Bibliography.
—Friends and associates.
—Illustrations.
—Illustrations—Library resources.
—Indexes.

—Influence.
—Influence—Bibliography.
—Interviews.
—Juvenile literature.
—Knowledge and learning.
—Knowledge—Cooking.
—Knowledge—England.
—Knowledge—Europe.
—Knowledge—France.
—Knowledge—Japan.
—Knowledge—Literature.
—Knowledge—London (England)
—Knowledge—Manners and customs.
—Knowledge—Medicine.
—Knowledge—Naval art and science.
—Knowledge—Navigation.
—Knowledge—Occultism.
—Knowledge—Performing arts.
—Knowledge—Psychology.
—Knowledge—Spiritualism.
—Literary style.
—Manuscripts—Catalogs.
—Manuscripts—Facsimiles.
—Parodies, imitations, etc.
—Parodies, imitations, etc.—Bibliography.
—Parodies, imitations, etc.—History and criticism.
—Parodies, imitations, etc.—Juvenile fiction.
—Periodicals.
—Philosophy.
—Quotations.
—Settings.
—Societies, etc.
—Societies, etc.—History—20th century.
—Societies, etc.—History—20th century—Sources.
—Societies, etc.—Periodicals.
—Sources.

—Stage history.

—Technique.

—Television adaptations.

—Translations into Danish—Bibliography.

—Translations into Swedish—Bibliography.

—Translations into Yiddish.

—Travel—Australia.

—Travel—United States.

Doyle, Arthur Conan, Sir, 1859-1930. Adventures of Sherlock Holmes.

—Bibliography.

Doyle, Arthur Conan, Sir, 1859-1930. Complete Sherlock Holmes.

—Indexes.

Doyle, Arthur Conan, Sir, 1859-1930. Return of Sherlock Holmes.

—Bibliography.

Doyle, Arthur Conan, Sir, 1859-1930. Sign of the four.

—Bibliography.

Dracula, Count (Fictitious character)

—Bibliography.

—Comic books, strips, etc.

—Comic books, strips, etc.—Periodicals.

—Congresses.

—Dictionaries—French.

—Drama.

—Fiction.

—Handbooks, manuals, etc.

—Juvenile drama.

—Juvenile fiction.

—Juvenile literature.

—Miscellanea.

—Name.

—Pictorial works.

—Poetry.

Espionage in literature.

—Bibliography.
—Bibliography—Catalogs.
—Dictionaries.
—Indexes.
—Maps.
—Social aspects.
Espionage in motion pictures.
Fan magazines. *
—Directories.
—Indexes.
—Periodicals.
Fanzines—see: Fan magazines.
Fleming, Ian, 1908-1964.
—Bibliography.
—Bibliography—Catalogs.
—Characters—James Bond.
—Characters—James Bond—Bibliography.
—Characters—James Bond—Congresses.
—Characters—James Bond—Dictionaries.
—Characters—James Bond—Maps.
—Correspondence.
—Criticism and interpretation.
—Film adaptations.
—Interviews.
—Knowledge—Occultism.
—Knowledge—Science.
—Library.
—Philosophy.
—Political and social views.
—Settings.
G-8 (Fictitious character)
Gangster films. *
—Caricatures and cartoons.
—Catalogs.
—China—Hong Kong—History and criticism.
—Egypt.

—Encyclopedias.
—Exhibitions.
—France—History and criticism.
—Great Britain—History and criticism.
—History and criticism.
—History and criticism—Juvenile literature.
—History and criticism—Periodicals.
—India.
—Israel.
—Italy—History and criticism.
—Japan—History and criticism.
—Miscellanea.
—Pictorial works.
—United States—Catalogs.
—United States—History and criticism.
—United States—History and criticism—Juvenile
 literature.
—United States—Plots, themes, etc.
Gangster television programs. *
—United States—History and criticism.
Gibson, Walter B. (Walter Brown), 1897-1985.
—Bibliography.
—Characters—Shadow.
Gothic fiction (Literary genre) *
—21st century—History and criticism.
—Bibliography.
—Bio-bibliography.
—Film adaptations—Congresses.
—History and criticism.
—History and criticism—Congresses.
Gothic fiction (Literary genre), American. *
—History and criticism.
—History and criticism—Handbooks, manuals, etc.
Gothic fiction (Literary genre), Australian. *
—History and criticism.
Gothic fiction (Literary genre), Canadian. *

—History and criticism.
Gothic fiction (Literary genre), English. *
    —History and criticism.
    —History and criticism—Handbooks, manuals, etc.
Gothic fiction (Literary genre), French. *
    —History and criticism.
Gothic fiction (Literary genre), German. *
    —History and criticism.
Gothic fiction (Literary genre), Italian. *
    —History and criticism.
Gothic fiction (Literary genre), Russian. *
    —19th century.
    —History and criticism.
Gothic fiction (Literary genre), Spanish. *
    —History and criticism.
Gothic literature. *
    —Great Britain—History and criticism.
    —History and criticism.
    —Ukraine.
    —United States—History and criticism.
Gothic revival (Literature)
    —Australia.
    —Bibliography.
    —Bio-bibliography.
    —Bio-bibliography—Dictionaries.
    —Canada.
    —China.
    —Congresses.
    —Dictionaries.
    —Encyclopedias.
    —England—History and criticism.
    —England—London.
    —English-speaking countries.
    —English-speaking countries—Bibliography.
    —English-speaking countries—History—20th
        century.

—Europe.

—France.

—Germany.

—Great Britain.

—Great Britain—Bibliography.

—Great Britain—Handbooks, manuals, etc.

—Great Britain—History.

—Great Britain—History—18th century.

—Great Britain—History—18th century—
Bibliography.

—Great Britain—History—19th century.

—Great Britain—History—20th century.

—Great Britain—Sources.

—Great Britain—Study and Teaching.

—Handbooks, manuals, etc.

—History and criticism.

—History and criticism—Congresses.

—History and criticism—Periodicals.

—Influence.

—Ireland.

—Italy.

—Netherlands.

—New England.

—New Zealand.

—Norway.

—Ontario.

—Periodicals.

—Peru.

—Portugal.

—Portugal—Bibliography.

—Québec (Province)

—Russia.

—Scotland.

—Southern states.

—Spain.

—Study and teaching—Great Britain.

—Study and teaching—United States.
—Sweden.
—United States.
—United States—Abstracts.
—United States—Bibliography.
—United States—Handbooks, manuals, etc.
—United States—History—19th century.
—United States—History—20th century.
—United States—Study and teaching.
Hand-to-hand fighting, Oriental, in motion pictures—see: Martial arts films—History and criticism.
Heroes in art.
—Catalogs.
—Congresses.
—Exhibitions.
—Juvenile literature.
Heroes in literature.
—Bibliography.
—Congresses.
—Dictionaries—French.
—Exhibitions.
—Handbooks, manuals, etc.
—Juvenile literature.
—Study and teaching—United States.
Heroes in mass media.
—Case studies.
—Congresses.
—Dictionaries.
—Encyclopedias.
—History—20th century.
—United States—History—20th century
Heroes in motion pictures.
Hogan, Robert J.—Characters—G-8.
Holmes, Sherlock (Fictitious character)
—Appreciation—Japan.
—Bibliography.

—Bibliography—Catalogs.
—Bibliography—Exhibitions.
—Bibliography—Indexes.
—Chronology.
—Comic books, strips, etc.
—Comic books, strips, etc.—History and criticism.
—Comic books, strips, etc.—Juvenile literature.
—Criticism and interpretation.
—Dictionaries.
—Drama.
—Drama—Bibliography.
—Fiction.
—Handbooks, manuals, etc.
—In literature.
—Juvenile fiction.
—Juvenile literature.
—Library resources.
—Literary collections.
—Maps.
—Miscellanea.
—Parodies, imitations, etc.
—Periodicals.
—Periodicals—Indexes.
—Pictorial works.
—Poetry.
—Quotations, maxims, etc.
—Societies, etc.
—Societies, etc.—History—20th century—Sources.
Holmes, Sherlock (Fictitious character) in art.
Holmes, Sherlock (Fictitious character) in mass media.
Horror—Juvenile literature.
Horror—Juvenile poetry.
Horror—Literary collections.
Horror—Periodicals.
Horror comic books, strips, etc. *
—Great Britain—History and criticism.

—History and criticism.
—History and criticism—Periodicals.
—Italy—Dictionaries.
—Japan.
—Periodicals.
—Themes, motives.
—United States.
—United States—History and criticism.

Horror films. *
—Asia—Cross-cultural studies.
—Asia—History and criticism.
—Australia—History and criticism.
—Authorship.
—Bibliography.
—Biography.
—Brazil—History and criticism.
—Canada—History and criticism.
—Catalogs.
—Catalogs—Juvenile literature.
—Catalogs—Periodicals.
—Congresses—Drama.
—Dictionaries.
—Dictionaries—French.
—Dictionaries—German.
—Dictionaries—Italian.
—Encyclopedias.
—Europe—History and criticism.
—Examinations, questions, etc.
—Germany—History.
—Germany—History and criticism.
—Great Britain.
—Great Britain—History and criticism.
—Great Britain—Plots, themes, etc.
—History and criticism.
—History and criticism—Bibliography.
—History and criticism—Juvenile literature.

—History and criticism—Periodicals.
—Humor.
—Hungary—History and criticism.
—Interviews.
—Italy—Catalogs.
—Italy—History and criticism.
—Japan—Encyclopedias.
—Japan—History and criticism.
—Juvenile fiction.
—Juvenile literature.
—Korea (South) —History and criticism.
—Mexico—History and criticism.
—Mexico—Posters—Catalogs.
—Miscellanea.
—Parodies, imitations, etc.
—Parodies, imitations, etc.—Drama.
—Periodicals.
—Periodicals—History.
—Plots, themes, etc.
—Poetry.
—Posters—Exhibitions.
—Production and direction.
—Production and direction—Drama.
—Production and direction—Germany—History.
—Production and direction—Juvenile literature.
—Production and direction—United States.
—Psychological aspects.
—Reviews.
—Singapore.
—Social aspects—Germany.
—Spain—History and criticism.
—Spain—History and criticism—Congresses.
—Study and teaching.
—United States.
—United States—Catalogs.
—United States—History and criticism.

—United States—History and criticism—Handbooks, manuals, etc.
Horror in art.
    —Bibliography.
    —Exhibitions.
    —Juvenile literature.
    —Periodicals.
Horror in literature.
    —Congresses.
    —Psychological aspects.
Horror in mass media.
    —Bibliography.
    —Congresses.
    —Periodicals.
Horror plays. *
    —History and criticism.
Horror plays, American. *
Horror plays, English. *
    —History and criticism.
Horror plays, European. *
    —History and criticism.
Horror plays, French. *
    —History and criticism.
Horror plays, Italian. *
Horror radio programs. *
    —Encyclopedias.
    —United States—History.
Horror tales. *
    —Appreciation—Drama.
    —Appreciation—Scotland.
    —Authorship.
    —Authorship—Comic books, strips, etc.
    —Authorship—Juvenile literature.
    —Authorship—Periodicals.
    —Bibliography.
    —Bibliography—Catalogs.

—Bibliography—Periodicals.
—Bio-bibliography.
—Bio-bibliography—Juvenile literature.
—Collectibles—Catalogs.
—Dictionaries.
—Dictionaries—Italian.
—Drama.
—Geography—Guidebooks.
—History and criticism.
—History and criticism—Bibliography.
—History and criticism—Comic books, strips, etc.
—History and criticism—Congresses.
—History and criticism—Handbooks, manuals, etc.
—History and criticism—Periodicals.
—Illustrations.
—Miscellanea.
—Periodicals.
—Publishing—Great Britain—History—19th century.
—Publishing—United States—History—20th
 century.
—Reference books—Bibliography.
—Stories, plots, etc.
—Technique.
—Technique—Juvenile literature.
—Technique—Miscellanea.
—Translations into Czech.
—Translations into English.
—Translations into German.
—Translations into Hungarian.
—Translations into Italian.
—Translations into Spanish.
—Translations into Swedish.
—Women authors.
Horror tales, American. *
—20th century—History and criticism.
—Adaptations.

—Appreciation.
—Bibliography.
—Bio-bibliography.
—Book reviews—Periodicals.
—Comic books, strips, etc.
—Dictionaries.
—Encyclopedias.
—Examinations—Study guides.
—Hawaii.
—History and criticism.
—History and criticism—Bibliography.
—History and criticism—Congresses.
—History and criticism—Handbooks, manuals, etc.
—History and criticism—Juvenile literature.
—History and criticism—Periodicals.
—History and criticism—Theory, etc.
—Illustrations.
—Indiana.
—Juvenile fiction.
—Louisiana—New Orleans.
—Maine—Miscellanea.
—Miscellanea.
—New England.
—Periodicals.
—Poetry.
—Southern States.
—Study and teaching.
—Study and teaching (Secondary)
—Tennessee—Memphis.
—Texas—San Antonio.
—Translations into Czech.
—Translations into French.
—Translations into German.
—Translations into Hungarian.
—Translations into Spanish.
—Translations into Turkish.

—West (U.S.)—Miscellanea.
—Women authors.
—20th century.
Horror tales, Argentine. *
Horror tales, Australian. *
—History and criticism.
Horror tales, Brazilian. *
—History and criticism.
Horror tales, Canadian. *
—History and criticism.
—History and criticism—Theory, etc.
—Nova Scotia—Cape Breton Island.
Horror tales, Catalan. *
Horror tales, Chilean. *
Horror tales, Chinese. *
—History and criticism.
Horror tales, Czech. *
Horror tales, Dutch. *
Horror tales, English. *
—Adaptations.
—Adaptations—Juvenile literature.
—Bibliography.
—Bio-bibliography.
—Criticism, Textual.
—Dictionaries.
—Encyclopedias.
—Examinations—Study guides.
—Film adaptations.
—First editions—Bibliography.
—History and criticism.
—History and criticism—Bibliography.
—History and criticism—Congresses.
—History and criticism—Handbooks, manuals, etc.
—History and criticism—Juvenile literature.
—History and criticism—Periodicals.
—History and criticism—Theory, etc.

—Manuscripts—Facsimiles.
—Miscellanea.
—Periodicals.
—Stories, plots, etc.
—Study and teaching.
—Translations into Czech.
—Translations into German.
—Translations into Hungarian.
—Translations into Swedish.
—Women authors.
Horror tales, European. *
—History and criticism.
Horror tales, Finnish. *
Horror tales, French. *
—History and criticism
—Stories, plots, etc.
—Translations into English.
Horror tales, Galician. *
Horror tales, German. *
—History and criticism.
—Switzerland.
Horror tales, Greek (Modern) *
Horror tales, Hungarian. *
Horror tales, Italian. *
—History and criticism.
—Italy—Liguria.
—Italy—Rome.
—Italy—Tuscany.
Horror tales, Japanese. *
—History and criticism.
—Japan—Tokyo.
—Translations into English.
Horror tales, Korean. *
—Periodicals.
Horror tales, Mauritian (English) *
Horror tales, Mexican. *

—20th century.
—Mexico—Nuevo León (State)
Horror tales, Peruvian. *
Horror tales, Philippine (English) *
Horror tales, Polish. *
    —History and criticism.
    —Silesia—History and criticism.
Horror tales, Portuguese. *
    —Bibliography.
    —History and criticism.
Horror tales, Russian. *
    —History and criticism.
    —Translations into English.
Horror tales, Scottish. *
Horror tales, Spanish. *
    —History and criticism.
    —Spain—Andalusia.
    —Translations into English.
Horror tales, Spanish American. *
Horror tales, Uruguayan. *
Horror television programs. *
    —Catalogs.
    —Dictionaries.
    —Encyclopedias.
    —History and criticism.
    —Illinois—Chicago—History and criticism.
    —Miscellanea.
    —United States—Catalogs.
    —United States—History and criticism.
James Bond films. *
    —Caricatures and cartoons.
    —Drama.
    —Encyclopedias.
    —History and criticism.
    —History and criticism—Congresses.
    —History and criticism—Juvenile literature.

—Miscellanea.
—Pictorial works.
—Social aspects.
Law in art.
    —Catalogs.
    —Exhibitions.
    —History.
    —United States—Exhibitions.
Law in literature.
    —Bibliography.
    —Congresses.
    —Dictionaries.
    —History.
    —Juvenile literature—Abstracts.
    —Periodicals.
Law in mass media.
Law in motion pictures.
Legal stories. *
    —Authorship.
    —Bibliography.
    —England—London.
    —History and criticism
    —History and criticism—Congresses.
    —History and criticism—Theory, etc.
Legal stories, American. *
    —Bibliography.
    —History and criticism.
    —History and criticism—Juvenile literature.
    —Stories, plots, etc.
Legal stories, Burmese. *
Legal stories, Chinese. *
    —China.
    —History and criticism.
Legal stories, Czech. *
Legal stories, English. *
    —Bibliography.

—History and criticism.
—Stories, plots, etc.
Legal stories, Philippine (English) *
Legal stories, Portuguese. *
Mafia—Fiction.
Mafia in art.
Mafia in literature.
Mafia in motion pictures.
Marple, Jane (Fictitious character)
      —Fiction.
      —Drama.
Martial arts films. *
      —History and criticism.
Murder—Fiction.
Murder in art.
      —Exhibitions.
Murder in literature.
      —Bibliography.
      —Congresses.
      —Encyclopedias.
Murder in motion pictures.
      —Congresses.
Noir fiction. *
      —History and criticism.
      —History and criticism—Congresses.
Noir fiction, American. *
      —Appreciation—Germany.
      —Bibliography.
      —Bio-bibliography.
      —Dictionaries.
      —Film adaptations.
      —History and criticism.
      —History and criticism—Bibliography.
Noir fiction, Canadian. *
Noir fiction, Danish. *
      —Translations into English.

Noir fiction, English. *
    —Bibliography.
    —Film adaptations.
    —History and criticism.
Noir fiction, Italian. *
    —History and criticism.
    —History and criticism—Congresses.
    —Translations into English.
Noir fiction, Russian. *
    —Translations into English.
Noir fiction, Turkish. *
    —Translations into English.
Operator 5 (Fictitious character)
Penny dreadfuls. *
    —Bibliography.
    —Bibliography—Exhibitions.
    —Catalogs.
    —Exhibitions.
    —History and criticism.
Police—Fiction.
Police in literature.
    —Bibliography.
    —Congresses.
    —Dictionaries.
    —Periodicals.
Prisoners as authors.
    —Biography—Dictionaries.
    —Japan.
    —Netherlands.
    —Periodicals.
    —Puerto Rico.
    —United States.
    —Uruguay.
Prisons in literature.
Private investigators in art.
Private investigators in literature.

—Bibliography.
—Chronology.
—Dictionaries.
—Encyclopedias.
—Examinations, questions, etc.
—Handbooks, manuals, etc.
—Indexes.
—Juvenile literature.
—Maps.
—Miscellanea.
—Societies, etc.
Shadow (Fictitious character)
—Bibliography.
—Comic books, strips, etc.
—Comic books, strips, etc.—Periodicals.
—Fiction.
Sherlock Holmes films. *
—History and criticism.
—Stories, plots, etc.
Sherlock Holmes television programs. *
—History and criticism.
Spies in literature.
—Bibliography.
—Bibliography—Catalogs.
—Dictionaries.
—Indexes.
—Social aspects.
Spies in mass media.
Spy films. *
—Caricatures and cartoons.
—Catalogs.
—Dictionaries—Italian.
—Drama.
—Exhibitions.
—Great Britain—History and criticism.
—History and criticism.

—History and criticism—Indexes.
—Italy—Dictionaries.
—Italy—History and criticism.
—Parodies, imitations, etc.
—Social aspects.
—United States—History and criticism.
—United States—Miscellanea.
Spy stories. *
—Authorship.
—Bibliography.
—Bio-bibliography.
—Book reviews—Periodicals.
—History and criticism.
—History and criticism—Indexes.
—Periodicals.
—Periodicals—History.
—Periodicals—Indexes.
—Stories, plots, etc.
—Technique.
Spy stories, American. *
—Bibliography.
—Bio-bibliography.
—Bio-bibliography—Dictionaries.
—Dictionaries.
—Handbooks, manuals, etc.
—History and criticism.
—Periodicals.
Spy stories, Chinese. *
Spy stories, English. *
—Bibliography.
—Bibliography—Catalogs.
—Bio-bibliography.
—Bio-bibliography—Dictionaries.
—Dictionaries.
—Film adaptations.
—Handbooks, manuals, etc.

—History and criticism.
—History and criticism—Congresses.
—History and criticism—Theory, etc.
Spy stories, French. *
—Bibliography.
—History and criticism.
Spy stories, French-Canadian. *
—History and criticism.
Spy stories, German. *
—History and criticism.
Spy stories, Hungarian. *
Spy stories, Japanese. *
Spy stories, Korean. *
Spy stories, Romanian. *
Spy stories, Russian. *
Spy television programs. *
—Great Britain.
—Great Britain—History and criticism.
—United States.
—United States—History and criticism.
—United States—Miscellanea.
Steele, Curtis—Characters—Operator 5.
Stout, Rex, 1886-1975.
—Bibliography.
—Characters—Nero Wolfe.
—Nero Wolfe—Periodicals.
—Correspondence.
—Criticism and interpretation.
—Periodicals.
Terrorism in literature.
—Congresses.
Terrorism in mass media.
—Bibliography.
—Congresses.
—History—20th century.
—History—20th century—Congresses.

—Periodicals.
—Psychological aspects.
—United States.
Terrorism in motion pictures.
Terrorism on television.
Trials—Drama.
Violence in art.
    —Catalogs.
    —Congresses.
    —Exhibitions.
Violence in literature.
    —Bibliography.
    —Congresses.
    —History—Congresses.
    —History and criticism.
Violence in mass media.
    —Bibliography.
    —United States.
    —Venezuela.
Violence in motion pictures.
    —Congresses.
    —Exhibitions.
    —Juvenile literature.
Violence on television.
    —Bibliography.
    —China.
    —Congresses.
    —Cross-cultural studies.
    —Europe.
    —Great Britain.
    —Handbooks, manuals, etc.
    —Indonesia.
    —Juvenile literature.
    —Periodicals.
    —Psychological aspects.
    —Social aspects.

—Social aspects—Chile.
—Social aspects—Germany.
—Social aspects—United States.
—United States.
—United States—Juvenile literature.
—Venezuela.
Wolfe, Nero (Fictitious character)
—Fiction.
—Periodicals.

2-1. CLASSIFICATION NUMBERS
INTRODUCTION

This section is arranged by classification number, with an index of subjects at the end of the chapter. The Library of Congress classes criticism and anthologies into their respective national literatures, or, if none predominates, into PN (general literature). Most of the numbers listed herein consist of two parts, general classification plus subject cutter (which is immutable); to these must be added a first or second cutter (for main entry), and a publication date. Note that anthologies are established under title main entries, with added entries for their editors. Thus, a 1987 anthology of American mystery stories entitled *Deadly Games* might be classed in PS648.D4D43 1987.

General criticism of mystery and detective literature is classed in PN3448.D4, specific criticism of national literatures being classed into their respective tables (PS374.D4 for American detective fiction, PR830.D4 for British, etc.). Anthologies are similarly classed into PN6071.D45/PN6120.95.D45, PS648.D4, and PR1309.D4/PR1111.C7, respectively. Most mystery anthologies with even half of their stories by American writers are actually classed into PS648.D4. Collections of stories by one author are classed with that author's literature number, as is criticism on a specific writer. Criticism on two writers is classed under the first author's literature number; criticism on three or more authors is considered general or national criticism. There is no consistency in the assignment of subject cutters in the various national literatures—for mystery fiction, for example, one can find any range from D4-D7. Similarly, there is no consistency in the development of appropriate subject headings, which LC generates as needed.

2-2. MYSTERY CLASSIFICATION NUMBERS

CLASS GV (RECREATION. LEISURE)

Games and amusements—Parties. Party games and stunts—Puzzles—Other, A-Z.

GV1507
.D4—Detective and mystery puzzles

CLASS N (ART)

Drawing. Design. Illustration—Drawing for reproduction
—Illustration—Special subjects, A-Z

NC961.7
.D46—Detective and mystery fiction

—Periodical illustration—Special subjects, A-Z

NC968.5
.H6—Horror tales

CLASS P (LANGUAGES AND LITERATURE)

Philology. Linguistics—Communication. Mass Media—Special aspects—Other, A-Z

P96
    .C74-.C742—Crime and criminals
    .D4-.D42—Detectives
    .H46-.H462—Heroes
    .H59-.H592—Holmes, Sherlock
    .H65-.H652—Horror
    .M85-.M852—Murder
    .T47-.T472—Terrorism
    .V5-.V52—Violence

CLASS PC (ROMANIC LANGUAGES)

CATALAN LITERATURE

Texts—Prose. Prose fiction—Special, A-Z

PC3930
    .D5—Detective and mystery stories

CLASS PE (ENGLISH PHILOLOGY AND LANGUAGES)

Modern English—Language—Grammar—Readers—Special subjects, A-Z

PE1127
    .A29—Adventure
    .V5—Violence

CLASS PG (SLAVIC, BALTIC, AND ALBANIAN LANGUAGES)

BULGARIAN LITERATURE

History—Prose—Fiction—Special types of fiction, A-Z

PG1012.3
    .D48—Detective and mystery stories

BELARUSIAN LITERATURE

Collections—Prose—Fiction—Special topics or types, A-Z

PG2834.636
    .D48—Detective and mystery stories

RUSSIAN LITERATURE

Literary history and criticism—Prose fiction—Special kinds of fiction—Other, A-Z

PG3098
    .D46 015—Detective and mystery stories
    .G68—Gothic fiction

CZECH LITERATURE

Collections—Prose—Fiction—Special. By form or subject, A-Z

PG5031.6
    .D47—Detective and mystery stories
    .L44—Legal stories

POLISH LITERATURE

Collections—Prose—Special. By form or subject, A-Z

PG7148
   .C75—Crime
   .D47—Detective and mystery stories
   .H67—Horror

CLASS PL (LANGUAGES OF EASTERN ASIA, AFRICA, OCEANIA)

JAPANESE LITERATURE

History—Special topics, A-Z

PL721
   .C74—Crime
   .D45—Detective and mystery stories

History—Prose. Fiction—By period—Shōwa period, 1945-1989—Special topics, A-Z

PL747.82
   .D45— Detective and mystery stories

History—Prose. Fiction—By period—Heisei period, 1989- — Special topics, A-Z

PL747.87
   .D45—Detective and mystery stories

Collections—By period—Shōwa period, 1926-1989—Special topics, A-Z

PL755.67
    .D45—Detective and mystery stories

Collections—By period—Heisei period, 1989- —Special topics, A-Z

PL755.87
    .D45—Detective and mystery stories

KOREAN LITERATURE

History—Special topics, A-Z

PL957.5
    .D48—Detective and mystery stories

CHINESE LITERATURE

History—Special topics, A-Z

PL2275
    .D48—Detective and mystery stories
    .H47—Heroes and heroines
    .L38—Law. Legal novels

Collections—Fiction—Special topics, A-Z

PL2629
    .D48—Detective and mystery stories
    .H47—Heroes and heroines
    .L38—Law. Legal novels

CLASS PN (GENERAL LITERATURE)

Theory. Philosophy. Esthetics—Relation to and treatment of special elements and subjects—Other special—Topics, A-Z. [Class here works that are not limited to one form, nor to one national literature.]

PN56

    .A3—Adventure
    .C7—Crime
    .D4—Death
    .G7—Grotesque
    .H6—Horror
    .L33—Law
    .M85—Murder
    .R48—Revenge
    .T45—Terrorism
    .V53—Violence

Literary history—Juvenile literature—History and criticism—Special topics, A-Z

PN1009.5

    .D43—Death
    .H47—Heroes
    .V54—Violence

Drama—Special types

PN1952—Detective and mystery plays

Drama—Broadcasting—Radio broadcasts—Special topics, A-Z

PN1991.8
>.D47—Detective and mystery programs
>.H66—Horror radio programs

Drama—Broadcasting—Television broadcasts—Special topics, A-Z

PN1992.8
>.D48—Detective and mystery programs
>.H67—Horror
>.S67—Spy television programs
>.V55—Violence

Drama—Motion Pictures—Special topics, A-Z

PN1995.9
>.A3—Adventure films
>.C37—Charlie Chan films
>.C66—Crime films
>.D37—Death [in films]
>.D4—Detective and mystery films
>.G3—Gangster films
>.H3—Hand-to-hand fighting [in films]
>.H44—Heroes [in films]
>.H6—Horror films
>.I47—Indiana Jones films
>.J3—James Bond films
>.J8—Justice. Law [in films]
>.J87—Juvenile delinquency [in films]
>.M23—Mafia [in films]
>.M835—Murder [in films]
>.O84—Outlaws [in films]
>.P57—Police films
>.S297—Serial murderers [in films]
>.S5—Sherlock Holmes films
>.S68—Spy films

.S87—Suspense. Thrillers
.T46—Terrorism [in films]
.V47—Villains [in films]
.V5—Violence [in films]

PROSE. PROSE FICTION.

Prose. Prose fiction—Technique. Authorship—Special forms, subjects, etc. —Other, A-Z

PN3377.5
    .A37—Adventure stories
    .C75—Crime writing
    .D4—Detective and mystery stories
    .H67—Horror tales
    .S87—Suspense fiction

Prose. Prose fiction—Special topics—Special races, classes, types, etc., in fiction—Other, A-Z

PN3426
    .L37—Lawyers

Prose. Prose fiction—Special kinds of fiction. Fiction genres—Other, A-Z, [criticism]

PN3448
    .A3—Adventure stories
    .D4—Detective and mystery stories
    .L4—Legal novels
    .S66—Spy stories
    .S86—Suspense fiction

Collections of general literature—By subject, A-Z. [anthologies]

PN6071
    .A38—Adventure stories
    .B76—Brigands and robbers
    .D4—Death
    .D45—Detective and mystery stories
    .G24—Gambling
    .H4—Heroes
    .H727—Horror
    .M14—Mafia
    .P68—Prisons
    .R42—Revenge
    .R55—Rogues and vagabonds
    .S64—Spy stories. Spies
    .S78—Substance abuse
    .S92—Suspense
    .V5—Violence

Collections of general literature—Poetry—Special. By subject or form, A-Z

PN6110
    .C88—Crime. Criminals
    .H2—Heroism
    .P8—Prisons and prisoners
    .T5—Terror and wonder

Collections of general literature—Drama—Special. By subject or form, A-Z

PN6120
    .M9—Mystery plays (Modern)

Collections of general literature—Fiction—Special. By subject or form, A-Z [anthologies]

PN6120.95
    .D45—Detective and mystery stories

[the other cutters for PN6120.95 are the same as for PN6071]

Collections of general literature—Wit and humor—Special topics, A-Z [anthologies]

PN6231
    .C73—Crime. Criminals
    .E75—Espionage
    .M163—Mafia
    .P59—Police
    .R45—Revenge
    .T555—Terrorism

CLASS PQ (ROMANCE LITERATURE)

FRENCH LITERATURE

History—Special subjects, classes, etc. [criticism]

PQ145.1
    .D33—Death
    .H4—Heroes

PQ145.4
    .P7—Prisons

History—By period—20th century—Special topics, A-Z

PQ307
> .H4—Heroes
> .M87—Murder
> .P68—Prisons
> .V55—Violence

History—Prose and prose fiction—Special—Prose fiction—Special topics, A-Z [criticism]

PQ637
> .A37—Adventure stories
> .D4—Detective and mystery stories
> .V56—Violence

Collections—Prose—Special forms, subjects, etc., A-Z [anthologies]

PQ1276
> .D4—Detective and mystery stories

ITALIAN LITERATURE

History—Prose—Special—Prose fiction—Special forms and topics, A-Z [criticism]

PQ4181
> .A38—Adventure stories
> .D4—Detective and mystery stories

Collections—Prose—By subject, A-Z [anthologies]

PQ4249.6
> .D45—Detective and mystery stories
> .H66—Horror tales

SPANISH LITERATURE

History—Prose—General—Prose fiction—Special kinds, A-Z [criticism]

PQ6147
    .A38—Adventure stories
    .D47—Detective and mystery stories

Collections—Prose—Prose fiction—Special forms, A-Z [anthologies]

PQ6256
    .D47—Detective and mystery stories
    .H66—Horror tales

MEXICAN LITERATURE

Collections—Prose—Fiction—Special—By form or subject, A-Z [anthologies]

PQ7276.5
    .D43—Death
    .D48—Detective and mystery stories
    .H67—Horror tales
    .M87—Murder
    .V54—Violence

ARGENTINIAN LITERATURE

Collections—Prose—Fiction—Special—By form or subject, A-Z [anthologies]

PQ7776.5
.D43—Death
.D48—Detective and mystery stories
.H67—Horror tales
.M87—Murder
.V54—Violence

CLASS PR (ENGLISH LITERATURE)

HISTORY OF ENGLISH LITERATURE [criticism]

History—Special topics—Treatment of special classes. By subject, A-Z

PR151
.L37—Lawyers
.V56—Villains

History—By period—Modern—Special topics, A-Z

PR408
.C75—Criminals
.G68—Gothic literature
.V54—Violence

History—By period—17th century—Special topics, A-Z

PR438
.D44—Death

History—By period—18th century—Special topics, A-Z

PR448
.C75—Crime
.G6—Gothic literature

History—By period—19th century—Special topics, A-Z

PR468
    .A29—Adventure
    .D42—Death
    .M85—Murder
    .M87—Mystery

History—Drama—By period—Elizabethan era (1550-1640)—Special topics, A-Z

PR658
    .D4—Death
    .H42—Heroes
    .R45—Revenge

History—Drama—By period—20th century—Special topics, A-Z

PR739
    .D42—Death
    .D48—Detective and mystery stories

History—Prose—By form—Prose fiction. The novel—Special topics. A-Z [criticism]

PR830
    .A38—Adventure stories
    .C68—Courtroom fiction
    .C74—Crime
    .D37—Death
    .D4—Detective and mystery stories
    .H4—Heroes and heroines
    .L39—Law. Lawyers
    .P59—Police
    .P7—Prisons

.S65—Spy stories
.S87—Suspense
.T3—Tales of terror. Gothic tales. Horror tales
.T47—Terrorism

History—Prose—By form—Prose fiction. The novel—By period—18th century—Special topics. A-Z [criticism]

PR858
.D4—Detective and mystery stories

[other cutters for PR858 same as for PR830]

History—Prose—By form—Prose fiction. The novel—By period—19th century—Victorian era—Special topics. A-Z [criticism]

PR878
.D4—Detective and mystery stories.

[other cutters for PR878 same as for PR830]

History—Prose—By form—Prose fiction. The novel—By period—20th century—Special topics. A-Z [criticism]

PR888
.D4—Detective and mystery stories.

[other cutters for PR888 same as for PR830]

History—Prose—By form—Prose fiction. The novel—By period—21st century—Special topics. A-Z [criticism]

PR890
.D4—Detective and mystery stories.

[other cutters for PR890 same as for PR830]

COLLECTIONS OF ENGLISH LITERATURE [anthologies]

General collections—Special topics (Prose and verse), A-Z

PR1111
 .C7—Crime
 .G67—Gothic revival
 .G7—Grotesque

Drama—Special forms, A-Z

PR1259
 .D4—Detective and mystery plays
 .H67—Horror plays

Prose (General)—Special subjects and forms, A-Z

PR1309
 .A38—Adventure stories
 .C7—Crime. Criminals
 .D4—Detective and mystery stories
 .H55—Holmes, Sherlock (Fictitious character)
 .H6—Horror stories
 .P45—Penny dreadful
 .S7—Spy stories

AUSTRALIAN LITERATURE

History and criticism—History—Treatment of special subjects, classes, etc. —Classes, A-Z

PR9605.6
 .P75—Prisoners

CLASS PS (AMERICAN LITERATURE)

HISTORY OF AMERICAN LITERATURE [criticism]

History —Other classes of authors, A-Z

PS153
.P74—Prisoners

History—Treatment of special subjects—Other, A-Z

PS169
.H4—Heroes
.L37—Law

By period—19th century—Special topics, A-Z

PS217
.D4—Death
.L37—Law

By period—20th century—Special topics, A-Z

PS228
.D43—Death
.L37—Law

History—Prose—Special topics, A-Z

PS366
.P75—Prisoners
.S95—Swindlers and swindling

History—Special forms—Prose—Prose fiction—Special forms
and topics, A-Z. [criticism]

PS374

    .A35—Adventure stories
    .D34—Death
    .D4—Detective and mystery stories
    .D5—Dime novels
    .G68—Gothic revival
    .H67—Horror tales
    .L34—Law
    .P57—Police
    .V53—Victims

COLLECTIONS OF AMERICAN LITERATURE [anthologies]

Collections—Special topics (Prose and verse), A-Z

PS509

    .A3—Adventure stories
    .C7—Crime. Criminals
    .D4—Death
    .H59—Horror
    .M83—Murder
    .P6—Poe, Edgar Allan

Collections—Poetry—Special—By subject, A-Z

PS595

    .D42—Death
    .H62—Holmes, Sherlock (Fictitious character)
    .M683—Murder
    .V55—Violence

Collections—Prose (General)—Special forms and topics, A-Z

PS648

    .A36—Adventure stories
    .C7—Crime stories
    .D4—Detective and mystery stories
    .D55—Dime novels
    .H4—Heroes
    .H6—Horror tales
    .L3—Law and Lawyers
    .R48—Revenge
    .S85—Spy stories

CLASS PT (GERMANIC LITERATURES)

GERMAN LITERATURE

History—Prose—Prose fiction—Special kinds, A-Z [criticism]

PT747

    .A38—Adventure stories
    .D4—Detective and mystery stories
    .D5—Dime novels

History—Prose—Prose fiction—Special topics, A-Z [criticism]

PT749

    .B7—Brigands and robbers
    .D39—Death

Collections—Prose fiction—Short stories. "Novellen" — Special forms, subjects, etc., A-Z [anthologies]

PT1340

    .D4—Detective and mystery stories
    .H6—Horror tales
    .L3—Lawyers. Judges

.V5—Violence

DUTCH LITERATURE

Collections—Special forms—Prose—Special forms and topics, A-Z

PT5532
    .D4—Detective and mystery stories

SCANDINAVIAN LITERATURE

History—Special forms—Prose and prose fiction—Special forms of prose and prose fiction, A-Z [criticism]

PT7083.5
    .D48—Detective and mystery stories

DANISH LITERATURE

History—Prose—Special forms—Prose fiction—Special topics—Other, A-Z [criticism]

PT7855
    .D46—Detective and mystery stories

NORWEGIAN LITERATURE

History—Prose—Special forms—Prose fiction—Special topics—Other, A-Z [criticism]

PT8564
    .D4—Detective and mystery stories

Collections—Prose—Fiction—Special subjects, A-Z [anthologies]

PT8723
.D4—Detective and mystery stories

SWEDISH LITERATURE

History—Prose—Special forms—Prose fiction—Special topics—Other, A-Z [criticism]

PT9487
.D4—Detective and mystery stories

Collections—Prose—Fiction—Special subjects, A-Z [anthologies]

PT9631
.D48—Detective and mystery stories

CLASS Z (LIBRARY SCIENCE AND BIBLIOGRAPHY)

Libraries—Library science—The collections. The books—Classification and notation—By subject or form, A-Z

Z697
.D48—Detective and mystery stories

National Bibliography—United States—American literature—Special topics, A-Z

Z1231
.A39—Adventure stories
.D47—Detective and mystery stories
.D55—Dime novels
.G66—Gothic revival

.S87—Suspense fiction

Subject bibliography—Fiction—Special topics, A-Z

Z5917

    .A39—Adventure stories
    .D5—Detective and mystery stories
    .G66—Gothic revival
    .H65—Horror tales
    .L3—Legal novels
    .S69—Spy stories

NOTE: the PZ1-4 classification, which was formerly used prior to the adoption of AACR2 to class "popular" fiction, was abandoned by LC at that time, but has continued to appear on books classified by the Library of Congress prior to that date (1980). The rests of the PZ classification, comprising PZ5 and above, remains in use to classify juvenile fiction of all nationalities.

2-3. INDEX TO CLASSIFICATION NUMBERS

Adventure films: PN1995.9.A3.
Adventure stories.

Bibliography. American literature: Z1231.A39; Subject bibliography: Z5917.A39.
Collections: PN6071.A38; American prose (general): PS648. A36; American prose and verse: PS509.A3; English prose (general): PR1309.A38.
Criticism: PN3448.A3; American prose fiction: PS374.A35; English 19th century literature: PR468.A29; English prose fiction: PR830.A38; French prose and prose fiction: PQ637. A37; German prose fiction: PT747.A38; Italian prose fiction: PQ4181.A38; Spanish prose fiction: PQ6147.A38.
English readers: PE1127.A29.
Technique. Authorship: PN3377.5.A37.
Theory, philosophy: PN56.A3.

Brigands and robbers in literature. Collections: PN6071.B76. Criticism: German prose fiction: PT749.B7.
Charlie Chan films: PN1995.9.C37.
Courtroom fiction. Criticism: English prose fiction: PR830. C68.
Crime and criminals.

Collections: American literature: PS509.C7; American prose (general): PS648.C7; English literature: PR1111.C7; English prose (general): PR1309.C7; Poetry (general): PN6110.C88; Polish prose: PG7148.C75; Wit and humor (general): PN6231. C73.

Criticism: English 18th century literature: PR448.C75; English modern literature: PR408.G68; English prose fiction: PR830. C74; English 20th century prose fiction: PR888.D4; Japanese literature: PL721.C74.

Mass media: P96.C74-.C742.

Technique. Authorship: PN3377.5.C75.

Theory, philosophy: PN56.C7.

Crime films: PN1995.9.C66.
Death in films: PN1995.9.D37.
Death in literature.

Collections: PN6071.D4; American poetry: PS595.D42; American prose and verse: PS509.D4; Argentinian prose fiction: PQ7776.5.D43; Mexican prose fiction: PQ7276.5.D43.

Criticism: American 19th century literature: PS217.D43; American 20th century literature: PS228.D43; American prose fiction: PS374.D34; English 16th century drama: PR658.D4; English 17th century literature: PR438.D44; English 19th century literature: PR468.D42; English 20th century drama: PR739.D42; English juvenile literature: PN1009.5.D43; English prose fiction: PR830.D37; French literature: PQ145.1.D33; German prose fiction: PT749.D39.

Theory, philosophy: PN56.D4.

Detective and mystery films: PN1995.9.D4.
Detective and mystery plays. Collections: PN6120.M9; English drama: PR1259.D4. Criticism: PN1952.
Detective and mystery puzzles: GV1507.D4.
Detective and mystery radio programs: PN1991.8.D47.

Detective and mystery stories.

Bibliography. American literature: Z1231.D47; Subject bibliography: Z5917.D5.

Classification and notation: Z697.D48.

Collections: General: PN6071.D45/PN6120.95.D45; American prose (general): PS648.D4; Argentinian prose fiction: PQ7776.5.D48; Belarusian prose fiction: PG2834.636. D48; Chinese fiction: PL2629.D4; Czech prose fiction: PG5031.6.D47; Dutch prose: PT5532.D4; English prose and verse: PR1111.C7; English prose (general): PR1309.D4; French prose: PQ1276.D4; German prose fiction: PT1340.D4; Italian prose fiction: PQ4249.6.D45; Japanese prose fiction (1945-1989): PL755.67.D45; Japanese prose fiction (1989-): PL755.87.D45; Mexican prose fiction: PQ7276.5.D48; Norwegian prose fiction: PT8723.D4; Polish prose: PG7148. D47; Spanish prose fiction: PQ6256.D47; Swedish prose fiction: PT9631.D48.

Criticism: General: PN3448.D4; American prose fiction: PS374. D4; Bulgarian prose fiction: PG1012.3.D48; Catalan prose fiction: PC3930.D5; Chinese literature: PL2275.D48; Danish prose: PT7855.D46; English 19th century literature: PR468. M87; English 20th century drama: PR739.D48; English prose fiction: PR830.D4; English 18th century prose fiction: PR858.D4; English Victorian era prose fiction: PR878.D4; English 20th century prose fiction: PR888.D4; English 21st century prose fiction: PR890.D4; French prose and prose fiction: PQ637.D4; German prose fiction: PT747.D4; Italian prose fiction: PQ4181.D4; Japanese literature: PL721.D45; Japanese prose fiction (1945-1989): PL747.82.D45; Japanese prose fiction (1989-): PL747.87.D45; Korean literature: PL957.5.D48; Norwegian prose fiction: PT8564.D4; Russian prose fiction: PG3098.D46; Scandinavian prose fiction: PT7083.5.D48; Spanish prose fiction: PQ6147.D47; Swedish prose fiction: PT9487.D4.

Drawing. Design. Illustration: NC961.7.D46.

Mass media: P96.D4-.D42.
Technique. Authorship: PN3377.5.D4.

Detective and mystery television programs: PN1992.8.D48.
Dime novels. Bibliography: American literature: Z1231.D55.
 Collections: American prose (general): PS648.D55; English
 prose (general): PR1309.P45. Criticism: American prose
 fiction: PS374.D5; German prose fiction: PT747.D5.
Espionage—see: Spy stories.
Gambling in literature. Collections: PN6071.G24.
Gangster films: PN1995.9.G3.
Gothic literature, Gothic revival.

Bibliography. American literature: Z1231.G66; Subject bibliog-
 raphy: Z5917.G66.
Collections: English prose and verse: PR1111.G67.
Criticism: American prose fiction: PS374.G68; English modern
 literature: PR408.G68; English 18th century literature:
 PR448.G6; Russian prose fiction: PG3098.G68.

Grotesque in literature. Collections: English prose and verse:
 PR1111.G7. Theory, philosophy: PN56.G7.
Hand-to-hand fighting in films: PN1995.9.H3.
Heroes.

Collections: PN6071.H4; American prose (general): PS648.H4;
 Chinese fiction: PL2629.H47; Poetry (general): PN6110.H2.
Criticism: American literature: PS169.H4; Chinese literature:
 PL2275.H47; English 16th century drama: PR658.H42;
 English juvenile literature: PN1009.5.H47; English prose
 fiction: PR830.H4; French literature (general): PQ145.1.D33;
 French 20th century literature: PQ307.H4.
Mass media: P96.H46-.H462.

Heroes in films: PN1995.9.H44.
Holmes, Sherlock. Collections: American poetry: PS595.H62;

English prose (general): PR1309.H55. Mass media: P96. H59-.H592.

Holmes, Sherlock films: PN1995.9.S5.
Horror films: PN1995.9.H6.
Horror in television programs: PN1992.8.H67.
Horror plays. Collections: English drama: PR1259.H67.
Horror radio programs: PN1991.8.H66.
Horror tales.

Bibliography: Z5717.H65.
Collections: General: PN6071.H727; American prose (general): PS648.H6; American prose and verse: PS509.H59; Argentinian prose fiction: PQ7776.5.H67; English prose (general): PR1309.H6; German prose fiction: PT1340.H6; Italian prose fiction: PQ4249.6.H66; Mexican prose fiction: PQ7276.5.H67; Polish prose: PG7148.H67; Spanish prose fiction: PQ6256.H66.
Criticism: American prose fiction: PS374.H67; English prose fiction: PR830.T3.
Mass media: P96.H65-.H652.
Periodical illustration: NC968.5.H6.
Technique. Authorship: PN3377.5.H67.
Theory, philosophy: PN56.H6.

Indiana Jones films: PN1995.9.I47.
James Bond films: PN1995.9J3.
Justice and law in films: PN1995.9.J8.
Juvenile delinquency in films: PN1995.9.J87.
Law and lawyers in literature.

Bibliography: Z5917.L3.
Collections: American prose (general): PS648.L3; Chinese fiction: PL2629.L38; Czech prose fiction: PG5031.6.L44; German prose fiction: PT1340.L3.
Criticism: PN3426.L37 [lawyers]; PN3448.L4 [legal novels]; American literature: PS169.L37; American 19th century liter-

ature: PS217.L37; American 20th century literature: PS228.
L37; American prose fiction: PS374.L34; Chinese literature:
PL2275.L38; English literature: PR151.L37; English prose
fiction: PR830.L39.
Theory, philosophy: PN56.L338.

Mafia in films: PN1995.9.M23.
Mafia in literature. Collections: PN6071.M14; Wit and humor
(general): PN6231.C73.
Murder in films: PN1995.9.M835.
Murder in literature.

Collections: American poetry: PS595.M683; American
prose and verse: PS509.M83; Argentinian prose fiction:
PQ7776.5.M87; Mexican prose fiction: PQ7276.5.M87.
Criticism: English 19th century literature: PR468.M85; French
20th century literature: PQ307.M87.
Mass media: P96.M85-.M852.
Theory, philosophy: PN56.M85.

Outlaws in films: PN1995.9.O84.
Penny dreadfuls. Collections: English prose (general): PR1309.
P45.
Poe, Edgar Allan. Collections: American prose and verse:
PS509.P6.
Police films: PN1995.9.P57.
Police in literature. Collections: Wit and humor: PN6231.P59.
Criticism: American prose fiction: PS374.P57; English prose
fiction: PR830.P59.
Prisons and prisoners in literature.

Collections: PN6071.P68. Poetry (general): PN6110.P8.
Criticism: American literature: PS153.P74 [prisoners as
authors]; American literature: PS366.P75; Australian literature: PR9605.6.P75; English prose fiction: PR830.P7; French
literature (general): PQ145.4.P7; French 20th century litera-

ture: PQ307.P68.

Revenge in literature. Collections: American prose: PS648. R48; Wit and humor: PN6231.R45. Criticism: English 16th century drama: PR658.R45. Theory, philosophy: PN56. R48.

Rogues and vagabonds in literature. Collections: PN6071. R55.

Serial murderers in film: PN1995.9.S297.

Spy films: PN1995.9.S68.

Spy stories.

Bibliography: Z5917.S69.

Collections: PN6071.S64; American prose: PS648.S85; English prose (general): PR1309.S7; Wit and humor (general): PN6231.E75.

Criticism: PN3448.S66; English prose fiction: PR830.S65; English 20th century literature: PR888.S65.

Spy television programs: PN1992.8.S67.

Suspense fiction.

Bibliography. American literature: Z1231.S87.

Collections: General: PN6071.S92.

Criticism: PN3448.S86; English prose fiction: PR830.S87.

Technique. Authorship: PN3377.5.S87.

Suspense films/Thrillers: PN1995.9.S87.

Swindlers and swindling in literature. Criticism: American literature: PS366.S95.

Tales of terror—see: Horror tales.

Terror and wonder in poetry: PN6110.T5.

Terrorism in films: PN1995.9.T46.

Terrorism in literature. Collections: Wit and humor (general): PN6231.T555. Criticism: English prose fiction: PR830.T47.

Theory, philosophy: PN56.T45.

Terrorism in mass media: P96.T47-.T472.

Victims in literature. Criticism: American prose fiction: PS374.
V53; English literature: PR151.V56.

Villains in films: PN1995.9.V47.

Violence in films: PN1995.9.V5.

Violence in literature.

Collections: PN6071.V5; American poetry: PS595.V55; Argentinian prose fiction: PQ7776.5.V54; German prose fiction: PT1340.V5; Mexican prose fiction: PQ7276.5.V54.

Criticism: English juvenile literature: PN1009.5.V54; English modern literature: PR408.V54; French 20th century literature: PQ307.V55; French prose and prose fiction: PQ637. V56.

English readers: PE1127.V5.

Mass media: P96.V5-.V52.

Theory, philosophy: PN56.V53.

Violence in television programs: PN1992.8.V55.

3-1. AUTHOR MAIN ENTRIES AND LITERATURE NUMBERS
INTRODUCTION

Publication in 1978 of the second edition of the *Anglo-American Cataloging Rules*, and the subsequent adoption of these rules by the Library of Congress in 1980, resulted in many changes in author main entries. In simplified form, AACR2 requires that catalogers use a contemporary writer's name as it actually appears on most of his or her books. Prior to AACR2, LC sometimes used common forms of names, but just as frequently adopted convoluted variations which bore little resemblance to the originals.

On the surface, AACR2 seems a logical simplification of previously abstruse cataloging rules, but problems have arisen in practice. The first changes were made in 1980, with a massive retrospective "sweep" through MARC (LC's giant database), OCLC, and the other library databases; a second large "sweep" was conducted in the summer of 1987 in OCLC, and such automated comparisons with LCs Name-Authority File will apparently be necessary for the indefinite future. Since LC does not normally recatalog books without reason, a great many authors who are dead or inactive, and whose status does not give them high literary visibility, continue to be listed in the *National Union Catalog* (and OCLC) under forms which are obsolete under AACR2; these names will be changed (if ever) only when a book by or about that author is newly cataloged by LC. Some libraries have arbitrarily assigned AACR2 forms to such writers when cataloging their books in OCLC; these names may differ slightly or radically from those already used by LC through 1980, from forms adopted after 1980, by LC or others, or from those which LC may ultimately choose, at some vague future date. What began with the best of intentions as a "great simplification" has actually spawned greater inconsistencies than the system it replaced.

The Library of Congress must share some of the blame for the haphazard way in which the rules have been applied. On occasion, it will choose forms which clearly contradict AACR2 rules, or (more commonly) it will continue to use forms not precisely correct. For example, Douglas Menville, an editor, critic, and novelist, is cataloged by LC as Douglas Alver Menville, despite the fact that he never uses a middle name or initial; this form derives from his first published book, which was an exact reproduction of his thesis, middle name included. Although clearly erroneous under AACR2, it has not been changed by the Library of Congress. One can only presume that LC has made a conscious choice with certain middle-level writers to leave their entries as they existed prior to AACR2, on the theory that few users will care or even notice. This is unfortunate, since no one outside of the Library of Congress reviews these changes or is even aware of them until after they occur.

AACR2 also provides for the addition of dates to main entries to distinguish writers with the same names from each other; when dates cannot be determined, no further effort is made to separate them. The Library of Congress, however, sometimes adds such dates to previously-established main entries years after the original authority was first created, to resolve conflicts posed by newer main entries about which it has less information.

The main entries listed below have been checked in LCs Name-Authority File through the fall of 2011, and are correct as of that time. A date of birth (or even a day of birth, if necessary) may be added to a name to resolve conflicts. Note that in early 2006, LC revised its policy to allow the option of adding death dates to open dates to avoid the idea of "wrong" or "misleading" headings that imply the deceased person is still living. More complete forms of an author's name are sometimes added in parentheses to differentiate similar names [*e.g.*, Compton, D. G. (David Guy), 1930-]; the parenthesis or hyphen is considered terminating punctuation in such entries, no period being added. OCLC sometimes differs from AACR2 in placing titles such as "Sir" or "Mrs." after the author's given name, and we have followed such practice here.

AACR2 also issued new filing rules in 1978, changing to a system which closely resembles computer filing practices. Thus, blank spaces and most punctuations file ahead of anything else, numbers and symbols ahead of letters, each word being treated as a separate entity for filing purposes. This in turn has changed the way in which cutter numbers are assigned to both authors and titles in the literature schedules. Authors whose names were affected by the filing changes, and whose books were cataloged for the first time after 1980, have received literature numbers which put their names in proper alphabetical order under the new rules; but previously-established authors who had already received permanent literature numbers were not moved, and under LC's policy of leaving well enough alone, will not be. This has resulted in many discrepancies in the tables, most obviously with authors whose names begin with "Mc"; under the old rules, such names were filed as if spelled "Mac," subject cutters being assigned appropriately. Under AACR2, these names are now filed in strict order, and the subject cutters have changed to "C" for those authors who have been assigned numbers for the first time post-1980.

LC also decided that only one literature number would be assigned to each author, even if his or her main entries were split under more than one name; this may sometimes result in an author's literature number being out of sequence under the new rules (see, for example, the Authority record for William Arden, but whose literature number continues to be generated from his real name, Dennis Lynds; such anomalies are common under AACR2). Note that the alternate literature numbers assigned by LC between 1969-1980 to PZ3 and PZ4 classifications are not regarded by LC as permanent unless confirmed by later assignments. For a fuller explanation of LC's procedures regarding the assignment of classification numbers for literature authors, see its *Classification and Shelflisting Manual* (Instruction sheet F 632).

In theory, the Library of Congress assigns literature numbers by language, nationality, and period, in that order. Under each period, authors are given numbers which put their names in strict alphabetical order (note again, however, that the change in filing rules in 1978 may affect the sequence of these names—and their classification numbers). American literature, for example, has two spans of numbers for the twentieth century, PS3500-3549 for authors active between 1900-1960, and PS3550-3576 for those active between 1961-2000. Those authors active after 2000 have a new range, PS3600-3626. The demarcations between these boundaries are often vague and ill-defined. PS3500, PS3550, and PS3600 are reserved for anonymous works, and for authors whose names consist only of punctuation or initialisms. PS3551-3576 and PS3601-3626 correspond, on a letter by number basis, to each letter of the English alphabet, PS3551, for example, standing for all American writers active in the latter half of the twentieth century whose surnames begin with "A."

Cutter numbers (from tables originally designed by Charles Cutter) complete the classification, providing a unique and unchangeable identification for each literary author (prior to 1900, authors may sometimes be given a span of numbers, particularly those with large bodies of work). The initial letter of the cutter corresponds to the second letter of the author's surname (or, in some foreign classifications, to the first changing element of the author's name). The number part of the classification is derived from the third letter of the author's name, and is expanded to whatever length may be necessary to create a unique number while maintaining proper alphabetical sequence. Very generally, the number "3" corresponds to the letter "a," "4" to "e," "5" to "i," "6" to "o," "7" to "r," "8" to "u," and "9" to "y"; these are not fixed, and may be adjusted to fit particular circumstances. For example, Edmund Cooper has the number PR6053.O5469; this falls between O53 (for Michael Cooney) and O55 (for Giles Cooper). Each digit of the number represents a further subdivision, not some greater amount. This becomes more obvious when one looks closely at the tables.

The author's literature number is immutable once assigned; a second cutter is used to create a similar number for each of the writer's literary works. Hence, Robert A. Heinlein's novel, *Friday*, could be classed in PS3515.E288F7 1987, for a printing issued in 1987. All of an author's fiction, drama, poetry, and other literary productions are assigned numbers which place them in strict alphabetical sequence, with some exceptions (explained at the end of this section); books on other subjects, including literary subjects, receive classification numbers appropriate to those subjects, and are not classed as literature.

The literature numbers provided below are those actually developed by LC as permanent or alternate numbers through late 2011, unless the latter are clearly erroneous (perhaps a half dozen); the alternate numbers may eventually change (when confirmed) if the author's main entry has changed, or if some other conflict has since developed, but most will remain the same. Where no literature number exists, or where only juvenile numbers (PZ7+) have been assigned, we use the word "none." LC does not normally catalog mass market paperback fiction; however, many writers with cloth or trade paperback editions to their credit have been assigned classification numbers. We also include here (in brackets) bibliography numbers from the "Z" schedule, for the few authors who have them. The "Z" schedule was the first to be developed at LC, in the late 1890s, and it remains the most primitive schedule, in both style and function. Essentially, it lists authors in alphabetical order by main entry, assigning whole and subdivided numbers in a span from Z8000-

8999. Many academic libraries have abandoned these numbers, preferring to class bibliographies with other nonfiction books about the author. Note that writers may have more than one valid literature number, if they have written original books in more than one language (Vladimir Nabokov wrote in Russian, French, and English, and thus has three numbers). There are also several authors who have accidentally been assigned more than one number by LC, without priority; we list both numbers until the conflict is resolved.

* * * * * * *

The adoption of RDA: Resource Description & Access rules in mid-2010, with a possible implementation date of 2013, promises once again to alter the way main author entries are handled by all participating libraries, including the Library of Congress. National testing in the U.S. was coordinated by the three national libraries (LC, NLM, & NAL), and there was participation from libraries of all types, as well as by groups such as the Continuing Resources Cataloging Committee within ALA. The U.S. RDA Test Coordinating Committee recommended that RDA be implemented by LC, NAL, and NLM no sooner than January 2013, pending satisfactory progress/completion of the tasks and action items identified by the Committee.

100/600/700 RDA changes: the main changes that may affect form of main entry for personal authors include:

More frequent use of identifiers such as "occupation" to create unique headings; terms such as "Jr." would now be included as well; the months used in dates would be spelled out: e.g., Smith, John, 1980 January 15- ; hyphens would be used before death dates, and hyphen after birth dates, abandoning the current abbreviations "b." (for "born") and "d." (for "death"); the word "active" would replace the AACR2 "fl." and RDA words "flourished"; the use of "active" would no longer be limited to pre-twentieth-century authors.

3-2. MYSTERY AUTHOR MAIN ENTRIES AND LITERATURE NUMBERS

50 Cent (Musician)	PS3600.A2
À Beckett, Arthur William, 1844-1909.	none
A. P.	PR6100.A1
A. T. R.	PS3601.T7
Aalben, Patrick.	none
Aalborg, Gordon.	PR9619.3.A22
Aames, Avery.	PS3601.A215
Aanrooy, Jacques.	none
Aaron, Chester.	PS3551.A57
Aaron, David, 1938-	PS3551.A6
Aaron, Richard, 1960-	PR9199.4.A17
Aarons, Edward S. (Edward Sidney), 1916-1975.	PS3501.A79
Aarons, Will B.	PS3501.A79
Aasheim, Ashley.	none
Ab Hugh, Dafydd.	PS3551.B19
Abad, José, 1967-	PQ6651.B255
Ábalos, Rafael, 1956-	PQ6651.B325
Abanes, Richard.	PS3601.B353
Abarbanell, Jacob Ralph, 1852-1922.	none
Abarca, Alfredo E. (Alfredo Ernesto)	PQ7798.1.B35
Abasolo, José Javier, 1957-	PQ6651.B33
Abbey, Edward, 1927-1989.	PS3551.B2
Abbey, Kieran, 1890-1962.	PS3535.E474
Abbey, Lynn.	PS3551.B23
Abbey, Margaret.	PR6051.B28
Abbey, Ruth.	none
Abbot, Anthony, 1893-1952.	PS3529.U65
Abbot, Francis.	none
Abbot, Rick.	PS3569.H3427
Abbott, Alice.	none
Abbott, Alice Irving.	none
Abbott, Bruce, 1910?-1970	PS3535.E12
Abbott, George, 1887-1995.	PS3501.B23

Abbott, J. H. M. (John Henry Macartney), 1874- PR9619.3.A24
1953.
Abbott, Jeff.   PS3601.B366
Abbott, John.   PS3551.B258
Abbott, Keith, 1944-   PS3551.B26
Abbott, Megan E., 1971-   PS3601.B37
Abbott, Margot.   PS3551.B263
Abbott, Richard.   PR5485.A37
Abbott, Rosa—see: Parker, Rosa Abbott.
Abbott, Sandra.   none
Abbott, Tony.   none
Abdoh, Salar.   PS3551.B2687
Abdullaev, Chingiz.   PG3478.B28
Abdullah, Achmed, 1881-1945.   PS3501.B3
Abe, Kōbō, 1924-1993.   PL845.B4
                                                      [Z8004.75]
Abécassis, Eliette.   PQ2661.B43
Abel, Dorothy, 1941-   PS3551.B335
Abel, Joel S.   none
Abel, Kenneth.   PS3551.B336
Abel-Halvorsen, Sharon.   none
Abella, Alex.   PS3551.B3394
Aber, Linda Williams.   none
Abercrombie, Barbara.   PS3551.B345
Abercrombie, Lynn.   none
Abercrombie, Neil.   PS3551.B375
Abió, Rufus O.   none
Abish, Walter.   PS3551.B5
Ableman, Paul.   PR6051.B5
Ablow, Keith R.   PS3551.B58
Abnett, Dan.   PR6051.B56
About, Edmond, 1828-1885.   PQ2151
Abraham, C. S.   none
Abraham, Daniel.   PS3601.B677
Abrahams, Gerald, 1907-   none
Abrahams, Peter, 1947-   PS3551.B64
Abrahams, Robert D. (Robert David), 1905-   PS3501.B882
Abram, Arthur.   none
Abramo, J. L.   PS3601.B73
Abrams, Tom.   PS3551.B713
Abramson, Mark, 1952-   PS3601.B758
Abramson, Traci Hunter.   PS3601.B76
Abresch, Peter E.   PS3551.B75
Abrevaya, Gustavo, 1952-   PQ7798.41.B74
Abse, Dannie.   PR6001.B7
Abshire, Richard.   PS3551.B84
Abu-Jaber, Diana.   PS3551.B895
Acevedo, Mario.   PS3601.C48
Acker, J. Alex.   PS3601.C54
Acker, Kathy, 1948-1997.   PS3551.C44
Acker, Rick, 1966-   PS3601.C545
Ackerman, Morris.   PS3551.C493
Ackerman, Sheila.   PR6051.C57
Ackroyd, Peter, 1949-   PR6051.C64

Acre, Stephen, 1904-1969.	PS3513.R866
Adair, Cherry, 1951-	PS3601.D348
Adair, Gilbert.	PR6051.D287
Adair, Liz.	PS3601.D35
Adair, Robin, 1936-	PS3601.D355
Adam, Nicholas.	none
Adam, Paul, 1958-	PR6051.D3156
Adamov, Bob.	PS3601.D3665
Adams, Alina.	PS3601.D367
Adams, Alph A.	PS3551.D3243
Adams, Bronte.	PR6051.D333
Adams, Cleve F. (Cleve Franklin), 1895-1949.	PS3501.D21735
Adams, Clifton.	PS3551.D34
Adams, D. J. (Debi J.)	PS3601.D37
Adams, Daniel, 1956 Jan. 22-	PS3601.D373
Adams, Deborah, 1956-	PS3551.D345
Adams, Douglas, 1952-2001.	PR6051.D3352
Adams, Ellery.	PS3601.D374
Adams, Harold, 1923-	PS3551.D367
Adams, Herbert, 1874-1958.	PR6001.D284
Adams, Ian, 1937-	PR9199.3.A25
Adams, J. V. (James Vincent), 1932-	PS3551.D3734
Adams, Jane, 1960-	PR6051.D3367
Adams, Joey, 1911-1999.	none
Adams, John Festus, 1930-	PR6051.D337
Adams, Kelly.	PS3551.D3756
Adams, Laura, 1960-	PS3561.A41665
Adams, Linda Paulson.	PS3551.D377
Adams, Lorraine.	PS3601.D38
Adams, Morley.	none
Adams, Nathan M.	none
Adams, Riley, 1971-	PS3619.P343
Adams, Samuel Hopkins, 1871-1958.	PS3501.D317
Adams, Stephen P.	PS3551.D39532
Adams, Will, 1963-	PR6101.D365
Adamson, Isaac.	PS3551.D39538
Adamson, Lydia.	PS3551.D3954
Adamson, Mary Jo.	none
Adcock, Thomas Larry, 1947-	PS3551.D397
Addeo, Edmond G., 1936-	none
Addiego, John.	PS3601.D46
Addison, Gwen.	none
Addison, Henry Robert, 1805?-1876.	none
Addleman, D. R.	none
Adeniyi, Kola.	PR9387.9.A3317
Adiga, Aravind.	PR9619.4.A35
Adkins, Bill.	none
Adkins, Jan.	PS3551.D52
Adleman, Robert H., 1919-	PS3551.D57
Adler, David A.	PS3551.D592
Adler, Elizabeth (Elizabeth A.)	PR6051.D56
Adler, Warren.	PS3551.D64
Adler-Olsen, Jussi.	PT8176.1.D54
Adorjan, Carol.	PS3551.D67

Adrian, Jack.	none
Aeby, Jacquelyn.	PS3557.R3338
Aellen, Richard.	PS3551.E45
Afrika, Tatamkulu.	PR9369.3.A37
Agarwal, Deepa, 1947-	PR9499.3.A384
Agel, Jerome.	PS3551.G43
Agnew, Spiro T., 1918-1996.	PS3551.G58
Agniel, Lucien D.	none
Aguilar, J. M. (José Manuel), 1968-	PQ6701.G837
Aguirre-Sacasa, Roberto.	PS3601.G85
Agunwa, William.	PR6051.G86
Ahern, Jerry.	none
Ahern, Jerry, 1946-	none
Aickman, Robert.	PR6051.I3
Aiken, Ginny.	PS3551.I339
Aiken, Joan, 1924-2004.	PR6051.I35
Aiken, John, 1913-	PR6051.I36
Aikman, David, 1944-	PS3551.I37
Ainsworth, Harriet—see: Cadell, Elizabeth.	
Ainsworth, William Harrison, 1805-1882.	PR4002-4003
	[Z8020.2]
Aird, Catherine.	PR6051.I65
Airth, Rennie, 1935-	PR9369.3.A47
Akagawa, Jirō, 1948-	PL845.K228
Akhmanov, Mikhail.	PG3491.3.K476
Akínlàdé, Kọlá.	PR9387.9.A3887
Akinyemi, Rowena.	none
Akunin, B. (Boris)	PG3478.K78
Alam, Glynn Marsh, 1943-	PS3551.L213
Alan, Douglas.	PS3601.L3267
Alan, Ray.	PR6051.L2
Alan, Robert.	PS3601.L3277
Albahari, David, 1948-	PG1419.1.L335
Albano, Peter.	PS3551.L244
Albarella, Joan, 1944-	PS3551.L244
Alben, Alex.	PS3551.L256
Albert, Marvin H.	PS3551.L26
Albert, Neil.	PS3551.L2634
Albert, Susan Wittig.	PS3551.L2637
Albiac, Gabriel.	PQ6651.L322
Albrand, Martha.	PS3501.L245
Albright, Letha, 1952-	PS3601.L34
Alcock, Terri, 1945-	PR9199.3.A914
Alcorn, Alfred.	PS3551.L29
Alcorn, Randy C.	PS3551.L292
Alcorn, Steve.	PS3601.L343
Alcott, Cynthia.	none
Alcott, Louisa May, 1832-1888.	PS1015-1018
	[Z8024.8]
Aldanov, Mark Aleksandrovich, 1886-1957.	PG3476.A327
Alden, Jami.	PS3601.L3446
Alden, Laura.	PS3601.L3448
Alderman, Tom.	none
Alderson, T. A., 1955-	PS3551.L337

Alding, Peter.	PR6060.E43
Aldridge, James, 1918-	PR9619.3.A5
Aldridge, Sarah.	PS3551.L345
Aldyne, Nathan.	PS3551.L346
Aleas, Richard.	PS3601.L353
Aleksandrov, Nikolaĭ.	PG3478.L37
Aleksandrova, N. (Natali‹a›)	PG3491.3.L455
Aleshina, Svetlana.	PG3491.3.L457
Aleshkovskiĭ, I‹U›z.	PG3478.L443
Alexander, Bruce, 1932-2003.	PS3553.O55314
Alexander, Catherine, d. 1992.	PS3551.L34857
Alexander, David, 1907-1973.	PS3551.L3492
Alexander, David M.	PS3551.L349
Alexander, Fern.	none
Alexander, Gary, 1941-	PS3551.L3554
Alexander, Hannah.	PS3551.L35558
Alexander, Jan, 1937-	PS3552.A476
Alexander, Joan.	PR6051.L36
Alexander, Karl.	PS3551.L3569
Alexander, Lawrence.	PS3551.L35696
Alexander, Marsha.	none
Alexander, Martin.	none
Alexander, Patrick, 1926-	PR6051.L37
Alexander, Robert, 1952-	PS3576.I5118
Alexander, Skye.	PS3551.L35756
Alexander, Sue, 1933-	PS3551.L3576
Alexander, Tasha, 1969-	PS3601.L3565
Alexander, Vanessa.	PR6051.L38
Alexie, Sherman, 1966-	PS3551.L35774
Alfieri, Annamaria.	PS3601.L3597
Alfonsi, Alice.	PS3601.L36
Alger, Horatio, 1832-1899.	PS1029.A3
	[Z8027.15]
Ali, Rahsaan, 1972-	PS3601.L378
Alibrandi, Tom.	none
Aline, Countess of Romanones, 1923-	PS3551.L364
Alington, Adrian, 1895-1958.	PR6001.L48
Allain, Marcel, 1885-1969.	PQ2601.L57
Allan, Barbara.	PS3601.L4
Allan, Dennis, 1900-1978.	PS3511.O186
Allan, Dina.	none
Allan, Francis.	PS3501.L4775
Allan, Joan.	none
Allan, Stella.	PR6051.L475
Allardyce, Paula—see: Blackstock, Charity.	
Allbeury, Ted.	PR6051.L52
Allbritten, Esri.	PS3601.L415
Allegretto, Michael.	PS3551.L385
Alleman, Richard.	PS3551.L386
Allen, Anita.	PS3551.L387
Allen, Charlotte Vale, 1941-	PS3551.L392
Allen, Conrad, 1940-	PR6063.I3175
Allen, Drue.	PS3601.L418
Allen, E. C.—see: Ward, Elizabeth C.	

Allen, Elisabeth Offutt.	none
Allen, Garrison.	PS3551.L39227
Allen, Glen Scott, 1950-	PS3601.L4185
Allen, Grant, 1848-1899.	PR4004.A2
Allen, Harper.	none
Allen, Henry.	PS3551.L3928
Allen, Irene, 1960-	PS3551.L3935
Allen, Jan.	none
Allen, John—see: Perry, Ritchie, 1942-	
Allen, Kate, 1957-	PS3551.L3956
Allen, Michael Derek, 1939-	PR6051.L5395
Allen, Nancy Campbell, 1969-	PS3551.L39644
Allen, Ralph, 1931-	PS3551.L3929
Allen, Robin, 1964-	PS3601.L4354
Allen, Steve, 1921-2000.	PS3501.L5553
Allen, Thomas B.	PS3551.L43
Allen, Tricia.	PS3601.L437
Allen, Woody.	PS3551.L44
Allende, Isabel.	PQ8098.1.L54
Allerton, Mark, b. 1881.	PR6001.L67243
Alleyn, Susanne, 1963-	PS3551.L4484
Allin, Lou, 1945-	PR9199.4.A46
Allingham, Margery, 1904-1966.	PR6001.L678
Allington, Maynard.	PS3551.L449
Allis, Sarah.	PS3551.L45
Allison, Ariel.	PS3601.L447
Allison, Clyde.	none
Allison, E. M. A.	PS3551.L454
Allison, Glen.	PS3601.L448
Allison, Jennifer.	none
Allman, Kevin.	PS3551.L462
Allred, Tara C. (Tara Christine), 1976-	PS3601.L46
Allyn, Douglas.	PS3551.L49
Allyson, Alan.	PR6051.L59
Almazán, Alejandro, 1971-	PQ7298.41.L48
Almquist, Gregg.	none
Alpert, Hollis, 1916-	PS3551.L7
Alpert, Mark, 1961-	PS3601.L67
Alsobrook, Rosalyn, 1952-	none
Alston, E. B.	none
Alt, Madelyn.	PS3601.L75
Alten, Steve.	PS3551.L764
Alter, Robert Edmond.	PS3551.L767
Altman, John, 1969-	PS3601.L85
Altman, Steven-Elliot.	PS3601.L855
Altman, Thomas.	PR6052.L25
Alvarez, A. (Alfred), 1929-	PR6051.L9
Alvarez, Blanca, 1957-	PQ6651.L778
Alverson, Charles E.	PS3551.L86
Alvtegen, Karin, 1965-	PT9876.1.L92
Alwyn, Cynthia G.	PS3601.L88
Amann, Jürg, 1947-	PT2661.M14
Amare, Rothayne—see: Byrne, Stuart J.	
Amato, Angela.	PS3551.M18

Amberg, Jay.   PS3551.M19
Amberhill, Bevan.   PR9199.3.A42
Amberley, Richard.   PR6051.M3
Ambler, Eric, 1909-1998.   PR6001.M48
Ambrose, David.   PR6051.M45
Ambrose, Marty.   PS3601.M368
Ames, Edna.   none
Ames, Delano, 1906-   PS3501.M415
Ames, J. Edward.   none
Ames, Jeffrey.   none
Ames, Jennifer, 1902-1971.   PR9619.3.G727
Ames, Leslie, 1912-   PR9199.3.R5996
Ames, Norma.   none
Amey, Linda, 1948-   PS3551.M46
Amidon, Stephen.   PS3551.M52
Amiel, Joseph, 1937-   PS3551.M53
Amis, Kingsley.   PR6001.M6
                                                     [Z8032.52]
Amis, Martin.   PR6051.M5
Ammaniti, Niccolò, 1966-   PQ4861.M54
Amo, Gary.   PS3551.L39227
Amos, Alan.   PS3521.N5347
Amos, Diane.   PS3601.M67
Ampuero, Roberto, 1953-   PQ8098.1.M68
Anable, Stephen.   PS3601.N33
Anan'ev, Gennadiĭ.   PG3478.N32
Anaya, Rudolfo A.   PS3551.N27
                                                     [Z8003.26]
Anders, Donna.   PS3551.N335
Anders, Karen.   none
Andersen, C. Paul, 1936-   PS3601.N49
Andersen, Ian.   PS3551.N346
Andersen, Jessica S., 1973-   PS3601.N43
Andersen, Susan, 1950-   PS3551.N34555
Anderson, B. Kent, 1963-   PS3601.N455
Anderson, Catherine (Adeline Catherine)   PS3551.N34557
Anderson, David Lynn, 1948-   PS3601.N533
Anderson, Donald B. (Donald Bruce), 1975-   PS3601.N542
Anderson, Edward, 1905-1969.   PS3501.N218
Anderson, Frances.   none
Anderson, Frederick Irving, 1877-1947.   PS3501.N2265
Anderson, Gerald D., 1944-   PS3601.N5436
Anderson, J. R. L. (John Richard Lane), 1911-   PR6051.N3934
Anderson, Jack, 1922-2005.   PS3551.N365
Anderson, Jack Albin, 1924-   PS3551.N367
Anderson, James, 1936-2007.   PR6051.N393
Anderson, Jeffrey (Jeffrey Scott)   none
Anderson, Jessica.   PR9619.3.A57
Anderson, Kevin J., 1962-   PS3551.N37442
Anderson, Lin.   PR6101.N344
Anderson, M. T.   PS3551.N37449
Anderson, Mary Desiree, 1902-   PR6001.N46
Anderson, Patrick, 1936-   PS3551.N377
Anderson, Paul (W. Paul)   PR9199.4.A53

Anderson, Poul, 1926-2001.	PS3551.N378
	[Z8035.55]
Anderson, Rex.	PS3551.N379
Anderson, Sheryl J., 1958-	PS3551.N3947
Anderson, Sue Lynn.	none
Anderson, V. S.	PS3551.N395
Anderson, William C.	PS3551.N4
Anderson-Minshall, Diane.	PS3601.N5484
Andersson, C. Dean.	none
Andrau, Marianne, 1905-	PQ2601.N258
André, Alix.	PQ2601.N27
Andreae, Christine.	PS3551.N4134
Andreev, Oleg.	PG3478.N4135
Andreeva, Natali‹a›.	PG3491.3.N53
Andress, Lesley.	PS3569.A5125
Andrew, Joseph J.	PS3551.N4147
Andrew, Meredith.	PR9199.3.A513
Andrews.	PS3601.N5523
Andrews, Brian T.	PS3551.N4149
Andrews, Charlton, 1878-1939.	PS3501.N5615
Andrews, Donna.	PS3551.N4165
Andrews, Linda, 1967-	PS3601.N55267
Andrews, Lori B., 1952-	PS3601.N5527
Andrews, Mark.	none
Andrews, Mary Kay, 1954-	PS3570.R587
Andrews, Michael Alford.	PR6051.N466
Andrews, Patrick E.	none
Andrews, Phillip.	none
Andrews, Robert, 1937-	PS3551.N4524
Andrews, Russell.	PS3551.N4525
Andrews, Sarah.	PS3551.N4526
Andrews, V. C. (Virginia C.)	PS3551.N454
Andrews, Val.	PR6101.N35
Andrus, Jeff.	PS3551.N4564
Aneke, Ifeanyi U.	PR9387.9.A5597
Angell, Judie.	none
Anghelides, Peter.	none
Angsten, David.	PS3601.N5545
Angus, John.	PS3551.N49
Angus, Sylvia.	PS3551.N5
Ani, Friedrich, 1959-	PT2661.N48
Ankrum, Barbara.	none
Annandale, Barbara, 1925-	PR6051.N62
Anne, David, 1930-	PR6051.N63
Anne-Mariel, 1907-	PQ2625.A787154
Anscombe, Roderick.	PS3551.N67
Ansle, Dorothy Phoebe.	PR6001.N75
Anson, Barbara.	none
Anthony, David, 1929-	PS3551.N72
Anthony, Elizabeth.	none
Anthony, Evelyn.	PR6069.T428
Anthony, Mark, 1973-	PS3601.N556
Anthony, Michael David.	PR6051.N77
Anthony, Patricia.	PS3551.N727

Anthony, Peter, 1926-	none
Anthony, Piers.	PS3551.N73
Anthony, Robert.	none
Anthony, Tom.	PS3601.N568
Antieau, Kim.	PS3551.N745
Antonio, San—see: San-Antonio.	
Antonov, Anton.	PG3491.3.N763
Aparicio, Juan Pedro, 1941-	PQ6651.P26
Apodaca, Jennifer.	PS3601.P63
Apostolou, Anna.	PR6051.P614
Appel, Benjamin, 1907-1977.	PS3501.P6
Appel, William, 1939-	PS3551.P556
Appelman, William H.	PS3551.P5575
Appiah, Anthony.	PS3551.P558
Appignanesi, Lisa.	PR9199.3.A533
Appleton, Victor.	none
Applin, Arthur, 1883-	PR6001.P65
Aragón, Clyde James.	PS3551.R26
Aramburu, Fernando, 1959-	PQ6651.R26
Arbenina, Irina.	PG3491.3.R37
Arch, E. L., 1922-	PS3566.A933
Archer, A. A., 1899-1986.	PS3519.O712
Archer, Alex.	PS3565.D53
Archer, Betty.	PS3601.R386
Archer, Chris.	none
Archer, Frank, 1915-1975.	PS3565.C642
Archer, Geoffrey.	PR6051.R282
Archer, Jeffrey, 1940-	PR6051.R285
Archer, Zoe.	PS3601.R388
Ard, William, 1922-1962?	none
Ardamatskiĭ, Vasiliĭ, 1911-	PG3476.A637
Arden, Andrew.	PR6051.R294
Arden, William, 1924-2005.	PS3562.Y44
Ardies, Tom.	PS3551.R39
Ardman, Harvey.	none
Arent, Arthur.	PS3551.R4
Arenz, A. K.	PS3601.R465
Argula, Anne.	PS3566.O6
Aricha, Amos, 1933-	PS3551.R435
	PJ5054.A8
Aristides, Paris, 1958-	PA5649.A73
Arisugawa, Arisu, 1959-	none
Arjouni, Jakob.	PT2661.R45
Arkham, Candice.	PS3551.R437
Arkhangel'skiĭ, Aleksandr, 1962-	PG3491.3.R56
Arkwright, Richard.	PR4007.A68
Arlen, Michael, 1895-1956.	PR6001.R7
Arleo, Joseph.	PS3551.R45
Arley, Catherine.	PQ2661.R58
Arlington, J. C.	PS3551.R453
Arliss, Joen.	none
Armiñán, Jaime de.	PQ6651.R5
Armistead, John.	PS3551.R4662
Armitage, Aileen.	PR6051.R562

Armour, John, 1916-	PS3566.A34
Armour, Toby.	none
Armstrong, Anthony, 1897-1976.	PR6045.I565
Armstrong, Campbell.	PR6052.L25
Armstrong, Charlotte, 1905-1969.	PS3501.R566
Armstrong, Derek, 1959-	PS3601.R575
Armstrong, Diane, 1939-	PR9619.4.A76
Armstrong, F. W., 1947-	PS3573.R544
Armstrong, Kelley.	PR9199.4.A8777
Armstrong, Lori, 1965-	PS3601.R576
Armstrong, Timothy J.	PR6051.R614
Armstrong, Victor.	none
Armstrong, Vivien.	PR6051.R6144
Arnaldi, Jean.	none
Arnaldur Indriðason, 1961-	PT7511.A67
Arness, Christine, 1957-	PS3551.R4865
Arnold, Catherine.	none
Arnold, Elliott, 1912-1980.	PS3501.R5933
Arnold, Jean.	PS3551.R485
Arnold, JoAnn.	PS3601.R585
Arnold, Margot.	PS3551.R536
Arnold, Marilyn, 1935-	PS3551.R538
Arnold, N. Xavier.	PS3551.R544
Arnopoulos, Sheila McLeod.	PR9199.3.A637
Arnote, Ralph.	PS3551.R558
Arnothy, Christine, 1930-	PQ2661.R684
Arnott, Jake.	PR6051.R6235
Arnston, Harrison.	none
Aronson, Harvey.	PS3551.R6
Arriaga Jordán, Guillermo, 1958-	PQ7298.1.R753
Arrighi, Mel.	PS3551.R7
Arrigio, Frank.	none
Arrou-Vignod, Jean-Philippe, 1958-	PQ2661.R69476
Arroyo, Santana.	none
Arruda, Suzanne Middendorf, 1954-	PS3601.R74
Arsenault, Emily.	PS3601.R745
Arsenault, Mark.	PS3601.R75
Arsen'eva, Elena.	PG3478.R69
Arthur, Frank, 1902-	PR6001.R79
Arthur, Keri.	PR9619.4.A78
Arthur, Randall.	PS3551.R77
Arthur, Robert.	none
Arthurson, Wayne, 1962-	PR9199.4.A884
Arvay, Harry.	PR6051.R66
Arvin, Nick.	PS3601.R77
Arvin, Reed.	PS3551.R85
Arvonen, Helen.	none
Asbury, Herbert, 1891-1963.	none
Ascher, Joani.	PS3601.S29
Asensi, Matilde, 1962-	PQ6651.S386
Ash, Maureen, 1939-	PR9199.4.A885
Ash, William, 1917-	PR6051.S4
Ashbaugh, Nancy.	PS3551.S36
Ashbaugh, Regan C.	PS3551.S3614

Ashby, Amanda.   PR9619.4.A843
Ashby, Kay.   none
Ashdown, Clifford.   PR6001.S42
Ashe, B. D.   none
Ashe, Gordon, 1908-1973.   PR6005.R517
Ashe, Rosalind.   PR6051.S47
Asher, Beth, 1935-   PS3552.O45
Asher, Michael, 1953-   PR6051.S47
Asher, Miriam.   none
Ashford, F. U.   none
Ashford, Jane.   none
Ashford, Jeffrey, 1926-   PR6060.E43
Ashford, Lindsay Jayne.   PR6101.S545
Ashforth, Albert.   PS3551.S376
Ashley, 1985-   PS3601.S543
Ashley, Jennifer.   PS3601.S547
Ashley, Martin.   none
Ashley, Michael.   none
Ashley, Steven, 1940-   PS3563.A2555
Ashman, Howard.   none
Ashton, Ann, 1929-   PS3561.I417
Aston, Irene Ziegler, 1955-   PS3576.I29325
Ashton, Mark.   none
Ashton, Sharon—see: Van Slyke, Helen, 1919-
1979.
Ashwood-Collins, Anna.   PS3551.S47
Ashworth, Donna.   PS3551.S48
Asimov, Isaac, 1920-1992.   PS3551.S5
Asinof, Eliot, 1919-2008.   PS3551.S54
Askew, Alice.   PR6001.S59
Askew, Claude.   none
Asner, Jules, 1968-   PS3601.S63
Aspinall, Ruth.   none
Aspler, Tony, 1939-   PR9199.3.A76
Asprey, Robert B.   PS3551.S59
Assonne, Sedley Richard, 1961-   none
Astley, Juliet—see: Lofts, Norah, 1904-1983.
Astley, Neil.   PR6051.S74
Aswad, Betsy.   PS3551.S9
Atamanenko, Igor'+A1067.   PG3478.T33
Ateev, Alekseĭ.   PG3478.T44
Atcheson, George, 1923-   PS3551.T35
Aterovis, Josh.   PS3601.T43
Atherton, Charles R.   PS3601.T47
Atherton, Nancy.   PS3551.T426
Atkey, Bertram.   PS3501.T37
Atkins, Ace.   PS3551.T49
Atkins, Charles.   PS3551.T533
Atkins, Leo.   PS3558.A71824
Atkins, Linda Y.   PS3551.T544
Atkins, Meg Elizabeth.   PR6051.T5
Atkins, Raymond L.   PS3602.T4887
Atkins, Thomas R., 1939-   PS3551.T56
Atkinson, Deborah Turrell.   PS3601.T49

Atkinson, Gean B.	PS3601.T494
Atkinson, Hugh.	PR9619.3.A8
Atkinson, Kate.	PR6051.T56
Atkinson, Kristine.	PS3601.T498
Atkinson, Michael, 1962-	PS3601.T496
Atlee, Philip.	none
Atwater, James D., 1928-	PS3551.T77
Atwell, Sarah.	PS3601.T83
Atwill, Douglas.	PS3601.T85
Atwood, Margaret, 1939-	PR9199.3.A8
	[Z8046.947]
Atwood, Russell.	PS3551.T87
Aubert, Brigitte.	PQ2661.U168
Aubert, Rosemary.	PR9199.3.A9
Aubrey, Edmund—see: Ions, Edmund S.	
Aubrey, Frank.	PR6001.U27
Audemars, Pierre.	PR6051.U3
Audrenn, Jöel.	PQ2661.U33
Auerbach, Jessica.	PS3551.U384
August, Leo.	none
August, Michael.	none
Ault, Sandi.	PS3601.U45
Austen, Michael (Michael E.)	PR6051.U75
Auster, Paul, 1947-	PS3551.U77
Austin, Alex.	PS3551.U78
Austin, Cindy Brown.	PS3601.U855
Austin, Marilyn.	PS3551.U84
Austin, Marlene.	PS3601.U863
Austin, Max.	none
Austin, Raymond, 1932-	PR6101.U78
Austin, Richard, 1926-	PR6051.U84
Austin, F. Britten (Frederick Britten), 1885-1941.	PR6001.U8
Auswaks, Alex, 1934-	none
Autry, Curt.	PS3601.U87
Avallone, Michael.	PS3551.V3
Aveline, Claude, 1901-1992.	PQ2601.V45
	[Z8048.73]
Avery, Claire.	PS3601.V4656
Avery, Graham, 1930-	PR6051.V394
Avery, Ira.	PS3551.V4
Avi, 1937-	PS3551.V5
Aviv, Zohar.	PJ5054.A9245
Avocato, Lori.	none
Awni, Margery.	none
Axelrod, George.	PS3501.X4
Axelrood, Larry, 1960-	PS3551.X45
Axinn, Donald E.	PS3551.X5
Axler, James.	PS3551.X54
Axler, Leo.	none
Axton, David, 1945-	PS3561.O55
Ayres, Don (Don R.)	PS3551.Y717
Ayres, E. C.	PS3551.Y72
Ayres, Paul, 1916-1975.	PS3501.A79
Ayers, Ronald.	none

Ayling, Keith, b. 1898.	none
Ayoob, Michael.	PS3601.Y66
Ayoub, Susanne.	PT2701.Y68
Ayres, Katherine.	none
Ayres, Noreen.	PS3551.Y74
Azolakov, Antoinette, 1944-	PS3551.Z66
Azusa, Rintarō, 1933-	none
Azzarello, Brian.	none
Azzopardi, Trezza.	PR6051.Z96
Baantjer, A. C.	PT5881.12.A2
Babbin, Jacqueline.	PS3552.A173
Babcock, Dwight V. (Dwight Vincent), 1909-	PS3503.A139
Babcock, Nicholas—see: Lewis, Tom, 1940-	
Babcock, Richard.	PS3552.A174
Babkin, Boris.	PG3479.B3382
Babson, Marian.	PS3552.A25
Babula, William.	PS3552.A252
Bacarr, Jina.	PS3552.A2544
Baccalario, Pierdomenico.	PQ4862.A18
Bach, Leo.	none
Bach, Richard.	PS3552.A255
Bacheller, Irving, 1859-1950.	PS1054.B3
	[Z8054.5]
Bachman, Richard.	PS3561.I483
Bachmann, Lawrence Paul, 1912-2004.	PS3503.A159
Bacon, Charlotte, 1965-	PS3552.A27
Badal, Joseph H.	PS3602.A355
Baddock, James.	PR6052.A3128
Baden, Michael M.	PS3602.A358
Badenoch, Andrea.	PR6052.A3129
Badgley, Anne V.	PS3552.A315
Badke, William B., 1949-	PS3552.A318
Baer, Judy.	PS3552.A33
Baer, Robert.	PS3602.A38
Baer, Will Christopher.	PS3552.A3323
Bagby, George, 1906-	PS3537.T3184
Bagdon, Paul.	PS3602.A39
Bagley, Desmond, 1923-1983.	PR6052.A315
Baglio, Ben M.	none
Bagshawe, Louise.	PR6052.A317
Bagshawe, Tilly.	PR6102.A525
Bahadur, Krishna Prakash, 1924-	none
Bahal, Aniruddha, 1967-	PR9499.3.B175
Bahr, Edith-Jane.	PS3552.A36
Bahr, Jerome.	PS3503.A413
Bailey, C. K. (Cherrann K.)	PS3602.A53
Bailey, Dale.	PS3602.A54
Bailey, Elizabeth.	PR6052.A31857
Bailey, F. Lee (Francis Lee), 1933-	PS3552.A366
Bailey, Frankie Y.	PS3552.A368
Bailey, H. C. (Henry Christopher), 1878-1961.	PR6003.A374
Bailey, Hilary, 1936-	PR6052.A3186
Bailey, Jo.	PS3552.A3722
Bailey, Linda, 1948-	none

Bailey, Michèle.	PR6052.A3188
Bailey, Robert, 1938-	PS3552.A37388
Bailey, Robert E., 1947-	PS3602.A55
Bailey, Sean Michael.	PS3602.A5533
Bailor, John E.	PS3602.A557
Bain, Darrell, 1939-	PS3602.A559
Bain, Donald, 1935-	PS3552.A376
Bainbridge, Beryl, 1932-2010.	PR6052.A3195
Bainbridge, Chuck.	none
Bair, Patrick.	PR6052.A32
Baird, Thomas, 1923-	PS3552.A39
Baisden, Michael.	PS3552.A3925
Baker, Abbey Pen.	PS3552.A3984
Baker, Calvin, 1972-	PS3552.A3997
Baker, Carlos, 1909-1987.	PS3552.A4
Baker, Deb, 1953-	PS3602.A586
Baker, Donna.	PR6052.A327
Baker, Elliott.	PS3552.A424
Baker, Ivon, 1928-	PR6052.A334
Baker, James Robert.	PS3552.A4278
Baker, John F., 1942-	PR6052.A338
Baker, Lise S.	PS3552.A43147
Baker, Lucinda, 1916-	PS3552.A4315
Baker, Nikki, 1962-	PS3552.A4327
Baker, Peter, 1921-	PR6003.A484
Baker, Robin, 1944-	PR6102.A5735
Baker, S. H. (Sarah H.)	PS3619.T693
Baker, Sam, 1966-	PR6102.A574
Baker, Susan, 1949-	PS3552.A4348
Baker, Susan P.	PS3602.A588
Baker, Sylvia, 1945-	PR6052.A366
Baker, T. N.	PS3602.A5885
Baker, Virginia.	none
Baker, Will, 1935-	PS3573.E199
Baker, William Howard.	PR6052.A37
Bakker, R. Scott.	PR9199.4.B356
Bakos, Susan Crain.	PS3552.A4383
Balaka, Bettina, 1966-	PT2662.A445
Balan, Bruce.	none
Balasch i Blanch, Enric, 1955-	PQ6702.A62
Balchin, Nigel, 1908-1970.	PR6003.A52
Baldacci, David.	PS3552.A446
Baldwin, Juanitta, 1927-	PS3552.A4513
Baldwin, Kim.	PS3602.A59537
Baldwin, Michael, 1930-	PR6052.A39
Baldwin, Richard L.	PS3552.A451525
Baldwin, Stanley C.	PS3552.A4517
Balester, Patrick.	PS3602.A59548
Balestrini, Nanni.	PQ4862.A37
Balfour, James.	none
Balham, Joe.	none
Ball, Brian, 1932-	PR6052.A42
Ball, David W.	PS3552.A45448
Ball, Donna.	PS3552.A4545

Ball, John Dudley, 1911-1989.	PS3552.A455
Ball, K. Randall, 1948-	none
Ball, Pamela.	PS3552.A4554
Ball, Terence.	PS3552.A45544
Ballard, Carol (Carol L.)	PS3602.A62
Ballard, J. G., 1930-2009.	PR6052.A46
	[Z8068.94]
Ballard, K. G., d. 1964.	PS3568.O85413
Ballard, Mignon Franklin.	PS3552.A466
Ballard, P. D., 1903-1980.	PS3503.A5575
Ballard, Pat (Patricia F.)	PS3552.A4664
Ballard, Todhunter, 1903-1980.	PS3503.A5575
Ballem, John Bishop.	PR9199.3.B36
Ballenger, Dean W.	none
Balliett, Blue, 1955-	none
Balling, L. Christian.	PS3552.A468
Ballinger, Bill S. (Bill Sanborn), 1912-	PS3552.A47
Ballinger, John.	PS3552.A47125
Ballinger, W. A.	PR6052.A37
Balmer, Edwin, 1883-1959.	PS3503.A55813
Balnave, James.	none
Balneaves, Elizabeth.	none
Balogh, Mary.	PR6052.A465
Baltzell, Karin Bundesen, 1941-	PS3602.A63
Baluja, Shumeet, 1971-	PS3602.A633
Balzo, Sandra.	PS3602.A634
Bambola, Sylvia.	PS3552.A47326
Banbury, Jen.	PS3552.A4737
Bandler, James.	PS3552.A47534
Bandy, Franklin, 1914-1987.	PS3552.A4754
Bane, Diana.	none
Bangs, John Kendrick, 1862-1922.	PS1064.B3
Baniewicz, Artur, 1963-	PG7202.A55
Banko, Daniel.	PS3552.A479
Bankoff, Peter N., 1947-	PS3552.A4793
Banks, Barbara.	PR6052.A484
Banks, Carolyn.	PS3552.A485
Banks, Iain, 1954-	PR6052.A485
Banks, Joan.	none
Banks, L. A.	PS3602.A64
Banks, Leslie E.	PS3602.A64
Banks, Oliver T.	PS3552.A488
Banks, Ray.	PR6102.A65
Banks, River, 1940-	PS3552.A489
Banks, Russell, 1940-	PS3552.A49
Banks, T. F.	PR9199.3.B367
Banning, John.	none
Bannister, Jo.	PR6052.A497
Bannon, Don.	none
Banscherus, Jürgen.	none
Bantock, Nick.	PR6052.A54
Banville, John.	PR6052.A57
Banville, Vincent.	PR6052.A572
Baptiste, Claire.	PR9272.9.B37

Bar-Zohar, Michael, 1938-   PR9510.9.B3
                                                       PJ5054.B324
Barak, Michael—see: Bar-Zohar, Michael, 1938-
Baraldi, Barbara.   PQ4902.A725
Baranay, Inez.   PR9619.3.B319
Baráth, Katalin, 1978-   PH3382.12.A728
Baratham, Gopal, 1935-2002.   PR6052.A594
Baratz-Logsted, Lauren.   PS3602.A754
Barber, Christine.   PS3602.A7595
Barber, Noel, 1909-   PR6052.A623
Barbieri, Maggie.   PS3602.A767
Barbour, Anne.   PS3552.A595
Barcelo, E. C.   none
Barclay, Alex.   PR6102.A75
Barclay, Ben.   none
Barclay, Ian.   PR6052.A626
Barclay, Linwood.   PR9199.3.B37135
Barcomb, Wayne, 1933-   PS3602.A775
Bard, Patrick.   PQ2662.A676
Bardin, John Franklin.   PS3503.A56374
Bardsley, Michael.   PS3552.A616
Barer, Helen.   PS3602.A77535
Barger, Ralph.   PS3602.A833
Bark, Conrad Voss—see: Voss Bark, Conrad.
Barken, A. H. (Aaron H.)   PS3552.A61665
Barker, Albert, 1900-   PS3503.A5655
Barker, Clive, 1952-   PR6052.A6475
Barker, Dudley.   PR6003.A679
Barker, Joseph, 1929-   PR6052.A6487
Barker, Pat, 1943-   PR6052.A6488
Barker, Trey R.   PS3602.A77555
Barker, Wade.   none
Barkley, Deanne.   PS3552.A6714
Barkworth, S.   PS3552.A6724
Barlay, Bennett, 1910-   PS3505.R89224
Barlay, Stephen.   PR6052.A654
Barling, Charles.   none
Barling, Tom.   none
Barlow, James, 1921-   PR6052.A66
Barlow, Linda.   PS3552.A67255
Barnaby, Peter.   none
Barnao, Jack.   PR9199.3.B3717
Barnard, Robert.   PR6052.A665
Barnes, Dallas L., 1941-   PS3552.A6738
Barnes, Eric.   PS3602.A8338
Barnes, Joanna, 1934-   PS3552.A674
Barnes, John, 1957-   PS3552.A677
Barnes, Jonathan.   PR6102.A768
Barnes, Julian.   PR6052.A6657
Barnes, Linda.   PS3552.A682
Barnes, Mark (Mark David)   PS3602.A77564
Barnes, Robert C.   none
Barnes, Trevor, 1955-   PR6052.A6688
Barnett, James, 1920-   PR6052.A69

Barnett, Mac.	PS3602.A83427
Barnett, Stan.	PS3602.A776
Barns, Glenn M.	PS3552.A717
Baroff, David.	PS3552.A7246
Baron, Aileen Garsson.	PS3602.A8345
Baron, Michael, 1952-	PS3602.A7774
Barone, Joe, 1942-	PS3602.A777415
Barone, Mike, 1924-	PS3551.L26
Barr, Elisabeth.	PR6052.A714
Barr, Emily.	PR6102.A77
Barr, Justin.	none
Barr, Nancy, 1972-	PS3602.A777435
Barr, Nevada.	PS3552.A73184
Barr, Robert.	PR6052.A715
Barr, Robert, 1850-1912.	PR4069.B38
Barr, Suzanne.	PS3602.A77745
Barrasso, Sibylle.	PS3602.A77746
Barratt, Robert.	none
Barre, Richard.	PS3552.A73253
Barrell, Jania.	none
Barrett, Dean.	PS3552.A7337
Barrett, Frank, 1848-1926.	PR4069.B55
Barrett, G. J. (Geoffrey John), 1928-1999.	PR6052.A7175
Barrett, Kathleen Anne.	none
Barrett, Lorna.	PS3602.A83955
Barrett, Margaret.	PR9199.3.B37373
Barrett, Max.	PR9619.3.B34
Barrett, Michael, 1924-	PR6052.A7215
Barrett, Neal.	PS3552.A7362
Barrett, Robert G.	PR9619.3.B342
Barrett, Susan, 1938-	PR6052.A723
Barrett, William E. (William Edmund), 1900-1986.	PS3503.A62873
Barrett-Lee, Lynne, 1959-	PR6102.A776
Barrie, J. M. (James Matthew), 1860-1937.	PR4070-4078 [Z8076]
Barrington, Pamela.	none
Barris, Chuck.	PS3552.A7367
Barritt, Christy.	PS3602.A77754
Barroll, Clare.	PS3552.A7369
Barron, Ann.	none
Barron, D. G. (Donald Gabriel)	PR6052.A725
Barron, Hugh.	none
Barron, Stephanie.	PS3563.A8357
Barroso, Miguel A.	PQ6652.A787
Barrow, Adam.	PS3552.A738
Barry, Brunonia.	PS3602.A777548
Barry, C. J.	PS3602.A777549
Barry, Charles—see: Bryson, Charles, 1877-	
Barry, Dave.	PS3552.A74146
Barry, Iris, 1895-1969.	PS3503.A643
Barry, Jerome, b. 1894	PS3503.A644
Barry, Loretta.	none
Barry, Mike, 1939-	PS3563.A434
Barry, Nora.	PS3552.A7425

Barry, Robert, 1938 Dec. 29-	PS3602.A7776
Barsov, Mikhail.	PG3479.R748
Bartell, Linda Lang.	none
Barth, Lois.	PS3552.A754
Barth, Richard, 1943-	PS3552.A755
Barthelme, Peter.	PS3552.A7633
Bartholomew, Cecilia.	PS3552.A764
Bartholomew, Nancy.	PS3552.A7645
Bartlett, James Y.	PS3552.A76539
Bartlett, Jean Anne.	none
Bartlett, L. L. (Lorraine L.)	PS3602.A83955
Barton, Beverly.	PS3552.A76777
Barton, Dan.	PS3552.A76785
Barton, Fredrick.	PS3552.A7687
Bartoy, Mitchell.	PS3602.A843
Bartram, George, 1931-	PS3553.A4335
Bartulin, Lenny.	PR9619.4.B38
Baruth, Philip E. (Philip Edward)	PS3552.A7794
Barwick, James.	PR6060.A453
Barwick, Tony, 1934-	PR6060.A453
Baryka, Marek.	none
Base, Ron.	PR9199.3.B3757
Basile, Gloria Vitanza.	none
Basmanova, Elena.	PG3479.S57
Bass, Jefferson.	PS3602.A8475
Bass, Milton R.	PS3552.A82
Bass, Ronald.	PS3552.A8215
Bassett, Jennifer.	none
Bastable, Bernard.	PR6052.A665
Bastion, Elisabeth.	PS3602.A8495
Batchelor, Reg, 1916-	PS3566.A34
Bateman, Colin, 1962-	PR6052.A773
Bateman, Marlene.	PS3602.A8535
Bateman, Tracey Victoria.	PS3602.A854
Bates, Karen Grigsby.	PS3602.A86
Bates, Quentin.	PR6102.A7847
Bates, Shelley.	PS3602.A875
Batonne, Eva, 1957-	PS3602.A894
Batshev, Vladimir.	PG3479.T73
Batta, Patricia K.	PS3602.A898
Batten, Jack.	PR9199.3.B37574
Battersby, Alan.	none
Battin, B. W.	none
Battison, Brian.	PR6052.A82
Battles, Brett.	PS3602.A923
Baucum, George M., 1932-	PS3602.A926
Baudino, Gael.	none
Bauer, Belinda, 1962-	PR6102.A796
Bauer, S. Wise.	PS3552.A83638
Bauer, Sydney, 1968-	PR9619.4.B386
Baughman, Lynnette.	PS3552.B38
Baum, L. Frank (Lyman Frank), 1856-1919.	PS3503.A923
Baumgold, Julie.	PS3552.A8453
Bavin, Bill.	none

Bawden, Nina, 1925-   PR6052.A84
Bax, Roger, 1908-   PR6073.I56
Baxt, George.   PS3552.A8478
Baxter, Cynthia.   PS3602.A975
Baxter, Glen.   PR6052.A8475
Baxter, Jean Rae.   PR9199.4.B39
Baxter, John, 1939-   PR9619.3.B36
Baxter, Mary Lynn.   PS3552.A8565
Baxter, Nancy Niblack.   PS3552.A857
Bay, Austin.   PS3552.A8586
Bay, Roger.   none
Bayard, Louis.   PS3552.A85864
Bayer, John.   PS3552.A85868
Bayer, Sandy.   PS3552.A85875
Bayer, William.   PS3552.A8588
Baylus, Robert F.   none
Bayne, Neil.   none
Bazal, Jean.   PQ2662.A9
Bazell, Josh.   PS3602.A994
Beach, Edward L. (Edward Latimer), 1918-2002.   PS3552.E12
Beach, Lynn.   none
Beakey, Chris.   PS3602.E2427
Beal, M. F. (Mary F.), 1937-   PS3552.E134
Beale, Elaine, 1962-   PS3552.E1366
Beall, Will.   PS3602.E243
Beam, Jack, 1949-   PS3552 .E1457
Bean, C. N.   none
Bean, Frederic, 1944-   PS3552.E152
Bean, Greg.   PS3552.E1525
Bear, David.   PS3552.E155
Bear, Greg, 1951-   PS3552.E157
Bearden, Milt.   PS3552.E172
Beardwood, Roger, 1932-   PR6052.E186
Beare, George.   PR9619.3.B38
Bearshaw, Brian, 1932-   none
Beasley, David R., 1931-   PR9199.3.B3762
Beason, Doug.   none
Beaton, M. C.   PR6053.H4535
Beattie, Tasman.   none
Beaty, David.   PR6003.E264
Beaudoin, Sean.   none
Beaufort, Simon.   PR6052.E2226
Beauman, Sally.   PR6052.E223
Beaumont, Charles, 1929-1967.   PS3552.E2316
Beaumont, Nicola.   PS3602.E2636
Bebris, Carrie.   PS3602.E267
Bechard, Gorman.   PS3552.E238
Beck, Glenn.   PS3602.E2685
Beck, Jessica.   PS3602.E2693
Beck, K. K.   PS3552.E248
Beck, Robert, 1918-1992.   PS3552.E25
Beck, William, 1949-   PS3602.E28
Becka, Elizabeth, 1963-   PS3602.E283
Becker, James.   PR6102.E236

Becker, Robin, M., 1967-	PS3602.E295
Becker, Stephen D., 1927-	PS3552.E26
Beckett, Jenifer.	PS3552.E27
Beckett, Simon.	PR6052.E286
Bedell, Geraldine.	PR6052.E293
Bedford, Jean, 1946-	PR9619.3.B452
Bedford, John, 1935-	PR6073.I47535
Bedford, Martyn.	PR6052.E31112
Bedford-Jones, H. (Henry), 1887-1949.	none
Beeby, Otto.	PR9619.3.B4
Beecham, Rose, 1958-	PR9639.3.B344
Beechcroft, William.	PS3552.E32
Beechey, Alan.	PR6052.E3155
Beeching, Jack.	PR6003.E295
Beede, John.	none
Beeding, Francis, pseud.	PR6003.E3
Beekman, E. M., 1939-	PS3552.E34
Beeman, Robin.	PS3552.E346
Beer, Olivier.	PQ2662.E334
Beevor, Antony, 1946-	PR6052.E323
Befeler, Mike.	PS3602.E37
Begg, Ken.	none
Beghel, Larry.	PR6052.E3255
Begiebing, Robert J., 1946-	PS3552.E372
Béguin, ReBecca.	PS3552.E374
Behm, Marc.	PS3552.E38
Behn, Noel.	PS3552.E4
Behr, Edward, 1926-2007.	PR6052.E327
Behrend, Arthur.	none
Beinhart, Larry.	PS3552.E425
Beirne, Gerard, 1962-	PR6052.E337
Beitia, Sara, 1977-	none
Belanger, Chuck.	none
Belfer, Lauren.	PS3552.E467
Belfort, Sophie.	PS3552.E474
Belgrave, Laura.	PS3552.E4745
Belinkie, Matt.	none
Bell, Albert A., 1945-	PS3552.E485
Bell, Alex.	PR6102.E435
Bell, Barbara, 1954-	PS3552.E4855
Bell, David, 1969 Nov. 17-	PS3602.E64544
Bell, Donna.	none
Bell, Gerard.	PR6052.E44
Bell, Glenn A.	PS3602.E453
Bell, James Scott.	PS3552.E5158
Bell, Josephine, 1897-1987.	PR6003.A525
Bell, Madison Smartt.	PS3552.E517
Bell, Malcolm, 1943-	PS3552.E5175
Bell, Michele Ashman, 1959-	PS3552.E5217
Bell, Nancy, 1932-	PS3552.E5219
Bell, Neil, 1887-1964.	PR6037.O843
Bell, Pauline.	PR6052.E443
Bell, Sara.	PS3602.E455
Bell, Ted.	PS3602.E6455

Bellah, James.	none
Bellairs, George, 1902-	PR6003.E4465
Bellak, George (George J.)	PS3552.E5317
Belle, Jove.	PS3602.E4574
Bellem, Robert Leslie, 1902-1968.	PS3503.E4438
Belletto, René.	PQ2662.E4537
Belli, Gioconda, 1948-	PQ7519.2.B44
Belliston, Rebecca.	PS3602.E458
Belloc, Hilaire, 1870-1953.	PR6003.E45
	[Z8087.7]
Bellon, Julie Coulter, 1969-	PS3602.E648
Bellow, Saul.	PS3503.E4488
	[Z8087.8]
Belmond, C. A.	PS3602.E46
Belsky, Dick.	PS3552.E5338
Belsky, Richard.	PS3552.E53385
Bel'ti⟨u⟩kov, Andreĭ.	PG3491.44.L59
Belzer, Richard.	PS3602.E6545
Benacquista, Tonino.	PQ2662.E4723
Benard, Cheryl, 1953-	PS3552.E5363
Benassi, Mark.	none
Benchley, Nathaniel, 1915-1981.	PS3503.E487
Benchley, Peter.	PS3552.E537
Benchley, T. Marie.	PS3602.E658
Bender, Carrie, 1953-	PS3552.E53845
Bendis, Brian Michael.	none
Benedek, Emily.	PS3602.E6615
Benedetti, Robert L.	PS3602.E6617
Benedict, Elizabeth.	PS3552.E5396
Benedict, John.	PS3602.E6625
Benedict, Laura, 1962-	PS3602.E6627
Benedict, Lynn, 1937-	PS3552.A476
Benedictus, David.	PR6052.E45
Bengen, Patti Ann.	PS3602.E4676
Benioff, David.	PS3552.E54425
Benison, C. C.	PR9199.3.B37783
Benjamin, Carol Lea.	PS3552.E54455
Benjamin, Paul, 1947-	PS3552.E5447
Benjamin, Peter, 1947-	PR6062.A778
Benjoya, Mitchell.	PS3552.E5454
Benke, Richard, 1942-	PS3602.E6643
Benn, James R.	PS3602.E6644
Benners, Bill, 1949-	PS3602.E664425
Bennet, Rick.	PS3552.E54753
Bennet, Robert Ames, 1870-1954.	PS3503.E54547
Bennett, Arnold, 1867-1931.	PR6003.E6
	[Z8089.3]
Bennett, Barbara Curry.	none
Bennett, Charles, 1899-1995.	PR6003.E63
Bennett, Cherie.	PS3552.E54574
Bennett, Dorothea.	PR6052.E52
Bennett, Dorothy.	none
Bennett, Dorothy, 1906-	PS3503.E5464
Bennett, Emerson, 1822-1905.	PS1094.B45

Bennett, Francis, 1941-	PR6052.E524
Bennett, Gregory Mantin.	none
Bennett, Hal, 1930-	PS3552.E546
Bennett, Jack, 1934-	PR9619.3.B476
Bennett, Janice.	none
Bennett, Jay, 1912-	PS3552.E5464
Bennett, John McGrew.	PS3552.E54735
Bennett, Margot, 1903-	PR6003.E646
Bennett, Mary Lou.	PS3552.E54739
Bennett, Mela Barrows.	PS3602.E469
Bennett, R. A. (Richard Alan), 1946-	PR6052.E5313
Bennett, Rebecca, 1935-	PS3552.E54752
Bennett, Robert D.	none
Bennett, Robert Jackson, 1984-	PS3602.E66455
Bennett, Ronan.	PR6052.E5315
Bennett, W. R.	none
Bennetts, Pamela.	PR6052.E533
Benoit, Charles.	PS3602.E668
Benoit, M. D., 1957-	PR9199.4.B466
Benoit, Margaret.	none
Benoît, Michel, 1940-	PQ2662.E4855
Benoît, Pierre, 1886-1962.	PQ2603.E583
Benrey, Ronald.	PS3552.E54764
Bensen, D. R. (Donald R.), 1927-1997.	PS3552.E54765
Benson, Ann.	PS3552.E547659
Benson, Ben.	PS3552.E5476595
Benson, Chris, 1953-	PS3552.E54766285
Benson, Daniel—see: Cooper, Colin.	
Benson, Edward Frederic, 1867-1940.	PR6003.E66
Benson, Eugene.	PR9199.3.B3787
Benson, O. G.	PS3552.E547663
Benson, Raymond, 1955-	PS3552.E547666
Bentinck, Henry.	none
Bentley, E. C. (Edmund Clerihew), 1875-1956.	PR6003.E7247
Bentley, John, 1908-	PR6003.E72475
Bentley, Joyce.	none
Bentley, Nicolas, 1907-1978.	PR6003.E7248
Bentley, Robert.	PS3552.E56
Benton, Caroline.	PR6102.E68
Benton, John, 1933-	PS3552.E57
Benton, Kenneth, 1909-	PR6052.E545
Benz, David.	PS3602.E725
Benzoni, Juliette.	PQ2662.E5
Berberian, Viken.	PS3602.E75
Berc, Shelley.	PS3552.E67
Berckman, Evelyn.	PS3552.E68
Bercovici, Eric.	PS3552.E6897
Bereg, Igor'+A1670.	none
Berenson, Alex.	PS3602.E75146
Berenson, Laurien.	PS3552.E6963
Beres, Michael.	PS3602.E7516
Beresford, J. D. (John Davys), 1873-1947.	PR6003.E73
Berg, Adam W.	none
Berg, Carol.	PS3602.E7523

Berger, Arthur Asa, 1933-	PS3602.E753
Berger, Bob.	PS3552.E71814
Berger, Eileen M.	PS3552.E7183
Berger, Karl, 1941-	PS3602.E7543
Berger, Thomas, 1924-	PS3552.E719
Berglund, Ingrid, 1966-	none
Bergman, Andrew.	PS3552.E7193
Bergon, Frank.	PS3552.E71935
Bergren, Lisa Tawn.	PS3552.E71938
Bergsma, Harold M.	PS3602.E7563
Bergstrom, Elaine.	none
Bergues Ramírez, Pablo.	PQ7390.B45
Berkeley, Anthony, 1893-1971.	PR6005.O855
Berkeley, Ellen Perry.	PS3602.E7565
Berkeley, Sara, 1967-	PR6052.E5875
Berkey, Brian Fair.	PS3552.E7217
Berkowitz, Ira.	PS3602.E7573
Berland, Nancy, 1941-	none
Berlin, Eric.	PS3552.E72484
Berliner, Ross.	PS3552.E7249
Berlinski, Claire.	PS3602.E758
Berlinski, David, 1942-	PS3552.E72494
Berman, Donald A., 1932-	PS3602.E7585
Bernanos, Georges, 1888-1948.	PQ2603.E5675
Bernard, D. V.	PS3602.E7594
Bernard, George.	none
Bernard, Jay, 1923-2006.	PR6069.A94
Bernard, Joel.	none
Bernard, Judd.	none
Bernard, Robert.	PS3563.A728
Bernard, Tom.	PS3602.E7595
Bernard, Trevor.	none
Berne, Karin.	none
Berne, Suzanne.	PS3552.E73114
Berney, Louis.	PS3552.E73125
Bernhard, Robert.	PS3552.E7314
Bernhardt, William, 1960-	PS3552.E73147
Bernier, John M.	none
Bernstein, Ken.	PS3552.E734
Berntsen, Gary.	PS3602.E7633
Berrenson, Marc.	none
Berrow, Norman.	PR6003.E74343
Berry, Carole.	PS3552.E743
Berry, Charlene A.	PS3552.E744
Berry, Hannah, 1982-	none
Berry, Jedediah.	PS3602.E76375
Berry, Linda, 1940-	PS3552.E74745
Berry, Steve, 1955-	PS3602.E764
Berson, Jon.	PS3552.E767
Bertematti, Richard.	PS3552.E7734
Bertrand, J. Mark, 1970-	PS3602.E7686
Besant, Walter, Sir, 1836-1901.	PR4104
Bessey, Siân Ann, 1963-	PS3552.E79495
Beste, R. Vernon.	PR6052.E75

Bester, Alfred.	PS3552.E796
Betit, Paul.	PS3602.E823
Betteridge, Don—see: Newman, Bernard, 1897-1968.	
Bettle, Janet.	PR6052.E84
Betts, Doris.	PS3552.E84
Betz, Ingrid.	none
Beukes, Lauren	PR9369.4.B485
Bevere, John.	PS3602.E8436
Beverley, Jo.	PR9199.3.B424
Bevill, C. L.	PS3602.E85
Bezuglov, Anatoliĭ Alekseevich.	PG3476.B459
Bhaṭṭa, Aśvinī.	PK1859.B46456
Bianchi, Eugene C.	PS3602.I16
Bianchi, Tony, 1952-	PR6102.I33
Bickers, Richard Townshend, 1917-	none
Bickham, Jack M.	PS3552.I3
Biddle, Cordelia Frances.	PS3552.I333
Biderman, Bob, 1940-	PS3552.I335
Bidulka, Anthony, 1962-	PR9199.4.B497
Biebel, David B.	PS3552.I3436
Bieber, Horst, 1942-	none
Biederman, Marcia, 1949-	PS3552.I344
Biedrzycki, David.	none
Biehl, Michael M., 1951-	PS3602.I34
Biery, Janet.	PS3602.I355
Bigelow, Bill.	PS3602.I36
Biggam, Simon R.	PR6102.I36
Biggers, Earl Derr, 1884-1933.	PS3503.I54 [Z8094.6]
Biggle, Lloyd, 1923-2002.	PS3552.I43
Biggs, Cheryl.	none
Bigsby, C. W. E.	PR6052.I35
Billheimer, John W.	PS3552.I452
Billing, Graham, 1936-2001.	PR9639.3.B5
Billingham, Mark.	PR6102.I44
Billingsley, ReShonda Tate.	PS3602.I445
Bilyeau, Nancy.	PS3602.I49
Binchy, Maeve.	PR6052.I7728
Binder, Sibylle Luise.	none
Binding, Tim.	PR6052.I77294
Bindloss, Harold, 1866-1945.	PR6003.I67
Bingham, Carson, 1920-2005.	PS3553.A79555
Bingham, John, 1908-	PR6053.L283
Bingham, Linda S., 1946-	PS3602.I54
Bingham, Robert, d. 1999.	PS3552.I496
Bingham, Roger.	none
Bingham, Stella.	PR6052.I777
Bingle, Donald J.	PS3552.I496
Bingley, Margaret.	PR6052.I7775
Binnie, Stewart.	PR6052.I778
Binns, Ottwell, 1872-	PR6003.I736
Binyon, T. J.	PS3552.I58
Bioy Casares, Adolfo.	PQ7797.B535
Birchfield, D. L., 1948-	PS3602.I725

Bird, Al.   PS3552.I69
Bird, Jessica.   PS3623.A73227
Bird, Kenneth.   none
Bird, Michael J.   PR6052.I7914
Birkegaard, Mikkel.   PT8177.12.I75
Birken, Gary A.   PS3552.I75432
Birkin, Charles.   none
Birkwood, Ilene.   PR9639.4.B57
Birmajer, Marcelo.   PQ7798.12.I635
Birmingham, John, 1964-   PR9619.3.B5136
Birmingham, Maisie.   PR6052.I7955
Birmingham, Ruth.   PS3569.O695
Birmingham, Stephen.   PS3552.I7555
Birznieks, Ilmars, 1932-   none
Bischoff, David.   PS3552.I759
Bishop, Carly.   PS3552.I7595
Bishop, Claudia, 1947-   PS3552.I75955
Bishop, George Victor.   PS3552.I7598
Bishop, Maggie, 1949-   PS3602.I76
Bishop, Mary.   none
Bishop, Paul.   PS3552.I7723
Bishop, Roland J.   PS3552.I77235
Bishop, Sandra, 1942-   none
Bishop, Sheila.   none
Bissell, Elaine.   PS3552.I7728
Bissell, Sallie.   PS3552.I772916
Bjorgum, Kenneth.   PS3552.J56
Blacher, Joan H.   PS3602.l225
Black Artemis.   PS3602.L24
Black, Baxter, 1945-   PS3552.L288
Black, Benjamin, 1945-   PR6052.A57
Black, Betty.   PS3552.L29
Black, Campbell.   PR6052.L25
Black, Cara, 1951-   PS3552.L297
Black, David, 1945-   PS3552.L32
Black, Donal James, 1924-   PR6052.L274
Black, Edwin.   PS3552.L323
Black, Ethan.   PS3552.L324
Black, Gavin, 1913-   PR6073.Y65
Black, Hermina.   PR6052.L29
Black, Ian Stuart, 1915-1997.   PR6052.L3
Black, Ingrid.   PR6102.L33
Black, Irene Loyd.   none
Black, Jaid.   PS3602.L285
Black, Jonathan, 1922-   PS3572.O42
Black, Laura.   PR6052.L32
Black, Ladbroke Lionel Day, 1877-   none
Black, Lionel, 1910-   PR6003.A679
Black, Lisa, 1963-   PS3602.E283
Black, Mansell.   PR6039.R518
Black, Michael A., 1949-   PS3602.L325
Black, Michelle.   PS3552.L34124
Black, Ronica.   PS3602.L325243
Black, Sean.   PR6102.L3335

Black, Stephanie, 1969-   PS3602.L32525
Black, Tony.   PR6102.L334
Black, Veronica.   PR6052.L335
Blackburn, John, 1923-   PR6052.L34
Blacker, Irwin R.   PS3552.L3423
Blacker, Terence.   PR6052.L3414
Blackledge, Ethel H.   none
Blackmore, Jane.   PR6052.L3415
Blackmur, L. L.   PS3552.L3426
Blackstock, Charity.   PR6070.O65
Blackstock, Lee—see: Blackstock, Charity.
Blackstock, Terri, 1957-   PS3552.L34285
Blackwell, Lawana, 1952-   PS3552.L3429
Blackwood, Algernon, 1869-1951.   PR6003.L3
Blagowidow, George.   PS3552.L344
Blain, W. Edward.   PS3552.L3448
Blaine, Michael.   PS3552.L3454
Blair, Allan—see: Bayfield, William John, 1871-
1958
Blair, Cynthia.   PS3552.L34624
Blair, Iain.   none
Blair, Jennifer.   none
Blair, John.   none
Blair, Kerry, 1958-   PS3552.L34628
Blair, Marcia.   none
Blair, Michael, 1946-   PR9199.4.B56
Blais, Marie Claire.   PQ3919.B6
                                                                 [Z8102.85]
Blaisdell, Anne, 1921-1988.   PS3562.I515
Blake, Ashley.   PS3602.L34
Blake, Christina Stead—see: Stead, Christina, 1902-1983.
Blake, Daniel, 1969-   PR6069.T345
Blake, James Carlos.   PS3552.L3483
Blake, Jennifer, 1942-   PS3563.A923
Blake, Katherine.   PS3552.L3485
Blake, Ken, 1921-2005.   PR6003.U35
Blake, Margaret, 1921-   PR6057.I538
Blake, Michelle.   PS3552.L3488
Blake, Nicholas, 1904-1972.   PR6007.A95
Blake, Nick, 1958-   none
Blake, Patrick, 1927-   PR6055.G55
Blake, Stephanie, 1923-   PS3566.E218
Blake, Vanessa, 1913-   none
Blake, Victoria.   PR6102.L35
Blake, William Dorsey.   none
Blakeston, Oswell.   PR6052.L35
Blanc, Nero.   PS3552.L365
Blanc, Suzanne.   PS3552.L365
Blanchard, Al.   PS3602.L355
Blanchard, Alice.   PS3552.L36512
Blanchard, Keith, 1966-   PS3602.L36
Blanchard, Nina.   PS3552.L36514
Bland, Eleanor Taylor.   PS3552.L36534
Bland, Jennifer, 1925-   PS3552.O845

Blank, Hannah I.	PS3602.L38
Blank, Martin.	PS3552.L3659
Blankenship, William D.	PS3552.L366
Blankfort, Michael, 1907-1982.	PS3503.L477
Blatte, Marc, 1951-	PS3602.L395
Blatty, William Peter.	PS3552.L392
Blaudez, Lena, 1958-	PT2702.L38
Blauner, Peter.	PS3552.L3936
Blaylock, James P., 1950-	PS3552.L3966
Blayn, Hugo, 1908-1960.	PR6011.E295
Blazer, J. S.	PS3552.L4
Blechta, Rick.	PR9199.3.B49
Blecker, Rhoda.	PS3602.L44
Bledsoe, Alex.	PS3602.L456
Bleeck, Oliver, 1926-	PS3570.H58
Bleecker, Theodore.	PS3552.L4185
Blevins, Meredith.	PS3602.L48
Blickle, Katrinka.	PS3552.L48
Blincoe, Nicholas.	PR6052.L55
Blish, Nelson Adrian, 1945-	PS3602.L57
Bliss, Lauralee.	PS3602.L575
Bliss, Miranda.	PS3602.L577
Blixt, David.	PS3602.L59
Blobel, Brigitte, 1942-	none
Bloch, Don.	PS3552.L55
Bloch, Jon P.	PS3602.L63
Bloch, Robert, 1917-1994.	PS3503.L718
	[Z8105.55]
Blochman, Lawrence Goldtree, 1900-	PS3503.L719
Block, Barbara.	PS3552.L614
Block, Brett Ellen.	PS3602.L64
Block, Lawrence.	PS3552.L63
Block, Paul.	PS3562.A259
Block, Valerie, 1964-	PS3552.L6345
Blodgett, Michael.	PS3552.L6355
Blom, K. Arne, 1946-	PT9876.12.L545
Bloodworth, Dennis.	PR6052.L59
Bloom, Edie.	none
Bloom, Elizabeth, 1969-	PS3569.A7882
Bloom, Matt, 1964-	PS3552.L6393
Bloom, Murray Teigh, 1916-	PS3552.L6394
Bloomfield, Anthony, 1922-	PR6052.L64
Bloomfield, Robert, 1912-	PS3509.D472
Bloomquist, Tim.	PS3552.L643
Blosil, Georgia Jensen.	PS3602.L67
Bloxham, Peter.	none
Bloxsom, Peter.	PR6052.L67
Bludis, Jack.	PS3602.L83
Blum, Bill.	PS3552.L834
Blum, Ralph, 1932-	PS3552.L84
Blum, Richard H.	PS3552.L842
Blumberg, Gary.	none
Blumenthal, John.	PS3552.L8485
Blumer, Adam, 1969-	PS3602.L87

Blundy, Anna, 1970-	PR6102.L86
Blunt, Giles.	PS3552.L887
Blunt, Ronald L.	PS3552.L889
Bly, Carol.	PS3552.L89
Bly, Stephen A., 1944-	PS3552.L93
Boán, Daniel, 1967-	PQ7798.412.O36
Board, Sherri L.	PS3552.O25
Boast, Philip.	PR6052.O19
Bobbs, Elspeth G. (Elspeth Grant), 1920-	PS3602.O26
Bobker, Lee R.	PS3552.O256
Bobkins, Denk.	none
Bocca, Geoffrey.	PR6052.O2
Bochco, Steven.	PS3602.O325
Böckl, Manfred.	PT2662.O253
Böckler, Michael.	none
Bodeen, DeWitt.	PS3503.O167
Bodelsen, Anders, 1937-	PT8176.12.O34
Bodman, Karna Small.	PS3602.O3257
Bodoin, Dorothy.	PS3602.O34
Boehringer, Heidi W.	PR6102.O37
Bogart, Stephen Humphrey.	PS3552.O4334
Bogart, William G.	none
Boggis, David.	none
Bogner, Norman, 1935-	PS3552.O45
Bogolin, Carol.	none
Bohan, Becky, 1952-	PS3552.O488
Bohan, Edmund.	PR9639.3.B59
Bohjalian, Chris, 1960-	PS3552.O495
Bohle, Edgar, 1909-	none
Boileau, Pierre, 1906-1989.	PQ2603.O27
Boileau-Narcejac.	PQ2603.O27
Boland, John, 1913-	PR6052.O36
Boland, John C.	PS3552.O575
Boland, Paul.	PS3602.O65
Bolaño, Roberto, 1953-2003.	PQ8098.12.O38
Boldrewood, Rolf, 1826-1915.	PR9619.2.B74
Bolea, Juan, 1959-	PQ6652.O52
Boles, Paul Darcy, 1916-	PS3552.O584
Bolger, Dermot, 1959-	PR6052.O384
Bolin, Janet.	PS3602.O6534
Boling, Janet.	PS3602.O654
Bolitho, Janie.	PR6052.O386
Bolt, Ben—see: Binns, Ottwell, 1872-	
Bolt, Carol.	PR9199.3.B58
Bolton, Carole.	PS3552.O5876
Bolton, Clyde.	PS3552.O5877
Bolton, S. J.	PR6102.O49
Bonanno, Bill.	PS3602.O656
Bonansinga, Jay R.	PS3552.O5927
Bond, Evelyn, 1926-	PS3558.E78
Bond, Larry.	PS3552.O59725
Bond, Michael.	PR6052.O52
Bond, Ruskin.	PR9499.3.B65
Bond, Stephanie.	PS3552.O59736

Bond, Walter.	none
Bondurant, Matt, 1971-	PS3602.O657
Bone, Timothy F.	PS3602.O65715
Bonett, Emery, 1906-	none
Bonett, John, 1906-	PR6005.O79
Bonfiglioli, Kyril.	PR6052.O574
Bonham, Frank.	PS3503.04315
Bonnamy, Francis.	PS3545.A6422
Bonnecarrère, Paul.	PQ2662.O5975
Bonner, Hilary.	PR6102.O56
Bonnot, Xavier-Marie, 1962-	PQ2702.O58
Bonsall, Crosby, 1921-1995.	none
Bontly, Thomas, 1939-	PS3552.O643
Boone, Mark Allen.	PS3552.O64384
Booth, Martin.	PR6052.O63
Booth, Stephen, 1952-	PR6052.O64
Boothby, Guy Newell, 1867-1905.	PR4149.B957
Booton, Kage.	PS3552.O68
Boray, Paul.	PS3561.E4246
Borden, Kate.	PS3602.O685
Borg, Todd.	PS3552.O737
Borgen, Johan, 1902-	PT8950.B713
Borgenicht, Miriam.	PS3552.O75
Borger, Judith Yates.	PS3602.O747
Borges, Jorge Luis, 1899-1986.	PQ7797.B635
Bork, Lisa, 1964-	PS3602.O755
Borland, Kathryn Kilby.	PS3552.O754
Borlik, Linda Stahl.	none
Born, James O.	PS3602.O76
Borneman, Ernest, 1915-	PR6003.O613
Bornemark, Kjell-Olof, 1924-	PT9876.12.O76
Borniche, Roger.	PQ2662.O6855
Bornschein, Dora.	PS3602.O766
Borodyni‹a›, Aleksandr, 1957-	PG3479.4.O674
Borowitz, Albert, 1930-	PS3552.O7547
Borthwick, J. S.	PS3552.O756
Borton, D. B.	none
Borton, Douglas.	none
Bosak, Steven.	PS3552.O7568
Bose, Rana.	PR9199.3.B5975
Bosetzky, Horst.	PT2662.O77
Bosse, Malcolm J. (Malcolm Joseph)	PS3552.O77
Boston, Jordanna.	PR9199.3.B598
Bosworth, Frank, 1916-	PS3566.A34
Böszörményi, Zoltán, 1951-	PH3382.12.O88
Boucher, Anthony, 1911-1968.	PS3545.H6172
Boucher, Bernard.	PR6052.O795
Boulds, Tammy L.	PS3602.O8895
Boulle, Pierre, 1912-1994.	PQ2603.O754
Bourdain, Anthony.	PS3552.O8328
Bourgeau, Art.	PS3552.O833
Bourjaily, Vance Nye.	PS3503.O77
Bourne, Hester.	none
Bourne, Sam, 1967-	PR6102.O92

Bouton, Mark.	PS3602.O894
Bova, Ben, 1932-	PS3552.O84
Bowden, Jean—see: Annandale, Barbara, 1925-	
Bowden, Susan, 1936-	PR9199.3.B628
Bowen, Gail, 1942-	PR9199.3.B629
Bowen, John, 1924-	PR6052.O85
Bowen, Kevin.	none
Bowen, Marjorie, 1888-1952.	PR6003.O676
Bowen, Michael, 1951-	PS3552.O864
Bowen, Peter, 1945-	PS3552.O866
Bowen, Rhys.	PR6052.O848
Bowen, Robert Sidney, 1900-	none
Bower, Mick, 1966-	none
Bowering, George, 1935-	PR9199.3.B63
	[Z8111.47]
Bowers, Elisabeth.	PS3552.O87197
Bowick, Dorothy Miiller.	PS3552.O8736
Bowie, Phil.	PS3602.O8975
Bowker, David.	PR6052.O879
Bowker, Richard.	PS3552.O8739
Bowler, Tim.	none
Bowling, Harry.	PR6052.O887
Bowman, David, 1957-	PS3552.O8757
Bowman, Eric, 1953-	PS3556.R599
Bowman, Jeanne, 1895-	PS3503.O8455
Bowman, Robert J.	PS3552.O8758
Bowne, Sam, 1925-	PS3552.O8765
Bowser, Jim.	none
Bowyer, John.	none
Box, C. J.	PS3552.O87658
Box, Edgar, 1925-	PS3543.I26
Boxer, Barbara.	PS3602.O923
Boyd, Austin, 1954-	PS3602.O928
Boyd, Bill (William Young)	PS3552.O884
Boyd, Donna, 1951-	PS3552.O87757
Boyd, Edward.	PR6052.O918
Boyd, John, 1919-	PS3571.P35
Boyd, Noah.	PS3602.O9326
Boyd, Randy.	PS3552.O8786
Boyd, W. Y.—see: Boyd, Bill (William Young)	
Boyd, William, 1952-	PR6052.O9192
Boyer, Bruce Hatton, 1946-	PS3552.O888
Boyer, Richard L.—see: Boyer, Rick.	
Boyer, Rick.	PS3552.O895
Boykin, Jerry.	PS3602.O955
Boylan, Clare.	PR6052.O9193
Boylan, Eleanor.	PS3552.O912
Boyle, Alistair.	PS3552.O917
Boyle, Ann.	none
Boyle, Gerry, 1956-	PS3552.O925
Boyle, Kay, 1902-1992.	PS3503.O9357
	[Z8111.92]
Boyle, Robert.	PR6052.O95
Boyle, Steve, 1955-	none

Boyle, T. Coraghessan.	PS3552.O932
Boyle, Thomas, 1939-	PS3552.O933
Boyll, Randall.	PS3552.O936
Boym, Svetlana, 1959-	PS3602.O974
Boyne, John, 1971-	PR6102.O96
Brace, Timothy, 1901-1969.	PS3531.R248
Brack, Robert, 1959-	none
Brackett, Beverley.	PS3602.R33
Brackett, Leigh.	PS3503.R154
Bradberry, James.	PS3552.R2127
Bradbury, Ray, 1920-	PS3503.R167
Bradbury, Wilbur.	PS3552.R213
Bradby, Tom.	PR6102.R33
Braddon, M. E. (Mary Elizabeth), 1837-1915.	PR4989.M4
Braddon, Russell.	PR6052.R25
Bradford, Barbara Taylor, 1933-	PS3552.R2147
Bradford, Kelly.	PS3552.R217
Bradford, Michael.	none
Bradley, C. Alan, 1938-	PR9199.4.B7324
Bradley, David, 1950-	PS3552.R226
Bradley, James, 1967-	PR9619.3.B655
Bradley, Jane, 1955-	PS3552.R2274
Bradley, John Ed.	PS3552.R2275
Bradley, Lynn.	PS3552.R2277
Bradley, Marion Zimmer.	PS3552.R228
Bradley, Michael—see: Blumberg, Gary.	
Bradley, Michael Anderson, 1944-	PR9199.3.B67
Bradshaw, Mel, 1947-	PR9199.4.B7325
Brady, Charles.	PS3552.R238
Brady, Elizabeth, 1945-	PR9199.3.B675
Brady, James, 1928-2009.	PS3552.R243
Brady, Joan, 1939-	PS3552.R2432
Brady, John, 1955-	PR6052.R2626
Brady, Leo, 1917-	PS3503.R233
Brady, Michael.	PS3552.R2436
Brady, Nicholas, 1935-	none
Brady, Rachel, 1975-	PS3602.R3437
Brady, Ryder.	PS3552.R245
Braff, Menalton, 1938-	PQ9698.12.R14
Braffet, Kelly, 1976-	PS3602.R3444
Bragan, Jeris E., 1946-	PS3552.R247
Brahms, Caryl, 1901-1982.	PR6001.B6
Brain, Leonard—see: Peck, Leonard, 1906-	
Brain, Robert, 1933-	PR9619.3.B65
Braithwaite, Kent.	PS3552.R2755
Braly, Malcolm, 1925-1980.	PS3552.R28
Bram, Christopher.	PS3552.R2817
Bramah, Ernest, 1869?-1942.	PR6037.M425
Bramble, Forbes, 1939-	PR6052.R2687
Bramwell, Charlotte, 1929-	PS3561.I417
Brand, Axel.	PS3573.H4345
Brand, Christianna, 1907-1988.	PR6023.E96
Brand, Fiona.	PR9639.4.B726
Brand, Max, 1892-1944.	PS3511.A87

Brand, Rebecca, 1939-	PS3553.H325
Brand, Susan.	PS3552.R293
Brandeis, Robin, 1961-	PS3602.R35
Brandel, Marc, 1919-	PS3503.R25784
Brandewyne, Rebecca.	PS3552.R296
Brandl, Dave.	PS3552.R298
Brandman, Michael.	PS3602.R356
Brandner, Gary.	PS3552.R313
Brandon, Beatrice.	PS3521.R527
Brandon, Jay.	PS3552.R315
Brandon, Paula.	PS3602.R36
Brandon, Ruth.	PR6052.R2765
Brandreth, Gyles Daubeney, 1948-	PR6052.R2645
Brandstetter, Alois.	PT2662.R258
Brandt, Ann, 1937-	PS3552.R3214
Brandt, Beverly.	PS3602.R3635
Brandt, Nat.	PS3552.R3233
Brandt, Roger.	none
Brandt, Tom—see: Dewey, Thomas Blanchard, 1915-	
Brandvold, Peter.	PS3552.R3236
Branham, Mary, 1929-	PS3552.R3238
Branon, Bill.	PS3552.R3253
Branston, Frank, 1939-	PR6052.R278
Brant, James.	PS3561.E4246
Brantley, Paige.	none
Branton, Matthew.	PR6052.R278
Brass, Perry.	PS3552.R336
Brasse, William.	none
Brat'i‹a› Alovy.	PG3491.46.R385
Braudy, Susan.	PS3552.R343
Braun, Lilian Jackson.	PS3552.R354
Braun, Matt, 1932-	PS3552.R355
Braunstein, Sarah, 1976-	PS3602.R3895
Brautigan, Richard.	PS3503.R2736
Braver, Gary.	PS3552.R3554
Brawer, Richard, 1943-	PS3552.R3559
Brawner, Daniel B.	PS3602.R395
Braxton, Hank.	none
Brayfield, Celia.	PR6052.R34
Brayne, Alan.	PR6102.R39
Brean, Herbert.	PS3503.R3
Breaznell, Gene.	PS3552.R3577
Brebner, Percy James, 1864-1922.	PR6003.R3265
Brechin, David.	none
Breckon, Ian, 1970-	PR6102.R43
Bredes, Don.	PS3552.R363
Breem, Wallace.	PR6052.R36
Breen, Jon L., 1943-	PS3552.R3644
Breen, Richard, 1936-	PS3552.R3646
Breeze, Paul A.	PR6052.R37
Breitenbach, Bert.	none
Brenna, Duff.	PS3552.R377
Brenna, Helen.	PS3602.R449
Brennan, Alice.	none

Brennan, Allison.   PS3602.R4495
Brennan, Carol.   PS3552.R3777
Brennan, Dan, 1917-   PS3503.R4474
Brennan, J. H.   PR6052.R412
Brennan, Jan—see: Brennan, J. H.
Brennan, Joseph Payne, 1918-   PS3503.R455
Brennan, Peter.   PS3552.R382
Brennan, Thomas.   PS3602.R454
Brent, Loring, b. 1892.   PS3545.O97
Brent, Madeleine.   PR6052.R419
Brent, Peter Ludwig.   PR6052.R42
Brent, R. L.   none
Breslin, Catherine.   PS3552.R388
Breslin, Jimmy.   PS3552.R39
Bretnor, Reginald.   PS3552.R395
Breton, Laurie.   PS3602.R4577
Breton, Thierry.   PQ2662.R4832
Bretonne, Anne-Marie.   none
Brett, Barbara.   none
Brett, Brian.   PR9199.3.B6926
Brett, David.   PR6052.R429
Brett, Hy.   PS3552.R398
Brett, John Michael—see: Brett, Michael, 1921-
Brett, Michael, 1921-   PS3552.R413
Brett, Mike—see: Brett, Michael, 1921-
Brett, Simon.   PR6052.R4296
Brett, Stephen, 1947-   PS3613.E788
Brewer, Gil, 1922-1983.   PS3552.R4177
Brewer, James D.   PS3552.R418
Brewer, Mark.   PS3552.R4213
Brewer, Steve.   PS3552.R42135
Brewster, Joy.   none
Brez, E. M.   PS3552.R44
Brezenoff, Steve—see: Brezenoff, Steven.
Brezenoff, Steven.   none
Briant, John H., 1930-   PS3552.R448
Briant, Shane.   PR9619.3.B6933
Brida, Jay.   PS3602.R5313
Bridge, Ann, 1889-1974.   PR6029.M35
Bridges, Roy, 1885-1952.   none
Bridges, Victor.   PR6003.R3754
Brieno, Linda.   none
Brierley, David.   PR6052.R4432
Bright, Elizabeth.   PS3552.R46234
Brightwell, Emily.   PS3552.R46443
Briley, John.   PS3552.R468
Brill, Marius.   PR6102.R55
Brill, Toni.   PS3552.R478
Brin, David.   PS3552.R4825
Brindley, Louise.   PR6052.R4447
Brine, Patricia, 1938-   PR9199.4.B743
Bringle, Mary.   PS3552.R485
Brink, Carol Ryrie, 1895-1981.   PS3503.R5614
Brinton, Henry, 1901-   PR6052.R4455

Briody, Thomas Gately.	PS3552.R4886
Brisco, Pat.	none
Briskin, Jacqueline.	PS3552.R49
Bristow, Gwen, 1903-1980.	PS3503.R576
Brite, Poppy Z.	PS3552.R4967
Britto, Anthony.	PS3552.R4972
Britton, Andrew, 1981-2008.	PS3602.R534
Britton, Christopher.	PS3552.R4975
Britton, Vickie.	PS3552.R52
Brix, Alexa.	none
Broach, Elise.	PS3602.R538
Broadbent, Tony.	PS3602.R54
Broadrick, Annette.	none
Brock, Lynn—see: McAllister, Alister, b. 1877.	
Brock, Rose.	PS3558.A513
Brock, Stuart, 1917-	PS3539.R565
Brockmann, Suzanne.	PS3552.R61455
Brockovich, Erin.	PS3602.R6325
Brod, D. C.	PS3552.R6148
Broder, Bill, 1931-	PS3552.R619
Brodeur, Paul.	PS3552.R62
Brodie, Gordon.	none
Brodie, Laura Fairchild.	PS3602.R63486
Brodrick, William, 1960-	PR6102.R63
Brody, Marc, d. 1986.	none
Brogan, Jan.	PS3602.R64
Brogan, Mike.	PS3602.R642
Broinowski, Alison.	PR9619.3.B7
Brokaw, Charles.	PS3602.R6424
Brome, Vincent, 1910-2004.	PR6052.R573
Bromell, Henry.	PS3552.R634
Bromley, Gordon.	none
Bronleewe, Matt.	PS3602.R64266
Bronte, Louisa, 1925-1982.	PS3552.R656
Brook, Meljean.	PS3602.R64274
Brooke, Anne, 1964-	PR6102.R646
Brooke, John, 1951 Aug. 27-	PR9199.3.B697
Brooke, P. J.	PR6102.R65
Brookes, Owen, 1940-1988.	PR6052.R5815
Brookhouse, Christopher, 1938-	PS3552.R658
Brookins, Carl.	PS3602.R643
Brookmyre, Christopher, 1968-	PR6052.R58158
Brookner, Anita.	PR6052.R5816
Brooks, Edwy Searles, 1889-1965.	PR6003.R4235
Brooks, Erik, 1972-	none
Brooks, Kate.	none
Brooks, Kevin.	none
Brooks, Vivian Collin, 1922-	PR6052.R5824
Brooks, Walter R., 1886-1958.	PS3503.R733
Brophy, Beth.	PS3602.R646
Brophy, Grace, 1941-	PS3602.R6463
Brosnan, Kate, 1948-	none
Brothers, Jay.	PS3552.R675
Brouwer, Sigmund, 1959-	PS3552.R6825

Brown, Antony. PR6052.R589
Brown, Barry S. PS3602.R666
Brown, Carolyn, 1948- PS3552.R685275
Brown, Carrie, 1950- PS3552.R68528
Brown, Carter, 1923-1985. PR9619.3.B725
Brown, Charles Brockden, 1771-1810. PS1130-1138
[Z8123.585]
Brown, Charles Manley, 1921- PS3602.R685
Brown, Christy, 1932-1981. PR6052.R5894
Brown, Conlan. PS3602.R689
Brown, Dale, 1956- PS3552.R68543
Brown, Dan, 1964- PS3552.R685434
Brown, Dee Alexander. PS3503.R79533
Brown, Don, 1960- PS3602.R6947
Brown, Elaine Meryl. PS3602.R696
Brown, Elizabeth. PS3552.R68546
Brown, Fredric, 1906-1972. PS3503.R8135
Brown, George Douglas, 1869-1902. PR4174.B6
Brown, J. Edward. PR9639.3.B695
Brown, James Ambrose, 1919- PR9369.3.B72
Brown, James Cooke, 1921- PS3552.R68565
Brown, Jim, 1956 Aug. 14- PS3602.R7
Brown, Jo Ann. PS3602.R714
Brown, John, 1924- PR6052.R6134
Brown, John Edward, 1920- PS3552.R6857
Brown, John W., 1933- PS3552.R688
Brown, L. Virginia. none
Brown, Lizbie. PR6052.R6136
Brown, Mark, 1947- PS3552.R6942
Brown, Mary Monroe. none
Brown, Molly. PR6052.R61434
Brown, P. A. none
Brown, R. D. none
Brown, Rae. none
Brown, Richard E. (Richard Eugene) PS3552.R6977
Brown, Rita Mae. PS3552.R698
Brown, Rosel George. PS3503.R828437
Brown, Russell, 1934- PS3552.R7145
Brown, Ryan, 1975- PS3602.R7228
Brown, Sandra, 1948- PS3552.R718
Brown, Steve, 1944- PS3552.R724
Brown, Tracy, 1974- PS3602.R723
Brown, Virginia, 1947- none
Brown, Wenzell, 1912- PS3503.R8365
Brown, Zenith Jones, 1898-1983. PS3511.O4113
Browne, Dennis James. PS3552.R745
Browne, Douglas G. (Douglas Gordon), 1884- PR6003.R49
Browne, Gerald A. PS3552.R746
Browne, Howard, 1907-1999. PS3503.R8436
Browne, Marshall. PR9619.3.B7594
Browne, Robert. PS3602.R7366
Browne, Robert Gregory. PS3602.R7367
Browner, John P. none
Browning, John. PR6052.R619

Brownlee, Nick.	PR6102.R73
Brownleigh, Eleanora.	none
Brownley, Megan.	none
Broyles, R. L. (Randall L.), 1931-	none
Brubaker, Ed.	none
Bruce, Alison.	PR6102.R83
Bruce, Anthony, 1939-	PR9199.4.B78
Bruce, Colin.	PS3552.R7917
Bruce, Gemma.	PS3556.R45
Bruce, Jean, 1921-	PQ2603.R914
Bruce, John Edward.	PS3503.R876
Bruce, Leo, 1903-1979.	PR6005.R673
Bruce, Maggie.	PS3602.R8325
Bruce, Victoria.	none
Bruen, Ken.	PR6052.R785
Bruheim, Magnhild, 1951-	PT8951.12.R84
Bruhns, Nina.	PS3602.R835
Brumbaugh, Renae.	none
Brundage, Elizabeth.	PS3602.R84
Brunel, Sigrid, 1939-	PS3552.R7996
Brunger, Scott.	PS3552.R7998
Brunner, John, 1934-1995.	PR6052.R8
Bruno, Anthony.	PS3552.R82
Bruns, Don.	PS3602.R86
Brunstetter, Wanda E.	PS3602.R864
Brush, E. Jonathan.	PS3602.R87
Brussolo, Serge, 1951-	PQ2662.R8565
Bruton, Eric.	none
Bryan, Bill.	PS3602.R925
Bryant, Dorothy, 1930-	PS3552.R878
Bryant, Jennifer.	none
Bryant, Peter, 1924-1966.	PR6057.E54
Bryant, Will.	PS3552.R898
Bryant-Woolridge, Lori.	PS3573.O6863
Bryce, Robert.	none
Bryers, Paul.	PR6052.R94
Brykczynski, Terry.	PS3552.R98
Brylawski-Miller, Laura, 1930-	PS3552.R993
Bryson, Charles, 1877-	PR6003.R99
Bucay, Jorge, 1949-	PQ7798.12.U188
Buchan, James.	PR6052.U215
Buchan, John, 1875-1940.	PR6003.U13
Buchan, Sinclair.	PR9619.3.B78
Buchan, Stuart.	PS3552.U317
Buchanan, Edna.	PS3552.U324
Buchanan, James David.	PS3552.U325
Buchanan, Marie.	PR6053.U79
Buchanan, Patrick.	PS3552.U33
Buchanan, William J., 1926-2005.	PS3552.U332
Buchard, Robert, 1931-	PQ2662.U25
Buck, Jerry.	PS3552.U3328
Buck, John L., 1951-	PS3552.U3335
Buck, Paul, 1946-	PR6052.U25
Buck, Pearl Sydenstricker, 1892-1973.	PS3503.U198

Buck, Rebecca S.   PR6102.U328
Buckalew, Walker.   PS3602.U263
Buckey, Sarah Masters, 1955-   none
Buckingham, Nancy.   PR6052.U26
Buckley, Andrew.   PS3552.U3385
Buckley, Carla (Carla S.)   PS3602.U2645
Buckley, Fiona.   PR6052.U266
Buckley, Julia, 1964-   PS3602.U2648
Buckley, Kristen.   PS3602.U265
Buckley, Michael.   none
Buckley, Michelle.   PS3602.U2664
Buckley, William F. (William Frank), 1925-2008.   PS3552.U344
Buckman, Peter.   PR6052.U267
Buckmaster, Henrietta.   PS3503.U227
Buckstaff, Kathryn.   PS3552.U3453
Buda, Rick.   PS3602.U33
Bude, John.   none
Budrys, Algis, 1931-2008.   PS3552.U348
Buell, John, 1927-   PR9199.3.B766
Buffa, Dudley W., 1940-   PS3552.U3739
Buffer, Joe.   none
Buffett, Jimmy.   PS3552.U375
Bugbee, M. Howe.   none
Buggé, Carole.   PS3552.U389
Buhl, Marc, 1967-   PT2662.U376
Bukiet, Melvin Jules.   PS3552.U398
Bukowski, Charles.   PS3552.U4
Bulgakova, Inna.   PG3479.4.U539
Bull, Bartle.   PS3552.U4226
Bull, James C.   PS3602.U394
Bullard, Nick.   none
Bulliet, Richard W.   PS3552.U44
Bullivant, Cecil Henry.   none
Bullock, Lotte.   none
Bulmer, Kenneth, 1921-2005.   PR6003.U35
Bulock, Lynn.   PS3552.U463
Bulosan, Carlos.   PR9550.9.B8
Bulwer-Lytton, Edward—see: Lytton, Edward Bulwer Lytton, Baron,
1803-1873.
Bumgarner, Barri L.   PS3602.U47
Bunich, Igor'.   PG3479.4.U6
Bunker, Edward, 1933-2005.   PS3552.U47
Bunkley, Anita R. (Anita Richmond)   PS3552.U4715
Bunn, T. Davis, 1952-   PS3552.U4718
Bunn, Thomas, 1944-   PS3552.U472
Bunting, Eve, 1928-   PS3552.U4735
Buntline, Ned, 1822 or 3-1886.   PS2156.J2
Bunzel, Reed.   none
Burbidge, T. J.   PR9199.4.B868
Burbridge, Roger T.   PS3602.U728
Burcell, Robin.   PS3602.U729
Burden, Pat.   PR6052.U614
Burdess, Wendy.   PR6102.U67
Burdett, John.   PR6052.U617

Burge, Milward Rodon Kennedy—see: Kennedy, Milward, b. 1894.
Burger, Neal R.   none
Burges, Dennis.   PS3602.U742
Burgess, Anthony, 1917-1993.   PR6052.U638
                                                         [Z8132.2]
Burgess, Barbara Hood.   PS3552.U714137
Burgess, Eric, 1912-   PR6052.U639
Burgess, Gelett, 1866-1951.   PS3503.U6
Burgess, Mallory.   none
Burgh, Anita, 1937-   PR6052.U6424
Burgin, Richard.   PS3552.U717
Burgoyne, Victoria.   none
Burkard, Linore Rose, 1960-   PS3602.U754
Burke, Alafair.   PS3602.U755
Burke, Alan Dennis.   PS3552.U7213
Burke, Bill, 1935-   PS3602.U75516
Burke, Declan.   PR6102.U74
Burke, J. F., 1915-   PS3503.U6126
Burke, James Lee, 1936-   PS3552.U723
Burke, Jan.   PS3552.U72326
Burke, John Frederick, 1922-   PR6003.U54
Burke, Jonathan, 1922-   PR6003.U54
Burke, Lee John.   none
Burke, Michael, 1939-   PS3602.U75525
Burke, Morgan.   PS3569.I5257
Burke, Sean, 1961-   PR6102.U75
Burke, Stewart.   PR6052.U64435
Burke, Thomas, 1887-1945.   PR6003.U55
Burkey, Dave.   none
Burkholz, Herbert, 1932-2006.   PS3552.U725
Burleson, Clyde W., 1934-   none
Burley, W. J. (William John)   PR6052.U647
Burman, Carina, 1960-   PT9876.12.U69
Burmeister, Jon.   PR9369.3.B8
Burnard, Marcella.   PS3602.U759
Burnell, Mark.   PR6052.U6546
Burnes, Caroline.   PS3558.A329
Burnett, W. R. (William Riley), 1899-1982.   PS3503.U6258
Burney, Claudia Mair, 1964-   PS3602.U7636
Burns, Alma.   none
Burns, Emily.   none
Burns, Monica.   PS3602.U76645
Burns, Rex.   PS3552.U7325
Burns, Ron.   PS3552.U73253
Burnside, John, 1955-   PR6052.U6683
Burrage, Alfred McLelland.   PR6003.U566
Burroughs, Rick.   PS3602.U7686
Burrows, Julie.   PR6052.U669
Burrows, Phillip.   none
Burstyn, Varda.   PR9199.4.B88
Burton, Anne, 1922-1985.   PR6073.O63
Burton, Anthony, 1934-   PR6052.U69
Burton, Betty, 1929-   PR6052.U693
Burton, Craig.   PS3552.U772

Burton, Mary (Mary T.)	PS3602.U7699
Burton, Miles, 1884-1964.	PR6037.T778
Burton, Milton T.	PS3602.U77
Busbee, Shirlee.	PS3552.U7895
Busby, Elaine.	PS3602.U83
Busby, Roger.	PR6052.U76
Busch, Frederick, 1941-2006.	PS3552.U814
Busch, Niven, 1903-1991.	PS3503.U746
Bush, Christine.	PS3552.U816255
Bush, Christopher, 1885-1973.	PR6003.U63
Bush, Nancy, 1953-	PS3602.I764
Bushell, Agnes.	PS3552.U8224
Bushkov, Aleksandr, 1956-	PG3479.4.U824
Bussi, Michel, 1965-	PQ2662.U845
Butcher, Jim, 1971-	PS3602.U85
Butcher, Kenneth.	PS3602.U855
Butcher, Shannon K.	none
Butler, Gerald.	none
Butler, Gwendoline.	PR6052.U813
Butler, Jack, 1944-	PS3552.U826
Butler, K. R.	PR6052.U816
Butler, Michael, 1941-	none
Butler, Ragan.	PR6052.U825
Butler, Richard, 1925-	PR6052.U85
Butler, William, 1929-	PS3552.U83
Butler, William Vivian, 1927-1987.	PR6052.U875
Butterworth, Michael, 1924-1986.	PR6052.U9
Buttimore, Anna Jones, 1968-	PR6060.O485
Button, C. F.	PS3602.U8927
Butyrskiĭ, Fedor.	PG3479.4.U878
Buzzelli, Elizabeth Kane, 1946-	PS3602.U985
Byars, Betsy Cromer.	PS3552.Y37
Byerrum, Ellen.	PS3602.Y36
Byers, Bruce, 1920-	none
Byers, Cal.	PS3602.Y37
Byfield, Barbara Ninde.	PS3552.Y65
Byrd, Adrianne.	PS3602.Y726
Byrd, Elizabeth.	PS3552.Y67
Byrd, Max.	PS3552.Y675
Byrd, Rhyannon.	none
Byrne, Beverly.	PS3552.Y69
Byrne, Kim.	PS3602.Y763
Byrne, Robert, 1930-	PS3552.Y73
Byrne, Stuart J.	none
Byrnes, Michael (Michael J.)	PS3602.Y768
Byrom, James, 1911-	none
Byron, Christopher.	PS3552.Y78
Caballero Ramos, Modesto.	PQ7499.3.C33
Cabiya, Pedro, 1971-	PQ7442.C33
Cabot, Meg.	PS3553.A278
Cabot, Meggin.	PS3553.A278
Cacek, P. D. (Patricia D.)	PS3553.A312
Cade, Alexander.	PR6053.A33
Cade, Robin, 1930-	PR9320.9.N5

Cadell, Elizabeth.	PR6005.A225
Cady, Dick.	PS3603.A375
Cafeo, Marie H. (Marie Helen), 1942-	PS3553.A3175
Cafesin, J., 1958-	PS3603.A377
Cafferty, Jake.	none
Cahill, Mary.	PS3553.A36
Cahill, Richard.	PS3603.A378
Caidin, Martin, 1927-1997.	PS3553.A38
Cail, Carol.	PS3553.A385
Caille, Julie.	none
Caillou, Alan, 1914-	PR6053.A347
Cain, Carolyn.	PS3603.A379
Cain, Chelsea.	PS3603.A385
Cain, James M. (James Mallahan), 1892-1977.	PS3505.A3113
Cain, Paul.	none
Cain, Steven, 1953-	PR9199.4.C3355
Cain, Tom.	PR6103.A365
Caine, Hamilton T.	PS3569.M645
Caine, Jeffrey, 1944-	PR6053.A35
Caine, Leslie.	PS3603.A39
Caine, Peter.	none
Caine, Rachel.	PS3603.O557
Caird, Janet.	PR6053.A36
Cairns, Alison.	PR6053.A373
Cairns, Colleen.	PS3553.A394
Cake, Patrick.	PS3553.A3944
Calandro, Ed, 1944-	PS3553.A39445
Calde, Mark A., 1945-	PS3553.A3946
Calder, James, 1957-	PS3603.A425
Calder, Robert.	PS3553.A3949
Caldwell, Celeste.	none
Caldwell, George S.	PS3553.A395
Caldwell, Ian, 1976-	PS3603.A435
Caldwell, Taylor, 1900-1985.	PS3505.A364
Calef, Noël, 1907-1968.	PQ2605.A317
Calhoun, B. B., 1961-	none
Calhoun, Bonnie S.	PS3603.A4387
Callaghan, Mary Rose.	PR6053.A382
Callahan, James.	none
Callahan, Jay.	none
Callahan, William R., 1931-	PR9199.4.C337
Callan, Michael Feeney.	none
Calland, Mary.	none
Callaway, Phil, 1961-	PS3603.A446
Callen, Paulette, 1947-	PS3553.A4237
Callison, Brian.	PR6053.A39
Calloway, Kate, 1957-	PS3553.A4245
Calmer, Ned.	PS3553.A425
Calnan, T. D., 1914-	none
Calvert, Candace, 1950-	PS3603.A4463
Calvert, Candy, 1950-	PS3603.A4463
Calvert, Robert Steven.	none
Calvin, Henry, 1922-	PR6058.A58
Calvin, June.	none

Calvo Poyato, José.	PQ6653.A4643
Camacho, George.	none
Cambards, Michelle, 1900-	PQ2605.A327
Cameron, Bill, 1963-	PS3603.A4475
Cameron, Dana.	PS3603.A449
Cameron, Eleanor Elford.	none
Cameron, Ian, 1924-	PR6066.A9
Cameron, Julia.	PS3553.A4333
Cameron, Kate.	PS3553.A4334
Cameron, Kenneth M., 1931-	PS3553.A4335
Cameron, Lou, 1924-	PS3553.A434
Cameron, Sara (Sara J.)	PR9230.9.C33
Cameron, Stella.	PS3553.A4345
Cameron, Sue, 1944-	PS3553.A4346
Cameron, Vicki.	PR9199.4.C347
Camilleri, Andrea.	PQ4863.A3894
Camp, Candace.	PS3553.A4374
Camp, John, 1944-	PS3569.A516
Camp, Roderic A.	PS3553.A4376
Camp, William, 1928-	PR6053.A46
Campanozzi, Lou.	PS3553.A4385
Campbell, Alice, b. 1887.	PR6005.A4115
Campbell, Bethany.	PS3553.A43954
Campbell, Bradley L.	PS3603.A463
Campbell, Chester D., 1925-	PS3603.A4695
Campbell, Colin.	PR6053.A4696
Campbell, Diana.	none
Campbell, Duncan, 1944-	PR6103.A49
Campbell, Gordon, 1942-	PS3603.A475
Campbell, Jeffrey.	PR6053.A4857
Campbell, Julie, 1908-1999.	none
Campbell, Karen.	PR6053.A487
Campbell, Karen, 1967-	PR6103.A53
Campbell, Marilyn, 1948-	PS3553.A4858
Campbell, Naomi.	PS3553.A4864
Campbell, P. J. (Patrick J.)	PR9199.4.C35
Campbell, R. T., 1914-1978.	PR6039.O26
Campbell, R. Wright.	PS3553.A4867
Campbell, Ramsey, 1946-	PR6053.A4855
Campbell, Robert—see: Campbell, R. Wright.	
Campbell, Scott.	none
Campbell, Will D.	PS3553.A488
Campbell-Slan, Joanna.	PS3603.A4845
Campion, Alexander.	PS3603.A4848
Canada, Wanda, 1941-	PS3603.A52
Canaday, John, 1907-1985.	PS3505.A53196
Canadeo, Anne, 1955-	PS3553.A489115
Canary, Glen.	none
Canby, C. C., 1937-	PS3603.A535
Canby, Vincent.	PS3553.A4894
Candy, Edward.	PR6064.E83
Cannan, Joanna, 1896-1961.	PR6005.A483
Cannell, Charles.	PR6043.I9
Cannell, Dorothy.	PS3553.A499

Cannell, Stephen J.	PS3553.A4995
Canning, Victor.	PR6005.A486
Cannon, Curt, 1926-2005.	PS3515.U585
Cannon, David Jack.	none
Cannon, Elliott.	none
Cannon, Julie, 1959-	PS3603.A549
Cannon, P. H. (Peter H.)	PS3553.A529
Cannon, Taffy.	PS3553.A5295
Canon, Jack.	none
Canon, Rachel.	PS3553.A537
Canter, MacKenzie.	PS3553.A545
Canterbury, Carolyn.	PS3603.A58
Cantore, Janice.	PS3603.A588
Cantrell, Lisa W.	PS3553.A548
Cantrell, Rebecca.	PS3603.A599
Çape, Tony.	PS3553.A5825
Čapek, Karel, 1890-1938.	PG5038.C3
Capes, Bernard Edward Joseph, d. 1918.	PR6005.A53
Caplan, Thomas.	PS3553.A584
Caple, Natalee, 1970-	PR9199.3.C314
Capon, Paul, 1912-1969.	PR6005.A4868
Capote, Truman, 1924-1984.	PS3505.A59
Caputi, Anthony Francis, 1924-	PS3553.A62
Caputo, Philip.	PS3553.A625
Carcaterra, Lorenzo.	PS3553.A653
Carco, Francis, 1886-1958.	PQ2605.A55
Card, Orson Scott.	PS3553.A655
Cardarelli, T. R. T.	none
Cardieri, Anthony J.	PS3603.A7347
Cardiff, Sara.	PS3553.A663
Carew, Henry.	PR6005.A4896
Carey, Benedict.	none
Carey, Bernice.	PS3525.A74525
Carey, Constance.	none
Carey, Diane.	PS3553.A6684
Carey, Webster.	none
Carfax, Catherine, 1928-	PR6056.A49
Cargill, Linda.	PS3553.A677
Carkeet, David.	PS3553.A688
Carl, JoAnna.	PS3569.A51977
Carl, Lee, 1929-	PS3603.A75
Carl, Lillian Stewart.	PS3603.A7523
Carleson, Donald V.	none
Carleton, Marjorie.	PS3505.A724
Carling, Finn.	PT8950.C3
Carlino, Lewis John.	PS3553.A7
Carlisle, D. M.	PR6053.A6838
Carlisle, Henry, 1926-	PS3553.A72
Carlisle, Kate, 1951-	PS3603.A7527
Carlon, Patricia, 1927-2002.	PR9619.3.C37
Carlotto, Massimo, 1956-	PQ4863.A7198
Carlow, Joyce.	none
Carlson, Melody.	PS3553.A73257
Carlson, P. M.	PS3553.A7328

Carlson, Steve, 1943-   PS3603.A7533
Carlton, Bea.   PS3553.A736
Carlton, Mitchell—see: Marshell, Mel, 1911-
Carlyle, Forrest.   PS3603.A7537
Carlyle, Liz.   PS3553.A739
Carmichael, Harry.   PR6029.G6
Carmichael, Judson Jack.   PS3603.A754
Carmichael, William, 1943-   PS3603.A7554
Carmon, Haggai.   PS3603.A7557
Carnac, Carol, 1894-1958.   PR6035.I9
Carnac, Nicholas.   PR6053.A6856
Carney, Charles.   none
Carney, Daniel, 1944-   PR6053.A687
Carney, William, 1922-   PS3553.A758
Carnoy, David.   PS3603.A7654
Carobini, Julie.   PS3603.A7657
Carofiglio, Gianrico, 1961-   PQ4903.A665
Carol, Robin.   none
Caroll, Robin.   PS3603.A7673
Carothers, A. J.   none
Carpenter, Carleton.   none
Carpenter, David, 1941-   PR9199.3.C35
Carpenter, Donald H., 1956-   PS3553.A7615
Carpenter, J. D.   PR9199.3.C356
Carpenter, Margaret, b. 1893.   none
Carpenter, P. L.   PS3603.A775
Carpentier, Charles.   PS3553.A7624
Carpozi, George.   none
Carr, Albert H. Z.   PS3553.A7627
Carr, Alex.   PS3569.I42125
Carr, Blair.   PS3553.A762745
Carr, Caleb, 1955-   PS3553.A76277
Carr, Carol K.   PS3603.A7726
Carr, Glyn, 1908-2005.   PR6037.T96
Carr, Jess.   PS3553.A763
Carr, John Dickson, 1906-1977.   PS3505.A763
Carr, Jolyon—see: Pargeter, Edith, 1913-1995.
Carr, Josephine.   PS3553.A76323
Carr, Kirby.   PS3553.A7632
Carr, Lauren.   PS3603.A774255
Carr, Lynn.   PS3603.A77426
Carr, Margaret, 1935-   PR6053.A697
Carr, Philippa, 1906-1993.   PR6015.I3
Carr, Robyn.   PS3553.A76334
Carrascal, José María, 1930-   PQ6653.A717
Carrel, Mark, 1916-   PS3566.A34
Carrell, J. L.—see: Carrell, Jennifer Lee.
Carrell, Jennifer Lee.   PS3603.A77438
Carrick, John, 1912-   none
Carrier, Roch.   PQ3919.2.C25
Carrier, Warren Pendleton.   PS3505.A7736
Carrington, Glenda.   none
Carrington, Tori.   PS3603.A77456
Carroll, Charles.   none

Carroll, J. R. (John R.), 1945-	PR9619.3.C3814
Carroll, James, 1943-	PS3553.A764
Carroll, Jerry Jay.	PS3553.A7642
Carroll, Jock.	none
Carroll, Jonathan, 1949-	PS3553.A7646
Carroll, Joy.	none
Carroll, Lois.	PS3603.A774585
Carroll, Margaret, 1960-	PS3603.A774587
Carroll, Martin, 1935-	PR6053.A697
Carroll, Robert—see: Alpert, Hollis, 1916-	
Carroll, Susan, 1952-	PS3553.A7654
Carroll, Terry, 1950-	PR9199.3.C394
Carson, Michael, 1946-	PR6053.A718
Carson, Nell.	PS3603.A77625
Carson, Paul, 1949-	PR6053.A719
Carson, Robert, 1909-1983.	PS3505.A77825
Carter, Alan, 1959-	PR9619.C37
Carter, Alberta Simpson.	none
Carter, Ally.	PS3603.A7765
Carter, Amanda.	none
Carter, Angela, 1940-1992.	PR6053.A73
Carter, Betty Smartt, 1965-	PS3553.A7733
Carter, Charlotte (Charlotte C.)	PS3553.A7736
Carter, Danita.	PS3603.A77695
Carter, Diana.	PR6053.A735
Carter, John.	none
Carter, John Franklin, 1897-1967.	PS3505.A7922
Carter, Maureen.	PR6103.A735
Carter, Nicholas.	none
Carter, Nick.	PS3507.E888
Carter, Noël Vreeland.	PS3553.A7827
Carter, Philip, 1949-	PS3573.I456288
Carter, Quentin.	PS3603.A7778
Carter, Robert A.	PS3553.A783
Carter, Ron, 1932-	PS3553.A7833
Carter, Sammi.	PS3562.E9752
Carter, Stephen L., 1954-	PS3603.A78
Carter, Steven, 1961-	PS3603.A779
Carter, Youngman, 1904-1969.	PR6005.A7643
Cartwright, Justin.	PR6053.A746
Caruso, Joseph George.	none
Carvalho, Bernardo, 1960-	PQ9698.13.A6525
Carver, Caroline, 1959-	PR6103.A78
Carvic, Heron.	PR6053.A75
Casals Aldama, Pedro, 1944-	PQ6653.A7266
Casanova, Mary.	PS3553.A78962
Casati Modignani, Sveva.	PQ4863.A777
Casberg, Melvin A., 1909-	PS3553.A78975
Case, Dave, 1961-	PS3603.A839
Case, David, 1937-	PS3553.A79
Case, Jim.	PS3613.E788
Case, John.	PS3553.A7914
Case, Peg.	none
Casebeer, Macey.	PS3553.A7922

Casey, Donis.	PS3603.A863
Casey, Elizabeth Lynn.	PS3603.A8633
Casey, Kathryn.	PS3603.A8635
Casey, Kevin.	PR6053.A814
Casey, Mervin.	none
Casey, Robert.	PS3553.A7936[sic]
Casey, Robert J. (Robert Joseph), 1890-1962.	PS3505.A8227
Cash, Dixie.	PS3603.A864
Cash, Nancy Sales.	PS3603.A8645
Cashman, John.	PS3553.A7936
Casillo, Charles.	PS3603.A8665
Casler, Ronald.	none
Casley, D. J.	PR6053.A8234
Caspary, Vera, 1899-1987.	PS3505.A842
Cass, Zoë.	PR6053.A824
Cassara, Ernest, 1925-	PS3553.A79528
Cassells, John, 1909-1975.	PR6007.U535
Cassels, Louis.	none
Cassiday, Bruce.	PS3553.A79555
Cassidy, Carla (Carla Bracale)	PS3553.A79558
Cassidy, John, 1922-	PS3553.A7956
Cassilis, Robert.	PR6053.A82413
Cassill, R. V. (Ronald Verlin), 1919-2002.	PS3553.A796
Castañeda, Marina.	PQ7298.413.A86
Castang, Viola.	none
Castell, Dianne.	PS3603.A8747
Castillo, Linda.	PS3603.A8758
Castle, Linda Lea.	PS3553.A81433
Castle, Frank.	none
Castle, Jayne.	PS3561.R44
Castle, Mort.	none
Castleman, Michael.	PS3603.A884
Casto, Nick, 1951-	PS3553.A8144
Castoire, Marie.	PS3553.A8148
Castro, Brian.	PR9619.3.C3922
Caswell, Helen Rayburn.	PS3505.A8565
Catanach, J. N.	PS3553.A8193
Cates, Emily.	none
Cates, Kimberly.	PS3553.A845
Catto, Max, 1909-	PR6005.A83
Caudwell, Sarah.	PR6053.A855
Cauffiel, Lowell.	PS3553.A938
Caulfield, Max, 1915-	none
Caunitz, William J.	PS3553.A945
Cavanagh, Thomas B.	PS3603.A8995
Cavanaugh, Jack, 1952-	PS3553.A965
Cave, Emma.	PR6053.A859
Cave, Hugh B. (Hugh Barnett), 1910-2004.	PS3505.A912
Cave, Julie, novelist.	PS3603.A89955
Cave, Patrick.	PR6103.A95
Cave, Peter, 1940-	PR6053.A865
Cave, Peter L.	none
Cavelti, Peter C. (Peter Christian), 1948-	PR9199.4.C387
Cavender, Chris.	PS3603.A94

Caveney, Philip.   PR6053.A87
Cawley, Robert.   none
Cawood, Chris.   PS3553.A975
Caxton, Tony.   PR6053.A94
Cebulash, Mel.   PS3553.E24
Cecil, Henry, 1902-1976.   PR6053.E3
Cecilione, Michael.   PS3553.E34
Ceder, Camilla.   PT9877.13.E42
Cederberg, Fred.   none
Celine, Marie, 1955-   PS3603.E45
Cerasini, Marc, 1952-   PS3553.E666
Ceren, Sandra Levy.   PS3603.E697
Chaber, M. E., 1910-   PS3505.R89224
Chabon, Michael.   PS3553.H15
Chabrey, François.   none
Chacko, David.   PS3553.H2
Chacón, Dulce, 1954-   PQ6653.H2
Chadbourn, Mark.   PR6053.H23
Chadwick, Cleo.   none
Chadwick, Elizabeth.   PR6053.H245
Chadwick, Jocelyn.   PS3505.H155
Chadwick, Joseph L.   none
Chafets, Ze'ev.   PS3553.H225
Chaikin, L. L., 1943-   PS3553.H2427
Chais, Pamela, 1930-   PS3553.H243
Chakraborti, Rajorshi.   PR9499.4.C433
Chalfant, Patrick.   PS3603.H336
Chalice, Ron Lynch.   PS3603.H3365
Chalker, Jack L.   PS3553.H247
Challinor, C. S. (Caroline S.)   PS3603.H3366
Challis, Joanna.   PR9619.4.C39
Challis, Mary, 1922-1985.   PR6073.O63
Chaloner, John, 1924-   PR6053.H283
Chamberlain, Anne.   PS3505.H232
Chamberlain, Diane, 1950-   PS3553.H2485
Chambers, Ava Lindsey.   PS3603.H343
Chambers, Christopher, 1963-   PS3603.H35
Chambers, Clem.   PR6103.H363
Chambers, Dana, 1895-1946.   PS3523.E365
Chambers, E. Whitman (Elwyn Whitman)—see: Chambers, Whitman,
1896-
Chambers, Peter, 1924-   PR6066.H463
Chambers, Robert, 1933-   PS3553.H26
Chambers, Robert W. (Robert William), 1865-1933. PS1280-1288
Chambers, Whitman, 1896-   PS3505.H275
Chambers, William E.   none
Chamoiseau, Patrick.   PQ3949.2.C45
Champion, David.   PS3553.H2649
Champion de Crespigny, Philip, Mrs.   PR6005.H26
Champion de Crespigny, Rose Key—see: Champion de Crespigny,
Philip, Mrs.
Champlin, Tim, 1937-   PS3553.H265
Chan, Cassandra.   PS3603.H35556
Chance, Jackie.   PS3603.H3559

Chance, John Newton.   PR6005.H28
Chance, Lisbeth, 1946-   PS3553.H266
Chance, Megan.   PS3553.H2663
Chance, Stephen, 1925-   PR6053.H3178
Chancellor, John.   PR6005.H285
Chandler, Bryn.   none
Chandler, David.   PS3553.H27
Chandler, Jessie.   PS3603.H3568
Chandler, Peter.   none
Chandler, Raymond, 1888-1959.   PS3505.H3224
                                                  [Z8159.15]
Chandra, Vikram.   PS3553.H27165
Chaney, Roy.   PS3603.H35726
Chang, Henry, 1951-   PS3603.H35728
Chang, Lee, 1935-   none
Chang, Leonard.   PS3553.H27244
Chantler, David Thomas.   PS3553.H275
Chao, Patricia, 1955-   PS3553.H2765
Chaplin, Elizabeth.   PR6063.C477
Chaplin, Patrice.   PR6053.H348
Chapman, Herb, 1951-   PS3603.H37
Chapman, Hester W., 1899-1976.   PR6005.H317
Chapman, John, 1947-   none
Chapman, Maristan.   PS3505.H424
Chapman, Raymond.   PR6005.H323
Chapman, Sally.   PS3553.H295
Chapman, Stan.   PS3553.H2953
Chapman, Steve.   PS3553.H2955
Chapman, Vannetta.   PS3603.H3744
Chappell, Helen, 1947-   PS3553.H299
Chaput, W. J.   PS3553.H314
Charbonneau, Eileen.   PS3553.H318
Charbonneau, Joelle.   PS3603.H3763
Charbonneau, Louis, 1924-   PS3575.O7
Charles, Hampton.   PR6053.H37212
Charles, Iona.   none
Charles, Kate.   PR6053.H37214
Charles, Nora.   PS3573.A42116
Charles, Paul, 1949-   PR6053.H372145
Charles, Robert, 1938-   PR6069.M53
Charles, Theresa.   PR6005.H3436
Charles, Will, 1919-   PS3545.I464
Charleston, Wally.   none
Charlton, John—see: Woodhouse, Martin, 1932-
Charnee, David.   PS3553.H3263
Charney, Noah.   PS3603.H3768
Charteris, Leslie, 1907-1993.   PR6005.H348
                                                  [Z8161.8]
Charyn, Jerome.   PS3553.H33
Chase, Allison.   none
Chase, Elaine Raco, 1949-   PS3553.H3333
Chase, Glen, 1935-   none
Chase, James Hadley, 1906-1985.   PR6035.A92
Chase, Linda, 1942-   PS3553.H33465

Chase, Marlene J.	PS3553.H3348
Chase, Naomi.	PS3603.H37945
Chase, Philip.	PS3556.R545
Chastain, Thomas.	PS3553.H3416
Chattam, Maxime, 1976-	PQ2703.H388
Chatterton, Martin.	none
Chatzēgiannidēs, Vangelēs.	PA5638.13.H36
Chavarría, Daniel, 1933-	PQ8520.13.H38
Chaze, Elliott.	PS3505.H633
Chazin, Suzanne.	PS3553.H3468
Cheatham, K. Follis (Karyn Follis), 1943-	PS3603.H427
Cheatham, Lillian.	PS3553.H348
Checketts, Cami, 1974-	PS3603.H434
Chehak, Susan Taylor.	PS3553.H34875
Chercover, Sean.	PS3603.H47
Cherginet‹s›, Nikolaĭ.	PG3479.5.H364
Cherkasov-Georgievskiĭ, V. G. (Vladimir	PG3479.5.H368
Georgievich)	
Cherne, Barbara, 1940-	PS3553.H3547
Chernenok, Mikhail.	PG3479.5.H3715
Chernozemsky, Vladimir.	PS3553.H35615
Chernykh, Ivan.	none
Chernyonok, Mikhail—see: Chernenok,Mikhail	
Cherry, Bob.	PS3553.H3563
Chesbro, George C.	PS3553.H359
Cheshire, Simon.	none
Chesney, Marion.	PR6053.H4535
Chesney, Weatherby.	PR6015.Y6
Chester, Alfred, 1928-1971.	PS3505.H679
Chester, George Randolph, 1869-1924.	PS3505.H684
Chester, Peter, 1924-	PR6066.H463
Chester, R. (Roy), 1936-	none
Chester, Samuel Beach.	none
Chesterton, G. K. (Gilbert Keith), 1874-1936.	PR4453.C4
Chetwynd-Hayes, R. (Ronald)	PR6053.H47
Chevalier, Paul, 1925-	PR6053.H473
Chevigny, Paul, 1935-	PS3553.H44
Cheyney, Jeanne.	none
Cheyney, Peter, 1896-1951.	PR6005.H48
Chiaverini, Jennifer.	PS3553.H473
Chicory, Nathaniel.	PS3553.H4743
Child, Lee.	PS3553.H4838
Child, Lincoln.	PS3553.H4839
Child, Roderick.	none
Childers, Erskine, 1870-1922.	PR6005.H52
Childs, Laura.	PS3603.H56
Childs, Marquis W. (Marquis William), 1903-1990.	PS3505.H774
Childs, Timothy, 1941-	PS3553.H488
Chimenti, Francesca.	PS3553.H489
Chinchinian, Harry.	PS3553.H48977
Chiodo, Daniel J.	none
Chiodo, Tom.	PS3553.H495
Chisholm, P. F., 1958-	PR6056.I519
Chittenden, Margaret.	PS3553.H533

Chiu, Tony.	PS3553.H54
Chizh, Anton.	PG3491.5.H575
Chmielewska, Joanna.	PG7162.H5
Choate, Jane McBride.	PS3553.H575
Ch'oe, Chae-hun, 1962-	PL994.18.C425
Chorlton, David.	PS3553.H62
Christensen, R. J. (Rachelle J.), 1978-	PS3603.H743
Christer, Sam.	PR6103.H75
Christian, John, 1930 Jan.6-	PR6054.I95
Christian, Mary Blount.	none
Christian, Nick—see: Pollitz, Edward A., 1937-	
Christiansen, Nancy.	none
Christie, Agatha, 1890-1976.	PR6005.H66
Christilian, J. D.	PS3553.H737
Christmas, Joyce.	PS3553.H745
Christner, D. W.	none
Christofferson, April.	PS3553.H749
Christopher, Cathy.	PR6053.H74
Christopher, Jay.	none
Christopher, John, 1922-	PR6053.H75
Christopher, Lawrence.	PS3603.H764
Christopher, Matt.	none
Christopher, Paul, 1949-	PS3558.Y36
Christy, Jim, 1945-	PS3553.H77
Chronister, Alan B.	none
Chubin, Barry.	PR9105.9.C55
Chudley, Ron, 1937-	PR9199.4.C489
Church, James, 1947-	PS3603.H88
Churchill, Jill, 1943-	PS3553.H85
Churchill, Luanna.	PS3553.H855
Churchward, John.	none
Chwedyk, Kathy.	none
Cileone, Augustus M.	PS3603.I43
Cinque, Jim.	none
Cioffari, Philip.	PS3603.I53
Ciotta, Beth.	PS3603.I58
Cirni, Jim, 1937-	PS3553.I76
Cirrone, Dorian.	none
Cisneros, Carlos, 1963-	PS3603.I86
Citro, Joseph A.	PS3553.I865
Ciullo, James A.	PS3603.I94
Clair, William R.	none
Claire, Edie.	PS3553.L2228
Clancy, Ambrose, 1948-	PS3553.L237
Clancy, Leo.	PR6053.L282
Clancy, Tom, 1947-	PS3553.L245
Clapperton, Richard.	none
Clare, Alys.	PR6053.L286
Clare, Baxter, 1959-	PS3553.L2487
Clare, Marguerite.	none
Clare, Pamela.	none
Claremon, Neil.	PS3553.L25
Clarins, Dana, 1937-	PS3557.I284
Clark, A. Carman, 1917-	PS3603.L355

Clark, Al C.—see: Goines, Donald, 1937-1974.
Clark, Alan (Alan M.)   PS3603.L3554
Clark, Barbara.   PS3603.L3555
Clark, Beverly, 1947-   PS3553.L2714
Clark, Carol Higgins.   PS3553.L278
Clark, Carolyn Chambers.   PS3553.L279
Clark, Cassandra.   PR6103.L3724
Clark, Cecily.   none
Clark, Clare.   PR6103.L3725
Clark, Dick, 1929-   PS3553.L2814
Clark, Douglas.   PR6053.L294
Clark, Eric, 1937-   PR6053.L295
Clark, Ernest.   none
Clark, Evert.   none
Clark, Gail.   PR6053.L298
Clark, Jack.   PS3603.L364
Clark, Katharine.   PS3556.L5838
Clark, Leigh.   PS3553.L28615
Clark, Lydia Benson.   none
Clark, Martin, 1959-   PS3553.L2865
Clark, Mary Higgins.   PS3553.L287
Clark, Mary Jane Behrends.   PS3553.L2873
Clark, Melissa, 1949-   PS3603.L3655
Clark, Mindy Starns.   PS3603.L366
Clark, Philip, fl. 1948-1949.   PS3505.L3666
Clark, Robert, 1952 Apr. 9-   PS3553.L2878
Clark, Wahida.   PS3603.L3695
Clark, William, 1916-1985.   PR6053.L324
Clark-Cross, Barbara.   none
Clarke, Anna, 1919-2004.   PR6053.L3248
Clarke, Colin.   none
Clarke, Edward.   PR6053.L3258
Clarke, Mary Andrea.   PR6103.L37455
Clarke, Richard A. (Richard Alan), 1951-   PS3603.L377
Clarke, Robert, 1916-   PS3566.A34
Clarke, Thomas Ernest Bennett, 1907-1989.   PR6005.L453
Clarkson, John, 1947-   PS3553.L3443
Clason, Clyde B.   PS3505.L44
Claudel, Philippe, 1962-   PQ2663.L31148
Claudia, Susan, 1924-   PS3560.O395
Clausen, Lowen.   PS3553.L349
Clausse, Suzanne, 1897-   PQ2605.L26
Clay, James.   PS3603.L387
Clay, Marilyn.   PS3603.L3877
Clay, Mary, 1950-   PS3603.L388
Clay, Patrick.   none
Claymore, Tod, 1898-1964.   PR6005.L762
Clayton, Donald D.   PS3553.L3874
Clayton, Mary.   PR6053.L376
Clayton, Richard—see: Haggard, William.
Cleary, Denis J.   none
Cleary, Jon, 1917-   PR9619.3.C54
Cleave, Paul, 1974-   PR9639.4.C54
Cleaver, Anastasia.   none

Cleeve, Brian Talbot, 1921-	PR6053.L43
Cleeves, Ann.	PR6053.L45
Cleife, Kenneth Philip Hubert.	PR6053.L47
Cleland, Jane K.	PS3603.L4555
Clemeau, Carol.	PS3553.L392
Clemens, Brian.	PR6053.L474
Clemens, Judy.	PS3603.L4579
Clemens, Kevin, 1957-	PS3603.L458
Clement, Alison, 1953-	PS3603.L46
Clement, Charles Baxter.	PS3552.L393
Clement, Dick.	none
Clement, Henry.	none
Clement, Blaize.	PS3603.L463
Clement, Peter, M.D.	PS3553.L3938
Clements, Abigail.	none
Clements, Andrew, 1949-	PS3553.L3957
Clements, Rory.	PR6103.L45
Clenott, Peter.	PS3603.L476
Clerc, Michel.	PQ2663.L4166
Clerk, Ernie.	PQ2663.L42
Cleveland, David Adams.	PS3603.L48
Clevely, Hugh, 1898-1964.	PR6005.L762
Cleverly, Barbara.	PR6103.L48
Clifford, Alan N.	PS3553.L436
Clifford, Eth, 1915-	none
Clifford, Francis.	PR6070.H66
Clifford, Nicholas Rowland.	PS3553.L4378
Clinch, Jon.	PS3603.L54
Clinch, Wendy.	PS3603.L545
Cline, C. Terry.	PS3553.L53
Cline, Edward.	PS3553.L544
Clinton-Baddeley, V. C. (Victor Clinton), 1900-1970.	PR6053.L5
Clipston, Amy.	PS3603.L58
Clive, Caroline, 1801-1873.	PR4454.C4
Clive, John.	PR6053.L53
Close, Robin.	PR6053.L56
Clothier, Peter, 1936-	PR6053.L57
Clouston, J. Storer (Joseph Storer), 1870-1944.	PR6005.L845
Cluster, Dick, 1947-	PS3553.L88
Clynes, Michael.	PR6054.O37
Coates, Robert M. (Robert Myron), 1897-1973.	PS3505.O1336
Cobb, Belton, 1892-1971.	PR6053.O15
Cobb, James H.	PS3553.O178
Cobb, L. B.	PS3603.O2255
Cobb, Sylvanus, 1823-1887.	PS1356.C57
Cobb, Thomas, 1854-1932.	PR6005.O125
Cobb, William, 1937-	PS3553.O198
Cobban, J. Maclaren (James Maclaren), 1849-1903.	PR4461.C29
Coben, Harlan, 1962-	PS3553.O225
Coble, Colleen.	PS3553.O2285
Coburn, Andrew.	PS3553.O23
Coburn, Laura.	none
Coburn, Michael, 1959-	PS3603.O278

Cochran, Alan.	PS3553.O247
Cochran, Brian David.	PS3603.O285
Cochran, Molly.	PS3553.O26
Cochrun, Thomas D.	PS3553.O274
Cockain, Frank.	none
Cockburn, Alexander.	PR6053.O219
Cockey, Tim, 1955-	PS3553.O277
Cody, James P.	none
Cody, Liza.	PR6053.O247
Cody, Matthew.	none
Cody, Patrick.	PR6053.O529
Cody, Paul, 1953-	PS3553.O335
Cody, Sandra Carey.	PS3603.O296
Coe, Marian.	PS3553.O345
Coe, Tucker.	PS3573.E9
Coel, Margaret, 1937-	PS3553.O347
Coelho, Paulo.	PQ9698.13.O3546
Coen, Franklin.	PS3505.O2
Coes, Ben.	PS3603.O2996
Coffey, Brian, 1945-	PS3561.O55
Coffey, Frank.	PS3553.O35
Coffey, Tom, 1958-	PS3553.O365
Coffey, William.	PR6103.O38
Coffin, Julie.	PR6053.O3
Coffin, M. T.	none
Coffman, D. M.	none
Coffman, Elaine.	PS3553.O39
Coffman, Virginia.	PS3553.O415
Coggeshall, Ina.	PS3553.O41545
Coggins, James Robert, 1949-	PR9199.4.C64
Coggins, Mark, 1957-	PS3553.O41555
Coggins, Paul.	none
Cogswell, Georgia.	none
Cohane, M. E.	none
Cohen, Anthea.	PR6053.O34
Cohen, Barney.	none
Cohen, Dana S.	PS3553.O4195
Cohen, Gabriel, 1961-	PS3603.O35
Cohen, Jeffrey, 1957-	PS3603.O358
Cohen, Jeffrey A. (Jeffrey Alan), 1962-	PS3603.O36
Cohen, Mark, 1958-	PS3603.O367
Cohen, Martin Samuel, 1953-	PS3553.O42449
Cohen, Matt, 1942-1999.	PR9199.3.C58
Cohen, Nancy J., 1948-	PS3553.O4258
Cohen, Octavus Roy, 1891-1959.	PS3505.O2455
Cohen, Paula, 1949-	PS3603.O37
Cohen, Paula Marantz, 1953-	PS3603.O372
Cohen, Robert, 1941-	PS3553.O4272
Cohen, Sheldon.	PS3603.O38
Cohen, Stanley, 1928-	PS3553.O43
Cohen, Stephen Paul.	PS3553.O433
Cohen, Steven Martin, 1953-	PS3553.O4334
Cohen, Stuart, 1958-	PS3553.O4337
Cohen, William S.	PS3553.O434

Cohler, David Keith.	PS3553.O4347
Cohn, Paul D.	PS3553.O4355
Coker, Carolyn.	PS3553.O4367
Colbert, Curt, 1947-	PS3603.O413
Colbert, James.	PS3553.O4385
Colbert, Larry L.	PS3603.O415
Colburn, Laura.	none
Colby, Lydia.	none
Colby, Robert.	PS3553.O4397
Cole, Allison.	PS3553.O449
Cole, Barry.	PR6053.O4
Cole, Burt, 1930-	PS3553.O45
Cole, G. D. H. (George Douglas Howard), 1889-	PR6005.O226
1959.	
Cole, Julian.	PR6103.O4415
Cole, Margaret, 1893-1980.	none
Cole, Martina.	PR6053.O413
Cole, Meredith.	PS3603.O4295
Cole, Sam, 1951-	PR9369.4.C65
Cole, Stephen, 1971-	none
Coleman, Clare.	none
Coleman, Darren.	PS3603.O433
Coleman, Evelyn, 1948-	PS3553.O47395
Coleman, Francis X. J.	none
Coleman, Lynn A.	PS3603.O4353
Coleman, Michael.	none
Coleman, Reed Farrel, 1956-	PS3553.O47445
Coleridge, Nicholas, 1957-	PR6053.O4218
Coles, Katharine.	PS3553.O47455
Coles, Manning.	PR6005.O334
Colgrove, David.	none
Collee, John.	PR6053.O423
Collett, Chris.	PR6103.O446
Collett, Dorothy.	none
Collett, Janet.	PS3603.O4395
Colley, Barbara.	PS3603.O44
Colley, I. B.	none
Collier, Iris.	PR6053.O4237
Collier, James Lincoln.	none
Collier, Jane.	none
Collier, Peter, 1939-	PS3553.O47465
Collignon, Jeff, 1953-	PS3553.O474673
Collin, Richard.	PS3553.O474694
Collingwood, Charles.	PS3553.O4747
Collingwood, Fred.	PS3603.O4524
Collins, Ace.	PS3553.O47475
Collins, Barbara, 1948-	PS3553.O474777
Collins, Brandilyn.	PS3553.O4747815
Collins, Cornelius J.	none
Collins, Eliza G. C.	PS3553.O474784
Collins, Gilbert, 1890-	PR6005.O36532
Collins, Hugh, 1951-	PR6103.O45
Collins, Jackie.	PR6053.O425
Collins, Jackson, 1939-	PS3553.O474795

Collins, Joan, 1933-	PR6053.O426
Collins, Judy, 1939-	PS3553.O47484
Collins, Kate, 1951-	PS3603.O4543
Collins, Larry.	PS3553.O47487
Collins, Max Allan.	PS3553.O4753
Collins, Michael, 1924-2005.	PS3562.Y44
Collins, Michael, 1964-	PR6053.O4263
Collins, Michelle.	none
Collins, Natalie R.	PS3603.O4545
Collins, Norman, 1907-	PR6005.O36534
Collins, Randall, 1941-	PS3553.O476
Collins, Robert J., 1924-	PS3553.O4763
Collins, Stephen, 1946-	none
Collins, Thomas.	none
Collins, Wilkie, 1824-1889.	PR4490-4498
	[Z8184.6]
Colquhoun, Keith.	PR6053.O435
Colt, Jennifer.	PS3603.O467
Colter, Frank.	none
Coltrane, James.	PS3573.O39
Combes, Mark, 1964-	PS3603.O4725
Combes, Sharon.	none
Comfort, Barbara.	PS3553.O4832
Comfort, Iris Tracy.	PS3553.O4834
Como, Robert P. (Robert Patrick), 1951-	PS3603.O483
Comport, Brian.	none
Compton, D. G. (David Guy), 1930-	PR6053.O45
Compton, David.	PS3553.O48395
Compton, Jodi.	PS3603.O486
Compton, Julie.	PS3603.O487
Comstock, Kathleen.	PS3553.O4853
Comstock, Mary Chase.	none
Conan, Allan, 1928-	PS3553.O4856
Conant, Susan, 1946-	PS3553.O4857
Conant-Park, Jessica.	PS3603.O525
Conard, Mark T., 1965-	PS3603.O532
Conaway, James.	PS3553.O486
Conaway, Jim C.	none
Condé, Maryse.	PQ3949.2.C65
Condé, Nicholas.	PS3553.O4867
Condon, Richard.	PS3553.O487
Confiant, Raphaël, 1951-	PQ3949.2.C66
Conger, Donald.	none
Conley, Martha.	PS3553.O492
Conley, Robert J.	PS3553.O494
Conlon, Edward, 1965-	PS3603.O5413
Conn, John F., 1949-	PS3603.O543
Connable, Alfred.	PS3553.O496
Connealy, Mary.	PS3603.O544
Connell, Candace.	PS3553.O498
Connelly, Mark, 1951-	PS3603.O5457
Connelly, Michael, 1956-	PS3553.O51165
Connelly, Valerie, 1947-	PS3603.O5464
Conner, K. Patrick.	PS3553.O5117

Conner, Robert, 1947-	PS3603.O547
Conners, Aaron.	PS3553.O5119
Conners, Bernard F.	PS3553.O512
Connington, J. J., 1880-1947.	PR6037.T4627
Connolly, Colm.	PR6053.O486
Connolly, Cyril, 1903-1974.	PR6005.O393
Connolly, J. J.	PR6053.O48644
Connolly, John, 1968-	PR6053.O48645
Connolly, Ray, 1940-	PR6053.O487
Connolly, Sheila.	PS3601.T83
Connolly, Vivian.	none
Connor, Bernadette Y.	PS3553.O51375
Connor, Beverly, 1948-	PS3553.O5138
Connor, John, 1963-	PR6103.O567
Connor, Nancy.	PS3603.O548
Connor, Ralph, 1860-1937.	PR9199.2.G6
Connors, Rose.	PS3603.O553
Conot, Robert E.	none
Conrad, Barnaby, 1922-	PS3553.O515
Conrad, Brenda, 1898-1983.	PS3511.O4113
Conrad, Joseph, 1857-1924.	PR6005.O4
	[Z8189.7]
Conrad, Linda.	PS3603.O5564
Conrad, Roxanne.	PS3603.O557
Conran, Shirley.	PR6053.O512
Conroy, Al, 1924-	PS3551.L26
Conroy, Richard Timothy.	PS3553.O51985
Conroy, Sarah Booth.	PS3553.O51987
Constable, Lawrence.	PR9639.3.C6
Constant, Jan, 1936-	PR6053.O5128
Constantine, Eddie, 1917-1993.	PQ2663.O593
Constantine, K. C.	PS3553.O524
Conte, Charles.	none
Conty, Jean-Pierre, 1912-	PQ2605.O49
Converse, Jane.	PS3553.O544
Conway, Joan Ditzel.	none
Conway, Keith.	none
Conway, Laura.	PR6001.N75
Conway, Martha.	PS3603.O565
Conway, Norman.	none
Conway, Peter, 1929-	none
Conway, Sara, 1962-	PS3603.O567
Conwell, Kent.	PS3553.O547
Cook, Alan L.	PS3603.O5685
Cook, Bruce, 1932-2003.	PS3553.O55314
Cook, Christopher, 1959-	PS3553.O55316
Cook, Dave F. (Dave Fuller), 1951-	PS3603.O5688
Cook, Eugenia.	none
Cook, J. S., 1967-	PR9199.3.S574
Cook, John Lennox, 1923-	PR6053.O5195
Cook, Judith, 1933-	PR6053.O5196
Cook, Kenneth, 1929-	PR9619.3.C57
Cook, Marshall, 1944-	PS3553.O55389
Cook, Pat (David Patrick)	PS3553.O55445

Cook, Robin, 1940-	PS3553.O5545
Cook, Stephen, 1949-	PR6053.O5242
Cook, Sy.	PS3553.O5546
Cook, Thomas H.	PS3553.O55465
Cook, Troy.	PS3603.O576
Cook, William Wallace, 1867-1933.	PS3505.O5593
Cooke, Cynthia.	PS3603.O578
Cooke, David C. (David Coxe), 1917-	PS3553.O555
Cooke, John Peyton, 1967-	PS3553.O5565
Cooke, Kaz, 1962-	PR9619.3.C572
Cooke, M. E.—see: Creasey, John.	
Cooke, W. Bourne, b. 1869.	none
Cooke, William P., 1934-	none
Cookman, Lesley.	PR6103.O68
Cookson, Catherine.	PR6053.O525
Cooney, Caroline B.	PS3553.O578
Cooney, Eleanor.	PS3553.O5786
Cooney, Ellen.	PS3553.O5788
Cooney, Linda A.	none
Cooney, Michael.	PR6053.O53
Coonts, Deborah.	PS3603.O5818
Coonts, Stephen, 1946-	PS3553.O5796
Cooper, Ben.	PS3553.O57977
Cooper, Brian, 1919-	PR6053.O546
Cooper, Bryan.	PR6053.O543
Cooper, Clarence L.	PS3553.O5799
Cooper, Colin.	PR6053.O5464
Cooper, Craig.	PS3553.O58
Cooper, Dominic, 1944-	PR6053.O5467
Cooper, Evelyn Barbara.	PR6053.O547
Cooper, Glenn, 1953-	PS3603.O582627
Cooper, Hugh Homfray.	PR6053.O555
Cooper, James Fenimore, 1789-1851.	PS1400-1448
	[Z8191.7]
Cooper, Jamie Lee.	PS3553.O588
Cooper, Jeffrey, 1950-	none
Cooper, Lettice Ulpha, 1897-	PR6005.O4977
Cooper, Louise Field, 1905-	PS3505.O62516
Cooper, Lynna, 1911-1986.	PS3553.O9645
Cooper, M. E. (Mary Ellen)	PS3553.O59547
Cooper, M. K. (Mae Klein)	PS3553.O5955
Cooper, Matthew, 1952-	PR6053.O574
Cooper, Morton.	PS3553.O62
Cooper, N. J. (Natasha J.), 1951-	PR6073.R47
Cooper, Natasha, 1951-	PR6073.R47
Cooper, Parley J.	PS3553.O622
Cooper, Roderick.	PR6053.O594
Cooper, Steven, 1961-	PS3603.O583
Cooper, Susan Rogers.	PS3553.O6235
Cooper, Tom.	none
Cooper, Will.	PS3553.O627
Cooper-Posey, Tracy, 1962-	PR9199.3.C646
Coovelis, Mark.	PS3553.O6327
Coover, Robert.	PS3553.O633

Cope, Todd F.	PS3603.O64
Copeland, John, 1928-	PS3553.O63357
Copeland, Lori.	PS3553.O6336
Copeland, Richard—see: McLeave, Hugh.	
Copeland, William.	PS3553.O634
Copling, Steve.	PS3603.O655
Copp, DeWitt S.	PS3553.O637
Copp, Rick.	PS3603.O65
Coppel, Alfred.	PS3553.O64
Copper, Basil.	PR6053.O658
Corace, Don, 1957-	PS3603.O73
Coram, Christopher, 1936-	none
Coram, Robert.	none
Corbett, James, 1887-1958.	PR6005.O615
Corbett, David, 1953-	PS3603.O732
Corbett, Sue.	none
Corby, Gary.	PR9619.4.C665
Corby, Jane, 1899-	PS3505.O6635
Corcoran, Tom, 1943-	PS3553.O6444
Cordell, Alexander.	PR6053.O67
Cordell, Melissa.	none
Corder, Eric, 1941-	PS3553.O645
Corin, Joshua.	PS3603.O74
Coriola, b. 1897.	PQ2613.A2764
Cork, Barry.	PR6053.O687
Cork, Vena.	PR6103.O745
Corlett, William.	PR6053.O7
Corley, Edwin.	PS3553.O648
Corley, Elizabeth.	PR6053.O713
Cormany, Michael.	PS3553.O6525
Cormier, Robert.	PS3553.O653
Corn, David.	PS3553.O656
Cornelison, Beth.	PS3603.O765
Cornelius, Kay.	PS3553.O65875
Cornford, Philip.	PR9619.3.C587
Cornuke, Robert, 1951-	PS3603.O7685
Cornwell, Bernard.	PR6053.O75
Cornwell, John, 1941-	PR6053.O76
Cornwell, Patricia Daniels.	PS3553.O692
Corpi, Lucha, 1945-	PS3553.O693
	PQ7079.2.C67
Corradi, Lou.	none
Correa, Arnaldo, 1938-	PQ7390.C626
Correa, Raul, 1961-	PS3603.O772
Corren, Grace, 1933-	PS3558.O76
Corrigan, John R.	PS3603.O773
Corriher, Kurt.	PS3603.O7734
Corrington, John William.	PS3553.O7
Corrington, Joyce H.	none
Corris, Peter.	PR9619.3.C595
Corsaro, Frank.	PS3603.O777
Cortez, Donn.	PS3603.O7836
Corwin, C. R.	PS3603.O79
Corwin, Miles.	PS3603.O793

Cory, Desmond, 1928-2001.	PR6053.O774
Coscarelli, Kate.	PS3553.O737
Cosgrave, Patrick.	PR6053.O775
Cosin, Elizabeth M.	PS3553.O748
Costa, Carol, 1940-	PS3603.O866
Costello, Mark.	PS3556.L5824
Costello, Matthew J. (Matthew John), 1948-	PS3553.O7632
Cote, Lyn.	PS3553.O76378
Cotelo, C. S.	none
Cothran, Betty.	none
Cotler, Gordon.	PS3553.O7643
Cottam, Francis, 1957-	PR6103.O88
Cotter, John—see: Couffer, Jack.	
Cotterill, Colin.	PR6053.O778
Cottrell, Jeanette.	PS3603.O87
Couch, Dick, 1943-	PS3553.O769
Couffer, Jack.	none
Coughlan, Eileen Patricia, 1960-	PR9199.3.C6577
Coughlin, Jack, 1966-	PS3603.O878
Coughlin, T. Glen.	PS3553.O775
Coughlin, William Jeremiah, 1929-	PS3553.O78
Coulson, Juanita.	PS3553.O83
Coulson, Robert.	PS3553.O84
Coulter, Catherine.	PS3553.O843
Coulter, Stephen, 1914-	PR6053.O8
Count, Ellen.	PS3553.O854
Court, Katherine, 1918-	PS3553.O8617
Courter, Gay.	PS3553.O86185
Courtier, Sidney Hobson.	PR9619.3.C5967
Courtis, Gerald.	none
Courtois, Wayne, 1954-	PS3603.O887
Courtoisie, Rafael, 1958-	PQ8520.13.O8
Cousin, Michel.	PQ2663.O84
Cousins, Caroline.	PS3603.O888
Cousins, E. G. (Edmund George), b. 1893.	PR6005.O819
Couto, Mia, 1955-	PQ9939.C68
Covadlo, Lázaro.	PQ7798.13.O86
Covert, Paul.	PS3553.O87
Coville, Bruce.	PS3553.O873
Covington, Dennis.	PS3553.O883
Cowan, Debra S.	none
Coward, Mat.	PR6053.O955
Cowen, Frances.	none
Cowen, Ron.	PS3553.O9
Cowley, Jason.	PR6053.O9627
Cox, Anne-Marie.	PR6053.O967
Cox, Carol.	PS3553.O9148
Cox, Elizabeth, 1942-	PS3553.O9183
Cox, Greg, 1959-	PS3603.O9
Cox, Michael, 1948-2009.	PR6103.O976
Cox, Richard Hubert Francis, 1931-	PR6053.O969
Coxe, George Harmon, 1901-	PS3505.O9636
Coyle, Cleo.	PS3603.O94
Coyle, Harold, 1952-	PS3553.O948

Coyle, John B.   none
Coyne, John.   PS3553.O96
Coyne, P. J.   PS3563.A82
Crabb, Ned.   PS3553.R18
Crabbe, Richard E.   PS3553.R18
Crace, Jim.   PR6053.R228
Craft, Francine.   none
Craft, Mary Beth.   PS3553.R214
Craft, Michael, 1950-   PS3553.R215
Craig, Alisa, 1922-2005.   PS3563.A31865
Craig, Bill, 1930-   PR6053.R25
Craig, Daniel Edward, 1966-   PS3603.R353
Craig, David, 1929-   PR6070.U23
Craig, James, 1964-   PR6103.R3475
Craig, Jasmine.   PS3553.R224
Craig, John, 1921-   PR9199.3.C68
Craig, Jonathan, 1919-1984.   none
Craig, Kit.   PS3568.E367
Craig, M. S. (Mary Shura), 1923-   PS3553.R226
Craig, Mary—see: Craig, M. S. (Mary Shura),
1923-
Craig, Peter, 1969-   PS3553.R229
Craig, Philip R., 1933-2007.   PS3553.R23
Craig, William, 1929-   PS3553.R25
Crais, Robert.   PS3553.R264
Cramer, Alan.   PS3603.R363
Cramer, Cahroul.   PS3553.R2665
Cramer, Rebecca.   PS3603.R3645
Crandall, Susan.   PS3603.R375
Crandolph, Augustus Jacob.   PR4518.C135
Crane, Caroline.   PS3553.R2695
Crane, Frances.   PS3505.R267
Crane, Hamilton.   PR6063.A7648
Crane, Robert, 1908-1990.   PS3513.L646
Craske, Darren.   PR6103.R37
Crater, Theresa, 1950-   PS3603.R388
Craven, Michael.   PS3603.R393
Crawford, Charles R., 1958-   PS3603.R3955
Crawford, Claudia.   none
Crawford, Dean.   PS3603.R3957
Crawford, Isis.   PS3603.R396
Crawford, Link.   none
Crawford, Louise.   PS3553.R2865
Crawford, Max, 1938-   PS3553.R293
Crawford, Oliver.   PS3553.R294
Crawford, Petrina.   none
Crawford, R. H. E.   PS3553.R2947
Crawford, Robert, 1935-   PR6068.A25
Crawford, Stanley G., 1937-   PS3553.R295
Crawford, William.   none
Cray, David.   PS3553.R315
Cray, Jordan.   PS3602.L883
Creasey, John.   PR6005.R517
Crecy, Jeanne, 1930-   PS3573.I4485

Creed, David, 1931-	PR6053.R435
Creed, John, 1961-	PR6063.C63
Creekmore, Donna.	PS3553.R338
Creighton, Jo Anne.	PS3505.H155
Creighton, John, pseud.	PS3505.H155
Crenshaw, Nadine.	PS3553.R433
Crespi, Camilla T.	PS3553.R435
Cresse, Gina.	PS3553.R437
Cresswell, Jasmine.	PR6053.R467
Crew, Cheryl Howard.	PS3603.R49
Crews, Sue B.	PS3603.R497
Crichton, Michael, 1942-2008.	PS3553.R48
Crichton, Wm. (William)	none
Crider, Bill, 1941-	PS3553.R497
Crisp, N. J.	PR6053.R497
Crisp, Quentin, 1908-	PR6005.R65
Crisp, William, 1942-	PS3553.R518
Crispin, Edmund, 1921-1978.	PR6025.O46
Cristofano, David.	PS3603.R578
Cristol, Jaymi.	none
Criswell, Millie.	PS3553.R5335
Crites, Susan.	PS3553.R536
Crockett, Linda, 1943-	PS3553.R5363
Crockett, Mark.	PS3603.R6354
Crockett, S. R. (Samuel Rutherford), 1860-1914.	PR4518.C3
Croft, Mike, 1965-	PR6103.R64
Croft, Sydney.	PS3603.R6356
Croft, Tom, 1948-	PS3553.R5373
Croft-Cooke, Rupert, 1903-	PR6005.R673
Crofts, Andrew.	none
Crofts, Freeman Wills, 1879-1957.	PR6005.R675
Crombie, Deborah.	PS3553.R5378
Cromie, Alice.	PS3553.R538
Cromie, Robert, 1856-1907.	PR4518.C554
Crompton, R. Z.	PS3553.R5392
Crone, Charles W.	PS3603.R66
Cronin, A. J. (Archibald Joseph), 1896-1981.	PR6005.R68
Cronin, Brendan Leo—see: Cronin, Michael, 1907-	
Cronin, George P., 1933-	none
Cronin, Justin.	PS3553.R542
Cronin, Michael, 1907-	PR6053.R57
Crosby, Ellen, 1953-	PS3603.R668
Crosby, John, 1912-	PS3553.R55
Crosby, Virginia.	PS3553.R556
Cross, Amanda, 1926-2003.	PS3558.E4526
Cross, Beverley, 1931-1998.	PR6005.R694
Cross, David—see: Chesbro, George C.	
Cross, E. B.	none
Cross, Gilbert B.	none
Cross, Gillian.	none
Cross, Jonathan.	none
Cross, Neil.	PR6053.R623
Cross, Ralph D.	none
Cross, William (William E.)	none

Crossen, Kendell Foster, 1910-   PS3505.R89224
Crossman, D. A. (David A.)   PS3553.R5728
Crosswell, Jack.   none
Crosthwaite, Bernie.   PR6053.R635
Crouch, Blake.   PS3603.R68
Croucher, Matt, 1983-   PR6103.R674
Croudace, Glynn.   PR6053.R64
Crow, C. P.   PS3553.R587
Crow, Donna Fletcher.   PS3553.R5872
Crow, Michael, 1948-   PS3563.O7714
Crowcroft, Peter.   none
Crowder, Herbert, 1925-   PS3553.R5878
Crowe, Cecily.   PS3553.R59
Crowe, John, 1924-2005.   PS3562.Y44
Crowleigh, Ann.   none
Crowley, Duane.   PS3553.R596
Crowther, Brad.   PS3603.R79
Crowther, Bruce, 1933-   PR6053.R657
Crowther, John, 1939-   PS3553.R67
Crowther, Peter, 1949-   PR6053.R658
Cruickshank, Charles Greig.   none
Cruikshank, Jeffrey L.   PS3603.R85
Cruise, Cameron.   none
Cruise, T. E.   none
Crum, Laura.   PS3553.R76
Crumb, Kit, 1952-   PS3603.R857
Crumbley, D. Larry.   PS3553.R77
Crumey, Andrew, 1961-   PR6053.R76
Crumley, James, 1939-2008.   PS3553.R78
Crump, David.   PS3553.R783
Cruse, Lonnie.   PS3603.R87
Crusie, Jennifer.   PS3553.R7858
Cruz, José da, 1945-   PQ8520.13.R7
Cruz, Mark.   none
Csabai, László, 1969-   PH3382.13.S33
Csampai, Sabine, 1952-   none
Cudahy, Sheila.   PS3553.U27
Cudlip, David R.   PS3553.U275
Cudlipp, Edythe.   none
Culbertson, Judi.   PS3553.U2849
Culea, John.   PS3553.U28495
Culhane, Patrick, 1948-   PS3553.O4753
Culiner, Jill.   PR9199.4.C845
Cullen, Anthony, 1920-   none
Culliford, Penny.   PR6103.U46
Cullin, Mitch, 1968-   PS3553.U319
Cullinan, Thomas.   PS3553.U33
Cullingford, Guy.   none
Cullum, Ridgwell, b. 1867.   PR6005.U4
Culpan, Maurice.   PR6053.U415
Culver, Carol, 1936-   PS3603.U628
Culver, Timothy J., 1933-2008.   PS3553.U42
Cumberland, Marten.   PR6005.U45
Cumming, Charles, 1971-   PR6103.U484

Cummings, Barbara, 1940-	PS3603.U655
Cummings, Doug M.	PS3603.U65555
Cummings, Jack, 1925-	PS3553.U444
Cummings, Jack, 1940-	PS3553.U4443
Cunningham, Albert Benjamin, 1888-1962.	PS3505.U418
Cunningham, Chet.	PS3553.U468
Cunningham, E. V., 1914-2003.	PS3511.A784
Cunningham, Elaine, 1957-	PS3553.U472
Cunningham, Elizabeth, 1953-	PS3553.U473
Cunningham, Jere.	PS3553.U475
Cunningham, Laura, 1947-	PS3553.U478
Cunningham, Peter, 1947-	PR6062.A778
Cunningham, Scott.	none
Cunningham, Will, 1959-	PS3553.U54
Cuomo, George.	PS3553.U6
Curlovich, John Michael, 1948-	PS3553.U66
Curnutt, Kirk, 1964-	PS3603.U76
Curnyn, Lynda.	PS3603.U764
Curran, Terrie.	PS3553.U666
Currington, O. J., 1924-	PR6053.U74
Curry, Avon—see: Annandale, Barbara, 1925-	
Curry, Tom, 1900-	PS3505.U9725
Curtis, Jack, 1922-	PS3505.U866
Curtis, Jack, 1942-	PR6053.U775
Curtis, James R., 1947-	PS3553.U713
Curtis, Marjorie.	PR6005.U762
Curtis, Mike, 1943-	none
Curtis, Peter—see: Lofts, Norah, 1904-1983.	
Curtis, Richard.	none
Curtis, Spencer.	none
Curtis, Susannah.	none
Curtis, Sydney Albert.	none
Curtis, Wade—see: Pournelle, Jerry, 1933-	
Curtiss, Ursula Reilly.	PS3505.U915
Curzon, Clare.	PR6053.U79
Cusack, John Beede—see: Beede, John.	
Cushman, Dan.	PS3553.U738
Cushman, Doug.	PS3603.U8245
Cussler, Clive.	PS3553.U75
Cuthbert, Margaret (Margaret Owens)	PS3553.U785
Cutler, Judith.	PR6053.U864
Cutler, Roland.	PS3553.U835
Cutler, Ronald.	PS3603.U86
Cutler, Stan.	PS3553.U84
Cutter, Leela.	PS3553.U86
Czuchlewski, David.	PS3553.Z83
Da Cruz, Daniel, 1921-	PS3554.A24
Daeninckx, Didier, 1949-	PQ2664.A417
Daffinrud, Paul.	PS3554.A247
Dager, Wendy, 1963-	PS3604.A3324
D'Agneau, Marcel.	none
Daheim, Mary.	PS3554.A264
Dahl, Arne, 1963-	PT9876.14.A35
Dahl, Kjell Ola, 1958-	PT8951.14.A443

Dahl, Roald.	PR6054.A35
Dahlen, K. J.	PS3604.A342
Dahler, Don.	PS3604.A343
Dahlquist, Gordon.	PS3604.A345
Dailey, Janet.	PS3554.A29
Dain, Catherine.	PS3554.A32
Dakan, Rick.	PS3604.A353
Dalby, Rob.	PS3554.A4148
Dale, Adrian, 1923-	none
Dale, Celia.	PR6054.A38
Dale, Jo Anne.	none
Dalessandro, James.	PS3554.A4164
Daley, Joseph A.	PS3554.A42
Daley, Kevin Vincent.	PS3604.A357
Daley, Robert, 1930-	PS3554.A43
Dalheath, David.	none
Dallas, John, 1909-1975.	PR6007.U535
Dallas, Sandra.	PS3554.A434
D'Almeida, Sarah.	none
Dalos, György.	PH3213.D256
D'Alpuget, Blanche, 1944-	PR9619.3.D24
Dalton, Chase.	PS3604.A425
Dalton, James, 1960-	PS3554.A443
Dalton, Joe, 1959-	PS3563.A95227
Dalton, John J.	PS3554.A443 [sic]
Dalton, Kit.	none
D'Alton, Martina.	PS3554.A438
Dalton, Moray.	PR6007.A494
Dalton, Pat.	PS3554.A444
Daly, Carroll John, 1889-1958.	PS3507.A4673
Daly, Conor.	PS3554.A4448
Daly, Elizabeth, 1878-1967.	PS3507.A4674
Daly, Michael, 1952-	PS3554.A454
Daly, Treve.	PS3570.H6433
Dámaso Martínez, Carlos, 1944-	PQ7798.23.A6915
D'Amato, Barbara.	PS3554.A4674
Damboa, Ibrahim M., 1950-	PR9387.9.D34
D'Ambrosio, Paul, 1959-	PS3604.A4397
Damien, Christine.	none
D'Ammassa, Don, 1946-	PS3604.A46
Damon.	PS3554.A488
Damore, Leo.	PS3554.A495
Damron, Carla.	PS3604.A47
Dams, Jeanne M.	PS3554.A498
Dan, Jerry.	PR6104.A77
Dan, Uri.	PJ5054.D248
Dana, Richard, 1916-	PS3566.A34
Dana, Rose, 1912-	PR9199.3.R5996
Dancer, Rex, 1939-2005.	PS3554.A514
D'Ancona, Matthew, 1968-	PR6104.A83
Dandola, John, 1951-	PS3554.A519
Dane, Clemence.	PR6001.S5
Dane, Eva.	none
Dane, Jordan.	none

Dangana, Moses J. (Moses Jiyah), 1957-	PR9387.9.D35
Daniel, David, 1945-	PS3554.A5383
Daniel, John, 1941-	PS3554.A553
Daniel, Mark, 1954-	PR6045.A469
Daniel, Roland.	none
Danielewski, Cynthia.	PS3604.A528
Daniels, A. Frederick (Albert Frederick)	none
Daniels, Angie.	PS3604.A529
Daniels, Casey.	none
Daniels, Claire.	PS3557.I718
Daniels, Dana.	none
Daniels, Dorothy, 1915-	PS3554.A563
Daniels, J.	PS3604.A533
Daniels, Jeffrey R.	PR6054.A52
Daniels, Les, 1943-	PS3554.A5637
Daniels, Philip.	PR6054.A522
Daniels, Jan—see: Ross, W. E. D. (William Edward Daniel), 1912-	
Daniels, Norman, 1910-	PS3554.A565
Danilin, Vitaliĭ.	PG3491.6.A525
Danilova, Anna.	PG3479.6.A49
Dank, Gloria.	PS3554.A5684
Danks, Denise.	PR6054.A524
Dansky, Richard E.	PS3604.A553
D'Anna, Eduardo, 1948-	PQ7798.14.A58
Dante, Kathleen.	PS3604.A57
Dantz, William R.	PS3554.A583
Danton, Rebecca, 1925-1982.	PS3552.R656
Danziger, Carla.	PS3604.A59
Darbon, Leslie.	PR6054.A64
Darby, Catherine.	PR6052.L335
Darby, Emma.	PS3554.A65
D'Arc, Bianca.	PS3604.A7247
Darcy, Emma.	PR6054.A694
Dard, Frédéric.	PQ2607.A558
Darden, Christopher A.	PS3554.A68
Dare, Lila.	PS3604.A735
Dark, James.	none
Darnton, John.	PS3554.A727
Darnton, Nina.	PS3604.A749
D'Arnuk, Nanisi Barrett, 1948-	PS3554.A728
Darrin, John.	PS3604.A765
Darrow, Marc.	PS3554.A768
Dartey, Léo.	PQ2607.A68
Dartt, G. L.	PR9199.4.D376
Darty, Peggy.	PS3554.A79
Dashkova, Polina.	PG3479.6.A823
Date, John H.	none
Date, S. V. (Shirish V.)	PS3554.A8237
Datesh, John Nicholas.	none
Daugharty, Janice, 1944-	PS3554.A844
Daughtridge, Mary Margret.	PS3604.A92
Davé, Robert.	PS3604.A94
Davenport, Diana.	PS3554.A8598
Davey, Chris, 1952-	PR6104.A84

Davey, Jocelyn.   PR6035.A64
David, James F.   PS3554.A9155
David-Neel, Alexandra, 1868-1969.   PQ2607.A927
Davidov, Len.   none
Davidsen, Leif, 1950-   PT8176.14.A8
Davidson, Avram.   PS3554.A924
Davidson, David Albert, 1908-   PS3507.A66596
Davidson, Diane, 1933-   PS3554.A9252
Davidson, Diane Mott.   PS3554.A925
Davidson, Hilary.   PS3604.A9466
Davidson, Jenny.   PS3604.A9467
Davidson, Lionel.   PR6054.A87
Davidson, MaryJanice.   PS3604.A949
Davidson, Muriel.   PS3554.A9258
Davidson, Rick.   PS3604.A9497
Davie-Martin, Hugh—see: McCutcheon, Hugh.
Davies, Adam.   PS3604.A953
Davies, David Stuart, 1946-   PR6104.A857
Davies, Freda.   PR6104.A86
Davies, Frederick.   PR6054.A879
Davies, Gwynneth.   none
Davies, Jack, 1913-1994.   PR6054.A884
Davies, L. P. (Leslie Purnell)   PR6054.A886
Davies, Lewis, 1967-   PR6054.A8864
Davies, Linda, 1963-   PR6054.A887
Davies, Martin.   none
Davies, Martin, 1965-   PR6104.A87
Davies, Melissa.   none
Davies, Rhys, 1901-1978.   PR6007.A78
Davis, Austin.   PS3604.A9555
Davis, Bart, 1950-   PS3554.A9319
Davis, Berrie.   PS3554.A932
Davis, Carol Anne.   PR6054.A89158
Davis, Charles, 1960-   PR6104.A88
Davis, Charles (Charles Raymond)   PS3604.A95616
Davis, Christopher, 1928-   PS3554.A933
Davis, Don.   PS3554.A93345
Davis, Dorothy Salisbury.   PS3554.A9335
Davis, Elizabeth—see: Davis, Lou Ellen, 1936-
Davis, Frederick C. (Frederick Clyde), 1902-1977.   PS3507.A728
Davis, George.   PR6054.A8917
Davis, Gordon, 1918-2007.   PS3515.U5425
Davis, Gordon, 1935-   none
Davis, Gwen.   PS3554.A9346
Davis, Howard Charles.   none
Davis, J. Madison.   PS3554.A934636
Davis, J. R.   none
Davis, Jo.   PS3604.A963
Davis, John Gordon.   PR6054.A8924
Davis, Justine.   none
Davis, Kaye, 1956-   PS3554.A934925
Davis, Kenn.   none
Davis, Krista.   PS3604.A9717
Davis, Kyra.   PS3604.A972

Davis, L. V.	none
Davis, Lindsey.	PR6054.A8925
Davis, Lisa E.	PS3554.A93535
Davis, Lou Ellen, 1936-	PS3554.A9355
Davis, Marc.	none
Davis, Mildred B.	PS3507.A7424
Davis, Nageeba.	PS3554.A93744
Davis, Patrick A.	PS3554.A937617
Davis, Phil.	none
Davis, Robert, 1941-	PS3554.A93766
Davis, Susan Page.	PS3604.A976
Davis, Thomas D., 1941-	PS3554.A937774
Davis, Thulani.	PS3554.A93779
Davis, Tom, 1970-	PS3604.A9775
Davis, Val.	PS3554.A937836
Davis, Wally, 1951-	PS3554.A93785
Davis-Goff, Annabel.	PS3554.A9385
Davison, Geoffrey.	PR6054.A895
Davison, Gilderoy, 1892-	none
Davison, Jean.	PS3554.A939
Davison, Norma.	none
Davison, Philip, 1957-	PR6054.A896
Davlin, Bennett Joshua.	PS3604.A9783
Davys, Tim.	PT9877.14.A88
Dawe, Carlton, 1865-1935.	none
Dawkins, Cecil, 1927-	PS3554.A943
Dawson, Clare, 1937-	none
Dawson, Clay, 1935-	none
Dawson, David F. L., 1941-	PR9199.3.D353
Dawson, Janet.	PS3554.A949
Dawson, Janis, 1936-	PS3568.O8473
Day, Chet.	none
Day, DeForest.	PS3554.A959
Day, Dianne.	PS3554.A9595
Day Lewis, C. (Cecil), 1904-1972.	PR6007.A95
Day, Marele.	PR9619.3.D382
Day, Marlis.	PS3554.A9653
Dayton, Gail.	PS3604.A9895
De Bernières, Louis.	PR6054.E132
De Bilio, Beth.	PS3554.E176
De Blasis, Celeste.	PS3554.E11144
De Borchgrave, Arnaud.	PR6054.E27
De Castrique, Mark.	PS3604.E124
De Cesco, Federica.	PT2664.E14
De Crespigny, Philip Champion, Mrs.—see: Champion de Crespigny, Philip, Mrs.	
De Felitta, Frank.	PS3554.E35
De Filippo, Eduardo, 1900-1984.	PQ4815.I48
De Ford, Miriam Allen, 1888-1975.	PS3507.E338
De Fraga, Geoff, 1913-	none
De Gramont, Sanche—see: Morgan, Ted, 1932-	
De Haven, Tom.	PS3554.E1116
De Jonge, Peter.	PS3554.E11354
De Kretser, Michelle.	PR9619.4.D4

De Larrabeiti, Michael. PR6054.E134
De La Torre, Lillian, 1902- PS3507.E1695
De la Valdène, Guy. PS3604.E1287
De Laguna, Frederica, 1906-2004. PS3507.E427
De Lauer, Marjel Jean. PS3554.E4414
De Lillo, Don—see: DeLillo, Don.
De Maria, Robert. PS3554.E455
De Marne, Denis. none
De Mazia, Justin, 1967- PR6104.E227
De Mille, James, 1833-1880. PS1534.D3
De Mille, Nelson, 1935- none
De Polnay, Peter, 1906-1984. PR6007.E635
De Pré, Jean-Anne, 1924-1999. PS3551.V3
De Reszke, David. none
De Rouen, Reed. none
De Sécary, Jean—see: Sécary, Jean de.
De St. Jorre, John, 1936- PR6054.E784
De Stefano, Anthony. none
De Toledano, Ralph, 1916-2007. PS3554.E85
De Villiers, Dirk. none
De Villiers, Gerald. none
De Vries, Anke—see: Vries, Anke de, 1936-
Deacon, Penny. PR6104.E234
Deal, Babs H. PS3554.E12
Deal, Borden, 1922-1985. PS3554.E13
Dean, Amber. PS3507.E1623
Dean, Anna. PR6104.E235
Dean, John, 1961- PR6104.E236
Dean, Maureen. PS3554.E1725
Dean, Robert G. (Robert George), 1930- none
Dean, S. F. X. PS3554.E1734
Dean, Scarlett. PS3604.E1538
Dean, Spencer, b. 1895. PS3545.I662
DeAndrea, William L. PS3554.E174
Deane, Jim. none
Deane, Norman, 1908-1973. PR6005.R517
Deane, Philip. PR9115.9.D4
Deane, Shirley. PR6054.E23
Dearborn, Dawn A. PS3554.E1748
Deaux, John. PS3554.E17545
Deauxville, Katherine. none
Deaver, Jeffery. PS3554.E1755
Debin, David. PS3554.E1762
DeBrosse, Jim. PS3554.E1768
DeChancie, John. PS3554.E1785
DeCicco, Joe. PS3604.E24
Decker, Jake. none
Decker, Rod, 1941- PS3554.E188
Decoin, Didier, 1945- PQ2664.E37
DeCure, John. PS3604.E28
Dee, Ed. PS3554.E32
Deeb, Mary-Jane. PS3554.E3433
Deere, Dicey. PS3554.E3553
Dees, Cindy. none

DeFelice, Jim, 1956-	PS3554.E357
DeFilippi, Jim, 1943-	PS3554.E365
Deford, Frank.	PS3554.E37
DeFuentes, Sean.	none
DeGrave, Philip.	PS3554.E416
DeHart, Terry.	PS3604.E3475
DeHaven, Tom.	PS3554.E1116
Deighton, Len, 1929-	PR6054.E37
Dekker, Anthony.	PR6054.E38
Dekker, Carl, 1924-2005.	PS3554.E43
Dekker, Ted, 1962-	PS3554.E43
Dekobra, Maurice, 1885-1973.	PQ2607.E22
Del Toro, Guillermo—see: Toro, Guillermo del, 1964-	
Delacorta—see: Odier, Daniel, 1945-	
Delacorta, 1945-	PQ2675.D5
Delacorte, Peter.	PS3554.E433
Delamer, John J., 1937-	PS3554.E4336
Delaney, Frank, 1942-	PR6054.E396
Delaney, Kathleen.	PS3604.E4226
Delaney, Laurence.	PS3554.E436
Delany, Vicki, 1951-	PR9199.4.D454
Delap, Richard.	none
Delffs, Dudley J.	PS3554.E4423
Delft, Japhet.	PR6054.E414
DeLillo, Don.	PS3554.E4425
Delinsky, Barbara.	PS3554.E4427
Dellosso, Mike.	PS3604.E446
Delman, David.	PS3554.E444
DeLoach, Nora.	PS3554.E44427
Delors, Catherine.	PS3604.E4473
DeLuca, Charles.	none
Del'vig, Polina.	PG3491.6.E59
Delving, Michael, 1914-1978.	PS3545.I528455
Demaine, Christy.	none
Demaine, Phyllis.	PS3554.E4467
DeMarco, Gordon.	PS3554.E448
DeMarco, Joseph R. G.	PS3604.E449
Demarest, Jaki.	PS3604.E454
Demarest, Judith H.	none
Demarest, Phyllis Gordon.	PS3507.E5344
DeMarinis, Rick, 1934-	PS3554.E4554
Demaris, Ovid.	PS3554.E4555
DeMers, John, 1952-	PS3604.E4615
Demijohn, Thom.	none
DeMille, Nelson.	PS3554.E472
Deming, Richard.	PS3554.E48
Demirjian, A., 1931-	PR9199.4.T69
Demirjian, Arto—see: Demirjian, A., 1931-	
DeMott, Joann.	PS3604.E47
DeMott, Wes.	PS3554.E4925
Dempsey, Al.	PS3554.E493
Demšar, Avgust.	PG1920.14.E57
Denbow, William.	none
Denby, Edwin, 1903-1983.	PS3507.E54339

Denby, Joolz.	PR6054.E467
Dengler, Sandy.	PS3554.E524
Denham, Bertie, Baron, 1927-	PR6054.E47
Denine, Teri.	PS3604.E5844
Denis, John.	none
Denisov, Vi‹a›cheslav.	none
Denker, Henry.	PS3507.E5475
Denning, Mark.	PS3554.E534
Dennis, Charles, 1946-	PR9199.3.D44
Dennis, Ralph.	PS3554.E539
Dennis, Robert C.	PS3554.E54
Denniston, Elinor, 1900-1978.	PS3511.O186
Dent, Lester, 1904-1959.	PS3507.E5777
Dentinger, Jane.	PS3554.E587
Denton, Bradley.	PS3554.E588
Denton, Jamie Ann.	PS3604.E595
Denton, Shannon Eric.	none
Denver, Paul.	none
DePalo, Anna.	none
DePietro, Peter.	PS3554.E622
DePoy, Phillip.	PS3554.E624
Depp, Daniel.	PS3604.E65
Depre, Cyndia.	PS3604.E66
DePree, Traci.	PS3604.E67
Deptula, Walter.	none
Dereske, Jo.	PS3604.E75
Derevi‹a›nko, Il'i‹a›, 1964-	PG3479.6.E724
Derham, Roger.	PR6104.E76
Derleth, August William, 1909-1971.	PS3507.E69
	[Z8226.7]
Dermody, Cate.	none
Derouin, R. E.	PS3554.E725
Derrick, Lionel.	none
Dershowitz, Alan M.	PS3554.E77
Derwent, Robert.	none
Des Cars, Guy.	PQ2607.E673
DeSario, Joseph P., 1950-	PS3554.E8353
DeSilva, Bruce.	PS3604.E7575
DesJardien, Teresa.	PS3554.E8363
Desjarlais, John, 1953-	PS3554.E11577
DeSmedt, Bill.	PS3604.E759
Desmond, Hugh.	none
Desmond, Rachel.	none
DeSoto, Lewis.	PR9369.4.D475
Deutcsh, Arthur V.	PS3554.E885
Deutermann, Peter T., 1941-	PS3554.E887
Deutschman, Deborah.	PS3554.E913
Deveraux, Jude.	PS3554.E9273
Deverell, Diana.	PS3554.E92734
Deverell, William, 1937-	PR9199.3.D474
Devereux, David, 1971-	PR6104.E89

Devi, Shakuntala—see: Shakuntala, Devi, 1939-
Devine, D. M.—see: Devine, Dominic, 1920-
Devine, David McDonald—see: Devine, Dominic, 1920-

Devine, Dominic, 1920-   PR6054.E9
Devine, Frances.   PS3604.E88635
Devine, Thea.   PS3554.E928175
Devlin, Frank.   PS3556.A775
DeVoe, Forrest.   PS3604.E887
Devon, D. G.   PS3554.E9282
Devon, Gary.   PS3554.E92824
Devon, Georgina, 1952-   none
Dewar, Evelyn.   PR6054.E93
Dewberry, Elizabeth.   PS3572.A936
DeWeese, Gene.   PS3554.E929
DeWeese, Jean—see: DeWeese, Gene.
Dewey, Donald, 1940-   PS3554.E9293
Dewey, Thomas Blanchard, 1915- PS3507.E883
Dewhurst, Eileen.   PR6054.E95
Dewhurst, Rick.   PR9199.4.D49
Dexter, Colin.   PR6054.E96
Dexter, Kristine.   PS3568.U7
Dexter, Pete, 1943-   PS3554.E95
Dexter, Ted.   PR6054.E967
Dey, Myrna, 1942-   PR9199.4.D4926
Dezenhall, Eric.   PS3604.E94
Dhondy, Farrukh.   PR6054.H55
Di Fiore, Frank.   none
Diaconú, Alina, 1945-   PQ7798.14.I115
Dial, Connie, 1944-   PS3604.I126
Dial, Joan, 1937-   PS3554.I223
Diamant, Anita.   PS3554.I227
Diamond, Ann, 1951-   PR9199.3.D494
Diamond, Dakota.   PS3604.I13
Diamond, Diana.   PS3554.I233
Diamond, Jacqueline, 1949-   PS3554.I24
Diamond, Stephen.   none
Dias, Dexter.   PR6054.I24
Díaz Eterović, Ramón, 1956-   PQ8098.14.I15
DiBartolomeo, Albert.   PS3554.I263
Dibb, C. E.   none
Dibble, David M.   PS3604.I19
Dibble, J. Birney (James Birney), 1925- none
Dibdin, Michael.   PR6054.I26
Dibner, Martin.   PS3507.I215
Dick, Alexandra—see: Erikson, Sibyl Alexandra.
Dick, Philip K.   PS3554.I3
Dick, R. A., 1898-1979.   PR6023.E774
Dickens, Charles, 1812-1870.   PR4550-4598
                               [Z8230]
Dickens, Frank.   none
Dickerson, Karle.   none
Dickey, Christopher.   PS3554.I318
Dickey, Eric Jerome.   PS3554.I319
Dickey, James.   PS3554.I32
Dickinson, David, 1946-   PR6104.I24
Dickinson, Matt.   PR6104.I26
Dickinson, Peter, 1927-   PR6054.I35

Dicks, Matthew.   PS3604.I323
Dickson, Athol, 1955-   PS3554.I3264
Dickson, Carter, 1906-1977.   PS3505.A763
Dickson, Jack.   PR6054.I3587
Didelot, Roger Francis, 1902-   PQ2607.I15
Didion, Joan.   PS3554.I33
Didkovs'ka, Dana.   PG3949.14.I34
Diehl, A. J., 1958-   PS3604.I344
Diehl, William.   PS3554.I345
Dierksen, Caryl.   none
Dietrich, Robert, 1918-2007.   PS3515.U5425
Dietrich, William, 1951-   PS3554.I367
Dietz, Denise.   PS3554.I368
Dietz, Laura.   PS3604.I374
Dietz, Lew, 1906-   none
Dietz, William C.   PS3554.I388
Díez, Rolo, 1940-   PQ7798.14.I28
DiFranco, Anthony Mario.   PS3604.I386
Diggs, Anita Doreen.   PS3604.I39
Dijon, Jon.   PS3554.I3959
Dill, Stuart.   PS3604.I456
Dillinger, James.   PS3552.A4278
Dillman, Darren.   PS3604.I4615
Dillon, Catherine.   none
Dillon, Eilis, 1920-1994.   PR6054.I42
Dillon, Martin, 1949-   PR6054.I43
Dillon, Millicent.   PS3554.I43
Dillon, Walter.   none
Dilnot, George, 1883-1951.   PR6007.I625
DiLucchio, Jane, 1953-   PS3604.I4635
Diment, Adam.   PR6054.I45
DiMercurio, Michael.   PS3554.I4374
Dimon, HelenKay.   PS3604.I467
DiMona, Joseph.   PS3554.I44
Dinallo, Gregory S.   PS3554.I46
Dinesen, Isak, 1885-1962.   PR9142.9.D55
     PT8175.B545
Dingwall, Wendy.   PS3604.I475
Dinsmore, Jeffrey.   none
Diotalevi, David A., 1951-   PS3604.I58
DiPego, Gerald.   PS3554.I63
Diplomat, 1897-1967.   PS3505.A7922
Dipper, Alan.   PR6054.I6
Dirckx, John H., 1938-   PS3554.I7
Dirgo, Craig.   PS3554.I74
Disch, Thomas M.   PS3554.I8
     [Z8232.5]
Dische, Irene.   PS3554.I825
     PT2664.I725
Disher, Garry.   PR9619.3.D56
DiSilverio, Laura A. H.   PS3604.I85
Disney, Doris Miles.   PS3507.I75
Disney, Dorothy Cameron.   PS3507.I76
Dison, David.   PR9369.4.D57

Ditfurth, Christian von.	PT2704.I84
Ditton, James, 1919-	none
Divakaruni, Chitra Banerjee, 1956-	PS3554.I86
Diver, Lucienne, 1971-	none
Divine, A. D. (Arthur Durham), 1904-1987.	PR9369.3.D6
Divine, Arthur Durham—see: Divine, A. D. (Arthur Durham), 1904-1987.	
Divine, David, 1904-1987.	PR9369.3.D6
Dix, Maurice Buxton.	none
Dixon, Collen.	PS3604.I94
Dixon, Franklin W.	PS3537.T817
Dixon, Gregory.	PS3604.I946
Dixon, H. Vernor (Harry Vernor), 1908-	none
Dixon, John, 1952-	PS3604.I947
Dixon, Louisa.	PS3554.I88
Dixon, Mark.	none
Dixon, Melvin, 1950-1992.	PS3554.I89
Dixon, Roger,1930-	PR6054.I95
Dixon, Stephen, 1936-	PS3554.I92
Dixson, Joseph I.	PS3604.I97
Dixson, Rosemary.	PS3554.I1935
Dobbins, Richard.	none
Dobbs, Michael, 1948-	PR6054.O23
Dobbyn, John F.	PS3604.O227
Dobler, Bruce.	PS3554.O16
Dobner, Maeva Park.	none
Dobson, Joanne, 1942-	PS3554.O19
Dobson, Margaret.	none
Dobson, William, 1924-1986.	PR6052.U9
Dobyns, Stephen, 1941-	PS3554.O2
Dodd, Christina.	PS3554.O3175
Dodd, D. O.	PR9199.4.D633
Dodd, Karen E.	none
Dodge, David, 1910-1974.	PS3507.O248
Dodge, Kirsten.	PS3604.O318
Dodge, Mary Louise.	none
Dodson, Brandt, 1958-	PS3604.O33
Dodson, Daniel Boone.	PS3554.O34
Dodson, DeAnna Julie, 1961-	PS3554.O3414
Doetsch, Richard.	PS3604.O343
Doherty, P. C.	PR6054.O37
Doherty, Robert.	PS3563.A95227
Doiron, Paul.	PS3604.O37
Dolan, Harry.	PS3604.O424
Dolan, Patrick.	none
Dold, Gaylord.	PS3554.O436
Doliner, Roy.	PS3554.O45
Dolley, Chris, 1954-	PS3604.O436
Dolson, Hildegarde.	PS3507.O662
Domatilla, John.	PR6054.O427
Domenica.	none
Domenici, Joe.	PS3604.O455
Dominic, R. B.	PS3562.A755
Domokos, Alex.	PR9199.4.D65

Donachie, David, 1944-   PR6053.O483
Donald, Anabel.   PR6054.O4587
Donald, Miles.   PR6054.O459
Donaldson, D. J.   PS3554.O4679
Donaldson, Norman.   none
Donaldson, Robert, 1919-   PR6054.O46
Donaldson, Stephen R.   PS3554.O469
Donavan, John, 1905-1986.   PR6025.O683
Donegan, Greg, 1959-   PS3563.A95227
Donelson, Dave.   PS3604.O545
Dong, Eugene.   PS3554.O4694
Donlay, Philip S.   PS3604.O55
Donne, Maxim—see: Duke, Madelaine.
Donnelly, Jane.   PR6054.O54
Donnelly, Keith.   PS3604.O56325
Donoghue, Emma, 1969-   PR6054.O547
Donoghue, P. S.   PS3515.U5425
Donohue, John J., 1956-   PS3604.O565
Donohue, Keith.   PS3604.O5654
Donovan, Dick, 1843-1934.   PR5101.M363
Donovan, Felicia.   PS3604.O5667
Donovan, Kate.   PS3604.O5668
Donovan, Truly.   PS3554.O564
Donskoĭ, Sergeĭ, 1955-   none
Dont‹s›ova, Dar'i‹a›.   PG3479.6.O65
Doody, Margaret Anne.   PR9199.3.D556
Doogan, Mike.   PS3604.O5675
Dooley, H. H.   PS3554.O57
Dooley, Roger Burke, 1920-   PS3507.O7254
Dooling, Richard.   PS3554.O583
Doolittle, Jerome.   PS3554.O584
Doolittle, Sean, 1971-   PS3604.O568
Doonan, William, 1965-   PS3604.O64
Dor, Milo, 1923-2005.   PT2607.O74
Doran, T. M.   PS3604.O734
Dorer, Frances.   none
Dorer, Nancy.   none
Dorf, Fran.   PS3554.O6715
Dorland, Michael.   PR9199.3.D558
Dorling, H. Taprell (Henry Taprell), 1883-1968.   PR6007.O72
Dorn, Thea, 1970-   PT2664.O6597
Dorner, Marjorie.   PS3554.O677
Dorph, Christian, 1966-   PT8176.14.O69
Dorrell, Linda.   PS3604.O77
Dorrell, Mike.   none
Dorsey, Christine.   none
Dorsey, Tim.   PS3554.O719
Doss, James D.   PS3554.O75
Dostoyevsky, Fyodor, 1821-1881.   PG3325-3328
Dot‹s›enko, Viktor (Viktor Nikolaevich)   PG3479.6.O83
Doty, Carolyn.   PS3554.O79
Doty, William L. (William Lodewick), 1919-   PS3507.O748
Doubtfire, Dianne.   PR6054.O78
Doudera, Vicki, 1961-   PS3604.O895

Doudera, Victoria—see: Doudera, Vicki, 1961-
Dougherty, Kathleen.   none
Doughty, Louise, 1963-   PR6054.O795
Douglas, Arthur, 1926-   PR6058.A55456
Douglas, Arthur, 1928-   PR6054.O82
Douglas, Carole Nelson.   PS3554.O8237
Douglas, Charlotte.   PS3604.O9254
Douglas, Gavin.   PR6007.O863
Douglas, George—see: Brown, George Douglas, 1869-1902.
Douglas, Graeme.   none
Douglas, Gregory A.   none
Douglas, John, 1947-   PS3554.O8257
Douglas, John E.   PS3554.O8258
Douglas, Kirk, 1916-   PS3554.O82625
Douglas, Laramee.   PS3604.O9275
Douglas, Lauren Wright, 1947-   PS3554.O8263
Douglass, Donald McNutt.   none
Doulgeris, James.   PS3604.O9327
Doumani, Carol.   PS3554.O86
Douthwaite, L. C. (Louis Charles), 1878-   none
Dovell, Michael, 1941-   PS3554.O8855
Dovey, Ceridwen.   PR9369.4.D68
Dow, Rosey.   PS3554.O89
Dowd, Siobhan.   PR6104.O88
Dowdee, John.   none
Dowdell, Dorothy.   PS3554.O895
Dowling, Gregory.   PR6054.O862
Dowling, Richard, 1846-1898.   PR4613.D45
Dowling, Terry.   PR9619.3.D674
Downey, Timothy.   PS3554.O934
Downie, Leonard.   PS3604.O944
Downie, Ruth, 1955-   PR6104.O94
Downing, David, 1946-   PR6054.O868
Downing, Jane.   PR9619.3.D677
Downing, Sybil.   PS3554.O9348
Downing, Warwick, 1931-   PS3554.O935
Downs, Jeff, 1969-   PS3604.O95
Downs, Robert, 1980-   PS3604.O9526
Downs, Susan K.   PS3604.O953
Downs, Tim.   PS3604.O954
Doxey, William.   PS3554.O974
Doyle, Adrian Conan.   PR6054.O89
Doyle, Arthur Conan, Sir, 1859-1930.   PR4620-4624
                                                        [Z8240]

Doyle, Bill H., 1968-   none
Doyle, David W.   PS3554.O97434
Doyle, Gerry, 1976-   PS3604.O9548
Doyle, James T., 1928-   PS3554.O9744
Doyle, Peter, 1951-   PR9619.3.D69
Doyle, Richard, 1948-   PR6054.O94
Doyle, Rose.   PR6054.O96
Doyle, Stephanie.   none
Doyle, T. J.—see: Doyle, Thomas J., 1930-
Doyle, Thomas J., 1930-   PS3554.O977

Drabble, John Frederick, 1906-   PR6054.R23
Drachman, Theodore S.   PS3507.R1723
Dracup, Angela.   PR6054.R26
Drago, Ty.   PS3604.R34
Draine, Betsy, 1945-   PS3604.R343
Drake, Abby.   PS3604.R345
Drake, David.   PS3554.R196
Drake, Francis (Francis Vivian)   none
Drake, Nick, 1961-   PR6054.R264
Drake, Rebecca.   none
Drake, Shannon.   PS3557.R198
Drake, Terrance S.   PS3604.R3554
Dramann, Ann.   none
Draper, Alfred.   PR6054.R28
Draper, Hastings, 1926-   PR6060.E43
Draper, Jessica.   PS3604.R37
Dreher, Sarah.   PS3554.R36
Dresden, Thomas.   none
Drew, John H., 1949-   PS3554.R44
Drew, Mary Anne, 1920-2005.   PS3553.A79555
Drew, Wayland, 1932-1998.   PR9199.3.D74
Drexler, J. F., 1916-   PS3566.A34
Dreyer, Eileen.   PS3554.R486
Drinnan, Neal, 1964-   PR9619.3.D78
Driscoll, Peter, 1942-   PR6054.R53
Driver, C. J.   PR6054.R55
Driver, Lee.   PS3554.R545
Droge, Edward F.   PS3554.R57
Droubay, M.   none
Druett, Joan.   PR9639.3.D68
Drugov, Aleksandr.   PG3491.6.R84
Drumm, D. B.   none
Drummond, Charles—see: Giles, Kenneth.
Drummond, Ivor.   PR6062.O516
Drummond, J.—see: Chance, John Newton.
Drummond, Jack, 1951-   PR6104.R88
Drummond, John Keith.   PS3554.R75
Drummond, June.   PR9369.3.D7
Drummond, William.   none
Drury, David M. (David Michael), 1951-   PS3604.R87
Drury, Joan M., 1945-   PS3554.R827
Drusiani, Eros.   none
Druxman, Michael B., 1941-   PS3554.R86
Drvenkar, Zoran, 1967-   PT2664.R84
Dryden, Alex.   PR6104.R95
D'Souza, Tony.   PS3604.S66
Du Bois, Theodora, b. 1890.   PS3507.U145
Du Boisgobey, Fortuné, 1821-1891.   PQ2220.D6
Du Brul, Jack B.   PS3554.U223
Du Maurier, Daphne, 1907-1989.   PR6007.U47
Duane, Allan.   PS3554.U23
DuBay, Sandra.   none
Dublin, D. H.   PS3604.U256
DuBois, Brendan.   PS3554.U2564

Dubosarsky, Ursula, 1961-	none
Dubowski, Cathy East.	PS3554.U2637
DuBreuil, Linda.	none
DuBurke, Randy.	PS3554.U2648
Duchin, Peter.	PS3604.U34
Duckworth, Michael.	none
Dudley, Ernest.	PR6054.U354
Dudley, Karen.	PR9199.3.D8315
Duell, Marie.	PR6053.U79
Duerden, Nick.	PR6054.U36
Duff, Gerald.	PS3554.U3177
Duff, William.	PS3554.U3186
Duffy, David L.	PS3604.U377
Duffy, Margaret.	PR6054.U397
Duffy, Maureen.	PR6054.U4
Duffy, Shirley Surrette.	PS3604.U379
Duffy, Stella.	PR6054.U415
Duffy, Sue.	PS3604.U38
Dufreigne, Jean-Pierre, 1942-	PQ2664.U3449
Dugoni, Robert.	PS3604.U385
Duke, Francis.	none
Duke, Madelaine.	PR6054.U45
Duke, Winifred.	PR6007.U39
Dukthas, Ann.	PR6054.O37
Dulany, Harris, 1940-	PS3554.U42
Dumas, Claire.	PQ2664.U382
Dunant, Sarah.	PR6054.U45756
Dunaway, Laramie.	PS3554.U4632
Dunbar, Anthony P.	PS3554.U46336
Dunbar, Catherine.	PR6054.U45758
Dunbar, Inga.	PR6054.U4579
Dunbar, Sophie.	PS3554.U46337
Duncan, Alice, 1945-	PS3554.U463394
Duncan, Dave, 1933-	PR9199.3.D847
Duncan, David, 1913-1999.	PS3507.U6215
Duncan, Diana.	none
Duncan, Elizabeth J.	PR9199.4.D863
Duncan, Francis.	none
Duncan, Lois, 1934-	PS3554.U464
Duncan, Patrick Sheane.	PS3554.U467
Duncan, Robert Lipscomb, 1927-	PS3554.U465
Duncan, Sharon, 1936-	PS3604.U536
Duncan, W. Glenn.	none
Duncan, W. Murdoch (William Murdoch), 1909- 1975.	PR6007.U535
Duncker, Patricia, 1951-	PR6054.U477
Dundee, Wayne D.	PS3554.U4655
Dunford, Warren, 1963-	PR9199.3.D867
Dungan, Marilyn.	PS3554.U4666
Dunham, Mikel.	PS3554.U4684
Dunham, Tracy.	PS3554.U4686
Dunlap, Susan.	PS3554.U46972
Dunleavy, Steve.	PS3554.U46974
Dunmore, Spencer, 1928-	PR6054.U53

Dunn, Adam.	PS3604.U557
Dunn, Alan, 1954-	PR6104.U544
Dunn, Carola.	PR6054.U537
Dunn, Joeming W.	none
Dunn, Joseph Allan Elphinstone, 1872-1941.	PR6007.U5615
Dunn, Mark P.	PS3604.U55
Dunn, Matthew, 1968-	PR6104.U54494
Dunn, Mike.	none
Dunn, Sharon, 1965-	PS3604.U57
Dunne, Bernard.	none
Dunne, Colin, 1937-	PR6054.U554
Dunne, Dominick.	PS3554.U492
Dunne, H. P. (Harry Powers), 1942-	none
Dunne, John Gregory, 1932-2003.	PS3554.U493
Dunne, Lee, 1934-	PR6054.U555
Dunne, Patrick (Patrick John)	PR6104.U547
Dunne, Thomas L.	PS3554.U4936
Dunnegan, T. L., 1949-2006.	PS3604.U574
Dunnett, Alastair MacTavish, 1908-	PR6054.U557
Dunnett, Dorothy.	PR6054.U56
Dunnett, Kaitlyn.	PS3555.M414
Dunning, John, 1942-	PS3554.U494
Dunning, Lawrence.	none
Duns, Jeremy, 1973-	PR6104.U565
Dunsany, Edward John Moreton Drax Plunkett,	PR6007.U6
Baron, 1878-1957.	
Dupuy, Frank C.	none
DuQuesne, Aisha.	PR6104.U67
Durand, Loup.	PQ2664.U6734
Durant, Isadore, 1945-	PS3554.U667
Duras, Marguerite.	PQ2607.U8245
Durbin, Charles.	PR6054.U66
Durbridge, Francis.	PR6054.U7
Durgin, Doranna.	PS3554.U674
Durham, Guy.	PS3554.U683
Durham, Laura.	PS3604.U735
Duris, Gene.	none
Durrant, Digby.	PR6054.U73
Dürrenmatt, Friedrich.	PT2607.U493
	[Z8246.2]
Durst, Paul.	PS3554.U695
Dušek, Milan, 1938-	PG5039.14.U75
Dust, C. C.	PS3604.U76
Dutton, Charles J. (Charles Judson), b. 1888.	PS3507.U9295
Dutton, James S.	none
Duvall, Chanson.	PS3604.U79
Dvoracek, Delray K.	PS3604.V67
Dvorkin, David.	PS3554.V67
Dwiggins, Toni.	PS3554.W54
Dwyer, Deanna—see: Koontz, Dean R. (Dean Ray), 1945-	
Dwyer, K. R., 1945-	PS3561.O55
Dwyer, Liam D., 1923-	PR9199.4.D887
Dwyer-Joyce, Alice.	PR6054.W9
Dye, Suzanne.	none

Dyer, Charles H., 1952-	PS3604.Y45
Dyer, Mary Heron.	PS3554.Y42
Dykes, Lew.	none
Dymmoch, Michael Allen.	PS3554.Y6
Dymov, Sergeĭ.	PG3479.6.Y56
Dyshev, Andreĭ.	PG3479.6.Y69
Dyson, John, 1943-	PR9639.3.D9
Dyson, Wanda L.	PS3604.Y77
Eachus, Irv.	PS3555.A25
Eagle, Kathleen.	PS3555.A385
Earl, Lawrence.	PR6055.A69
Earley, Pete.	PS3605.A76
Early, Jack.	PS3555.A693
Early, Robert, 1940-	PR9369.3.E17
Earnest, Mark.	PS3605.A77
Eason, Lynette.	PS3605.A79
East, Michael, 1916-	PR9619.3.W4
East, Roger.	none
Eastburn, Joseph.	PS3555.A6958
Easterman, Daniel.	PR6055.A82
Eastland, Sam.	PS3605.A85
Eastman, Robert.	PS3555.A73
Easton, Douglas.	none
Eastvale, Margaret.	none
Eastwood, Helen, b. 1892.	PR6009.A76
Eastwood, James, 1918-	PR6055.A84
Eatock, Marjorie, 1927-	PS3555.A75
Eaton, Anthony, 1972-	PR9619.4.E28
Eaton, Tom.	PR9369.4.E37
Eberhardt, Michael C.	PS3555.B465
Eberhart, Mignon Good, 1899-1996.	PS3509.B453
Ebershoff, David.	PS3555.B4824
Ebersohn, Wessel.	PR9369.3.E24
Ebert, Roger.	PS3555.B52
Eberz, Matthew.	PS3605.B47
Ebisch, Glen Albert, 1946-	PS3605.B57
Ebsen, Buddy, 1908-2003.	PS3605.B74
Eccles, Marjorie.	PR6055.C33
Echard, Margaret.	PS3509.C3
Echenoz, Jean.	PQ2665.C5
Eckblad, Jonathan.	none
Eckhardt, Kristin.	PS3557.A2426
Eco, Umberto.	PQ4865.C6
Ecton, Emily.	none
Eddenden, A. E.	PR9199.3.E32
Eddings, David.	PS3555.D38
Eddy, Pamela, 1956-	PS3605.D38
Eddy, Paul, 1944-2009.	PR6055.D32
Edell, Stephen Anthony.	PR9199.3.E34
Eden, Cynthia.	PS3605.D4535
Eden, Dorothy, 1912-1982.	PR9639.3.E38
Eden, Francis J. S.	none
Eden, Matthew.	PR9199.3.E33
Edgar, Janet.	PS3605.D456

Edgar, Josephine, 1907-1991.	PR6015.O857
Edgar, Ken, 1924-	PS3555.D45
Edgar, Stanley Walter.	none
Edge, Harry.	none
Edgehill, S. D.	PS3605.D458
Edgerton, Clyde, 1944-	PS3555.D47
Edghill, India.	PS3555.D474
Edghill, Rosemary.	PS3555.D475
Edgley, Leslie, 1912-	PS3509.D472
Edmonds, Harry, 1891-1989.	none
Edmonds, Lucinda.	PR6055.D63
Edmonson, Roger.	PS3555.D64
Edouard, Dianne.	PS3555.D66
Edric, Robert, 1956-	PR6055.D7
Edson, John Thomas.	PR6055.D8
Edugyan, Esi.	PR9199.4.E35
Edward, John (John J.)	PS3555.D82
Edwards, Alexander.	none
Edwards, Anne, 1927-	PS3555.D87
Edwards, Anne K., 1940-	PS3605.D87
Edwards, Cassie.	PS3555.D875
Edwards, Charman—see: Edwards, Frederick Anthony, 1896-	
Edwards, Denis, 1948-	PR9639.3.E416
Edwards, Dyfed.	PB2298.E235
Edwards, Frank John.	PS3605.D883
Edwards, Frederick Anthony, 1896-	PR6009.D72
Edwards, Gillian Mary, 1918-	none
Edwards, Grace F. (Grace Frederica)	PS3555.D99
Edwards, Jane, 1932-	PS3555.D933
Edwards, Josh, 1935-	none
Edwards, Kim, 1958-	PS3555.D942
Edwards, L. Ray (Lonnie Ray), 1965-	PS3605.D889
Edwards, Louis, 1962-	PS3555.D945
Edwards, Martin, 1955-	PR6055.D894
Edwards, Michael B.	PS3605.D89
Edwards, Mike.	none
Edwards, Paul.	PS3555.D96
Edwards, Paul M.	PS3605.D896
Edwards, R. T.	PS3557.O85
Edwards, Rachelle.	PR6055.D948
Edwards, Rex.	PR6055.D95
Edwards, Ruth Dudley.	PR6055.D98
Edwards, Samuel, 1914-1988.	PS3513.E8679
Edwardson, Åke, 1953-	PT9876.15.D93
Effinger, George Alec.	PS3555.F4
Efimov, Igor' Markovich.	PG3479.7.F49
Egan, Jennifer.	PS3555.G292
Egan, K. J.	PS3554.A4448
Egan, Lesley, 1921-1988.	PS3562.I515
Egeland, Tom, 1959-	PT8951.15.G413
Egerton-Thomas, Christopher.	none
Egghart, Chris.	PS3605.G49
Egiazarov, Aleksandr.	PG3491.7.G53
Egleton, Clive.	PR6055.G55

Eglin, Anthony.	PS3605.G53
Eguda, Peter Iwoba.	PR9387.9.E3215
Ehly, Ehren M.	none
Ehrenfeld, David.	none
Ehrhart, Peggy.	PS3605.H746
Ehrlich, Collis.	none
Ehrlich, Jack.	none
Ehrlich, Max, 1909-1983.	PS3509.H663
Ehrlichman, John.	PS3555.H74
Ehrman, Kit.	PS3605.H76
Eichler, Selma.	PS3555.I226
Eickhoff, Randy Lee.	PS3555.I23
Eidson, Bill.	PS3555.I34
Eidson, Tom, 1944-	PS3555.I36
Einstein, Charles.	PS3555.I58
Eisenberg, Hershey.	PS3555.I796
Eisler, Barry.	PS3605.I85
Eitel, Jerry.	PS3605.I88
Ekin, Des.	PR6055.K56
Ekman, Kerstin, 1933-	PT9876.15.K55
Ekstrom, Jan, 1923-	PT9876.15.K74
Elam, Jason.	PS3605.L26
Elbrecht, Joyce, 1927-	PS3555.L24
Elder, Evelyn.	PR6021.E66
Elder, Mark.	PS3555.L33
Eldridge, Jim, 1944-	PR6055.L29
Elegant, Robert S.	PS3555.L37
Elgeshin, Konstantin.	PG3479.7.L44
Elgin, Elizabeth.	PR6055.L37
Elgin, Mary, 1917-1965.	PR6055.L4
Eliade, Mircea, 1907-1986.	PC839.E38
Elias, Albert J.	none
Elias, Gerald.	PS3605.L389
Elias, Robert, 1950-	PS3605.L39
Eli'av, Ḥayim, 1936-	PJ5055.2.L538
Eliot, Anne, 1903-1979.	PS3553.O473
Eliot, Jessica.	none
Eliot, Marc.	none
Elkins, Aaron J.	PS3555.L48
Elkins, Charlotte.	PS3555.L485
Eller, John.	PS3555.L53
Ellerbeck, Rosemary.	PR6070.H689
Ellery, Jan.	none
Ellin, Stanley.	PS3555.L56
Ellington, Richard.	PS3509.L545
Elliot, Bruce.	none
Elliot, Jason, 1965-	PR6105.L5855
Elliot, John Michael.	none
Elliott, Bruce.	none
Elliott, Carter.	PS3605.L445
Elliott, Cathy, 1950-	PS3605.L444
Elliott, Chris, 1960-	PS3605.L4453
Elliott, James.	PS3555.L586
Elliott, Jane.	none

Elliott, Richard.   none
Elliott, Sumner Locke.   PR9619.3.E44
Elliott, Thornton.   PS3555.L5932
Ellis, Bret Easton.   PS3555.L5937
Ellis, Carol, 1945-   none
Ellis, David, 1967-   PS3555.L59485
Ellis, Julie, 1933-   PS3555.L597
Ellis, Kate, 1953-   PR6055.L495
Ellis, Leigh.   none
Ellis, Mel, 1912-   PS3555.L615
Ellis, Nishawnda.   PS3605.L4684
Ellis, Rhian.   PS3555.L6156
Ellis, Robert, 1954-   PS3605.L469
Ellis, Ron, 1941-   none
Ellis, Scott.   PS3555.L6157
Ellis, Walter.   PR3555.L45
Ellis, Warren.   PS3555.L61717
Ellis, Wesley.   none
Ellis, William.   PR6055.L52
Ellison, Harlan.   PS3555.L62
Ellory, R. J.—see: Ellory, Roger Jon.
Ellory, Roger Jon.   PR6105.L65
Ellroy, James, 1948-   PS3555.L6274
Ellson, Hal.   PS3509.L668
Elm, Joanna.   PS3555.L6278
Elman, Richard M.   PS3555.L628
Elmore, Joel Saunders.   PS3605.L478
Elrod, P. N. (Patricia Nead)   PS3555.L68
Else, Barbara.   PR9639.3.E496
Else, Chris, 1942-   PR9639.3.E5
Elsinck.   PT5881.15.L77
Elsna, Hebe.   PR6001.N75
Elsner, Alan.   PS3605.L76
Elton, Ben.   PR6055.L79
Elward, James.   PS3555.L84
Elwood, Roger.   PS3555.L85
Ely, David, 1927-   PS3555.L9
Ely, Ron.   PS3555.L93
Elzey, Susan Dean.   PS3605.L92
Emberey, Ivor.   PR6105.M54
Emberland, Terje, 1956-   none
Emerson, Earl W.   PS3555.M39
Emerson, Kathy Lynn.   PS3555.M414
Emerson, Sally, 1952-   PR6055.M42
Emerson, Scott, 1959-   none
Emery, Anne.   PR9199.4.E47
Emery, Robert J.   PS3605.M49
Emley, Dianne.   PS3605.M54
Emmerton, Anton.   none
Emmet, E. R. (Eric Revell)   none
Emmons, Josh.   PS3605.M574
Emsley, Lloyd.   none
Enderle, Dotti, 1954-   none
Endfield, Mercedes, 1922-   PS3572.O42

Endō, Shūsaku, 1923-1996.	PL849.N4
Endore, S. Guy, 1901-1970.	PS3509.N374
Enefer, Douglas.	PR6055.N35
Engel, Howard, 1931-	PR9199.3.E49
Engel, Mitch.	PS3605.N4426
Engelhard, Jack.	PS3555.N395
Enger, L. L.	PS3555.N422
Enger, Thomas, 1973-	PT8952.15.N44
England, Edward Harold.	none
England, George Allan, 1877-1936.	PS3509.N4
England, Jane, 1897-	PR6009.N52
Englander, Seymour.	none
Englehart, Steve.	PS3555.N4257
Engleman, Paul, 1953-	PS3555.N426
Englert, Jonathan.	PS3605.N48
English, Ernest Ivan.	none
English, Jean M. (Jean Martin), 1937-	PS3555.N428
English, Robert.	PR9619.3.E54
Engstrom, Elizabeth.	PS3555.N48
Enikeeva, D. D. (Dili‹a› Dĕrdovna)	PG3479.7.N388
Ennis, Catherine, 1937-	PS3555.N6
Enright, Tracey.	PS3605.N753
Ephron, Delia.	PS3555.P48
Ephron, G. H.	PS3555.P49
Ephron, Hallie.	PS3605.P49
Epperson, S. K.	PS3555.P6187
Epping, Randy Charles.	PS3605.P645
Epstein, Carole.	PR9199.3.E65
Epstein, Charlotte.	PS3555.P645
Epstein, Edward Jay, 1935-	PS3555.P652
Epstein, Edward Z.	none
Erdman, Paul, 1932-2007.	PS3555.R4
Erel, Aran.	PJ5055.2.R388
Ergas, Elizabeth.	none
Erhart, Margaret.	PS3555.R426
Erickson, John R., 1943-	PS3555.R428
Erickson, K. J.	PS3555.R433
Erickson, Lynn.	PS3555.R45
Ericson, Liz.	none
Ericson, Walter, 1914-2003.	PS3511.A784
Erikson, Sibyl Alexandra.	none
Eriksson, Kjell, 1953-	PT9876.15.R5155
Eringer, Robert.	PS3555.R48
Erlanger, Michael, 1915-2002.	PS3555.R5
Ermansons, Egīls.	PG9049.15.R57
Ernst, Kathleen, 1959-	PS3605.R77
Ernst, Paul, b. 1886.	none
Erskine, Barbara.	PR6055.R7
Erskine, Margaret.	PR6045.I5467
Ervin, Sharon, 1941-	PS3605.R86
Erwin, Vicki Berger, 1951-	none
Escott, John.	none
Eskapa, Shirley.	PR6055.S4
Esler, Anthony.	PS3555.S52

Eslick, Tom.	PS3605.S57
Esmond, Harriet.	PR6055.S5
Esser, Robin, 1933-	PR6055.S7
Essex, William, 1932-	none
Estabrook, Barry.	PS3555.S7
Estep, Maggie.	PS3555.S754
Esteven, John, 1888-1954.	PS3537.H64
Estey, Dale.	PR9199.3.E8
Estleman, Loren D.	PS3555.S84
Estow, Daniel.	none
Etchells, Olive.	PR6055.T34
Etheridge, A. I.	none
Etheridge, Christine.	none
Eubank, Judith.	PS3555.U18
Eugenides, Jeffrey.	PS3555.U4
Eulo, Ken.	PS3555.U56
Eustis, Helen.	PS3509.U66
Evanovich, Janet.	PS3555.V2126
Evans, Alan, 1930-	PR6055.V13
Evans, Annaliese.	PS3605.V363
Evans, Bill, 1960 July 16-	PS3605.V364
Evans, Christy.	PS3605.V3647
Evans, Cicely Louise.	PS3555.V213
Evans, Elaine.	none
Evans, Eric C. (Eric Charles)	PS3555.V216
Evans, Geraldine.	PR6055.V17
Evans, Jimmie Ruth.	PS3610.A43
Evans, John P.	none
Evans, Jon, 1973-	PS3605.V365
Evans, Jonathan.	PR6056.R43
Evans, Justin.	PS3605.V366
Evans, Kenneth.	none
Evans, Kenneth L.	PS3555.V218
Evans, Liz.	PR6055.V194
Evans, Mary Anna.	PS3605.V369
Evans, Penelope, 1959-	PR6055.V215
Evans, Peter, 1933-	PR6055.V218
Evans, Philip.	PR6055.V22
Evans, Stan, 1931-	PR9199.4.E934
Evans, Stuart, 1934-1994.	PR6055.V24
Evans, Tabor.	PS3555.V27
Evans, Warren M., 1923-	PS3555.V277
Evenson, Brian, 1966-	PS3555.V326
Everett, Percival L.	PS3555.V34
Everett, Peter.	PR6055.V34
Everett-Green, Evelyn, 1856-1932.	PR4699.E844
Everitt, Bridget.	PR6055.V35
Evers, Crabbe.	PS3552.R33
Evers, Forrest.	PS3560.U336
Everson, David H., 1941-	PS3555.V385
Everson, Eva Marie.	PS3605.V47
Eversz, Robert.	PS3555.V39
Ewan, Chris, 1976-	PR6105.W36
Ewen, Pamela Binnings, 1944-	PS3605.W46

Ewing, Rita.	PS3555.W54
Ex, Sant.	none
Exbrayat, 1906-1989.	PQ2609.X2
Eyerly, Jeannette.	PS3555.Y4
Eyers, John.	PR6055.Y47
Eyre, Elizabeth.	PR6009.Y74
Eyre, Katherine Wigmore.	PS3555.Y675
Eyre, Marie.	none
Faber, Bonnie.	none
Faber, Doris, 1916-	none
Fabian, Ruth.	none
Fabio.	PS3556.A23
Fackler, Elizabeth.	PS3556.A28
Facos, James, 1924-	PS3556.A3
Fadiman, Edwin.	PS3511.A333
Faecke, Peter, 1940-	PT2666.A4
Fagerholm, Monika, 1961-	PT9876.16.A4514
Fagyas, M.	PS3556.A34
Faherty, Terence.	PS3556.A342
Fahy, Christopher.	PS3556.A346
Fahy, Warren.	PS3606.A275
Faigen, Anne G.	PS3556.A32325
Fair, A. A., 1889-1970.	PS3513.A6322
Fairbairn, Douglas, 1926-	PS3556.A362
Fairbairn, Roger, 1906-1977.	PS3505.A763
Fairbanks, Nancy, 1934-	PS3606.A36
Fairburn, Eleanor M.	PR6056.A49
Fairburn, James.	none
Fairchild, Elisabeth.	PS3556.A3626
Fairchild, William.	PR6011.A395
Fairfax, Jane.	none
Fairfield, Roy P.	PS3556.A365
Fairlawn, James.	none
Fairlie, Gerard, b. 1899.	PR6011.A43
Fairman, Paul W.	none
Fairstein, Linda A.	PS3556.A3654
Fairweather, Lori.	PS3556.A3656
Fairweather, Nancy.	none
Faith, Barbara.	PS3556.A3659
Falco, Edward.	PS3556.A367
Falcone, L. M. (Lucy M.), 1951-	none
Falconer, Duncan.	PR6106.A525
Falkirk, Richard, 1929-	PR6062.A47
Fallada, Hans, 1893-1947.	PT2607.I6
Fallis, Greg.	PS3556.A39
Fallon, Ann C.	PS3556.A395
Fallon, Martin, 1929-	PR6058.I343
Fane, Julian, 1927-2009.	PR6056.A57
Fanning, Diane.	PS3606.A55
Fantoni, Barry.	PR6056.A59
Farah, Nuruddin, 1945-	PR9396.9.F3
Farber, Erica.	none
Farell, Anne.	PS3556.A713
Farinetti, Gianni, 1953-	PQ4866.A7665

Farjeon, B. L. (Benjamin Leopold), 1833-1903.   PR4699.F17
Farjeon, J. Jefferson (Joseph Jefferson), 1883-1955. PR6011.A74
Farmer, Jerrilyn.   PS3556.A719
Farmer, Joan.   PR6056.A675
Farmer, Philip José.   PS3556.A72
Farnol, Jeffery, 1878-1952.   PR6011.A75
Farndale, Nigel.   PR6106.A758
Farnsworth, Christopher.   PS3606.A726
Farnsworth, Clyde H.   PS3556.A724
Farnsworth, Mona.   none
Farr, Caroline, 1923-1985.   PR9619.3.B725
Farran, Christopher, 1942-   PS3606.A73
Farrant, Sarah.   PR6056.A736
Farrar, Helen.   none
Farrar, Stewart.   PR6056.A74
Farrell, Gillian B.   PS3556.A7675
Farrell, Kirby, 1942-   PS3556.A77
Farrell, Marjorie.   none
Farrell, Maud.   PS3556.A7713
Farrell, Tom, 1925-   PS3606.A737
Farrelly, Gail E.   PS3556.A7724
Farrelly, Rita K.   PS3556.A7726
Farrère, Claude, 1876-1957.   PQ2611.A78
Farrimond, John.   PR6056.A76
Farrington, Fielden, 1909-   PS3511.A7395
Farris, David, 1954-   PS3606.A74
Farris, John.   PS3556.A777
Farrow, David A. (David Ashby)   PS3556.A7778
Farrow, John, 1947-   PR9199.3.F455
Fasman, Jon.   PS3606.A775
Fast, Howard, 1914-2003.   PS3511.A784
Fast, Jonathan.   PS3556.A779
Fast, Julius, 1919-2008.   PS3556.A78
Fate, Robert.   PS3606.A84
Faulcon, Robert, 1948-2009.   PR6058.O442
Faulkner, Colleen.   PS3556.A93
Faulks, Sebastian.   PR6056.A89
Faust, Joe Clifford, 1957-   PS3556.A972
Faust, Ron.   PS3556.A98
Fawcett, Edgar, 1847-1904.   PS1657
Fawcett, Quinn.   PS3556.A992
Fawkes, L. T.   none
Faye, Lyndsay.   PS3606.A96
Feagan, Stephanie.   none
Fearing, Kenneth, 1902-1961.   PS3511.E115
Fearn, John Russell, 1908-1960.   PR6011.E295
Feather, Jane.   PS3556.E22
Featherstone, Ann.   PR6106.E17
Feddersen, Connie.   none
Fedler, Joanne.   PR9369.4.F43
Feegel, John R.   PS3556.E32
Feehan, Christine.   PS3606.E36
Feely, Terence.   PR6056.E35
Feibleman, Peter S., 1930-   PS3556.E4

Feierstein, Ricardo.	PQ7798.16.E36
Feiffer, Jules.	PS3556.E42
Feinsod, Ethan.	PS3556.E432
Feinstein, Elaine.	PR6056.E38
Feinstein, John.	PS3556.E433
Fekete, Ján, 1945-	PG345439.16.E38
Felber, Ron.	none
Feld, Bernard, 1947-	PS3556.E453
Feldman, Ellen, 1941-	PS3572.I38
Feldmeyer, Dean, 1951-	none
Felix, Charles.	PR4699.F183
Fell, Doris Elaine.	PS3556.E4716
Fellowes, Kate.	PS3606.E3887
Femling, Jean.	PS3556.E475
Fenady, Andrew J.	PS3556.E477
Fenech, Karen.	PS3606.E54
Fenisong, Ruth.	PS3511 .E376
Fenn, George Manville, 1831-1909.	PR4699.F1844
Fennario, David.	PR9199.3.F45
Fennelly, Tony.	PS3556.E49
Fennerton, William, 1921-	PR6056.E485
Fennessy, Aidan.	PR9619.3.F44
Fenno, Jack.	PS3556.E496
Fenton, Julia.	PS3556.E56
Fenton, Kate.	PR6056.E54
Fenton, Margaret.	PS3606.E585
Fenty, Philip.	none
Fenwick, Elizabeth, 1920-	PS3511.E435
Ferguson, Alane.	none
Ferguson, Anthony.	PR6056.E57
Ferguson, Austin.	PS3556.E68
Ferguson, Chris.	PS3556.E69
Ferguson, Danny T.	PS3606.E365
Ferguson, James, 1936-	none
Ferguson, Jo Ann.	PS3556.E714
Ferguson, John Alexander, 1873-	PR6011.E64
Ferguson, Pamela.	PR6056.E619
Ferguson, Tom, 1943-2006.	PS3556.E718
Ferguson, W. B. M. (William Blair Morton), 1882- 1967.	none
Ferm, Betty.	PS3556.E724
Ferone, Joseph.	none
Ferraiolo, Jack D.	none
Ferrand, Georgina.	PR6056.E68
Ferrarella, Marie.	none
Ferraris, Zoë.	PS3606.E738
Ferrars, E. X.	PR6003.R458
Ferrars, Elizabeth, 1907-1995.	PR6003.R458
Ferrell, Keith.	PS3556.E72574
Ferrenz, Barbara J.	PS3606.E76
Ferrigno, Robert.	PS3556.E7259
Ferris, Gordon, 1949-	PR6106.E769
Ferris, Jean Erskine.	none
Ferris, Monica.	PS3566.U47

Ferris, Paul, 1929-	PR6056.E74
Ferris, Tom, 1936-	none
Ferris, Wally.	PS3556.E75
Fesperman, Dan, 1955-	PS3556.E778
Fessier, Michael, 1907-1988.	PS3556.E78
Fetzer, Amy J.	PS3556.E8927
Feuchter, Roy.	none
Feuer, Laurelle.	PS3606.E84
Fforde, Jasper.	PR6106.F67
Fick, Carl.	PS3556.I32
Fickling, G. G., 1925-	PS3556.I327
Fiddimore, David, 1944-	PR6106.I33
Fiechter, Jean-Jacques.	PQ2666.I374
Fiedler, Jacqueline.	none
Fiedler, Jean.	none
Field, Evan.	PS3556.I374
Field, Penelope.	PS3557.I16
Field, Ruth Baker.	none
Fieldhouse, Karl.	PS3606.I35
Fielding, A. (Archibald), 1900-	PR6011.I3
Fielding, Helen, 1958-	PR6056.I4588
Fielding, Joy.	PR9199.3.F518
Fields, Alan.	none
Fields, Jan.	none
Fiffer, Sharon Sloan, 1951-	PS3606.I37
Figueras, Marcelo, 1962-	PQ7798.16.I336
Filgate, Macartney—see: Macartney-Filgate, Terence.	
Filostrat, Christian.	PS3606.I45
Finch, Carol.	none
Finch, Charles (Charles B.)	PS3606.I526
Finch, Kay.	PS3606.I53
Finch, Matthew.	none
Finch, Phillip.	PS3556.I456
Finder, Joseph.	PS3556.I458
Findley, Ferguson, 1910-	none
Findley, Timothy.	PR9199.3.F52
Fine, Peter Heath.	PS3556.I4635
Finger, Gerrie Ferris.	PS3606.I534
Fink, John.	PS3556.I475
Finlay, Iain.	PR9619.3.F46
Finney, Jack.	PS3556.I52
Finney, Patricia, 1958-	PR6056.I519
Fiorato, Marina.	PR6106.I67
Fiore, Carmen Anthony, 1932-	PS3556.I57
Fischer, Bruno, 1908-1992.	PS3511.I687
Fischer, Erwin, 1928-	PT2666.I75
Fischer, John.	none
Fischer, Marie Louise, 1922-	PT2621.E672
Fish, Robert L.	PS3556.I79
Fisher, Alan (Alan E.)	PR6056.I773
Fisher, David E., 1932-	PS3556.I813
Fisher, Eve.	PS3606.I7725
Fisher, George.	none
Fisher, Graham, 1920-	PR6056.I777

Fisher, Michael R.   PS3556.I81423
Fisher, Nancy.   none
Fisher, Norman, 1910-   PR6056.I795
Fisher, R. Darryl.   PS3556.I81432
Fisher, Rudolph, 1897-1934.   PS3511.I7436
Fisher, Stephen Gould—see: Fisher, Steve, 1912-1980.
Fisher, Steve, 1912-1980.   PS3511.I7438
Fishman, Hal.   PS3556.I81455
Fiske, Dorsey.   PS3556.I81463
Fister, Barbara.   PS3556.I81466
Fitch, Stona.   PS3556.I816
Fitt, Mary, 1897-1959.   PR6011.I787
Fitz, Jean DeWitt.   PS3556.I82
Fitzek, Sebastian, 1971-   PT2706.I89
Fitzgerald, Arlene J.   PS3556.I829
Fitzgerald, Conor.   PR9120.9.F58
Fitzgerald, Kitty.   PR6056.I855
Fitzgerald, Michael, 1918-   PS3556.I8344
Fitzgerald, Nigel, 1906-   PR6056.I856
Fitzgerald, Paul.   none
Fitzgerald, Penelope.   PR6056.I86
Fitzgerald, Tom.   PS3556.I84
FitzGibbon, Constantine, 1919-   PR6011.I88
Fitzhugh, Bill.   PS3556.I8552
Fitzjames, Phoebe.   none
Fitzmaurice, Eugene.   PS3556.I87
Fitzpatrick, Flo.   PS3606.I886
Fitzpatrick, Janine.   none
Fitzsimmons, Cortland, 1893-1949.   PS3511.I96
Fitzsimons, Christopher.   PR6056.I916
Fitzwater, Judy.   PS3556.I899
Flacco, Anthony.   PS3606.L33
Flagg, Fannie.   PS3556.L26
Flagg, John.   none
Flagg, Jonas.   none
Flaherty, Joe.   PS3556.L28
Flanagan, John (John Anthony)   PR9619.4.F63
Flanagan, Richard, 1961-   PR9619.3.F525
Flander, Scott.   PS3556.L346
Flannery, Sean.   PS3556.L37
Fleet, Charles.   none
Fleetwood, Hugh.   PR6056.L38
Fleetwood, Wade B.   PS3556.L4223
Fleischer, Ludwig Roman, 1952-   PT2666.L417
Fleishman, Jeffrey.   PS3606.L457
Fleischman, Sid, 1920-2010.   PS3556.L42269
Flem-Ath, Rose.   PR9199.3.F562
Fleming, Anne.   PR6056.L39
Fleming, Charles.   PS3606.L46
Fleming, Dorothy, 1925-   PS3556.L443
Fleming, H. K. (Horace Kingston), 1901-2000.   PS3511.L4417
Fleming, Ian, 1908-1964.   PR6056.L4
Fleming, Irene, 1939-   PS3557.A414
Fleming, James, 1944-   PR6056.L42

Fleming, Jane.	none
Fleming, Joan, 1908-	PR6011.L46
Fleming, Kathleen Anne.	PS3556.L4464
Fleming, May Agnes, 1840-1880.	PR9199.2.F57
Fleming, Nichol, 1939-1995.	PR6056.L42
Fleming, Thomas J.	PS3556.L45
Fletcher, Aaron.	PR9639.3.F56
Fletcher, Adrian.	none
Fletcher, David, 1940-1988.	PR6052.A616
Fletcher, Dirk.	PS3553.U468
Fletcher, Dorothy.	none
Fletcher, Frances.	PS3511.L447
Fletcher, Harry Lutf Verne, 1902-	PR6011.L484
Fletcher, Joël.	PR9199.3.F5627
Fletcher, Joseph Smith, 1863-1935.	PR6011.L5
Fletcher, Leigh.	none
Fletcher, Lucille.	PS3556.L517
Fletcher, Mary (Mary Mann)	none
Fletcher, Meredith.	none
Flett, Alfred.	PR9639.3.F57
Fliegel, Richard.	none
Flinn, Elaine.	PS3606.L565
Flint, Shamini, 1969-	PR6106.L56
Flood, Charles Bracelen.	PS3556.L58
Flood, John, 1962-	PS3556.L5824
Flood, Robert J.	none
Flora, Fletcher, 1914-1969.	none
Flora, Kate, 1949-	PS3556.L5838
Florence, Ronald.	PS3556.L5853
Flores, Janis.	PS3556.L586
Florian, S. L.	none
Flower, Amanda.	PS3606.L683
Flower, Pat.	PR9619.3.F54
Flowers, Charles.	none
Floyd, Bill, 1968-	PS3606.L687
Fluke, Joanne, 1943-	PS3556.L685
Flynn, Brian.	PR6011.L8
Flynn, Carol Houlihan, 1945-	PS3556.L78
Flynn, Connie.	none
Flynn, Don.	PS3556.L84
Flynn, Gillian, 1971-	PS3606.L935
Flynn, J. M.—see: Flynn, Jay.	none
Flynn, Jay.	PS3556.L87
Flynn, Joseph.	PS3556.L872
Flynn, Lucine Hansz.	PS3556.L88
Flynn, Vince.	PS3556.L94
Flynt, Ray.	PS3606.L96
Foden, Giles, 1967-	PR6056.O27
Fogarty, Fitzgerald.	none
Fogarty, Michael, 1939-	PR6056.O3
Fogelson, Genia.	none
Foglia, Leonard.	PS3556.O36
Fois, Marcello, 1960-	PQ4866.O43
Fokker, Nicholas, 1908-	PS3556.O37

Foley, Gaelen.	PS3556.O3913
Foley, Helen.	PR6056.O4
Foley, Lorette.	none
Foley, Louise Munro.	none
Foley, Rae, 1900-1978.	PS3511.O186
Foley, Tom (Thomas C.)	PS3556.O3918
Follett, Edwina.	none
Follett, James, 1939-	PR6056.O44
Follett, Ken.	PR6056.O45
Folsom, Allan.	PS3556.O398
Fong, C. K., 1920-2005.	PS3553.A79555
Fonseca, Rubem.	PQ9698.16.O46
Fontana, D. C.	PS3556.O48
Fontana, Joe, 1939-	PS3556.O49
Fontes, Justine.	none
Foote, Shelby.	PS3511.O348
Foote-Smith, Elizabeth.	PS3556.O63
Footman, Robert.	PS3556.O64
Footner, Hulbert, 1879-1944.	none
Foran, Charles, 1960-	PR9199.3.F5669
Foran, Phil.	none
Forand, Claude, 1954-	PQ3919.2.F587
Forbes, Bryan, 1926-	PR6056.O63
Forbes, Colin, 1923-2006.	PR6069.A94
Forbes, Daniel, 1931-	PR6061.E675
Forbes, DeLoris.	PS3556.O6615
Forbes, Edith, 1954-	PS3556.O662
Forbes, Elena.	PR6106.O67
Forbes, Leslie.	PR6056.O654
Forbes, Stanton, 1923-	PS3556.O67
Ford, Clyde W.	PS3606.O724
Ford, Florence.	none
Ford, G. M. (Gerald M.)	PS3556.O6978
Ford, George.	none
Ford, Harriett, 1946-	PS3606.O735
Ford, Hilary, 1922-	PR6053.H75
Ford, Jack, 1950-	PS3606.O736
Ford, Jeffrey, 1955-	PS3556.O6997
Ford, Leslie, 1898-1983.	PS3511.O4113
Ford, Mackenzie.	PR6106.O73
Ford, Peter Shann.	PS3556.O7127
Ford, Susan, 1957-	PS3606.O747
Forde, Nicholas.	none
Foreman, Dave, 1946-	PS3556.O7223
Fores, John, 1916-	PR6056.O68
Forest, Stephen.	PS3556.O7242
Forester, Bruce M., 1939-	PS3556.O7249
Forester, C. S. (Cecil Scott), 1899-1966.	PR6011.O56
Forma, Warren.	PS3556.O7325
Forman, Steven M.	PS3606.O74775
Formichella, Joe, 1955-	PS3606.O7478
Forrest, Christopher.	PS3606.O7483
Forrest, David.	PR6056.O684
Forrest, Elizabeth.	none

Forrest, Katherine V., 1939-	PS3556.O737
Forrest, Richard, 1932-	PS3556.O739
Forrest, Steven, 1949-	PS3606.O7485
Forrest, Wilma.	none
Forrest, V. K.	PS3606.O74855
Forrest-Webb, Robert, 1929-	PR6056.O692
Forrester, Larry.	PR6056.O693
Forrester, Stan.	PS3556.O7393
Forster, Gwynne.	PS3556.O742
Forster, Margaret, 1938-	PR6056.O695
Forster, Rebecca, 1952-	none
Forster, Suzanne.	PS3556.O7443
Forstot, Marilyn, 1942-	none
Forsyth, Frederick, 1938-	PR6056.O699
Forsythe, Cathy.	PS3556.O7446
Forvé, Guy.	none
Fosburgh, Lacey, 1942-	PS3556.O7545
Foss, Patrick (Patrick W.)	PS3606.O749
Fossum, Karin, 1954-	PT8951.16.O735
Foster, Alan Dean, 1946-	PS3556.O756
Foster, Bennett.	PS3511.O6812
Foster, Iris—see: Posner, Richard.	
Foster, L. L., 1958-	PS3556.O767
Foster, Levin Wilson, 1907-1992.	PS3556.O765
Foster, Lori, 1958-	PS3556.O767
Foster, Marion, 1924-	PR9199.3.F574
Foster, R. Francis (Reginald Francis), 1896-	PR6011.O7
Foster, Richard, 1910-	PS3505.R89224
Foster, Robert.	PS3556.O7714
Foster, Tony.	PR9199.3.F577
Foth, Kitty.	PS3556.O775
Fotheringham, Peter Moir.	PR6056.O83
Fought, Catherine Ann.	PS3556.O78
Fountain, Nigel.	none
Fowler, Christopher.	PR6056.O846
Fowler, Connie May.	PS3556.O8265
Fowler, Dennis.	none
Fowler, Earlene.	PS3556.O828
Fowler, Sydney, 1874-1965.	PR6045.R45
Fowles, Anthony.	PR6056.O847
Fowlkes, Frank V., 1941-	PS3556.O873
Fox, Addison.	PS3606.O877
Fox, Anthony.	PS3556.O877
Fox, Clayton.	PS3556.O8773
Fox, George.	PS3556.O88
Fox, James M., 1908-	PS3521.N6
Fox, Jimmy.	PS3606.O95
Fox, Kathryn, 1966-	PS3606.O9526
Fox, Norman A., 1911-1960.	PS3511.O968
Fox, Peter F.	PR6056.O865
Fox, Stuart, 1950-	PS3556.O9557
Fox, Zachary Alan.	PS3556.O972
Foxall, P. A.	PR6056.O875
Foxall, Raymond.	PR6056.O88

Foxx, Aleister.	PR9199.3.F63
Foxx, Jack, 1943-	PS3566.R67
Foy, George.	PS3556.O99
Fradkin, Barbara Fraser, 1947-	PR9199.4.F698
Fraï, Maksim, 1965-	PG3480.R27
Frake, Ann Gustafson.	PS3556.R258
Fraley, Craig.	PS3556.R268
Fraley, Oscar, 1914-	PS3556.R275
Frances, Stephen, D.	PR6056.R265
Francis, Clare.	PR6056.R268
Francis, David, 1958-	PR9619.4.F73
Francis, Dick.	PR6056.R27
Francis, Dorothy Brenner.	PS3556.R327
Francis, Felix.	PR6056.R273
Francis, H. G.	none
Francis, Patry.	PS3606.R3645
Francis, Paul, 1953-	PS3555.N426
Francis, Pauline.	none
Francis, Richard, 1945-	PR6056.R277
Francis, Robin.	none
Francisco, Ruth.	PS3606.R366
Francome, John.	PR6056.R282
Frani‹u›k, Vladimir, 1931-	none
Frank, Jacquelyn.	PS3606.R3796
Frank, Larry.	PS3556.R33426
Frank, Steven J.	PS3556.R33445
Frankau, Gilbert, 1884-1952.	PR6011.R26
Frankau, Pamela, 1908-1967.	PR6011.R28
Frankel, Neville.	PS3556.R3355
Frankel, Robert.	none
Frankel, Sandor, 1943-	PS3556.R3356
Frankel, Valerie.	PS3556.R3358
Frankland, Noble, 1922-	PR6106.R453
Frankle, Judith—see: Couffer, Jack.	
Franklin, Ariana.	PR6064.O73
Franklin, Charles, 1909-1976.	PR6071.U8
Franklin, Donald.	none
Franklin, Eugene, 1914-1987.	PS3556.R337
Franklin, Harry.	none
Franklin, June.	none
Franklin, Keith.	none
Franklin, Max, 1915-1983.	PS3554.E48
Franklin, Steve.	PS3556.R34
Franzen, Jonathan.	PS3556.R352
Frase, H. Michael.	PS3556.R3528
Fraser, Anthea.	PR6056.R286
Fraser, Antonia, 1932-	PR6056.R2863
Fraser, Christine Marion.	PR6056.R2864
Fraser, Guy.	none
Fraser, James, 1924-	PR6073.H49
Fraser, Jean.	none
Fraser, John, 1932-	PR6056.R292
Fraser, Margot, 1936-	PS3556.R3545
Fraser, Sylvia.	PR9199.3.F7236

Frash, Bill.	PS3556.R35464
Frasier, Anne.	PS3606.R425
Frates, Kent F.	PS3606.R4263
Frayn, Michael.	PR6056.R3
Frazee, Steve, 1909-1992.	PS3556.R358
Frazer, Margaret.	PS3556.R3586
Frazer, Robert Caine, 1908-1973.	PR6005.R517
Frazier, Charles, 1950-	PS3556.R3599
Frazier, Kit, 1965-	PS3606.R428
Freadhoff, Chuck.	PS3556.R365
Frede, Richard.	PS3556.R37
Frederick, K. C., 1935-	PS3556.R3755
Fredericks, Harriet.	none
Frederics, Jocko.	none
Frederics, Macdowell—see: Frede, Richard.	
Fredman, John.	PR6056.R38
Fredman, Mike.	PR6056.R383
Fredrickson, Jack.	PS3606.R437
Fredrickson, Michael.	PS3556.R3826
Freeborn, Brian.	PR6056.R394
Freeborn, Richard.	PR6056.R395
Freed, Donald, 1932-	PS3556.R383
Freedman, J. F.	PS3556.R3833
Freeling, Nicholas.	PR6056.R4
Freely, Maureen, 1952-	PS3556.R3836
Freeman, Barbara Constance.	none
Freeman, Brian, 1963-	PS3606.R4454
Freeman, Castle, 1944-	PS3556.R3838
Freeman, Gwen.	PS3606.R44545
Freeman, Jayne.	none
Freeman, Lucy, 1916-	PS3556.R392
Freeman, Martha, 1956-	none
Freeman, R. Austin (Richard Austin), 1862-1943.	PR6011.R43
Freemantle, Brian.	PR6056.R43
Frei, Pierre, 1930-	PT2666.R3592
Freire, Espido, 1974-	PQ6656.R42
Freireich, Valerie J.	none
Freivalds, John.	PS3556.R394
Fremlin, Celia.	PR6056.R45
French, Fergus.	none
French, Linda—see: Mariz, Linda, 1948-	
French, Nicci.	PR6056.R456
French, Richard P.	PS3556.R43
French, Tana.	PR6106.R457
Frerker, Jack.	PS3606.R74
Freveletti, Jamie.	PS3606.R486
Frey, Charles Weiser—see: Findley, Ferguson, 1910-	
Frey, James N.	PS3556.R4474
Frey, Stephen W.	PS3556.R4477
Freydont, Shelley.	PS3556.R45
Freytag, Joseph.	none
Freytag, Josephine.	none
Fried, Amelie, 1958-	none
Fried, Barbara.	none

Friedlander, Mark P.	PS3556.R495
Friedman, Bruce Jay, 1930-	PS3556.R5
Friedman, Hal.	PS3556.R52
Friedman, Kinky.	PS3556.R527
Friedman, John M., 1914-	PS3556.R5264
Friedman, Lisa K.	none
Friedman, Mickey.	PS3556.R53
Friedman, Philip, 1944-	PS3556.R545
Friedman, Roy.	PS3556.R56
Friedman, Stuart, 1913-	none
Friend, Catherine.	PS3556.R5662
Friend, Oscar J. (Oscar Jerome), 1897-1963.	PS3511.R745
Frimansson, Inger, 1944-	PT9876.16.R5725
Frimmer, Steven.	PS3556.R5687
Frisby, Mister Mann.	PS3606.R575
Frizell, Bernard.	PS3556.R59
Froetschel, Susan.	PS3556.R59353
Froissard, Lily Powell.	PR6066.O93
Frome, David, 1898-1983.	PS3511.O4113
Frome, Shelly, 1935-	PS3606.R59
Frommer, Sara Hoskinson.	PS3556.R5944
Froscher, Jon.	PS3556.R5956
Frøslev, Ole, 1943-	PT8176.16.R64
Frost, G. H.	none
Frost, Gregory.	PS3556.R59815
Frost, Jason, 1952-	PS3554.U4632
Frost, Jeaniene.	PS3606.R653
Frost, Joan Van Every.	none
Frost, Mark, 1953-	PS3556.R599
Frost, Scott.	PS3556.R62
Fruchter, Norm, 1937-	PS3556.R77
Fruttero, Carlo.	PQ4866.R8
Fry, Pete, 1914-	PR6061.I44
Fry, Stephen, 1957-	PR6056.R88
Frye, Alexandra.	PS3556.R877
Fuchs, Jake.	PS3556.U3133
Fuchs, Michael Stephen.	PR6106.U24
Fuentes, Carlos.	PQ7297.F793
Fuentes, Erica.	none
Fuentes, Roberto.	none
Fuentes Pulido, Eugenio, 1958-	PQ6656.U47
Fuerst, James W. (James William)	none
Fulford, Paul A.	none
Fulk, David.	none
Fuller, Dean.	PS3556.U38
Fuller, H. E.	none
Fuller, Jack.	PS3556.U44
Fuller, Kathleen.	PS3606.U553
Fuller, Peter.	none
Fuller, Roger, 1905-1976.	PS3539.R124
Fuller, Roy, 1912-1991.	PR6011.U55
Fuller, Samuel, 1911-	PS3511.U6622
Fullerton, Alexander, 1924-	PR6056.U435
Fullerton, John.	PR6056.U437

Fullilove, Eric James.	PS3556.R877
Fulmer, David.	PS3606.U56
Fulton, E. G.	none
Fulton, Eileen	PS3556.U5157
Fulton, Jennifer, 1958-	PS3556.U524
Funderburk, Robert, 1942-	PS3556.U59
Furber, Rosemary.	PR6106.U73
Furlong, Nicola.	PR9199.4.F87
Furman, Ben (Ben R.)	none
Furman, Susan.	PS3606.U76
Furness, Audrey.	none
Furnivall, Kate.	PR6116.U76
Furst, Alan.	PS3556.U76
Furutani, Dale.	PS3556.U778
Fusco, John.	PS3606.U83
Fusilli, Jim.	PS3606.U85
Futrelle, Jacques, 1875-1912.	PS3511.U97
Fyfield, Frances.	PR6056.Y47
Fyhrlund, Eric.	none
Gabaldon, Diana.	PS3557.A22
Gabbay, Tom.	PS3607.A226
Gablehouse, Gary L.	PS3607.A24
Gaboriau, Emile, 1832-1873.	PQ2257.G2
Gabriel, Marius.	PR6057.A273
Gachuhi, David.	PR9381.9.G23
Gadda, Carlo Emilio, 1893-1973.	PQ4817.A33
Gaddis, Peggy.	PS3513.A227
Gadney, Reg, 1941-	PR6057.A294
Gadol, Peter.	PS3557.A285
Gadziola, Rick.	PR9199.4.G333
Gaetz, Dayle, 1947-	none
Gaffney, Marguerite S.	PS3557.A29
Gage, Edwin.	PS3557.A326
Gage, Leighton.	PS3607.A3575
Gage, Nicholas.	PS3557.A33
Gaĭdukov, Sergeĭ.	PG3481.A354
Gaille, S. Scott.	PS3607.A3595
Gaiman, Neil.	PR6057.A319
Gainham, Sarah.	PR6057.A34
Gaitano, Nick.	PS3557.A3586
Galbraith, Ruth.	none
Galenorn, Yasmine, 1961-	PS3607.A413
Galgut, Damon, 1963-	PR9369.3.G28
Galit⟨s⟩kiĭ, Pëtr.	none
Gall, Sandy, 1927-	PR6057.A386
Gallacher, Tom.	PR6057.A388
Gallagher, P. B.	none
Gallagher, Patricia.	none
Gallagher, Richard.	none
Gallagher, Stephen.	PR6057.A3893
Gallant, Gladys S.	PS3557.A41167
Galli, Guy Morgan, 1970-	PS3607.A416
Gallico, Paul, 1897-1976.	PS3513.A413
Gallie, Menna.	PR6057.A394

Galligan, John.	PS3607.A4165
Gallison, Kate, 1939-	PS3557.A414
Gallon, Tom, 1866-1914.	PR6013.A46
Galloway, David D.	PS3557.A4155
Galloway, Sherry, 1967-	PS3557.A41568
Galster, Karen, 1976-	none
Galvin, John, 1963-	PR6057.A445
Galway, Robert Conington, 1920-	none
Gambino, Denise.	PS3557.A4475
Gamble, Geoffrey P.	PS3557.A449
Gamble, M. L.	none
Gamboa, Santiago, 1965-	PQ8180.17.A395
Gandolfi, Simon.	PR6057.A457
Gandt, Robert L.	PS3607.A447
Gangemi, Joseph.	PS3607.A46
Gangi, Theo.	PS3607.A47
Gannascoli, Joseph R.	PS3607.A555
Gannon, Michael, 1927-	PS3557.A518
Gano, John.	PR6057.A47
Ganpat, b. 1886.	PR6013.O455
Gansky, Alton.	PS3557.A5195
Gant, Jonathan, 1919-	PS3551.D34
Gant, Norman.	none
Gantzer, Hugh.	PR9499.3.G28
Gar, Robin.	none
Garanin, Andreĭ.	none
Garber, Joseph R.	PS3557.A64
Garbera, Katherine.	PS3607.A68
Garbo, Norman.	PS3557.A65
Garcia, Eric.	PS3557.A665
Garcia, Guy, 1955-	PS3557.A67
Garcia, Ricardo L.	PS3607.A725
Garcia-Aguilera, Carolina.	PS3557.A71124
García Calderón, Fernando, 1959-	PQ6657.A6538
García Lledó, Alberto, 1965-	PQ6707.A35744
García-Roza, L. A. (Luiz Alfredo)	PQ9698.17.A745
Garden, John—see: Fletcher, Harry Lutf Verne, 1902-	
Garden, Nancy.	PS3557.A711266
Gardiner, Dorothy, 1894-1979.	PS3513.A617
Gardiner, Judy, 1922-	PR6057.A627
Gardiner, Meg.	PR6107.A725
Gardiner, Wayne J.	none
Gardner, Alan.	none
Gardner, Ashley.	none
Gardner, Craig Shaw.	PS3557.A7116
Gardner, Erle Stanley, 1889-1970.	PS3513.A6322
	[Z8324.15]
Gardner, John, 1926-2007.	PR6057.A63
Gardner, Lee.	none
Gardner, Lisa.	PS3557.A7132
Gardner, Lynn, 1938-	PS3557.A7133
Gardner, Theodore Roosevelt.	PS3557.A7146
Gardner, Willard Boyd, 1963-	PS3607.A73
Garey, Berton D., 1944-	PS3557.A7148

Garfield, Brian, 1939-	PS3557.A715
Garfield, Henry.	PS3557.A7152
Garfield, Leon.	PR6057.A636
Garfield, Valerie.	none
Garforth, John.	none
Garin, Maksim.	none
Garland, Ardella, 1962-	PS3560.O242
Garland, Bob.	PS3557.A71572
Garland, Nicholas—see: Katz, Herbert M.	
Garlington, Philip, 1943-	PS3557.A7163
Garlock, Dorothy.	PS3557.A71645
Garn, Jake.	PS3557.A71663
Garner, Craig C.	none
Garner, David.	none
Garner, Hugh, 1913-1979.	PR9199.3.G3
Garner, James.	none
Garner, Laura.	PS3607.A76
Garner, Sharon K.	PS3557.A71669
Garner, Tracee Lydia.	none
Garner, William, 1920-	PR6057.A675
Garnet, A. H.	PS3557.A7167
Garnett, Bill.	PS3557.A7165
Garnett, Griffin T., 1914-	PS3557.A7168
Garrett, George, 1929-2008.	PS3557.A72
Garretson, Jerri.	none
Garrett, Randall.	PS3557.A7238
Garrett, Robert.	PS3557.A72
Garrison, Christian.	none
Garrison, Jim, 1921-1992.	PS3557.A735
Garrison, Joan, 1916-	PS3527.E598
Garrison, Paul, 1952-	PS3557.A738
Garrity.	none
Garros-Evdokimov.	PG3491.94.A775
Garth, David.	PS3513.A736
Garth, Ed.	none
Garton, Ray.	PS3557.A796
Garve, Andrew, 1908-	PR6073.I56
Garvey, Amy, 1967-	PS3607.A7826
Garvin, Richard M.	PS3557.A8
Garwood, Judith.	PS3557.A8424
Garwood, Julie.	PS3557.A8427
Gary, Vernon, 1954-	PS3557.A8442
Gascar, Pierre, 1916-1997.	PQ2613.A59
Gaseţ Tačāné.	none
Gash, Joe.	PS3557.R256
Gash, Jonathan.	PR6057.A728
Gask, Arthur, b. 1872.	PR6013.A757
Gaskell, Jane, 1941-	PR6057.A73
Gaskin, Catherine.	PR6057.A75
Gaskin, Sandy.	none
Gasner, Beverley.	PS3557.A84475
Gaspar, Stephen.	PR9199.4.G378
Gaspar de Alba, Alicia, 1958-	PS3557.A8449
Gast, Kelly P.	PS3557.A847

Gastine, Michel.	PQ2667.A7918
Gaston, Bill.	none
Gat, Dimitri V., 1936-	PS3557.A85
Gatenby, Rosemary.	PS3557.A86
Gates, Nancy Gotter.	PS3607.A7887
Gates, Natalie.	PS3557.A88
Gates, Olivia.	none
Gates, R. Patrick.	none
Gates, Tudor.	PR6057.A8
Gathje, Curtis.	PS3557.A885
Gatiss, Mark.	PR6107.A86
Gat‹s›ura, Gennadiĭ.	none
Gattzden, Matt.	none
Gauḍa, Tā. Bhā.	none
Gault, William Campbell.	PS3557.A948
Gaunt, Graham.	PR6057.A86
Gaus, P. L.—see: Gaus, Paul L.	
Gaus, Paul L.	PS3557.A9517
Gause-Jackson, Arlene.	PS3557.A9518
Gautreaux, Tim.	PS3557.A954
Gavin, Bernard.	PR6057.A87
Gavin, Catherine Irvine.	PR6013.A83
Gay, Virginia.	PR6057.A97
Gay, William.	PS3557.A985
Gayet, Caroline.	PQ2667.A98
Gayle, Kiniesha.	PS3607.A985756
Gaylin, Alison.	PS3607.A9858
Gaylord, Louise.	PS3607.A986
Geagley, Brad, 1950-	PS3607.E35
Gear, Kathleen O'Neal.	PS3557.E18
Gear, W. Michael.	PS3557.E19
Geary, Joseph.	PR6107.E28
Geary, Nancy.	PS3557.E228
Geary, Patricia.	PS3557.E23
Geason, Susan, 1946-	PR9619.3.G4
Gebhard, H. Harris.	none
Gebhard, Pat—see: Gebhard, Patricia.	
Gebhard, Patricia.	none
Geddes, D. Grant.	PS3607.E36
Geddes, Paul.	PR6057.E24
Gedge, Pauline, 1945-	PR9199.3.G415
Gedney, Mona, 1945-	none
Gee, Maggie, 1948-	PR6057.E247
Gee, Maurice.	PR9639.3.G4
Geffs, Tolman Farrah.	PS3607.E365
Genna, Giuseppe, 1969-	PQ4867.E498
Geisler, Barbara R.	PS3607.E37
Gelb, Alan.	PS3557.E365
Gelb, Jeff.	none
Gelien, Modena.	PS3557.E378
Gelinas, Robert E.	none
Geller, Laurence.	PS3607.E45
Geller, Michael.	PS3557.E3793
Geller, Shari, 1959-	PS3557.E395

Geller, Stephen.   PS3557.E4
Gellis, Roberta.   PS3557.E42
Gelsey, James.   none
Gemmell, David.   PR6057.E454
Genelin, Michael.   PS3607.E53
Gentle, Mary.   PR6057.E525
Gentry, Anita.   PS3557.E458
Gentry, Christine, 1954-   PS3607.E582
Genya, Monica.   none
George, Anne.   PS3557.E469
George, Elizabeth, 1949-   PS3557.E478
George, Jonathan, 1922-   PR6003.U54
George, Kara.   PS3557.E486
George, Kathleen, 1943-   PS3557.E487
George, Nelson.   PS3557.E493
George, Peter, 1924-1966.   PR6057.E54
George, Sara.   PR6057.E55
George, Theodore.   PS3557.E5
Gerahty, Digby George—see: Standish, Robert.
Gerard, Cindy.   PS3557.E625
Gérard, Francis, 1905-   PR6013.E67
Gerard, Morice, 1856-1929.   none
Gerard, Ron L.—see: Renauld, Ron.
Gerard, Philip.   PS3557.E635
Gerber, Linda C.   none
Gercke, Doris.   PT2667.E644
Germeshausen, Anna Louise.   none
Geron, Frank.   none
Gerritsen, Tess.   PS3557.E687
Gerrity, Dave.   none
Gerrity, David J.—see: Gerrity, Dave.
Gerson, Jack.   PR6057.E72
Gerson, Noel B. (Noel Bertram), 1914-1988.   PS3513.E8679
Gethin, David.   PR6057.E76
Gettel, Ronald E., 1931-   PS3557.E86
Ghelfi, Brent.   PS3607.H46
Gheorghiu, Virgil, 1916-   PQ2667.H4
                                                          PC839.G5
Ghosh, Amitav.   PR9499.3.G536
Giannetta, Sal.   PS3557.I134
Gibbins, David J. L.   PR6107.I225
Gibbon, Charles, 1843-1890.   PR4712.G145
Gibboney, Douglas Lee, 1953-   PS3557.I1391686
Gibbons, H. Scott.   none
Gibbons, Scott—see: Gibbons, H. Scott.
Gibbs, George F.   none
Gibbs, Henry.   PR6013.I254
Gibbs, Mary Ann.   PR6057.I234
Gibbs, Tony, 1935-   PS3557.I155
Gibson, George.   none
Gibson, Jo.   PS3556.L685
Gibson, Maggie.   PR6057.I275
Gibson, Miles.   PR6057.I28
Gibson, Walter B. (Walter Brown), 1897-1985.   PS3513.I2823

Gibson, William, 1948-   PS3557.I2264
Gibson-Jarvie, Clodagh.   PR6057.I3
Gideon, Robin.   PS3557.I2563
Gielgud, Val Henry, 1900-1981.   PR6013.I295
Giencke, Jill, 1959-   PS3557.I258
Giesbert, Franz-Olivier, 1949-   PQ2667.I28
Gifford, Barry, 1946-   PS3557.I283
Gifford, Thomas.   PS3557.I284
Gilbert, Anna.   PR6057.I49
Gilbert, Anthony, 1899-1973.   PR6025.A438
Gilbert, Dale L.   PS3557.I338
Gilbert, Harriett, 1948-   PR6057.I515
Gilbert, James.   none
Gilbert, Lois.   PS3557.I342235
Gilbert, Michael A.   PR9199.3.G5244
Gilbert, Michael Francis, 1912-2006.   PR6013.I3335
Gilbert, Sharon K., 1952-   PS3607.I42325
Gilbert, Sky, 1952-   PR9199.3.G5248
Gilbert, Stephen, 1912-1999.   PR6013.I3363
Gilboy, Peter.   PS3557.I34245
Gilchrist, Andrew, Sir, 1910-   none
Gilchrist, Ellen, 1935-   PS3557.I34258
Gilchrist, Jeri Lawrence, 1963-   PS3607.I4235
Gilchrist, Murray, 1868-1917.   PR6013.I3373
Gilchrist, Robert Murray—see: Gilchrist, Murray, 1868-1917.
Giles, D. N. (D. Nichole)   PS3607.I432
Giles, Kenneth.   PR6057.I53
Giles, Peter.   none
Giles, Raymond.   none
Giles, Stephen M.   none
Gilford, C. B.   PS3557.I345
Gilibert Vargas, Luis Ernesto.   PQ8180.417.I45
Gill, Anton.   PR6057.I537
Gill, B. M.   PR6057.I538
Gill, Bartholomew, 1943-   PS3563.A296
Gill, John.   PR6057.I55
Gill, Max.   none
Gillenwater, Sharon.   PS3557.I3758
Giller, Marc D. (Marc Daniel), 1968-   PS3607.I436
Giller, Norman.   none
Gillespie, Robert B.   PS3557.I3795
Gillette, Paul J.   PS3557.I385
Gillgannon, Mary.   none
Gilligan, Roy.   PS3557.I3883
Gilligan, Sharon, 1943-   PS3557.I38833
Gilling, Tom.   PR9619.3.G538
Gillis, Jackson.   PS3557.I394
Gillison, Samantha.   PS3557.I3945
Gillmore, Inez Haynes, 1873-1970.   PS3513.I594
Gilman, Charlotte Perkins, 1860-1935.   PS1744.G57
Gilman, David.   PS3557.I428
Gilman, Dorothy, 1923-   PS3557.I433
Gilman, J. D.   PR6057.I63
Gilman, James—see: Gilmore, Joseph L.

Gilman, Keith.   PS3607.I45213
Gilman, Laura Anne.   PS3557.I4545
Gilmer, Bryan, 1972-   none
Gilmer, J. Lance.   none
Gilmore, Christopher Cook.   PS3557.I458
Gilmore, Jim, 1930-   none
Gilmore, Joseph L.   PS3557.I459
Gilmour, David, 1949-   PR9199.3.G543
Gilmour, H. B. (Harriet B.), 1939-   PS3557.I462
Gilpatrick, Noreen.   PS3557.I46308
Gilpin, T. G.   PR6057.I635
Gilstrap, John.   PS3557.I4745
Giménez Bartlett, Alicia.   PQ6657.I3955
Gimenez, Mark.   PS3607.I456
Ginn, R. C. K.   none
Ginsberg, Debra, 1962-   PS3607.I4585
Giorello, Sibella.   PS3607.I465
Giovannetti, Alberto.   PQ4867.I6348
Giovinazzo, Buddy.   PS3557.I58
Gipe, George.   PS3557.I6
Girard, Bernard.   none
Girard, Danielle, 1970-   none
Girard, James Preston, 1944-   PS3557.I65
Girard, Paula Tanner.   PS3557.I68
Girdner, Jaqueline.   PS3557.I718
Girolami, Lisa.   PS3607.I474
Giroux, E. X.   PR9199.3.S49
Giroux, Leo.   PS3557.I73
Gischler, Victor, 1969-   PS3607.I48
Gist, Deeanne.   PS3607.I55
Gitlin, Todd.   PS3557.I82
Gittlin, Adam.   PS3607.I67
Giusti, Debby.   PS3607.I73
Giuttari, Michele, 1950-   PQ4867.I7998
Givens, David.   PS3607.I755
Givens, John.   PS3557.I85
Gladilin, Anatoliĭ Tikhonovich.   PG3481.L24
Gladkiĭ, Vitaliĭ.   PG3481.L244
Gladstone, William.   PS3607.L344
Glahn, Sandra, 1958-   PS3557.L293
Glaister, Lesley, 1956-   PR6057.L27
Glander, Don.   none
Glass, Joseph, 1946-   PS3557.L335
Glass, Leslie.   PS3557.L34
Glass, Suzanne.   PR6057.L3
Glatzer, Hal.   PS3607.L38
Glauser, Friedrich, 1896-1938.   PT2613.L39
Glavinic, Thomas.   PT2667.L53
Glazer, Melissa.   PS3607.L394
Glazner, Joseph Mark.   none
Gleason, MaryAnne.   PS3557.L4326
Gleason, Robert (Robert Herman)   PS3557.L433
Gleeson, Janet.   PR6107.L44
Gleiter, Jan, 1947-   PS3557.L4415

Glemser, Bernard, 1908-1990.	PS3513.L646
Glen, Alison.	PS3557.L4418
Glendinning, Ralph.	PS3557.L443
Glenn, Roy.	PS3607.L456
Glenn, Stormy.	PS3607.L457
Glidewell, Jeanne.	PS3607.L57
Gloag, John, 1896-1981.	PR6013.L5
Gloag, Julian.	PR6057.L6
Glockner Corte, Fritz.	PQ7298.17.L63
Glover, Sandra.	PR6107.L68
Gluck, Sinclair, b. 1887.	none
Gluckman, Janet, 1939-	PS3557.L8214
Glukhovskiĭ, Dmitriĭ.	PG3491.94.L85
Glut, Donald F.	PS3557.L87
Gluyas, Constance, 1920-	PR6057.L87
Glynn, Alan, 1960-	PR6107.L93
Gobbell, John J.	PS3557.O16
Gober, Dom.	none
Goda, Dee.	PS3569.C25
Goddard, Anthea.	PR6057.O28
Goddard, Elizabeth.	PS3607.O324
Goddard, Harry.	none
Goddard, Kenneth W. (Kenneth William)	PS3557.O285
Goddard, Robert.	PR6057.O33
Godden, Jon, 1906-1984.	PR6013.O18
Godden, Rumer, 1907-1998.	PR6013.O2
Goddin, Jeffrey.	none
Godey, John, 1912-2006.	PS3513.O155
Godfrey, Ellen.	PR9199.3.G593
Godwin, Glyn J.	PS3607.O327
Goff, Christine.	PS3607.O344
Goff, Oliver.	none
Goines, Donald, 1937-1974.	PS3557.O3255
Gold, Don.	PS3557.O327
Gold, Glen David, 1964-	PS3607.O43
Gold, Herbert, 1924-	PS3557.O34
Gold, Maya.	none
Goldberg, Ed, 1943-	PS3557.O3566
Goldberg, Gerald Jay.	PS3557.O357
Goldberg, Lee, 1962-	PS3557.O3577
Goldberg, Leonard S.	PS3557.O35775
Goldberg, Lucianne.	PS3557.O3579
Goldberg, Marshall.	PS3557.O358
Goldberg, Tod.	PS3557.O35836
Golden, Bruce, 1952-	PS3607.O452
Golden, Christopher.	PS3557.O35927
Goldenbaum, Sally.	PS3557.O35937
Goldfluss, Howard E.	PS3557.O363
Golding, Louis, 1895-1958.	PR6013.O3
Goldman, Francisco.	PS3557.O368
Goldman, Ivan G.	PS3557.O3686
Goldman, James.	PS3513.O337
Goldman, Jane, 1970-	PR6057.O43
Goldman, Joel.	none

Goldman, Lawrence.   PS3513.O338
Goldman, Mary Elizabeth Sue.   PS3607.O4545
Goldman, William, 1931-   PS3557.O384
Goldring, Kat.   PS3607.O47
Goldsborough, Robert.   PS3557.O3849
Goldsby, Gabrielle, 1972-   PS3607.O478
Goldsmith, John, 1947-   PR6057.O44
Goldsmith, Olivia.   PS3557.O3857
Goldstein, Arthur D.   PS3557.O388
Goldstein, Gary.   none
Goldstein, Jan, 1951-   PS3607.O4844
Goldstein, Paul, 1943-   PS3607.O4853
Goldstein, Susan T.   PS3607.O4857
Goldstein, William.   none
Goldstone, Lawrence, 1947-   PS3557.O426
Goldstone, Nancy Bazelon.   PS3557.O427
Goldstrand, Theresa.   PS3557.O4284
Goldthwaite, Eaton K.   PS3513.O355
Golemon, David Lynn.   PS3607.O4555
Goliszek, Andrew.   none
Golit‹s›yn, Maksim.   PG3491.96.L57
Goller, Nicholas,   PR6057.O46
Gollin, James.   PS3557.O445
Golub, Aaron Richard.   PS3557.O452
Golub, Marcia.   PS3557.O453
Gom, Leona, 1946-   PR9199.3.G6
Gombrowicz, Witold.   PG7158.G669
                                            PG7158.G6692

Gómez, Sergio, 1962-   PQ8098.17.O385
Gómez-Jurado, Juan.   PQ6707.O54
Gonzales, Deborah Martin.   none
Gonzalez, Gloria.   PS3557.O4744
González, José Antonio.   PQ6707.O5851
González Ledesma, F.   PQ6657.O5517
González Madrid, Juan Antonio, 1979-   PQ7498.417.O5958
Goodchild, George, b. 1888.   PR6013.O473
Gooden, Philip.   PR6057.O533
Goodfield, June, 1927-   PR6057.O537
Goodger, John.   PR9199.4.G665
Gooding, Kathleen.   none
Goodis, David, 1917-1967.   PS3513.O499
Goodkind, Terry.   PS3557.O5826
Goodliffe, Roy.   PS3607.O5638
Goodman, Carol.   PS3607.O566
Goodman, Jo, 1953-   PS3557.O58374
Goodman, Jonathan.   PR6057.O55
Goodman, Karl.   PS3557.O5838
Goodman, Pete.   PS3607.O588
Goodnough, David.   PS3557.O586
Goodrich, David L.   PS3557.O588
Goodrum, Charles A.   PS3557.O59
GoodWeather, Hartley, 1943-   PR9199.3.K4422
Goodwill, Susan, 1957-   PS3607.O59226
Goodwin, Jason, 1964-   PR6107.O663

Goodwin, Jo-Ann.	PR6057.O582
Goodwin, Vincent.	none
Gordon, A. C.	none
Gordon, Alan (Alan R.)	PS3557.O649
Gordon, Alison.	PR9199.3.G617
Gordon, Charmaine.	PS3607.O5934
Gordon, Dan, 1947-	PS3557.O65455
Gordon, David Arthur.	PS3557.O6546
Gordon, Diana.	PR6057.O65
Gordon, Donald, 1924-	PR6066.A9
Gordon, Ethel Edison.	PS3557.O655
Gordon, Gaelyn, 1939-	PR9639.3.G67
Gordon, Giles, 1940-2003.	PR6057.O67
Gordon, Gordon.	none
Gordon, Howard, 1961-	PS3607.O5937
Gordon, John V.	none
Gordon, Josie.	none
Gordon, Mildred.	none
Gordon, Nadia.	PS3607.O594
Gordon, Noah.	PS3557.O68
Gordon, Peter.	none
Gordon, Peter, 1950-	none
Gordon, Richard, 1921-	PR6057.O714
Gordon, R. L. (Richard Laurence), 1920-1979.	PR9199.3.G63
Gordon, Victoria, 1942-	PR9619.3.A22
Gordon-Smith, Dolores.	PR6107.O676
Gordons.	PS3557.O725
Gore, Kristin, 1977-	PS3607.O5965
Gore, Steven.	PS3607.O5967
Gores, Joe, 1931-2011.	PS3557.O75
Goring, Anne.	PS3557.O757
Gorman, Carol.	none
Gorman, Edward.	PS3557.O759
Gorokhov, A. (Aleksandr)	PG3481.2.R667
Gorshkov, Valeriĭ.	PG3491.96.R78
Gortner, C. W.	PS3607.O78
Goshgarian, Gary.	PS3557.O77
Gosling, Paula.	PR6057.O75
Goss, Shelia M. (Shelia Marie)	PS3607.O854
Gostin, Jennifer, 1948-	PS3557.O792
Gotti, Victoria.	PS3557.O82
Gottlieb, Alan.	PS3557.O825
Gottlieb, Annie.	none
Gottlieb, Nathan.	none
Gottlieb, Paul, 1936-	PR9199.3.G6
Gottlieb, Samuel Hirsh, 1939-	PS3557.O832
Goudge, Eileen.	PS3557.O838
Gough, Laurence.	PR9199.3.G652
Goulart, Ron, 1933-	PS3557.O85
Gould, Chester.	none
Gould, Heywood.	PS3557.O86
Gould, Judith.	PS3557.O867
Gould, Steven.	PS3557.O8947
Gover, Robert, 1929-	PS3557.O92

Gowdy, Barbara.	PR9199.3.G658
Gowen, Kenneth K., 1924-	PS3607.O897
Gower, Iris.	PR6057.O845
Gowing, Nik.	PR6057.O847
Goyer, Tricia.	PS3607.O94
Goyne, Richard.	none
Grabenstein, Chris.	PS3607.R27
Grabien, Deborah.	PS3557.R1145
Grace, Alicia.	none
Grace, C. L.	PR6054.O37
Grace, Margaret, 1937-	PS3563.I4663
Grace, Nancy, 1959-	PS3607.R3266
Grace, Tom.	PS3557.R1177
Grady, James, 1949-	PS3557.R122
Grady, P. J.	PS3557.R1235
Grady, Shawn.	PS3607.R3285
Grae, Camarin.	PS3557.R125
Graeme, Bruce, 1900-	PR6019.E33
Graeme, Roderic, 1926-	PR6060.E43
Graf, Roger, 1958-	PT2667.R279
Graff, Keir, 1969-	PS3607.R7329
Graff, Mab.	PS3557.R128
Grafton, C. W. (Cornelius Warren), 1909-	PS3513.R1457
Grafton, Sue.	PS3557.R13
Graham, Barbara, 1948-	PS3607.R336
Graham, Bob, 1936-	PS3607.R3364
Graham, Burton.	none
Graham, C. S.	PS3566.R5877
Graham, Caroline, 1931-	PR6057.R232
Graham, Heather.	PS3557.R198
Graham, James, 1929-	PR6058.I343
Graham, John Alexander, 1941-	PS3557.R2
Graham, Mark, 1950-	PS3557.R2158
Graham, Michael (Michael A.)	PS3607.R345
Graham, Mitchell.	PS3607.R346
Graham, Neill, 1909-1975.	PR6007.U535
Graham, Robert, 1943 June 9-	PS3558.A353
Graham, Victoria.	PS3568.A4975
Graham, Winston.	PR6013.R24
Graham-Yooll, Richard.	PR6107.R3458
Grainger, Tom.	PR9199.3.G69
Gram, Dewey.	none
Gran, Sara.	PS3607.R362
Granbeck, Marilyn.	PS3558.E487
Grand, David, 1968-	PS3557.R247
Grandhi, Preetham, 1968-	PS3607.R3628
Grandower, Elissa.	PS3573.A9
Grangé, Jean-Christophe.	PQ2667.R329
Granger, Ann.	PR6057.R259
Granger, Bill.	PS3557.R256
Granotier, Sylvie.	PQ2667.R3412
Grant, Andrew, 1968-	PR6107.R366
Grant, Ben, 1927-	PS3558.E487
Grant, Charles.	none

Grant, Charles L.	PS3557.R265
Grant, David, 1942-	PR6070.H56
Grant, Helen, 1964-	PR6107.R368
Grant, James, 1933-	PR6057.R29
Grant, Jonathan, 1933-	PR6057.A728
Grant, Linda, 1942-	PS3573.I44975
Grant, Maxwell.	PR9619.3.G654
Grant, Maxwell, 1897-1985.	PS3513.I2823
Grant, Michael, 1940 Dec. 21-	PS3557.R2674
Grant, Pete.	PS3557.R2677
Grant, Richard, 1952-	PS3557.R268
Grant, Roderick, 1941-	PR6057.R323
Grant, S. A.	PS3557.R272
Grant, Tracy.	PS3607.R366
Grant, Vicki.	PR9199.4.G7265
Grant-Adamson, Lesley.	PR6057.R324
Granville, Edgar.	none
Grape, Jan.	PS3607.R373
Gratus, Jack.	none
Gravatt, Glenn G.	none
Graversen, Pat.	PS3557.R2866
Graves, Evelyn.	none
Graves, Geoffrey.	none
Graves, Jane, 1958-	PS3607.R386
Graves, Keith.	none
Graves, Paula.	none
Graves, Ralph.	PS3557.R2887
Graves, Richard L.	PS3557.R289
Graves, Samantha.	none
Graves, Sarah.	PS3557.R2897
Gray, A. W. (Albert William)	PS3557.R2914
Gray, Andrew.	PR9369.3.G69
Gray, Angela.	none
Gray, Berkeley, 1889-1965.	PR6003.R4235
Gray, Caroline.	PR9320.9.N5
Gray, Dulcie.	PR6013.R364
Gray, Fred A.	PS3607.R394
Gray, Gallagher.	PS3557.R2944
Gray, Ginna.	PS3557.R2945
Gray, James.	PS3557.R2948
Gray, John, 1946-	PR9199.3.G753
Gray, Linda Crockett.	PS3553.R5363
Gray, Malcolm, 1927-	PR6069.T77
Gray, Nicholas Stuart.	PR6057.R327
Gray, P. D.	PS3557.R2967
Gray, Simon, 1936-2008.	PR6057.R33
Gray, Stephen, 1941-	PR9369.3.G7
Grayson, Elizabeth.	PS3623.I875
Grayson, Emily.	PS3557.R337
Grayson, George, 1967-	PS3557.R338
Grayson, Richard.	PR6057.R55
Grayson, Rupert, 1897-	PR6013.R39
Grayson, Ruth.	none
Graziunas, Daina.	PS3557.R352

Greaney, Mark.   PS3607.R4285
Greanias, Thomas.   PS3607.R4286
Greatorex, Wilfred, 1921-   PR6057.R337
Greaves, Jimmy, 1940-   none
Greber, Judith.   PS3557.R356
Greeley, Andrew M., 1928-   PS3557.R358
Green, Anna Katharine, 1846-1935.   PS2731-2732
Green, Betsy Brannon, 1958-   PS3607.R43
Green, Chloe, 1967-   PS3557.R363
Green, Chris Marie.   PS3607.R4326
Green, Christine.   PR6057.R338
Green, Crystal.   PS3607.R4326
Green, Edith Piñero.   PS3557.R367
Green, Evelyn Everett—see: Everett-Green, Evelyn, 1856-1932.
Green, F. L. (Frederick Lawrence), 1902-1953.   PR6013.R414
Green, George Dawes.   PS3557.R3717
Green, Gerald.   PS3513.R4493
Green, Hilary, 1937-   PR6057.R3425
Green, Jane, 1968-   PR6057.R3443
Green, Janet.   none
Green, John, 1977-   none
Green, Judith Andrews.   none
Green, Julien, 1900-1998.   PQ2613.R3
Green, Kate.   PS3557.R3729
Green, Maury.   none
Green, Norman, 1954-   PS3607.R44
Green, Simon R., 1955-   PR6107.R44
Green, Thomas J.   PS3557.R3756
Green, Tim, 1963-   PS3557.R37562
Green, Vincent S.   PS3557.R37566
Green, William M. (William Mark), 1929-   PS3557.R3757
Greenan, Russell H.   PS3557.R376
Greenaway, Gladys, 1901-   PR6057.R365
Greenbaum, Leonard.   PS3557.R3765
Greenberg, David, 1943-   none
Greenberg, Martin Harry.   none
Greenburg, Dan.   PS3557.R379
Greene, Carolyn.   PS3607.R4526
Greene, Graham, 1904-1991.   PR6013.R44
Greene, Harris.   PS3557.R38
Greene, L. Patrick.   none
Greene, Michele, 1962-   none
Greener, Richard, 1941-   PS3607.R4535
Greenfield, Irving A.   PS3557.R3942
Greenfield, Richard Pierce.   none
Greenland, Francis.   none
Greenland, Shannon.   none
Greenlaw, Linda, 1960-   PS3607.R457
Greenleaf, Stephen.   PS3557.R3957
Greenlee, Sam, 1930-   PS3557.R396
Greenlief, K. C.   PS3607.R46
Greenwald, Nancy.   PS3557.R3967
Greenwood, D. M. (Diane M.)   PR6057.R376
Greenwood, John, 1921- 1986.   PR6058.I5

Greenwood, Kerry.	PR9619.3.G725
Greenwood, L. B.	PS3557.R3975
Greer, Ben.	PS3557.R399
Greer, Gaylon E.	PS3607.R47
Greer, Robert O.	PS3557.R3997
Greer, Woody.	none
Gregg, Andy.	PS3607.R48
Gregg, Cecil Freeman, 1898-	PR6013.R457
Gregorio, Michael.	PR6107.R4447
Gregory, Daryl.	PS3607.R48836
Gregory, Deborah, 1949-	none
Gregory, Jackson, 1882-1943.	PS3513.R562
Gregory, James.	none
Gregory, Jill.	PS3557.R4343
Gregory, Susanna, 1958-	PR6057.R3873
Gregson, J. M.	PR6057.R3876
Greig, Maysie, 1902-1971.	PR9619.3.G727
Greiman, Lois.	PS3557.R4369
Greis, Martin A.	PS3607.R498
Gresham, Elizabeth, 1904-1985.	none
Gresham, Jack.	PS3607.R4986
Gresham, Stephen.	none
Greth, Roma.	PS3557.R48
Grex, Leo, 1908-	PR6013.R718
Grey, Anthony.	PR6057.R454
Grey, Dorien.	PS3557.R48165
Grey, Leslie.	PS3557.R4828
Grey, Loren.	PS3557.R483
Grey, Naidra.	PR6057.R456
Grey, Robin, 1904-1985.	none
Grey, Sandra, 1969-	PS3607.R4996
Gribble, Leonard R. (Leonard Reginald), 1908-	PR6013.R718
Grice, Julia.	PS3557.R4873
Grierson, Edward, 1914-1975.	PR6013.R72
Grierson, Francis Durham, b. 1888.	PR6013.R725
Griffey, Jackie.	PS3607.R544
Griffin, Annie.	PS3553.H295
Griffin, Gerald, 1803-1840.	PR4728.G8
Griffin, Gerald G.	none
Griffin, H. Terrell.	PS3607.R547
Griffin, John.	none
Griffin, Nicholas, 1971-	PR6057.R49
Griffin, Robert J.	none
Griffin, Samuel Franklin.	none
Griffin, W. E. B.	PS3557.R489137
Griffith, Bill, 1941-	PS3557.R256
Griffith, George Chetwynd.	PR4728.G83
Griffith, Kathryn Meyer.	PS3607.R5488
Griffith, Nicola.	PS3557.R48935
Griffith, Roslynn.	none
Griffiths, Arthur, 1838-1908.	PR4728.G84
Griffiths, Bill (William G.)	PS3607.R549
Griffiths, Elly.	PR6107.R534
Griffiths, John, 1940-	PR6057.R513

Griffiths, Niall, 1966-	PR6107.R54
Griffiths, Peter, 1944-	PR6057.R517
Griggs, Vanessa Davis.	PS3557.R48954
Grimes, Lee.	none
Grimes, Martha.	PS3557.R48998
Grimes, Terris McMahan.	none
Grimes, Tom, 1954-	PS3557.R489985
Grimsey, Len.	none
Grimsley, Jim, 1955-	PS3557.R4949
Grimwood, Jon Courtenay.	PR6107.R56
Grimwood, Ken.	PS3557.R497
Grindal, Richard.	PR6057.R55
Grindle, Lucretia W.	PS3557.R526
Griner, Paul.	PS3557.R5314
Grin'kov, V. V.	PG3481.4.I57
Grippando, James, 1958-	PS3557.R534
Grisham, John.	PS3557.R5355
Grisman, Arnold.	PS3557.R536
Grissom, Ken.	PS3557.R5366
Groom, Arthur John Pelham.	none
Groom, Carola, 1957-	PR6057.R58
Groom, Winston, 1944-	PS3557.R56
Groot, Tracy, 1964-	PS3557.R5655
Gross, Andrew, 1952-	PS3607.R654
Gross, Claudia, 1956-	PT2707.R78
Gross, Gwendolen, 1967-	PS3557.R568
Gross, Ken, 1938-	PS3557.R583
Gross, Leonard.	PS3557.R585
Gross, Shelly.	PS3557.R62
Gross, Tudor.	none
Grossman, David.	PJ5054.G728
Grossman, Gary H.	PS3607.R667
Grossman, Jeni, 1951-	PS3607.R67
Grossman, Paul.	PS3607.R674
Grote, Paul, 1946-	none
Groundwater, Beth.	PS3607.R677
Grove, Fred.	PS3557.R7
Grove, Marjorie J.	none
Grubb, Davis, 1919-1980.	PS3513.R865
Gruber, Frank, 1904-1969.	PS3513.R866
Gruber, Helmut, 1928-	PS3557.R78
Gruber, Michael, 1940-	PS3607.R68
Gruenfeld, Lee.	PS3557.R8
Gruley, Bryan.	PS3607.R74
Gruppe, Henry.	PS3557.R85
Grytten, Frode, 1960-	PT8951.17.R97
Guaspari, John.	PS3557.U233
Gudenkauf, Heather.	PS3607.U346
Gudger, S. I.	PS3557.U26
Güemes, César, 1963-	PQ7298.17.U24
Guène, Faïza.	PQ3989.3.G84
Guenter, C. H., 1924-	none
Guest, James W.	PS3557.U3449
Guest, Judith.	PS3557.U345

Guibert, Hervé.	PQ2667.U4612
Guild, Nicholas.	PS3557.U357
Guilfoile, Kevin.	PS3607.U48
Guillory, Lloyd J., 1925-	PS3557.U365
Guillou, Jan, 1944-	PT9876.17.U38
Guiver, Patricia.	PS3607.U543
Gulik, Robert Hans van, 1910-1967.	PR9130.9.G8 [Z8375.3]
Gull, Cyril Arthur Edward Ranger, 1876-1923.	PR6013.U54
Gulliver, Hal, 1935-	PS3557.U45
Gulliver, Sam.	PR6057.U46
Guliashki, Andrei.	PG1037.G8
Gunesekera, Romesh.	PR9440.9.G86
Gunn, Elizabeth, 1927-	PS3557.U4854
Gunn, James E., 1923-	PS3513.U797
Gunn, John, 1925-	PR9619.3.G765
Gunn, Victor.	PR6003.R4235
Gunn, Virginia S.	PS3557.U487
Gunning, Sally.	PS3607.U548
Gunter, Archibald Clavering, 1847-1907.	PS1769.G27
Gunther, Max, 1927-	PS3557.U53
Günther, Ralf, 1967-	none
Gur, Batya.	PJ5054.G637
Gurr, David, 1936-	PR9199.3.G795
Gussin, Patricia.	PS3607.U73
Gustainis, Justin.	PS3607.U785
Gutcheon, Beth Richardson.	PS3557.U844
Guthrie, A. B. (Alfred Bertram), 1901-1991.	PS3513.U855
Guthrie, Al.	PS3557.U847
Gutman, Amy, 1960-	PS3557.U885
Gutteridge, Don, 1937-	PR9199.3.G84
Gutteridge, Lindsay, 1923-	PR6057.U84
Gutteridge, Rene.	PS3557.U887
Guttridge, Peter.	PR6107.U88
Guyan, Linda Himes.	PS3607.U93
Guymon, Shannon, 1972-	PS3607.U96
Gwyn, Aaron.	PS3607.W96
Gwyn, Richard, 1956-	PR6057.W85
Gwynne, P. N.	PS3557.W95
Haas, Ben.	PS3558.A17
Haas, Charlie.	PS3558.A173
Haas, Derek, 1970-	PS3608.A235
Haas, Joseph, 1929-1971.	PS3558.A177
Habe, Hans, 1911-1977.	PT2615.A18
Haber, Julian Stuart.	PS3608.A238
Haberkorn, Jim, 1951-	PS3608.A2386
Habersham, Elizabeth.	PS3558.A6247938
Habila, Helon, 1967-	PR9387.9.H26
Hachey, Michael.	PS3608.A246
Hacker, Shyrle.	none
Hackforth-Jones, Gilbert, 1900-	PR6015.A1534
Hackman, Gene.	PS3558.A3114
Hackworth, David H.	PS3558.A31154
Haddad, C. A.	PS3558.A3117

Haddam, Jane, 1951-	PS3566.A613
Haddock, Lisa, 1960-	PS3558.A31195
Haddock, Nancy.	PS3608.A275
Haddon, Mark.	PR6058.A26
Haddrill, Marilyn, 1950-	PS3558.A31197
Hadik, Louise.	PS3608.A28
Hadley, J. B.	none
Hagan, Arthur P.	PS3558.A322
Hagan, Chet.	PS3558.A3223
Hagan, Patricia.	PS3558.A3226
Hagan, Robert C.	PS3608.A34
Hagberg, David.	PS3558.A3227
Hagen, Agnes M.	none
Hagenbach, Keith.	PR6058.A365
Hager, Jean.	PS3558.A3232
Haggard, Raymond.	PR6058.A37
Haggard, William.	PR6053.L38
Hahn, Harriet, 1919-	PS3558.A3235
Hahn, Mary Downing.	PS3558.A32358
Haiblum, Isidore.	PS3558.A324
Haig, Alec.	PS3558.A326
Haig, Brian.	PS3608.A54
Haig, Robert.	PR6058.A39
Haigh, Raymond.	PR6058.A418
Hailey, Arthur.	PR9199.3.H3
Hailey, J. P.	PS3558.A3275
Haïm, Victor.	PQ2668.A36
Haining, Peter.	none
Haines, Carolyn.	PS3558.A329
Haines, Harry, 1932-	PS3608.A54485
Haines, Jess.	none
Haines, Kathryn Miller.	PS3608.A5449
Hains, Richard.	PR6108.H43
Haire-Sargeant, Lin.	PS3558.A3325
Hak, Otto.	PR9199.4.H347
Haldeman, Joe W.	PS3558.A353
Haldimon, Madelaine.	none
Hale, Arlene.	PS3515.A262
Hale, Bruce.	none
Hale, Christopher.	none
Hale, Gena.	PS3622.I45
Hale, Jennifer.	none
Hale, John, 1926-	PR6058.A438
Hale, Rebecca M.	PS3608.A54576
Hale, Michael, 1949-	PS3558.A35713
Halegua, Lillian.	PS3558.A3572
Haley, James L.	PS3558.A3577
Haley, Wendy.	none
Haligon, Richard.	none
Hall, Adam.	PR6039.R518
Hall, Angus.	PR6058.A4447
Hall, Connie—see: Hall, Constance.	
Hall, Constance.	none
Hall, David C.	PS3558.A365

Hall, Douglas, 1929-	PR9199.3.H317
Hall, Elliott, 1978-	PR9199.4.H356237
Hall, F. H., 1926-	PS3558.A3666
Hall, Gimone, 1940-	none
Hall, Gregory, 1948-	PR6058.A4474
Hall, James W. (James Wilson), 1947-	PS3558.A369
Hall, Jenni, 1939-	none
Hall, Jennifer.	PS3558.A3688
Hall, Linda, 1950-	PS3558.A3698
Hall, Lynn.	PS3558.A36987
Hall, M. R.	PR6108.A485
Hall, Marjory, 1908-	none
Hall, Mary Bowen.	PS3558.A37166
Hall, Matthew.	PS3558.A37168
Hall, Oakley M.	PS3558.A373
Hall, Parnell.	PS3558.A37327
Hall, Patricia, 1940-	PR6058.A46
Hall, Patrick, 1932-	PR6058.A47
Hall, Richard Walter.	PS3558.A3735
Hall, Robert Lee.	PS3558.A3739
Hall, Rodney, 1935-	PR9619.3.H285
Hall, Roger, 1919-2008.	PS3558.A374
Hall, Russ, 1949-	PS3558.A37395
Hall, Simon.	none
Hall, Simon, 1969-	PR6108.A493
Hall, Steven.	PS3558.A375
Hall, Steven, 1975-	PR6108.A494
Hall, Tarquin.	PR6108.A495
Hallahan, William H.	PS3558.A378
Hallas, Richard, 1897-1943.	PR6021.N417
Halleran, Tucker.	PS3558.A3795
Halley, Laurence.	PR6058.A534
Halliday, Brett.	PS3507.R615
Halliday, Dorothy—see: Dunnett, Dorothy.	
Halliday, Fred, 1939-	PS3558.A385
Halliday, Michael, 1908-1973.	PR6005.R517
Halliday, Sylvia.	PS3558.A3864
Halligan, Marion, 1940-	PR9619.3.H287
Hallinan, Timothy.	PS3558.A3923
Hallquist, F. Jacquelyn.	PS3558.A394
Halls, Geraldine.	PR9619.3.H29
Hallums, James.	none
Halsey, Harlan Page—see: Old Sleuth, 1839?-1898.	
Halstead, Thayer.	none
Hamamura, John.	PS3608.A549436
Hamand, Maggie, 1953-	PR6058.A5455
Hambly, Barbara.	PS3558.A4215
Hamer, Bob.	PS3608.A57
Hamill, Denis.	PS3558.A4217
Hamill, Desmond.	PR6058.A549
Hamill, Edson T.	none
Hamill, Pete, 1935-	PS3558.A423
Hamill, Stuart.	none
Hamilton, Adam, 1927-	PS3558.E487

Hamilton, Alex.   PR6058.A552
Hamilton, Alistair—see: Beattie, Tasman.
Hamilton, Barbara, 1951-   PS3558.A4215
Hamilton, Bruce, 1900-1974.   PR6015.A425
Hamilton, Charles, 1875-1961.   PR6015.A43
Hamilton, Denise.   PS3608.A68
Hamilton, Donald, 1916-2006.   PS3515.A42514
Hamilton, Hugo.   PR6058.A5526
Hamilton, Ian, 1938-2001.   PR6058.A553
Hamilton, Jessica.   PS3558.A443
Hamilton, Julia, 1956-   PR6058.A5535
Hamilton, Laurell K.   PS3558.A443357
Hamilton, Lyn.   PR9199.3.H323
Hamilton, Masha.   PS3558.A44338
Hamilton, Michael.   none
Hamilton, Nan.   PS3558.A4434
Hamilton, Patrick, 1904 Mar. 17-1962.   PR6015.A4644
Hamilton, Peter F.   PR6058.A5536
Hamilton, Roger.   none
Hamilton, Steve.   none
Hamilton, Steve, 1961-   PS3558.A44363
Hamilton, Violet.   none
Hamman, Henry.   PS3558.A4475
Hammer, David L.   PS3558.A44825
Hammerschmitt, Marcus, 1967-   PT2668.A46
Hammesfahr, Petra.   PT2668.A463
Hammett, Dashiell, 1894-1961.   PS3515.A4347
                                                       [Z8385]
Hammil, Joel.   PS3558.A4488
Hammond, Gerald, 1926-   PR6058.A55456
Hammond, Jim, 1943-   PS3608.A6958
Hammond, Marc.   none
Hammond, Warren.   PS3608.A69585
Hammonds, Michael, 1942-   none
Hampson, June.   PR6108.A526
Hampton, Brenda (Brenda M.)   PS3608.A6959
Hampton, Jay.   none
Hampton, Lynette Hall.   none
Hampton, Ruth E.   none
Hamrick, Janice.   PS3608.A69655
Hancock, Karen.   PS3608.A698
Hancock, Michelle, 1964-   PS3608.A6983
Hancock, Sybil.   none
Hand, Dana.   PS3608.A69845
Handberg, Ron.   PS3558.A4625
Handeland, Lori.   PS3558.A4625245
Handler, David, 1952-   PS3558.A4637
Handley, Alfred.   none
Hänel, Wolfram.   none
Haney, Lauren.   none
Hanin, Daliyah.   PS3608.A7148
Hanley, Clifford.   PR6058.A58
Hanley, Elizabeth—see: DuBreuil, Linda.
Hanley, William, 1931-   PS3558.A47

Hanlon, Robert, 1932-	PS3608.A7155
Hanna, David.	none
Hanna, Edward B.	PS3558.A4757
Hanna, Frances.	PS3515.A486
Hanna, Janice.	PS3608.A71556
Hannah, Barry.	PS3558.A476
Hannah, Darci.	PS3608.A7156
Hannah, Janet, 1939-	PS3558.A47624
Hannah, Kristin.	PS3558.A4763
Hannah, Sophie, 1971-	PR6058.A5928
Hannam, Joyce.	none
Hannon, Ezra, 1926-2005.	PS3515.U585
Hannon, Irene.	PS3558.A4793
Hannuksela, David.	PS3558.A4798
Hansen, B. J.	PS3558.A5125
Hansen, Jeanne, 1943-	none
Hansen, Jennie L., 1943-	PS3558.A51293
Hansen, Jim Michael, 1949-	PS3608.A72225
Hansen, Joseph, 1923-2004.	PS3558.A513
Hansen, Matthew Scott, 1953-	PS3608.A7225
Hansen, Ron, 1947-	PS3558.A5133
Hansen, Valerie.	PS3608.A7224
Hanshew, Thomas W., 1857-1914.	PS1784.H5457
Hansl, Arthur.	PS3558.A51363
Hanson, Mary Catherine.	PS3558.A53
Hanson, Rick, 1949-	PS3558.A54375
Hanson, Vic J.	PR6058.A598
Harbinson, W. A. (William Allen), 1941-	PR6058.A618
Harcourt, Palma.	PR6058.A62
Hardaway, Robert M., 1946-	PS3608.A7252
Hardie, Titania.	PR6108.A723
Hardin, J. D.	none
Hardin, Robert.	PS3558.A62317
Harding, Georgina, 1955-	PR6108.A724
Harding, Paul, 1946-	PR6054.O37
Harding, Robyn.	PR9199.4.H366
Harding, William Harry.	PS3558.A62344
Hardwick, Gary.	PS3558.A62368
Hardwick, Michael, 1924-1991.	PR6058.A673
Hardwick, Mollie.	PR6058.A6732
Hardwick, Phil.	PS3558.A64254
Hardy, Robin.	PR6058.A6754
Hardy, Robin, 1955-	PS3558.A62387
Hardy, Ronald.	PR6058.A676
Hardy, William M.	PS3558.A624
Hare, Cyril, 1900-	PR6005.L3115
Hargrave, Leonie.	PS3558.A62416
Harington, Donald.	PS3558.A6242
Harkins, Eugene.	PS3608.A743
Harkins, Sterling.	none
Harkness, Lucy, 1969-	PR6058.A6866
Harknett, Terry, 1936-	none
Harlick, R. J., 1946-	PR9199.4.H368
Harlin, Christina.	PS3608.A7435

Harling, Robert.	PR6058.A6867
Harlow, Jennifer, 1983-	PS3608.A7443
Harmidarow, Walter J., 1963-	PR9199.3.H3456
Harmon, Margaret.	none
Harmon, Nikki.	PS3558.A62453
Harmon, Susan.	PS3558.A62457
Harmyk, Peter Scott.	PS3558.A62473
Harp, Andy.	PS3608.A763
Harper, B. H. B. (Bena Harlene Brewer)	PS3608.A77
Harper, Beverley.	PR9619.3.H3235
Harper, Brian.	none
Harper, David, 1931-	PS3553.O648
Harper, Karen (Karen S.)	PS3558.A624792
Harper, Lynette.	none
Harper, Paul, 1944 Nov. 6-	PS3562.I51193
Harper, Philip.	PS3558.A62484
Harper, Richard.	none
Harper, Stephen, 1924-	PR6058.A6875
Harper, Steven (Steven Piziks)	PS3616.I97
Harper, Tom, 1977-	PR6120.H644
Harrar, George, 1949-	PS3558.A624924
Harrigan, John J.	PS3608.A7815
Harrigan, M. E.	PS3608.A7814
Harrigan, Stephen, 1948-	PS3558.A626
Harrington, Denis J., 1932-	PS3558.A6277
Harrington, Joseph, 1903-	PS3515.A7125
Harrington, Joyce.	PS3558.A6284
Harrington, Kent A., 1952-	PS3558.A62944
Harrington, Kim, 1974-	none
Harrington, R. E.	PS3558.A6295
Harrington, William, 1931-	PS3558.A63
Harris, Alfred, 1928-	PS3558.A633
Harris, Andrea.	none
Harris, C. S.	PS3566.R5877
Harris, Charlaine.	PS3558.A6427
Harris, Charlie Avery.	none
Harris, E. Lynn.	PS3558.A64438
Harris, Ellen.	PS3608.A7828
Harris, Evelyn.	none
Harris, Fred R., 1930-	PS3558.A64455
Harris, Gardiner.	PS3608.A78285
Harris, Herbert.	none
Harris, Hyde—see: Harris, Timothy, 1946-	
Harris, Jana, 1947-	PS3558.A6462
Harris, Jeane, 1948-	PS3558.A6463
Harris, Joanne, 1964-	PR6058.A68828
Harris, John, 1916-1991.	PR6058.A6886
Harris, Jonathan, 1962-	PS3608.A783
Harris, Lee.	none
Harris, Lee, 1935-	PS3562.E23
Harris, Leonard, 1929-	PS3558.A6467
Harris, Lisa, 1969-	PS3608.A78315
Harris, Lori L.	none
Harris, Lynn.	PS3608.A78325

Harris, MacDonald, 1921-1993.	PS3558.E458
Harris, Marilyn, 1931-	PS3558.A648
Harris, Max F.	none
Harris, Paul, 1972-	PR6108.A766
Harris, Raina Wissing, 1952-	none
Harris, Randolph.	none
Harris, Richard, 1926-	PS3558.A653
Harris, Robert, 1957-	PR6058.A69147
Harris, Rosemary.	PS3608.A78328
Harris, Rosemary, 1923-	PR6058.A6915
Harris, Thomas, 1940-	PS3558.A6558
Harris, Timothy, 1946-	PS3558.A657
Harris, Walter.	PR6058.A6919
Harris, Yvonne L.	PS3608.A78329
Harris-Burland, John Burland, 1870-1926.	PR6015.A6473
Harrison, Barbara.	none
Harrison, C. C.	PS3608.A7833
Harrison, Chip.	PS3552.L63
Harrison, Colin, 1960-	PS3558.A6655
Harrison, Cora.	PR6058.A6883
Harrison, David, 1966-	PR6108.A776
Harrison, Emma.	none
Harrison, Harry, 1925-	PS3558.A667
Harrison, Jamie, 1960-	PS3558.A6712
Harrison, Janis (Janis Anne)	PS3558.A67132
Harrison, Jim, 1937-	PS3558.A67
	[Z8387.92]
Harrison, Joel.	none
Harrison, Kim.	PS3608.A78355
Harrison, M. John (Michael John), 1945-	PR6058.A6942
Harrison, Mike (Mike S.), 1945-	PR9199.4.H3735
Harrison, Payne.	PS3558.A6718
Harrison, Rashad.	PS3708.A7837
Harrison, Ray.	PR6058.A69424
Harrison, Sam.	PS3558.A6719
Harrison, Shirley (Shirley Baker Donham)	none
Harrison, Stuart, 1958-	PR9639.3.H324
Harrison, William, 1933-	PS3558.A672
Harriss, Will.	PS3558.A673
Harrod-Eagles, Cynthia.	PR6058.A6945
Harsch, Rick, 1959-	PS3558.A67557
Harstad, Donald.	PS3558.A67558
Hart, Carolyn G.	PS3558.A676
Hart, Craig (Craig Alan)	PS3608.A784
Hart, Ellen.	PS3558.A6775
Hart, Erin, 1958-	PS3608.A785
Hart, Gary, 1936-	PS3558.A6776
Hart, Griffin.	PS3558.A679
Hart, Jeanne.	PS3558.A6816
Hart, John, 1965-	PS3608.A78575
Hart, Jon.	none
Hart, Josephine.	PR6058.A694845
Hart, Norman Phillip.	none
Hart, Roy.	PR6058.A694857

Hart, Stan.	none
Hart, Ted.	PR6058.A69486
Hart, Tom.	none
Hart-Davis, Duff.	PR6058.A6949
Harte, Marie.	PS3608.A787159
Hartenfels, Jerome, 1934-	PR6058.A69494
Hartland, Michael.	PR6058.A69496
Hartley, A. J. (Andrew James)	PR6108.A787
Hartley, Norman.	PR6058.A69497
Hartman, Cherry.	PS3558.A7117
Hartman, Claire.	PS3608.A7873
Hartman, Dane.	none
Hartman, Honor.	PS3610.A43
Hartman, Keith, 1966-	PS3558.A71245
Hartmann, Betsy.	PS3608.A7875
Hartmann, Michael, 1944 July 24-	PR6058.A6955
Hartov, Steven.	PS3558.A7146
Hartshorne—see: Blum, Richard H.	
Hartzmark, Gini.	PS3558.A7157
Harvard, Jane.	PS3557.R2659
Harvester, Simon, 1909-1975.	PR6013.I254
Harvey, Alyxandra.	none
Harvey, Clay.	PS3558.A71824
Harvey, Jack, 1960-	PR6068.A57
Harvey, James Neal.	PS3558.A7183
Harvey, John, 1938-	PR6058.A6989
Harvey, John D.	PS3608.A789
Harvey, Kathryn.	PS3573.O5877
Harvey, Kenneth J.	PR9199.3.H3495
Harvey, Michael T.	PS3608.A78917
Harvey, Philip D., 1938-	PS3608.A78919
Harvill, Ken, 1967-	PS3608.A7893
Harwin, Patricia.	PS3608.A78935
Harwood, John, 1946-	PR9619.4.H37
Harwood, Ronald, 1934-	PR6058.A73
Harwood, Seth.	PS3608.A7894
Hasburgh, Patrick.	PS3608.A7897
Hasford, Gustav.	PS3558.A7233
Haskell, John, 1958-	PS3608.A79
Haskins, Michael.	PS3608.A84
Haslam, Chris.	PR6108.A84
Hasler, Susan.	PS3608.A847
Hasluck, Alexandra, Lady.	PR6058.A75
Hasluck, Nicholas P.	PR9619.3.H337
Hassan, Marwan, 1950-	PR9199.3.H3625
Hassler, Jon.	PS3558.A726
Hastings, Beverly.	none
Hastings, Brook.	PS3515.A82868
Hastings, Graham, 1926-	PR6060.E43
Hastings, Laura.	PS3569.E43
Hastings, Macdonald.	PR6058.A79
Hastings, Michael, 1938 Jan. 30-	PR9510.9.B3
Hastings, Michael, 1938 Sept. 2-	PR6058.A816
Hastings, Phyllis, 1913-	PR6058.A82

Haswell, Margaret Rosary.	PS3558.A7275
Hatch, Denison.	PS3558.A73
Hatfield, Kate.	PR6058.A824
Hathaway, Mavis—see: Avery, Ira.	
Hathaway, Robin.	PS3558.A7475
Hathaway-Nayne, Anne.	none
Hatton, Joseph, 1841-1907.	PR4759.H78
Hatvary, George Egon.	PS3558.A754
Hauf, Michele.	PS3608.A867
Haughey, Thomas Brace.	PS3558.A7565
Haus, Illona.	PR9199.3.H3684
Hauser, Thomas.	PS3558.A759
Häusser, Alexander, 1960-	PT2708.A97
Hautala, Rick, 1949-	none
Hautman, Pete, 1952-	PS3558.A766
Havens, Candace, 1963-	PS3608.A878
Havighurst, Marion, d. 1974.	PS3515.A869
Haviland, Diana.	PS3558.A784
Havill, Steven.	PS3558.A785
Hawke, Richard, 1955-	PS3608.A886
Hawke, Simon.	PS3558.A8167
Hawkes, Ellen.	PS3558.A817
Hawkes, Robert.	PR9199.3.H365
Hawkey, Raymond.	PR6058.A886
Hawking, Lucy.	PR6108.A95
Hawkins, D. James (Derek James), 1947-	PR9199.4.H386
Hawkins, Edward H.	PS3558.A823
Hawkins, Frank N.	none
Hawkins, Odie.	PS3558.A82317
Hawksley, Elizabeth.	PR6058.A8965
Hawksley, Humphrey.	PR6058.A95
Hawn, Elizabeth.	PS3608.A894
Hawthorne, Julian, 1846-1934.	PS1845-1848 [Z8392.9]
Hawthorne, Nathaniel, 1804-1864.	PS1850-1898 [Z8393]
Hawthorne, Sally.	PS3558.A8238
Hawthorne, Violet.	PS3558.A824
Hawton, Hector, 1901-	PR6015.A7924
Hawvermale, Lance, 1972-	PS3615.R585
Hay, Jacob.	PS3558.A826
Hay, Mary Cecil, 1840?-1886.	PR4769.H14
Hayden, G. Miki.	PS3558.A8287
Hayden, L. C.	PS3558.A82875
Hayden, Laura.	PS3558.A8288
Hayder, Mo.	PR6058.A9776
Hayes, Helen, 1900-1993.	PS3558.A8298
Hayes, J. M.	PS3558.A8315
Hayes, John R.	PS3608.A94
Hayes, Jonathan, 1960-	PS3608.A932
Hayes, Joseph, 1918-2006.	PS3515.A942
Hayes, Lee (Lee A.)	PS3608.A9425
Hayes, Mary-Rose.	PR6058.A982
Hayes, Ralph.	none

Hayes, Roy. PS3558.A836
Hayes, Teddy. PS3558.A8377
Hayeunickx, Robert d'. none
Hayles, Brian, 1930-1978. PR6058.A9853
Haymaker, Lafayette. PS3558.A844
Hayman, James. PS3608.A9445
Hayman, Mark. none
Haymon, S. T. PR6058.A9855
Haynes, Betsy. none
Haynes, Brian. none
Haynes, Conrad. PS3558.A84875
Haynes, Dana. PS3558.A84875
Haynes, Darleen. PS3608.A95
Hays, Edward M. PS3558.A867
Hays, K. D. PS3604.O426
Hays, Lee. none
Hays, Tony. PS3558.A877
Haysom, Derrick. none
Hayter, Sparkle, 1958- PR9199.3.H39
Haythorne, John, 1928- PR6066.A719
Hayward, David. none
Haywood, B. B. PS3608.A9874
Haywood, Gar Anthony. PS3558.A885
Hazo, Samuel John. PS3515.A9877
Head, Lee. PS3558.E15
Head, Matthew, 1907-1985. PS3505.A53196
Headley, Victor. PR9265.9.H39
Headrick, Robert J. PS3552.R354
Headworth, Paul. PS3608.E235
Heal, Anthony. PR6058.E166
Heald, Tim. PR6058.E167
Healey, Ben. PR6058.E17
Healey, Judith Koll. PS3608.E236
Healy, Erin M. PS3608.E245
Healy, J. F. (Jeremiah F.), 1948- PS3558.E2347
Healy, R. Austin. PS3558.E238
Heaps, Leo. PS3558.E24
Heard, Gerald, 1889-1971. PR6015.E19
Heard, Nathan C. PS3558.E25
Hearn, Bonnie, 1945- PS3608.E26
Hearn, Daniel. PS3558.E2545
Hearst, Patricia, 1954- PS3558.A3739
Heath, Catherine. PR6058.E217
Heath, David J. PS3608.E277
Heath, JoEllen. PS3608.E283
Heath, Monica. PS3558.E264
Heath, Roy A. K. PR9320.9.H4
Heath, Terrence, 1936- PR9199.3.H44
Heath, W. L. (William L.), 1924- PS3558.E27
Heatter, Basil, 1918- PS3515.E164
Heaven, Constance. PR6058.E23
Hebden, Mark, 1916-1991. PR6058.A6886
Heber, R. W. PR6058.E26
Heberden, M. V. (Mary Violet), 1906-1965. PR6015.E244

Hébert, Anne.	PQ3919.H37
Hebert, Brandon.	PS3608.E284
Hecht, Ben, 1894-1964.	PS3515.E18
Hecht, Daniel.	PS3558.E284
Hechtman, Betty, 1947-	PS3608.E288
Heck, Peter J.	PS3558.E313
Hecker, Josef Ludwig, 1910-	PT2617.E213
Heckler, Jonellen.	PS3558.E315
Heckman, Victoria.	PS3608.E296
Heddon, James.	none
Hedges, Joseph, 1936-	none
Hedrich, Cleda.	PS3558.E347
Heffernan, William, 1940-	PS3558.E4143
Hegarty, Frances.	PR6056.Y47
Heggan, Christiane.	PS3608.E345
Hegner, William.	PS3558.E42
Hegwood, Martin.	PS3558.E4233
Hehl, Eileen.	none
Heidenreich, Gert.	PT2668.E32
Heidish, Marcy.	PS3558.E4514
Heighton, Steven, 1961-	PR9199.3.H4443
Heimer, Mel, 1915-1971.	PS3558.E453
Hein, Christoph, 1944-	PT2668.E3747
Heinzmann, David.	PS3608.E383
Heiss, Rolland L.	PS3558.E463
Heitzmann, Kristen.	PS3558.E468
Heldman, Gladys.	PS3558.E474
Heldt, Morris.	PS3608.E44
Heley, Veronica.	PR6070.H6915
Helgerson, Joel.	none
Heliodorus, of Emesa.	PA3998.H2
Helix, Daniel C., 1929-	PS3608.E446
Hellenga, Robert, 1941-	PS3558.E4753
Heller, Jean.	PS3558.F4758
Heller, Keith.	PS3558.E47614
Heller, Mandasue.	PR6108.E45
Heller, Murray.	PS3558.E47623
Hellmann, Libby Fischer.	PS3608.E46
Helm, Eric.	PS3558.E47655
Helm, Roger.	PS3608.E463
Helms, Richard W., 1955-	PS3608.E466
Helton, Peter.	PR6108.E47
Helú, Antonio.	none
Helwig, David, 1938-	PR9199.3.H445
Helwig, Maggie, 1961-	PR9199.3.H446
Hemingway, Amanda.	PR6058.E49188
Hemingway, Hilary.	PS3558.E479125
Hemingway, Joan.	none
Hemmingson, Michael A.	PS3558.E479154
Hemyng, Bracebridge, 1841-1901.	none
Henaghan, Jim—see: O'Neill, Archie.	
Henderson, C. J.	PS3558.E48244
Henderson, Christopher John.	none
Henderson, Dee.	PS3558.E4829

Henderson, Ellen.   none
Henderson, J. J.   PS3608.E526
Henderson, Jack.   PS3608.E527
Henderson, James, 1934-   PR6058.E4927
Henderson, Lauren, 1966-   PR6058.E4929
Henderson, Laurence.   PR6058.E493
Henderson, M. R.   PS3558.E487
Henderson, Patty G.   PS3558.E493
Henderson, T. T.   PS3558.E4938
Hendricks, Carl.   PS3558.E49516
Hendricks, Michael.   PS3558.E49518
Hendricks, Vicki.   PS3558.E495187
Hendricksen, Louise.   none
Hendrickson, Emily.   PS3558.E49519
Hendrix, Howard V., 1959-   PS3558.E49526
Hendryx, James B. (James Beardsley), 1880-1963. PS3515.E48
Henege, Thomas.   PS3558.E4954
Henehan, Kira, 1974-   PS3608.E545
Henissart, Paul.   PS3558.E4958
Henke, Shirl.   PS3558.E49586
Henkin, Harmon.   PS3558.E4959
Henle, Theda O.   PS3558.E496
Henn, Henry.   none
Henrick, Richard P.   PS3558.E49673
Henry, Angela.   PS3608.E5655
Henry, April.   PS3558.E4969
Henry, Diane, 1945-   PS3558.E49733
Henry, O., 1862-1910.   PS2649.P5
                                                               [Z8706.2]
Henry, Patti Callahan.   PS3608.E578
Henry, Sara J.   PS3608.E5796
Henry, Sue, 1940-   PS3558.E534
Hensley, Joe L., 1926-   PS3558.E55
Henson, D. B.   PS3608.E59
Henson, P. (Pauline)   PR9390.9.H46
Henstell, Diana.   none
Hentoff, Nat.   PS3558.E575
Hepinstall, Kathy.   PS3558.E577
Herbert, Frank.   PS3558.E63
Herbert, Ivor, 1925-   PR6058.E6
Herbert, James, 1943-   PR6058.E62
Herbert, Nan.   none
Herbert, Rosemary.   PS3608.E7296
Herbrand, Jan.   none
Herlin, Hans, 1925-1994.   PT2668.E748
Hériz, Enrique de.   PQ6658.E672
Herkert, Gabriella.   PS3608.E745
Herman, Gail, 1959-   none
Herman, J. B.   none
Herman, Kathy.   PS3608.E762
Herman, George, 1928-   PS3558.E677
Herman, Richard.   PS3558.E684
Hermans, Daniëlle, 1963-   PT6467.18.E76
Hermanson, Eric.   PS3608.E764

Hernandez, Paul A., 1958-	PS3558.E6877
Hernbrode, Gerry, 1935-	PS3608.E76866
Herndon, Nancy R.	none
Hernon, Peter, 1947-	PS3558.E69
Heron, Echo.	PS3558.E698
Heron, James.	none
Herráez, Miguel.	PQ6658.E766
Herren, Greg.	PS3608.E77
Herrick, Marian J.	none
Herrick, Steven.	PR9619.3.H39
Herring, Peg.	PS3558.E75478
Herring, Peter C.	none
Herron, Mick.	PR6108.E77
Herron, Rita B.	none
Herron, Shaun.	PR6058.E68
Herschensohn, Bruce, 1932-	PS3608.E777
Hersey, John, 1914-1993.	PS3515.E7715
Hershatter, Richard L. (Richard Lawrence), 1923-	none
Hershman, Morris, 1926-	PS3558.E78
Herst, Roger.	PS3558.E793
Hervey, Evelyn, 1926-2011.	PR6061.E26
Hervey, Michael.	none
Herz, Wilfried Viktor.	none
Herzog, Arthur.	PS3558.E796
Hesky, Olga.	PR6058.E69
Hesla, Stephen.	PS3558.E7965
Hess, Joan.	PS3558.E79785
Hess, Kamelle.	none
Hettche, Thomas.	PT2668.E866
Heussaff, Anna.	PB1399.H48
Hewens, Frank E.	none
Hewitt, Pat, 1942-	PS3558.E834
Hewson, David, 1953-	PR6058.E96
Heyer, Georgette, 1902-1974.	PR6015.E795 [Z8402.4]
Heyman, Evan Lee.	none
Heywood, Joseph.	PS3558.E92
Hiaasen, Carl.	PS3558.I217
Hichens, Robert Smythe, 1864-1950.	PR6015.I4
Hick, P. J.	PS3608.I27
Hickam, Homer H., 1943-	PS3558.I224
Hickman, Hal.	PR9369.3.H55
Hickman, Katie.	PR6058.I27
Hicks, Mack R.	PS3608.I28
Hicks, Randall, 1956-	PS3608.I285
Hiestand, Jo A.	PS3608.I33
Higashino, Keigo, 1958-	PL871.I33
Higgins, George V., 1939-1999.	PS3558.I356
Higgins, Jack, 1929-	PR6058.I343
Higgins, Joan.	PS3558.I3573
Higgins, Joanna, 1945-	PS3558.I3574
Higgins, Margaret.	none
Higgins, Marie (Phyllis Marie)	PS3608.I366
Higgs, Eric C.	PS3558.I3623

High, Bernard G.   PS3558.I3624
Highland, Dora—see: Avallone, Michael.
Highland, Frederick, 1945-   PS3558.I3645
Highsmith, Domini, 1942-   PR6073.I4159
Highsmith, Patricia, 1921-1995.   PS3558.I366
Hightower, Lynn S.   PS3558.I372
Higley, T. L.   PS3608.I375
Higman, Anita.   PS3558.I374
Higman, Dennis J.   none
Higson, Charles, 1958-   PR6058.I364
Hilaire, Frank.   PS3558.I38
Hilary, Richard.   none
Hilburn, Lynda.   PS3608.I418
Hild, Jack.   none
Hilderbrand, Elin.   PS3558.I3384355
Hildick, E. W. (Edmund Wallace), 1925-   PR6058.I37
Hilger, Christine, 1962-   PS3558.I3384378
Hill, A. W. (Andrew Warren), 1951-   PS3608.I4248
Hill, Albert Fay.   none
Hill, Archie.   PR6058.I376
Hill, Bonnie Hearn, 1945-   PS3608.E426
Hill, Carol, 1942-   PS3558.I3845
Hill, Christopher, fl. 1974-   PR6058.I38
Hill, David Campbell.   PS3558.I3855
Hill, Donna, 1921-   PS3558.I3865
Hill, Donna (Donna O.)   PS3558.I3864
Hill, Gerri.   PS3558.I3878
Hill, Grace Livingston, 1865-1947.   PS3515.I486
Hill, Headon, 1857-1927.   PR6013.R27
Hill, Ingrid.   PS3558.I3886
Hill, Jane, 1964 April 2-   PS3608.I434
Hill, Joe.   PS3608.I4342
Hill, John Spencer, 1943-   PR9199.3.H4787
Hill, Kaye C.   PR6108.I443
Hill, Laban Carrick.   none
Hill, Marion Moore, 1937-   PS3608.I4348
Hill, Owen.   PS3608.I437
Hill, Pamela, 1920-   PR6058.I446
Hill, Peter, fl. 1976-   PR6058.I4465
Hill, R. Lance.   PR9199.3.H48
Hill, Reginald.   PR6058.I448
Hill, Richard, 1941 Oct. 15-   PS3558.I443
Hill, Russell.   PS3558.I4435
Hill, Sam, 1953-   PS3608.I4377
Hill, Susan, 1942-   PR6058.I45
Hill, Suzette A.   PR6108.I453
Hill, Tobias, 1970-   PR6058.I4516
Hilldrup, Robert P., 1933-   none
Hillerman, Tony.   PS3558.I45
Hilley, Joseph H.   PS3608.I439
Hillhouse, Raelynn.   PS3608.I44
Hilliard, Maurice, 1931-   PR6058.I455
Hillier, Jennifer.   PS3608.I446
Hills, Kathleen.   PS3608.I455

Hillstrom, Tom.	PS3558.I4535
Hilton, Christopher.	none
Hilton, James, 1900-1954.	PR6015.I53
Hilton, John Buxton.	PR6058.I5
Hilton, Matt, 1966-	PR6108.I48
Hime, James L.	PS3608.I47
Himes, Chester B., 1909-1984.	PS3515.I713
Himmel, Richard.	PS3515.I7147
Hinck, Sharon.	PS3608.I53
Hinde, Thomas, 1926-	PR6058.I524
Hine, Al.	PS3558.I48
Hines, Jeanne.	PS3558.I527
Hines, Joanna.	PR6058.I529
Hines, T. L.	PS3608.I5726
Hinger, Charlotte, 1940-	PS3558.I534
Hinkel, M. L.	none
Hinkemeyer, Michael T.	PS3558.I54
Hinkle, Vernon.	PS3558.I5445
Hinojosa, Jose Luis.	PS3608.I575
Hinojosa, Rolando.	PQ7079.2.H5
	PS3558.I545
Hinrichsen, Ronda Gibb.	PS3608.I577
Hinshelwood, Tom.	PR6058.I5323
Hintze, Naomi A.	PS3558.I55
Hinxman, Margaret.	PR6058.I537
Hinze, Vicki.	PS3558.I574
Hirahara, Naomi, 1962-	PS3608.I76
Hiriart, Hugo, 1942-	PQ7298.18.I7
Hirschberg, Cornelius.	PS3558.I665
Hirschfeld, Burt, 1923-	PS3558.I67
Hirschfeld, Corson.	PS3558.I672
Hirschhorn, Richard Clark.	PS3558.I675
Hirschson, Yakov M.	PJ5129.H5215
Hirsh, M. E.	PS3558.I69
Hirshberg, Glen, 1966-	PS3608.I77
Hirt, Howard.	PS3558.I73
Hischak, Thomas S.	PS3558.I76
Hitchcock, Alfred, 1899-1980.	none
	[Z8408.8]
Hitchcock, Colleen.	PS3608.I83
Hitchcock, Jane Stanton.	PS3558.I82
Hitchcock, Mark, 1959-	PS3608.I84
Hitchcock, Raymond.	PR6058.I7
Hitchens, Dolores, 1907-1973.	PS3515.I955
Hite, Molly, 1947-	PS3558.I833
Hitt, Frisco.	PT2668.I8
Hivert-Carthew, Annick.	PS3558.I87
Hjortsberg, William, 1941-	PS3558.J6
Hoag, Tami.	PS3558.O333
Hoar, Jere R.	PS3558.O33565
Hobbs, Jonathan.	none
Hobhouse, Christina, 1941-	PR6058.O18
Hobson, Hank, 1908-	none
Hobson, Polly.	PR6058.O24

Hoch, Edward D., 1930-2008.   PS3558.O337
Hochstein, Peter.   none
Hockenberry, John.   PS3558.O34182
Hockensmith, Steve.   PS3608.O29
Hocker, Karla, 1946-   PS3558.O34183
Hocking, Anne.   PR6025.E744
Hocking, Mary.   PR6058.O26
Hodder, Mark, 1962-   PR6108.O28
Hodder-Williams, Christopher, 1926-1995.   PR6058.O267
Hoddinott, Derek.   PR6015.O146
Hodel, Michael P.   PS3558.O3419
Hodge, Jane Aiken.   PS3558.O342
Hodges, Mike.   PR6108.O328
Hodgson, Barbara, 1955-   PS3558.O34345
Hodgson, Ken.   PS3558.O34346
Hodgson, William Hope, 1877-1918.   PR6015.O253
Høeg, Peter, 1957-   PT8176.18.O335
Hoesel, Don.   PS3608.O4765
Hofer, G. Henry (Gunter Henry), 1926-   PS3558.O34394
Hoff, B. J., 1940-   PS3558.O34395
Hoff, Benjamin, 1946-   PS3608.O477
Hoff, Ellis.   PR9199.3.H545
Hoffa, Helynn.   PS3558.O34443
Hoffenberg, Jack.   PS3558.O3445
Hoffman, Alice.   PS3558.O3447
Hoffman, Blair.   PS3558.O34476
Hoffman, Cara.   PS3608.O4775
Hoffman, Chandra.   PS3608.O4776
Hoffman, David, 1936-   PR9199.4.H64
Hoffman, Jilliane, 1967-   PS3608.O478
Hoffman, L. F. (Lynn F.)   PS3558.O3454
Hoffman, L. P.   PS3618.O47824
Hoffman, Louise.   PS3558.O3462
Hoffman, Margaret, 1949-   PS3558.O34623
Hoffman, Moshe.   PR9510.9.H64
Hoffman, William, 1925-   PS3558.O34638
Hofland, Karin.   PS3608.O4795
Hogan, Chuck.   PS3558.O34723
Hogan, James P.   PR6058.O348
Hogan, Michael, 1950-   PS3608.O4826
Hogan, Ray, 1908-1998.   PS3558.O3473
Hogan, Robert Goode, 1930-   PR6058.O352
Hogan, Robert J.   PS3515.O2469
Hogg, Gil.   PR9639.3.H6
Högstrand, Olle E., 1933-   PT9876.18.O327
Hohlbein, Wolfgang, 1953-   PT2668.O3795
Hoklin, Lonn.   none
Hoklotubbe, Sara Sue, 1952-   PS3608.O4828
Holbrook, Teri.   none
Holdefer, Charles, 1959-   PS3558.O347746
Holden, Anne.   PR6058.O426
Holden, Craig.   PS3558.O347747
Holden, Dalby, 1926-   PR6058.A55456
Holden, William C., 1942-   PS3558.O347754

Holder, Serena F., 1948-	PS3558.O347755
Holding, Elisabeth Sanxay, 1889-1955.	PS3515.O3418
Holding, Ian.	PR9390.9.H65
Holl, Kristi.	none
Holland, David, 1959-	PS3558.O3482
Holland, Isabelle.	PS3558.O3485
Holland, Norman.	PR6015.O38
Holland, Norman Norwood, 1927-	PS3558.O34857
Holland, Rebecca.	none
Holland, Robert—see: Katz, Robert, 1933-2010.	
Holland, Robert, M.A.	none
Holland, Sheila.	none
Holland, Thomas D.	PS3608.O48454
Holland, Tom.	PR6058.O4439
Holland, William E.	PS3558.O3492
Hollands, Judith Winship.	none
Holles, Robert, 1926-	PR6058.O446
Holliday, Liz.	PR6058.O44654
Holliday, V. K. (Vynette)	PS3608.O48478
Hollihan, Keith.	PR9199.4.H6455
Hollingsworth, Gerelyn.	PS3558.O34977
Hollis, John, 1926-	PS3558.O3546
Hollon, Frank Turner, 1963-	PS3608.O494
Holly, Emma.	PS3608.O4943
Holly, Joan Carol Hunter, 1932-	none
Holman, Sheri.	PS3558.O35596
Holman, Susan R.	PS3558.O355957
Holme, Timothy.	PR6058.O45355
Holmes, Beth.	PS3558.O358
Holmes, Clare Frances.	PR6058.O45359
Holmes, H. H.—see: Boucher, Anthony, 1911-1968.	
Holmes, Michael, 1966-	PR9199.3.H5815
Holmes, Michele Paige.	PS3608.O4943546
Holmes, Nancy, 1921-	PS3558.O364
Holmes, Oliver W.	none
Holmes, Rupert.	PS3558.O367
Holmes, Shannon.	PS3608.O494356
Holt, A. J.	PS3558.O395
Holt, Anne, 1958-	PT8952.18.O386
Holt, Dick.	none
Holt, Gavin, 1891-	PR6035.O596
Holt, Glenn.	none
Holt, Hazel, 1928-	PR6058.O473
Holt, Henry.	none
Holt, Jerry, 1942-	PS3608.O4943594
Holt, Peter.	none
Holt, Robert Lawrence.	PS3558.O4163
Holt, Samuel.	PS3558.O42
Holt, T. D. (Thomas D.)	PS3608.O4943597
Holt, Victoria, 1906-1993.	PR6015.I3
Holt, Will.	none
Holt-White, W. (William), b. 1878.	PR6015.O48
Holton, Cathy.	PS3608.O494434

Holton, Chuck.	PS3608.O4944344
Holton, Hugh.	PS3558.O4373
Holton, Leonard, 1915-1983.	PS3573.I2
Holtzer, Susan.	PS3558.O4374
Holzer, Erika.	PS3558.O44
Holzer, Hans, 1920-2009.	none
Holzner, Nancy, 1961-	PS3603.O5468
Homer, Joel.	none
Homes, Geoffrey, 1902-1977.	PS3525.A4157
Homewood, Harry.	PS3558.O45
Hone, Joseph, 1937-	PR6058.O49
Honeycombe, Gordon.	PR6058.O5
Hong, Edna H. (Edna Hatlestad), 1913-2007.	PS3515.O4974
Honig, Donald.	PS3558.O5
Hoobler, Dorothy.	none
Hood, Christopher.	PR6058.O536
Hood, Jack B.	PS3608.O557
Hood, Mantle.	PS3558.O542
Hood, Rob N.	PS3608.O56
Hood, William, 1920-	PS3558.O545
Hook, Philip.	PR6058.O55
Hooper, Chloe, 1973-	PR9619.4.H66
Hooper, Kay.	PS3558.O587
Hooper, Tobe, 1943-	PS3608.O5955
Hoopes, Roy, 1922-	PS3558.O6323
Hoover, Terry.	PS3608.O6255
Hoover, Thomas.	none
Hope, Laura Lee.	none
Hopkins, Brian A.	PS3558.O63465
Hopkins, Julian, 1940-	PR6108.O645
Hopkins, Kenneth.	PR6015.O62
Hopkins, Lila.	PS3558.O63546
Hopkins, Robert S.	PS3558.O636
Hopkins, Roland.	PS3558.O6363
Hopley, George, 1903-1968.	PS3515.O6455
Hoppe, Joanne.	none
Hopwood, Jim.	none
Horan, Don.	none
Horan, Hume, 1934-	PS3558.O644
Horan, James David, 1914-	PS3558.O65
Horan, Richard, 1957-	PS3558.O662
Horansky, Ruby.	PS3558.O664
Horler, Sydney, 1888-1954.	PR6015.O66
Horn, Dara, 1977-	PS3608.O76
Horn, Phyllis, 1938-	PS3558.O686
Horn, Stephen, 1946-	PS3558.O68723
Horne, Geoffrey, 1916-	PR6015.O6824
Hornig, Doug.	PS3558.O68785
Hornsby, Wendy.	PS3558.O689
Hornung, E. W. (Ernest William), 1866-1921.	PR6015.O687
Horowitz, Renee B.	none
Horowitz, Anthony, 1955-	PR6058.O715
Horrock, Henry.	P3558.O6973
Horrock, Nicholas.	none

Horst, Joel.	none
Horstman, Thomas.	none
Horton, J. Royal (Jon Royal)	PS3558.O698
Horton, John.	none
Horton, Martha.	PS3608.O7725
Horváth, Ödön von, 1901-1938.	PT2615.O865
Horvitz, Leslie Alan.	none
Horwood, William.	PR6058.O719
Hosegood, Lewis, 1920-	PR6058.O7197
Hoshino, Tomoyuki, 1965-	PL871.O752
Hosken, Clifford James Wheeler, 1882-1949.	PR6015.O7625
Hoskins, Robert, 1933-	PS3558.O76
Hoskins, Susan M.	PS3558.O773
Hosp, David.	PS3608.O79
Hospital, Janette Turner, 1942-	PR9619.3.H674
Hossent, Harry.	none
Hotchkiss, Clarence.	PS3608.O84
Hotchner, A. E.	PS3558.O8
Hougan, Carolyn.	PS3558.O835
Hougan, Jim.	PS3558.O836
Hough, Charlotte, 1924-2008.	PR6058.O79
Hough, John T.	PS3558.O84
Hough, Robert, 1963-	PR9199.4.H66
Hough, S. B. (Stanley Bennett), 1917-	PR6058.O83
Houghton, Claude, 1889-1961.	PR6029.L4
Household, Geoffrey, 1900-1988.	PR6015.O7885
Housewright, David, 1955-	PS3558.O8668
Houston, David, 1938-	none
Houston, James D.	PS3558.O87
Houston, Margaret Bell.	PS3515.O79
Houston, Robert, 1940-	PS3558.O873
Houston, Victoria, 1945-	PS3608.O88
Howard, Clark.	PS3558.O877
Howard, Colin—see: Shaw, Howard.	
Howard, Gil.	PS3558.O88156
Howard, Hartley.	PR6029.G6
Howard, Jacki.	PS3608.O9235
Howard, James A. (James Arch), 1922-	none
Howard, Lesley.	PS3558.O882
Howard, Linda, 1950-	PS3558.O88217
Howard, Linden.	PR6058.O884
Howard, Mary, 1942-	PS3558.O88226
Howard, Maureen, 1930-	PS3558.O8823
Howe, Melodie Johnson.	PS3558.O8926
Howard, Tom, 1937-	PR9619.4.H69
Howard, Tracie.	PS3608.O94
Howatch, Susan.	PR6058.O912
Howe, J. M. (John M.)	none
Howe, James, 1946-	PS3558.O8923
Howe, Russell Warren, 1925-	PS3558.O8927
Howell, Dorothy (Dorothy A.)	PS3608.O9525
Howell, Jean.	none
Howell, Lis.	PR6108.O945
Howell, Patricia Hagan—see: Hagan, Patricia.	

Howland, Hal, 1951-	PS3608.O95728
Howlett, John, 1940-	PR6058.O96
Howley, Brendan.	PR9199.3.H685
Hoyle, Fred, Sir.	PR6058.O98
Hoyle, Geoffrey, 1942-	none
Hoyle, Trevor.	PR6058.O99
Hoyos, Andrés.	PQ8180.18.O795
Hoyt, Edwin Palmer.	PS3558.O97
Hoyt, Richard, 1941-	PS3558.O975
Hozy, Penny, 1947-	PR9199.4.H737
Hrabal, Bohumil, 1914-1997.	PG5039.18.R2
Hubbard, L. Ron (La Fayette Ron), 1911-1986.	PS3515.U1417
Hubbard, P. M. (Philip Maitland), 1910-	PR6058.U2
Hubbard, Regina—see: Hubbard, Richard.	
Hubbard, Richard,	none
Huber, Frederic Vincent, 1944-	PS3558.U237
Hubert, Tord, 1933-	PT9876.18.U2
Hudgin, Thomas L., 1939-	PS3608.U3256
Hudgins, Maria.	PS3608.U326
Hudson, Christopher, 1946-	PR6058.U313
Hudson, Jeffrey, 1942-2008.	PS3553.R48
Hudson, John Paul.	none
Huebner, Fredrick D.	PS3558.U3127
Huff, Afton.	none
Huff, T. E.	PS3558.U323
Huffman, Laurie.	PS3558.U34
Hufford, Susan.	PS3558.U343
Huggett, William Turner.	PS3558.U345
Huggins, David, 1959-	PR6058.U335
Huggins, James Byron.	PS3558.U346
Hughes, Declan, 1963-	PR6058.U343
Hughes, Dorothy B. (Dorothy Belle), 1904-1993.	PS3515.U268
Hughes, Mary Ellen.	PS3558.U3745
Hughes, Michael, 1950-	none
Hughes, Natalie McCoy.	PS3608.U3725
Hughes, Richard E.	PS3558.U388
Hughes, Rodney.	none
Hughes, Terry, 1933-	PR6058.U38
Hughes, William Harry.	none
Hugill, Robert.	none
Hugo, Richard, 1923-1982.	PS3515.U3
Hugo, Richard, 1947-	PS3558.U396
Hull, Richard, 1896-1973.	PR6015.U43
Hulland, J. R.	PR6058.U3924
Hume, David.	none
Hume, Fergus, 1859-1932.	PR4809.H87
Humes, Larry R.	none
Humphrey, David M.	PS3608.U47
Humphrey, Howard C.	PS3558.U4457
Humphrey, Joe.	PS3608.U473
Humphreys, C. C. (Chris C.)	PR9199.4.H85
Humphreys, James.	none
Humphreys, James, 1967-	none
Humphreys, Joel Don.	PS3558.U4654

Hunnings, Vicky.	PS3608.U56
Hunsicker, Harry.	PS3608.U566
Hunt, Alexa.	PS3608.U57
Hunt, Angela Elwell, 1957-	PS3558.U46747
Hunt, Arlene.	PR6108.U58
Hunt, Charlotte.	none
Hunt, David, 1939-	PS3558.U467654
Hunt, E. Howard (Everette Howard), 1918-2007.	PS3515.U5425
Hunt, James Patrick, 1964-	PS3608.U577
Hunt, Kyle, 1908-1973.	PR6005.R517
Hunt, La Jill.	PS3608.U5797
Hunt, Morgan.	PS3608.U5834
Hunt, Richard, 1938-	PR6058.U517
Hunter, Alan, 1922-2005.	PR6015.U565
Hunter, Catherine, 1957-	PR9199.3.H8255
Hunter, Chris.	none
Hunter, David, 1947-	PS3558.U46964
Hunter, Denise, 1968-	PS3608.U5925
Hunter, Ellen Elizabeth.	none
Hunter, Evan, 1926-2005.	PS3515.U585
Hunter, Fred.	PS3558.U476
Hunter, Gwen.	PS3608.U59278
Hunter, J. Michael (James Michael), 1963-	PS3608.U5929
Hunter, Jack D.	PS3558.U48
Hunter, Jessie Prichard.	PS3558.U4815
Hunter, Kate, 1964-	PS3608.U59295
Hunter, Ken, 1934-	PS3558.U4825
Hunter, Maddy.	PS3608.U5944
Hunter, Matthew.	PR6058.U538
Hunter, R. David.	PS3608.U5948
Hunter, Rex.	none
Hunter, Robin, 1935-2006.	PR6058.U54
Hunter, Seth.	PR6108.U59
Hunter, Stephen, 1946-	PS3558.U494
Hunter, Travis, 1969-	PS3558.U497
Hunvald, Henry.	PS3558.U53
Hurd, Douglas, 1930-	PR6058.U7
Hurd, Florence.	PS3558.U532
Hurd, Jimmy.	PS3608.U767
Hurka, Joseph.	PS3608.U768
Hurley, Graham.	PR6058.U717
Hurst, Heather Smith.	none
Hurst, Jim.	PS3558.U548
Hurst, Kathryn.	none
Hurt, Freda.	none
Hurwitz, Gregg Andrew.	PS3558.U695
Hurwood, Bernhardt J.	none
Huson, Paul.	none
Hustmyre, Chuck.	PS3608.U853
Huston, Charlie.	PS3608.U855
Huston, Fran.	PS3558.U78
Huston, James W.	PS3558.U8122
Hutchins, J. C., 1975-	PS3608.U859
Hutchinson, Mary Jane.	none

Hutson, Shaun, 1958-	none
Hutter, A. D.	none
Hutton, John, 1928-	PR6058.U859
Hutton, Malcolm.	PR6058.U8598
Huxley, Elspeth Joscelin Grant, 1907-1997.	PR6015.U92
Hyams, Edward, 1910-1975.	PR6015.Y33
Hyams, Joe.	PS3558.Y33
Hyatt, Betty Hale.	PS3558.Y337
Hyde, Anthony, 1946-	PR9199.3.H895
Hyde, Bill, 1934-	PS3558.Y354
Hyde, Christopher, 1949-	PS3558.Y36
Hyde, Eleanor.	PR6058.Y4
Hyde, Elisabeth.	PS3558.Y38
Hyland, Adrian.	PR9619.4.H95
Hyland, Henry Stanley.	PR6058.Y6
Hylton, Sara.	PR6058.Y63
Hyman, Ann.	PS3558.Y46
Hyman, Vernon Tom.	PS3558.Y49
Hyman, Jackie, 1949-	PS3554.I24
Hynd, Noel.	PS3558.Y54
Hyne, Charles John Cutcliffe Wright, 1866-1944.	PR6015.Y6
Hynes, Charles J.	PS3608.Y85
Hynes, James.	PS3558.Y55
Hyzy, Julie A.	PS3608.Y98
I‹A›kovlev, Alekseĭ.	PG3492.34.A39
I‹A›kovleva, Elena (Elena Viktorovna)	PG3482.A477
Iakovou, Takis.	PS3559.A45
I‹A›maleev, R.	PG3482.A4937
Iams, Jack, 1910-1990.	PS3517.A5
Iannuzzi, John Nicholas, 1935-	PS3559.A55
I‹A›roshenko, Elena.	PG3492.34.A76
Ibáñez, Julián, 1940-	PQ6659.B225
Ibargüengoitia, Jorge, 1928-1983.	PQ7298.19.B3
Ibe, Adimchinma, 1977-	PR9387.9.I125
Iceberg Slim, 1918-1992.	PS3552.E25
Ickler, Glenn.	PS3609.C55
Ifkovits, Nicholas.	PS3559.F44
Ignatius, David, 1950-	PS3559.G54
Ikezawa, Natsuki, 1945-	PL853.K45
Ikuta, Naochika, 1929-	none
Iles, Francis, 1893-1971.	PR6005.O855
Iles, Greg.	PS3559.L47
Il'in, Andreĭ.	PG3482.L478
Il'in, Anton.	PG3492.34.L53
Inchbald, Peter.	PR6059.N3
Ind, Allison, 1903-	PS3517.N2
Indiana, Gary.	PS3559.N335
Infante, Anne.	PR9619.3.I54
Ing, Dean.	PS3559.N37
Ingate, Mary.	PR6059.N47
Ingermanson, Randall Scott.	PS3609.N46
Ingersol, Jared, 1916-	PS3566.A34
Ingham, Daniel, 1926-2001.	PR6059.N516
Ingham, Richard, 1935-	PR6059.N52

Inglis, Gordon.   PR9199.4.I52
Ingraham, Jim.   PS3609.N467
Ingram, C. David.   PR6109.N456
Ingram, Grace.   PR6059.N54
Ings, Simon.   PR6059.N54
Inigo, Martin.   PR6063.I3175
Ink, India, 1961-   PS3607.A413
Innes, Hammond, 1913-1998.   PR6017.N79
Innes, Michael, 1906-1994.   PR6037.T466
Innes, Roy, 1939-   PR9199.4.I56
Inness-Brown, Elizabeth, 1954-   PS3559.N47
Innocenzi, Paul Claude.   PQ2669.N63
Ions, Edmund S.   PR6059.O5
Iraldi, James C.   none
Irby, Lee.   PS3609.R47
Ireland, David, 1927-   PR9619.3.I674
Iriarte, Alfredo, 1932-   PQ8180.19.R54
Irish, William, 1903-1968.   PS3515.O6455
Ironside, Elizabeth.   PR6059.R6
Irungu, Kiunjuri Edward.   PR9381.9.I785
Irvin, Kelly.   PS3609.R82
Irvine, Patricia McCune.   none
Irvine, R. R. (Robert R.)   PS3559.R65
Irvine, Robert P.   none
Irving, Clifford.   PS3559.R79
Irving, Clive.   PR6059.R914
Irving, Karen, 1957-   PR9199.3.I695
Irving-James, Thomas—see: James, T. I. (Thomas Irving)
Irving, John, 1942-   PS3559.R8
Irwin, Frances.   PR6059.R92
Irwin, Inez Haynes—see: Gillmore, Inez Haynes, 1873-1970.
Irwin, Robert, 1946-   PR6059.R96
Irwin, Wallace, 1876-1959.   PS3517.R87
Isaacman, Max.   PS3609.S225
Isaacs, Susan, 1943-   PS3559.S15
Isaak, David T. (David Thomas), 1954-   PS3609.S24
Isely, Reymoure Keith.   PR9199.3.I8
Isenberg, Jane.   PS3609.S46
Isherwood, Eve.   PR6109.S54
Ishiguro, Kazuo, 1954-   PR6059.S5
Isleib, Roberta.   PS3609.S57
Isler, Saul, 1934-   PS3609.S577
Ison, Graham.   PR6059.S6
Israel, Peter, 1933-   PS3559.S74
Itule, Bruce D., 1947-   PS3609.T85
I⟨U⟩denich, Marina.   PG3482.U28
I⟨U⟩rskai⟨a⟩, Elena.   PG3482.U773
Ives, John.   PS3559.V44
Izmaĭlov, Konstantin.   none
Izner, Claude.   PQ2709.Z64
Izzi, Eugene.   PS3559.Z9
Izzo, Jean-Claude.   PQ2669.Z95
Jablokov, Alexander.   PS3560.A116
Jack, Jeremiah.   none

Jackman, Stuart Brooke, 1922-   PR6019.AI8
Jack, Alex, 1945-   PS3560.A14
Jacks, Marie.   none
Jacks, Oliver.   PR6068.O98
Jackson, Basil, 1920-   PR9199.3.J37
Jackson, Blyden.   PS3560.A18
Jackson, Bruce, 1936-   PS3560.A212
Jackson, Clarence J.-L.—see: Bulliet, Richard W.
Jackson, Eileen.   PR6060.A226
Jackson, Everatt, 1942-   none
Jackson, James O.   PS3560.A2157
Jackson, Jon.   none
Jackson, Jon A.   PS3560.A216
Jackson, Joshilyn.   PS3610.A3525
Jackson, Ken.   PS3560.A22
Jackson, Lee, 1955-   PS3610.A3528
Jackson, Liam.   PS3610.A353
Jackson, Lisa.   PS3560.A223
Jackson, Loretta.   PS3560.A224
Jackson, Marian J. A.   PS3560.A228
Jackson, Muriel Resnik.   PS3568.E7
Jackson, Olive.   PS3560.A2416
Jackson, Renay, 1959-   PS3610.A3547
Jackson, Richard.   PS3610.A35475
Jackson, Robert C., 1923-   PS3560.A2434
Jackson, Sherryle Kiser.   PS3610.A35495
Jackson, Shirley, 1916-1965.   PS3519.A392
Jackson, Sibyl Avery.   PS3610.A355
Jackson, Steve, 1969-   PR6110.A27
Jacobs, Claire Rainwater.   PS3560.A2495
Jacobs, Eli.   PR9510.9.J328
Jacobs, Jonnie.   PS3560.A2543
Jacobs, Linda, 1952-   PS3610.A35645
Jacobs, Mark, 1951-   PS3560.A2549
Jacobs, Nancy Baker, 1944-   PS3560.A2554
Jacobs, Nick.   PS3610.A35647
Jacobs, Paula, 1930-   none
Jacobs, T. C. H. (Thomas Curtis Hicks), 1899-1976. PR6019.A336
Jacobson, Alan, 1961-   PS3560.A2585
Jacobson, Jeff (Jeffory)   PS3610.A356756
Jacovsky, Marilyn, 1949-   PS3560.A2848
Jacquemard-Sénécal.   PQ2670.A249
Jaffarian, Sue Ann, 1952-   PS3610.A359
Jaffe, Jody.   PS3560.A3125
Jaffe, Michele.   PS3560.A3136
Jaffe, Susanne.   PS3560.A316
Jaffee, Irving L.   none
Jaffee, Mary.   none
Jagninski, Tom.   PS3560.A337
Jagoda, Robert.   PS3560.A34
Jahn, Mike, 1943-   PS3560.A35
Jahn, Ryan David.   PS3560.A356
Jakeman, Jane.   PR6060.A435
Jakes, John, 1932-   PS3560.A37

Jakober, Marie.	PR9199.3.J376
Jakubowski, Maxim.	PR6060.A436
James, Bill, 1929-	PR6070.U23
James, Darrell, 1946-	PS3610.A429
James, David, 1958-	PS3619.T85
James, Dean (Darryl Dean)	PS3610.A43
James, Donald, 1931-2008.	PR6060.A453
James, Elle.	none
James, Henry, 1843-1916.	PS2110-2128
James, Leigh, 1918-	PS3560.A395
James, Margaret, 1922-	PR6052.E533
James, Meleri Wyn.	PB2298.J28
James, Miranda.	PS3610.A43
James, P. D.	PR6060.A467
James, Peter, 1948-	PR6060.A472
James, Rebecca, 1928-1996.	PS3560.A394
James, Robert.	none
James, Russell.	PR6060.A473
James, S. E.	PR9275.A583
James, Steven, 1969-	PS3610.A4545
James, Susan, 1944-	PS3560.A397
James, Susan S.	PS3610.A455
James, T. I. (Thomas Irving)	none
Jamesson, Peter.	PS3610.A47
Jamieson, Kerry.	PR9369.4.J36
Jamison, Amelia.	none
Jamison, Ellen.	none
Jamyang Norbu.	PR9499.3.J268
Jance, J. A.—see: Jance, Judith A.	
Jance, Judith A.	PS3560.A44
Janes, Diane.	PR6110.A54
Janes, J. Robert (Joseph Robert), 1935-	PR9199.3.J3777
Janeshutz, Trish, 1947-	PS3563.A31115
Janeway, Harriet.	none
Janifer, Laurence M.	PS3560.A52
Janson, Hank, 1908-	none
Jansson, Robert.	none
Jansson, Tove.	PT9875.J37
Janzen, Tara.	PS3563.C75
Japrisot, Sébastien, 1931-2003.	PQ2678.O72
JaQuavis.	PS3610.A69
Jardine, Quintin.	PR6060.A67
Jarvis, Edward.	PS3560.A6
Jarvis, Fred G.	PS3560.A63
Jarvis, Suzan.	none
Jason, Stuart.	none
Jauniere, Claudette.	none
Javits, Hank.	none
Javitt, Jonathan.	PS3610.A94
Jay, Charlotte, 1919-1996.	PR9619.3.H29
Jay, Simon, 1920-2007.	PR6060.A96
Jay, Stacey.	none
Jecks, Michael.	PR6060.E22
Jefferies, William, 1950-	PS3554.E1755

Jefferis, Barbara.	PR9619.3.J4
Jeffers, H. Paul (Harry Paul), 1934-2009.	PS3560.E36
Jeffers, Sunni.	PS3610.E36
Jefferson, Paul.	PS3560.E4
Jefferson, Roland S.	PS3560.E415
Jeffery, Ransom.	PS3560.E42
Jeffett, Elizabeth.	PS3610.E37
Jeffrey, Grant R.	PS3560.E436
Jeffreys, J. G.	PR6058.E17
Jeffries, J. M.	PS3560.E455
Jeffries, Roderic, 1926-	PR6060.E43
Jekoff, Christa.	none
Jelinek, Elfriede, 1946-	PT2670.E46
Jenkins, Dan.	PS3560.E48
Jenkins, Emyl.	PS3610.E544
Jenkins, Geoffrey, 1920-2001.	PR9369.3.J38
Jenkins, Jerry B.	PS3560.E485
Jenkins, Rebecca, 1961-	PR6060.E5189
Jenkins, Will, 1896-1975.	PS3519.E648
Jennifer, Susan, 1933-	PS3558.O76
Jennings, Dana Andrew.	PS3560.E5175
Jennings, Maureen.	PR9199.3.J397
Jennings, Phillip.	PS3610.E56
Jenoff, Pam.	PS3610.E562
Jensen, J. Arthur.	PS3610.E565
Jensen, Ruby Jean.	none
Jensen, Derrick, 1960-	PS3610.E56283
Jensen, Jane.	PS3560.E5919
Jenson, Martin.	none
Jeppesen, Travis, 1979-	PS3610.E67
Jepson, Edgar, 1863-1938.	PR6019.E55
Jepson, Selwyn, 1899-1989.	PR6019.E553
Jerina, Carol.	none
Jerkins, Grant.	PS3610.E69
Jerome, Owen Fox, 1897-1963.	PS3511.R745
Jesmer, Elaine, 1939-	PS3560.E77
Jessup, Richard.	PS3560.E8
Jeter, K. W.	PS3560.E85
Jevons, Marshall.	PS3560.E88
Jewell, Britt.	PS3560.E89
Jewell, Derek.	PR6060.E94
Jillette, Penn.	PS3610.I45
Jinks, Catherine.	PR9619.3.J48
Jobson, Hamilton.	PR6060.O22
Joe, Yolanda.	PS3560.O242
Joens, Michael R.	PS3560.O246
Joensuu, Matti Yrjänä, 1948-	PH355.J553
Joey.	none
Johann, Anna.	none
Johansen, Iris.	PS3560.O275
Johansen, Roy.	PS3560.O2756
Johler, Jens, 1944-	PT2670.O355
John, Cathie.	PS3560.O295
John, Hendrix.	PS3560.O32

John, Katherine.	PR6060.O237
John, Katherine, d. 1984.	none
John, Marie-Elena.	PR9275.A583
John, Owen, 1918-	PR6060.O24
John, Romilly.	PR6019.O39135
Johns, Derek, 1948-	PR6060.O26
Johns, Larry.	none
Johns, W. E. (William Earl), 1893-1968.	PR6019.O3914
Johnson, B. B.	PS3560.O3715
Johnson, Barbara, 1955-	PS3560.O37174
Johnson, Bett Reece.	PS3560.O37184
Johnson, Claire M. (Claire Margaret), 1956-	PS3610.O324
Johnson, Craig, 1961-	PS3610.O325
Johnson, D. E. (Dan E.)	PS3610.O328
Johnson, Diane, 1934-	PS3560.O3746
Johnson, Dolores.	PS3560.O3748
Johnson, E. Richard (Emil Richard), 1937-	PS3560.O376
Johnson, James Leonard, 1927-	PS3560.O379
Johnson, Jane, 1960-	PS3610.O3545
Johnson, Jason, 1969-	PR6110.O426
Johnson, Keith Lee.	PS3610.O359
Johnson, Ken, 1942-	PS3560.O3796
Johnson, Lisa Jones.	PS3610.O363
Johnson, Lois Walfrid.	PS3560.O37976
Johnson, Margaret, 1959-	PR6110.O44
Johnson, Mat.	PS3560.O38167
Johnson, Mendal W.	PS3560.O3817
Johnson, Norma Tadlock.	PS3560.O3819
Johnson, Pamela M.	PS3610.O37
Johnson, Richard A., 1946-	PR6060.O366
Johnson, Rique.	PS3610.O373
Johnson, Sandy, 1934-	PS3560.O38635
Johnson, Stanley, 1940-	PR6060.O37
Johnson, Steve, 1960-	none
Johnson, Wayne.	PS3560.O3866
Johnson, William Oscar.	none
Johnston, Brian, 1944-	PS3560.O3873
Johnston, Clint.	none
Johnston, Donald.	PS3560.O3875
Johnston, Dorothy, 1948-	PR9619.3.J672
Johnston, Fred, 1951-	PR6060.O389
Johnston, J. M.	PS3560.O3892
Johnston, Jane, 1927-	PS3560.O3893
Johnston, Joan, 1948-	PS3560.O3896
Johnston, Linda O.	PS3610.O387
Johnston, Norma.	PS3560.O3897
Johnston, Paul, 1957-	PR6060.O417
Johnston, Ronald, 1926-	PR6060.O43
Johnston, Velda.	PS3560.O394
Johnston, William, 1924-	PS3560.O395
Johnstone, William W.	PS3560.O415
Jokinen, Seppo, 1949-	PH355.J573
Jolliffe, Grace.	PR6110.O55
Jolowicz, Philip.	PS3610.O46

Jon, Montague. PR6060.O45
Jones, Able. PS3560.O4553
Jones, Annie, 1957- PS3560.O45744
Jones, Anthony P., 1958- PS3610.O585
Jones, Bret Austin. PS3610.O619
Jones, Brian, 1930- none
Jones, Bruce, 1944- PS3560.O4585
Jones, Cleo. PS3560.O465
Jones, Craig. PS3560.O466
Jones, D. J. H. PS3560.O474
Jones, Darynda. PS3610.O6236
Jones, Dennis, 1945- PR9199.3.J6276
Jones, Douglas C. (Douglas Clyde), 1924- PS3560.O478
Jones, Dylan, 1955- PR6060.O5117
Jones, E. Scott. PS3560.O4812
Jones, Edward R. PS3560.O4814
Jones, Elizabeth McDavid, 1958- none
Jones, Elwyn. PR6060.O512
Jones, Frank, 1937- none
Jones, Frankie J., 1953- PS3560.O4825
Jones, Geraint V. (Geraint Vaughan), 1938- PB2298.J5238
Jones, Harry, 1938- PS3560.O4837
Jones, Howard A. PS3610.O62535
Jones, J. D. F. PR6060.O5168
Jones, J. Sydney. PS3610.O62553
Jones, James, 1921-1977. PS3560.O49
Jones, John Handel. none
Jones, K. R. PS3610.O6258
Jones, L. Q. none
Jones, Larry. PS3560.O498
Jones, Liane, 1958- PR6060.O543
Jones, Madison, 1925- PS3560.O517
Jones, Matthew F. PS3560.O52244
Jones, Merry Bloch. PS3610.O6273
Jones, Mervyn, 1922-2010. PR6060.O56
Jones, Pauline Baird. PS3560.O52415
Jones, Philip M., 1919- PR9619.3.J688
Jones, R. W. (Roger William), 1941- PR6060.O576
Jones, Rennie. PS3560.O52474
Jones, Robert Gerallt. PB2298.J6142
Jones, Robert Page. none
Jones, Ryan D., 1962- PS3610.O628
Jones, Scott. PS3560.O534
Jones, Simmons, 1920- PS3560.O538
Jones, Solomon, 1967- PS3560.O5386
Jones, Stan, 1947- PS3560.O539
Jones, Stephen Graham, 1972- PS3560.O5395
Jones, Susanna, 1967- PR6110.O64
Jones, Terry, 1942- PR6060.O588
Jones, Tobias. PR6110.O643
Jones, Tristan, 1924- PR6060.O59
Jones, Veda Boyd. none
Jones, Victor, 1919- PR6060.O6
Jones, Weyman, 1928- PS3560.O5584

Jonnes, Christopher Bonn.	PS3610.O64
Jontos, Richard.	none
Jopson, Marion.	PR6060.O62
Jordan, B. B., 1955-	none
Jordan, Cathleen.	PS3560.O68
Jordan, Chris, 1951-	PS3566.H474
Jordan, David, 1939-	PR6060.O624
Jordan, Eric, 1930-	PS3560.O7215
Jordan, James, 1956-	PS3610.O6557
Jordan, Jennifer.	PR6060.O6247
Jordan, Jennifer L.	PS3560.O728
Jordan, Keeling.	PS3560.O74
Jordan, Lee.	PR9369.3.S3
Jordan, Leonard, 1935-	none
Jordan, Oakley.	PS3560.O7613
Jordan, Pat.	PS3560.O7615
Jordan, Richard Tyler, 1960-	PS3620.Y58
Jordan, River.	PS3610.O6615
Jorgensen, Christine T.	PS3560.O765
Joscelyn, Archie, 1899-1986.	PS3519.O712
Jose, Nicholas, 1952-	PR9619.3.J73
Joseph, Alan.	none
Joseph, Alison.	PR6060.O6315
Joseph, George, 1912-1989.	PR9639.3.J647
Joseph, Henry, 1948-	PS3560.O7728
Joseph, Marie.	PR6060.O636
Joseph, Mark.	PS3560.O776
Joshe, O. K.	PR9499.3.J598
Joss, Morag.	PR6060.O77
Jossel, Joylynn.	PS3610.O68
Jost, John.	none
Journet, Terence.	PR6060.O9
Jovanovich, William.	PS3560.O84
Joven, Enrique, 1964-	PQ6710.O84
Joyce, Brenda.	PS3560.O864
Joyce, Cyril.	none
Joyce, Graham, 1954-	PR6060.O93
Joyce, Marianne.	none
Joyce, T. Robert.	none
Judd, Alan, 1946-	PR6060.U32
Judson, D. Daniel, 1962-	PS3610.U532
Judson, William.	PS3560.U4
Jungk, Peter Stephan, 1952-	PT2670.U53
Jungersen, Christian.	PT8176.2.U47
Jungstedt, Mari, 1962-	PT9877.2.U64
Juniper, Alex.	PR9619.3.J76
Jurado López, Manuel, 1942-	PQ6660.U58
Jürgs, Michael.	none
Jurjevics, Juris, 1943-	PS3610.U76
Justus, Adalu, 1928-	PS3560.U86
Jute, André, 1945-	PR9369.3.J84
Kadlecek, Jo.	PS3611.A33
Kadota, Yasuaki, 1940-	none
Kadow, Jeannine.	PS3561.A36154

Kadrey, Richard. PS3561.A3616
Kaewert, Julie Wallin. PS3561.A3617
Kagen, Lesley. PS3611.A344
Kahn, James. PS3561.A37
Kahn, Michael A., 1952- PS3561.A375
Kahn, Roger. PS3561.A39
Kahn, Sharon, 1934- PS3561.A397
Kahn, Steve. none
Kahn, Wilma J. (Wilma Jean), 1950- PS3611.A354
Kail, Robert. none
Kains, Josephine. PS3557.O85
Kaiser, Ernst. PT2671.A385
Kaiser, Ronn. none
Kakonis, Tom E. PS3561.A4154
Kalb, Bernard. PS3561.A41628
Kalb, Marvin L. PS3561.A4163
Kalian, Cady. PS3611.A4336
Kalikoff, Beth. PS3611.A434
Kalikwu, Ikechukwu, 1972- PR9387.9.K3444
Kalinina, Dar'i‹a›. PG3482.5.L5734
Kalish, Robert. none
Kalla, Alec. PS3561.A41657
Kalla, Daniel. PR9199.4.K34
Kallen, Lucille. PS3561.A41662
Kallentoft, Mons, 1968- PT9877.21.A48
Kalliman, Samuel. PS3611.A443
Kallifatides, Theodor, 1938- PT9876.21.A45
Kalogridis, Jeanne. PS3561.A41675
Kalstein, Dave. PS3611.A457
Kamarck, Lawrence. PS3561.A417
Kamau, Pius K. PS3561.A41713
Kaminsky, Stuart M. PS3561.A43
Kamitses, Zoë. PS3561.A434
Kamm, Dorinda. none
Kandel, Susan, 1961- PS3611.A53
Kane, Abel. none
Kane, Andrea. PS3561.A463
Kane, Cornelius, 1964- PR9619.4.O54
Kane, Frank, 1912-1968. PS3521.A434
Kane, Henry. PS3521.A4347
Kane, John, 1946- PS3561.A4675
Kane, Jonathan, 1935- PR6073.I463
Kane, Kay. PS3611.A546
Kane, Mark none
Kane, Stephanie. PS3611.A548
Kangende, Kenneth, 1953- PR9405.9.K28
Kanon, Joseph. PS3561.A476
Kantner, Rob. none
Kantor, Hal. PS3561.A48
Kantor, Harry—see: Kantor, Hal.
Kantra, Virginia. none
Kaplan, Alexander. PS3561.A53
Kaplan, Andrew. PS3561.A545
Kaplan, Andrew, 1941- none

Kaplan, Arthur	PS3561.A547
Kaplan, Barry Jay.	none
Kaplan, Howard, 1950-	PS3561.A558
Kaplan, Janice.	PS3561.A5593
Karamesines, P. G. (Patricia G.), 1956-	PS3611.A73
Karasik, Arkadiĭ.	PG3482.5.R293
Karetnikova, Anna.	none
Kariŭki, Emmanuel.	PR9381.9.K33
Kark, Austen.	PR6061.A724
Karl, M. S.	PS3561.A6144
Karman, Mal.	none
Karney, Jack, 1911-	none
Karp, David, 1922-1999.	PS3561.A679
Karp, Larry.	PS3611.A7844
Karp, Marshall.	PS3561.A684
Karr, Jillian.	PS3561.A69278
Karr, Lee.	none
Karr, Leona.	PS3561.A6928
Karta, Nat—see: Norwood, Victor George Charles.	
Kartun, Derek.	PR6061.A78
Karyshev, Valeriĭ.	PG3482.6.A79
Kash, Marcia.	PR9199.3.K385
Kasminoff, Ross.	PS3553.A6995
Kassak, Fred.	PQ2671.A78
Kassel, Bill, 1947-	PS3561.A69967
Kasischke, Laura, 1961-	PS3561.A6993
Kastin, Darrell.	PS3611.A787
Kastle, Herbert D.	PS3561.A7
Katcher, Leo.	PS3561.A73
Katkov, Norman.	PS3521.A654
Kato, Arei.	none
Katsume, Azusa, 1932-	none
Katz, Candace.	PS3611.A7887
Katz, Herbert M.	PS3561.A754
Katz, Jon.	PS3561.A7558
Katz, Michael J., 1951-	PS3561.A772
Katz, Robert, 1933-2010.	PS3561.A773
Katz, Robert I., 1952-	PS3611.A813
Katz, William, 1940-	PS3561.A777
Katzenbach, John.	PS3561.A7778
Kaufelt, David A.	PS3561.A79
Kauffman, Reginald Wright, 1877-1959.	PS3521.A725
Kauffmann, Lane, 1921-1988.	PS3561.A824
Kaufman, Lynne.	PS3611.A838
Kaufman, Michael.	none
Kaufman, Michael T.	none
Kaufman, Pamela.	PS3561.A8617
Kaufman, Schuyler.	PS3611.A84
Kaufman, Thomas.	PS3611.A843
Kava, Alex.	PS3561.A8682
Kavaler, Rebecca.	PS3561.A8685
Kavanagh, Dan, 1946-	PR6061.A898
Kavanagh, Linda.	PS3611.A84

Kavanagh, Paul, 1938-   PS3561.A87
Kay, George.   none
Kay, Kenneth.   none
Kaye, Mandalyn.   none
Kay, Terry.   PS3561.A885
Kaye, H. R.   none
Kaye, John.   PS3561.A8857
Kaye, M. M. (Mary Margaret), 1908-2004.   PR6061.A945
Kaye, Marvin.   PS3561.A886
Kaye, Mavis.   PS3611.A89
Kaye, Sharon M.   PS3611.A918
Kazant‹s›ev, Kirill.   PG3492.52.Z364
Kean, Rob.   PS3561.E224
Keane, Christopher.   PS3561.E23
Keane, David, 1965-   none
Kearey, Charles, 1916-   PR6061.E215
Kearney, Robert.   PS3561.E2454
Kearsley, Susanna, 1966-   PR9199.3.K4112
Keating, H. R. F. (Henry Reymond Fitzwalter), PR6061.E26
1926-2011.
Keating, Henry—see: Keating, H. R. F. (Henry Reymond Fitzwalter),
1926-2011.
Keckhut, John.   PS3561.E253
Keddington, Dorothy M., 1943-   PS3561.E256
Keeble, John, 1944-   PS3561.E3
Keech, Scott.   PS3561.E333
Keegan, Alex.   PR6061.E328
Keegan, William.   PR6061.E33
Keeler, Harry Stephen, 1890-   PS3521.E265
Keeley, Edmund.   PS3561.E34
Keeling, Douglas J.   PS3561.E345
Keenan, James.   none
Keenan, Joe.   PS3561.E365
Keene, Carolyn.   PS3537.T817
Keene, Day.   PS3561.E37
Keene, Joseph E.   none
Keene, Tom.   PR6061.E42
Keener, Joyce.   none
Keenleyside, Hương.   none
Keevers, Thomas J.   PS3611.E35
Kehrer, Jürgen, 1956-   none
Keifetz, Norman.   PS3561.E3753
Keinzley, Frances, 1922-   PR6061.E45
Keitges, Julie.   none
Keith, Carlton, 1914-   PS3568.O2493
Keith, Eric, 1951-   PS3611.E368
Keizer, Gregg.   PS3611.E37
Kelby, N. M. (Nicole M.)   PS3561.E382
Kelhawk, Terry, 1955-   PS3611.E38
Kelland, Clarence Budington, 1881-1964.   PS3521.E3524
Kelleher, Ed.   none
Keller, Beverly.   PS3561.E385
Keller, Roland.   PS3561.E38576
Kelley, Nancy.   PS3611.E4434

Keller, Tsipi.	PS3611.E43
Kellerman, Faye.	PS3561.E3864
Kellerman, Jesse.	PS3561.E38648
Kellerman, Jonathan.	PS3561.E3865
Kelley, D. Ann.	PS3611.E437
Kelley, James.	none
Kelley, Karen.	PS3611.E443
Kelley, Lamar.	none
Kelley, Lee Charles.	PS3611.E4427
Kelley, Leo P.	PS3561.E388
Kelley, Norman, 1954-	PS3561.E3884
Kelley, Patrick A.	none
Kelley, William, 1929-	PS3561.E39
Kelln, Brad, 1970-	PR9199.4.K437
Kellogg, Marne Davis.	PS3561.E39253
Kelly, Bill.	none
Kelly, Clint.	PS3561.E3929
Kelly, David A. (David Andrew), 1964-	none
Kelly, Erin, 1976-	PR6111.E498
Kelly, Fred, 1926-	PS3561.E3933
Kelly, George C., 1849-1895.	none
Kelly, Gerald E.	PS3561.E3936
Kelly, Jack, 1949-	PS3561.E394
Kelly, Jane, 1949-	PS3561.E39424
Kelly, Jeffrey G.	PS3561.E39426
Kelly, Jim, 1957-	PR6111.E5
Kelly, John, 1921-	PS3561.E3944
Kelly, Lauren, 1938-	PS3565.A8
Kelly, Lelia.	PS3561.E39455
Kelly, Mary, 1927-	PR6061.E495
Kelly, Mary Anne.	PS3561.E3946
Kelly, Mitzi, 1958-	PS3611.E454
Kelly, Nora.	PS3561.E3947
Kelly, Patrick, 1917-	PR6051.L52
Kelly, Rod.	none
Kelly, Ronald, 1959-	none
Kelly, Sofie, 1958-	PS3611.E457
Kelly, Susan, 1949-	PS3561.E39715
Kelly, Susan B.	PR6061.E4965
Kelly, Terence, 1920-	PR6061.E497
Kelly, Thomas, 1961-	PS3561.E39717
Kelly, Tim J.	PS3561.E39718
Kelman, Judith.	PS3561.E39727
Kelner, Toni L. P.	PS3561.E39734
Kelton, Elmer.	PS3561.E3975
Kemal, Yaşar—see: Yaşar Kemel, 1922-	
Kemelman, Harry.	PS3561.E398
Kemp, Kenny.	PS3561.E39922
Kemp, Robert, 1908-1967.	PR6061.E533
Kemp, Sarah, 1924-1986.	PR6052.U9
Kemper, Dwight.	PS3611.E527
Kemper, Troxey, 1915-	PS3611.E527
Kempley, Walter.	PS3561.E422
Kemprecos, Paul.	PS3561.E4224

Kemske, Floyd, 1947-   PS3561.E4226
Kendall, David, 1940-   PR9199.3.K4176
Kendig, Ronie.   PS3611.E5344
Kendrick, Baynard Hardwick, 1894- none
Kendrick, Stephen, 1954-   PS3611.E54
Keneally, Thomas.   PR9619.3.K46
Kenneally, Christy.   PR6061.E595
Kennealy, G. P.   none
Kennealy, Jerry.   PS3561.E4246
Kennedy, Adam.   PS3561.E425
Kennedy, Adrienne.   PS3561.E4252
Kennedy, Conan.   PR6111.E54
Kennedy, Brian (Brian Melville), 1948- PR9199.4.K4584
Kennedy, Douglas, 1955-   PR6061.E5956
Kennedy, Ellen Edwards, 1947-   PS3611.E5587
Kennedy, Elliot.   PS3561.E4255
Kennedy, Kim.   none
Kennedy, Michael Dana.   PS3611.E57
Kennedy, Milward, b. 1894.   PR6021.E66
Kennedy, Nancy.   none
Kennedy, William, 1928-   PS3561.E428
Kennedy, William P.   PS3561.E429
Kenner, Julie.   PS3611.E665
Kenneth, Maxine.
Kennett, Shirley.   PS3561.E432
Kenney, Charles.   PS3561.E435
Kenney, Susan, 1941-   PS3561.E445
Kenny, Kathryn.   none
Kenny, Paul.   PQ2671.E58
Kenrick, Douglas M.   none
Kenrick, Tony, 1935-   PR9619.3.K49
Kenson, Stephen.   none
Kent, Alison.   PS3561.E5155
Kent, Bill, 1954-   PS3561.E516
Kent, Cameron.   PS3611.E6735
Kent, Christobel.   PR6111.E58
Kent, David, 1963-   PS3601.N455
Kent, Fortune.   PS3561.E517
Kent, Gordon.   PS3561.E5185
Kent, Graeme.   PR6061.E635
Kent, Lisa, 1942-   PS3561.E5199
Kent, Paul.   none
Kent, Trilby, 1982-   PR9199.3.K422
Kenyon, Michael.   PR6061.E675
Kenyon, Sherrilyn, 1965-   PS3563.A311145
Kenyon, T. K.   PS3611.E685
Kephart, Dean.   PS3561.E556
Kepler, Lars.   PT9877.21.E65
Kerley, Jack.   PS3611.E74
Kernahan, Coulson, 1858-1943.   PR6021.E727
Kernahan, Coulson, Mrs., 1857-1941. PR6021.E728
Kernick, Simon.   PR6111.E76
Kerr, Carole, 1935-   PR6053.A697
Kerr, James—see: Mugler, Frederick, 1923-

Kerr, M. E.	PS3561.E643
Kerr, Michael.	PR6061.E78
Kerr, Michael, 1933-	PS3558.O76
Kerr, Peter, 1940-	PR6111.E767
Kerr, Philip.	PR6061.E784
Kerr, Robert, 1899-	PS3561.E646
Kerrigan, Gene.	PR6111.E777
Kerrigan, John.	none
Kerrigan, Philip, 1959-	PR6061.E794
Kersey, Christine.	PS3611.E768
Kersh, Gerald, 1911-1968.	PR6021.E743
Kershaw, John.	PR6061.E84
Kessler, Leo, 1926-2007.	PR6061.E843
Ketchum, Jack, 1916-	PS3566.A34
Ketchum, Jack, 1946-	none
Keverne, Richard, 1882-1949.	PR6015.O7625
Key, Eileen.	PS3611.E965
Key, Sean A.	none
Keyes, Edward.	PS3561.E7694
Keyes, Frances Parkinson, 1885-1970.	PS3521.E86
Kezer, Glenn.	none
Khadra, Yasmina.	PQ3989.2.K386
Khashoggi, Soheir.	PS3561.H29
Khemir, Sabiha.	PR9408.T83
Khoury, Raymond.	PR6111.H68
Khristoforov, Igor', 1956-	PG3482.6.H747
Khrut‹s›kiĭ, Ėduard.	PG3482.6.H79
Kidd, Chip.	PS3611.I39
Kidde, Janet.	none
Kiecolt-Glaser, Janice K.	none
Kiefer, Warren, 1929-	PS3561.I34
Kieft, Raymond N.	PS3611.I398
Kiely, David M.	PR6061.I3297
Kiely, Tracy.	PS3611.I4453
Kienzle, William X.	PS3561.I35
Kiernan, Caitlín R.	PS3561.I358
Kiernan-Lewis, Susan.	PS3611.I446
Kiesling, Angela.	PS3611.I448
Kiggins, Alfred J.	PS3561.I3624
Kiger, Robert.	PS3611.I4495
Kihn, Greg.	PS3561.I363
Kijewski, Karen.	PS3561.I364
Kiker, Douglas.	PS3561.I366
Kilby, Janice Eaton, 1955-	none
Kilgore, Axel.	none
Kilgore, Evan.	PS3611.I4498
Kilgore, James William, 1947-	PS3561.I3675
Kilian, Michael, 1939-2005.	PS3561.I368
Killham, Nina.	PS3611.I45
Killian, Diana.	PS3611.I4515
Killick, Brian, 1928-	PR6061.I36
Killion, Gene.	PS3561.I385
Killoran, Geraldine.	none
Killough, Lee.	PS3561.I387

Kilmer, Nicholas. PS3561.I39
Kilpack, Josi S. PS3561.I412
Kilpatrick, Sarah. PR6061.I37
Kilroy, Claire, 1973- PR6111.I53
Kilworth, Garry. PR6061.I39
Kim, Chin-myŏng, 1957- PL992.415.C482
Kim, Don'o. PR9619.3.K53
Kim, Suki, 1970- PS3611.I457
Kim, Willyce. PS3561.I41547
Kimball, K. M. none
Kimball, Michael, 1949- PS3561.I4163
Kimberling, Nicole. PS3611.I4577
Kimberly, Alice. PS3611.I458
Kimbro, Jean, 1929- PS3561.I417
Kimbro, John M., 1929- PS3561.I417
Kimbrough, Katheryn, 1929- PS3561.I417
Kimmel, Bruce. PS3611.I4595
Kimpton, Diana. none
Kincaid, Taylor. none
Kinder, Kathleen. PR6061.I434
Kinder, R. M. (Rose Marie) PS3561.I429
Kindler, Seth. none
King, Alison, 1930- none
King, Atticus. PS3561.I4724
King, Benjamin, 1944- PS3561.I473
King, C. Daly, 1895-1963. PS3521.I514
King, Charles, 1934- PS3561.I4736
King, Christopher. none
King, Daren, 1972- none
King, Francis, 1923- PR6061.I45
King, Frank, b. 1892. none
King, Frank, 1936- PS3561.I4755
King, Graham, 1930-1999. PR9619.3.K54
PR6061.I455
King, Harold, 1945 Feb. 27- PS3561.I476
King, Irene, 1943- PS3561.I478
King, J. Robert (John Robert) PS3561.I4783
King, John, 1960- PR6061.I462
King, Jonathon. PS3611.I58
King, Katy. PS3611.I583
King, Larry, 1933- PS3561.I58335
King, Laurie R. PS3561.I4813
King, Marian Denman. PS3561.I4816
King, Pauline. PR6061.I467
King, Peter (Christopher Peter), 1922- PS3561.I4822
King, Peter T., 1944- PS3611.I584
King, Ross, 1962- PR6061.I475
King, Rufus, 1893-1966. PS3521.I5425
King, Sara. none
King, Stephen, 1947- PS3561.I483
King, Tabitha. PS3561.I4835
King, Tariq, 1983- PS3611.I5865
King, Terry Johnson. PR6061.I48
King-Wente, Sami. PS3561.I5325

Kingsbury, Kate.	PR9199.3.K44228
Kingsbury, Myra.	none
Kingsley, Bettina.	none
Kingsley, Gerry.	none
Kingsley, Johanna.	PS3561.I488
Kingsley, Michael J., 1918-1972.	PS3561.I49
Kingsley-Smith, Terence—see: Kingsley-Smith, Terry.	
Kingsley-Smith, Terry.	PS3561.I49
Kinkopf, Eric.	PS3561.I536
Kinsley, Peter.	none
Kinsman, Lawrence.	PS3561.I577
Kinyua, Kimani.	PS3611.I66
Kipling, Rudyard, 1865-1936.	PR4850-4858
	[Z8465]
Kipps, Charles.	PS3611.I68
Kirby, T. J.	none
Kirino, Natsuo, 1951-	PL855.I566
Kirk, Don.	PS3611.I75
Kirk, Lydia.	PS3561.I687
Kirk, Michael, 1928-1999.	PR6061.N6
Kirk, Philip, 1935-	none
Kirk, Russell.	PS3521.I665
Kirkbride, Ronald de Levington, 1912-	PS3521.I696
Kirkland, Martha.	PS3561.I7116
Kirkwood, James,1930-1989.	PS3561.I72
Kirkwood, Thomas.	PS3561.I74
Kirn, Walter, 1962-	PS3561.I746
Kirsch, Jonathan.	none
Kirst, Hans Hellmut, 1914-1989.	PT2621.I76
Kisor, Henry.	PS3611.I87
Kistler, Mary.	PS3561.I82
Kitakata, Kenzō.	PL855.I685
Kitchell, Jennifer A.	PS3611.I878
Kitchin, C. H. B. (Clifford Henry Benn), 1895-1967.	PR6021.I7
Kittle, Katrina.	PS3561.I864
Kittredge, Caitlin.	none
Kittredge, Mary, 1949-	PS3561.I868
Kivinov, Andreĭ.	PG3482.6.I87
Klaich, Dolores.	PS3561.L14
Klainer, Albert S.	none
Klainer, Jo-Ann.	PS3561.L15
Klasne, William, 1933-	PS3561.L245
Klausner, Lawrence D.	PS3561.L332
Klass, Perri, 1958-	PS3561.L248
Klavan, Andrew.	PS3561.L334
Klavan, Laurence.	PS3561.L3343
Klawans, Harold L.	PS3561.L336
Klein, Chuck, 1942-	PS3561.L3426
Klein, Daniel M.	PS3561.L344
Klein, Dave.	none
Klein, Dave, 1940-	PS3561.L3442
Klein, Georg, 1953-	PT2671.L4122
Klein, Jeffrey.	none
Klein, Zachary, 1948-	PS3561.L3768

Klein, Kathleen Gregory, 1946-	PS3611.L447
Kleinfeld, Lenny.	PS3611.L455
Kleinholz, Lisa.	none
Klempner, Joseph T.	PS3561.L3866
Klensch, Elsa.	PS3611.L46
Klim, Christopher, 1962-	PS3611.L555
Klimasewiski, Marshall N.	PS3611.L557
Klimova, Svetlana.	none
Kline, Christina Baker, 1964-	PS3561.L478
Kline, Suzy.	none
Kling, Christine.	PS3611.L56
Klinger, Henry.	PS3561.L5
Klingler, Erin.	PS3611.L563
Klinger, Leslie S.	PS3561.L499
Klop, Thomas.	PS3561.L635
Klose, Kevin.	PS3561.L65
Klugmann, Norbert, 1951-	PT2671.L8455
Knaak, Richard A.	PS3561.N25
Knapp, Gregory Cromwell.	PS3561.N3
Knebel, Fletcher.	PS3561.N4
Kneifl, Edith, 1954-	PT2671.N433
Knellwolf, Ulrich, 1942-	PT2671.N44
Kneubuhl, Victoria N. (Victoria Nalani)	PS3561.N418
Knickmeyer, Steve, 1944-	PS3561.N425
Knief, Charles.	PS3561.N426
Knight, Adam, 1908-1981.	PS3523.A71237
Knight, Alanna.	PR6061.N45
Knight, Bernard.	PR6113.E22
Knight, Clifford, b. 1886.	PS3521.N5335
Knight, Dakota.	PS3611.N563
Knight, Eric, 1897-1943.	PR6021.N417
Knight, Kathleen Moore.	PS3521.N5347
Knight, Kathryn Lasky.	PS3561.N485
Knight, L. A. (Leonard Alfred), b. 1895.	none
Knight, Phyllis.	PS3561.N488
Knight, Stephen, 1951-1985.	PR6061.N53
Knight, William E.	PS3561.N53
Knipe, J. A.	none
Knister, Barry.	none
Knode, Helen.	PS3611.N63
Knoerle, John.	PS3611.N635
Knoll, Anne.	none
Knopf, Chris.	PS3611.N66
Knott, Bill, 1927-	PS3561.N645
Knowler, John, 1932-	PR6061.N55
Knowles, David, 1966-	PS3561.N677
Knowlton, Edward Rogers.	none
Knox, Alexander.	PR9199.3.K58
Knox, Bill, 1928-1999.	PR6061.N6
Knox, Elizabeth.	PR9639.3.K57
Knox, Oliver.	PR6061.N63
Knox, Ronald Arbuthnott, 1888-1957.	PR6021.N6
Knox, Tom, 1963-	PR6070.H6555
Kobryn, A. P.	PS3561.O24

Koch, C. J. (Christopher J.), 1932-	PR9619.3.K64
Koch, Ed, 1924-	PS3561.O275
Koch, Eric, 1919-	PR9199.3.K6
Koehler, C. J.	PS3561.O318
Koenig, Joseph.	PS3561.O3345
Koenig, Laird.	PS3561.O335
Koenig, Sharolett.	PS3611.O364
Koestler, Arthur, 1905-1983.	PR6021.O4
Koger, Gail, 1950-	PS3611.O3655
Kohler, Sheila.	PR9369.3.K64
Kohler, Vince, 1948-2002.	PS3561.O358
Kohout, Pavel, 1928-	PG5038.K64
Koike, Mariko, 1952-	PL855.O3525
Kok, Marilyn R.	PS3561.O378
Kolarz, Henry, 1927-	PT2671.O38
Kolb, Ken.	PS3561.O39
Kolychev, Vladimir, 1968-	PG3492.56.L94
Komarnicki, Todd.	PS3561.O4523
Komo, Dolores.	PS3561.O4545
Kon, David.	none
Koning, Hans.	PS3561.O46
Konrad, James.	none
Konrath, Joe, 1970-	PS3611.O587
Konstantinov, Andreĭ.	PG3482.7.N668
Konstantinov, Vladimir, 1944-	none
Konvitz, Jeffrey.	PS3561.O53
Koontz, Dean R. (Dean Ray), 1945-	PS3561.O55
Koontz, I. Michael, 1963-	PS3611.O625
Kopf, Gail.	PS3561.O643
Koperwas, Sam.	PS3561.O64
Kopp, Nancy.	none
Kopperud, Gunnar, 1946-	PT8951.21.O45
Korda, Michael, 1933-	PS3561.O6566
Korelitz, Jean Hanff, 1961-	PS3561.O6568
Koret‹s›kiĭ, Danil.	PG3482.7.R374
Koretsky, Judy Lea.	PS3611.O74
Korkos, Alain.	PN6727.K664
Korman, Keith.	PS3561.O66
Kornbluth, C. M. (Cyril M.), 1924-1958.	PS3561.O67
Korolev, Anatoliĭ.	PG3482.7.R59439
Korotkin, Judith.	none
Korsh, Vadim.	none
Korzenko, Julie.	PS3611.O74915
Koryta, Michael.	PS3611.O749
Kosinski, Jerzy N., 1933-1991.	PS3561.O8
Koslowski, Rich.	PN6727.K665
Kosner, Alice.	none
Koster, R. M., 1934-	PS3561.O84
Kostoff, Lynn.	PS3561.O843
Kotzwinkle, William.	PS3561.O85
Kovačevski, Zoran.	PG1196.21.O9
Kovacs, Ed.	PS3611.O74943
Kowet, Don.	none
Kozak, Harley Jane, 1957-	PS3611.O75

Kozhevnikov, Vadim, 1909-1984.	PG3476.K67
Kozloff, Charles.	PS3561.O9
Krabbé, Tim.	PT5881.21.R26
Kramer, Greg, 1961-	PR9199.3.K692
Kraft, Bridget.	PS3611.R34
Kraft, Gabrielle.	none
Krajewski, Marek, 1966-	PG7170.R26
Kramer, Julie.	PS3611.R355
Kramnoĭ, Nikolaĭ.	none
Kranes, David.	PS3561.R26
Krasner, William, 1917-2003.	PS3561.R283
Kraus, Harry Lee, 1960-	PS3561.R2875
Kraus, Krandall.	PS3561.R2879
Krause, Kathalyn.	none
Kray, Kate.	PR3611.R38
Kray, Roberta.	PR6111.R39
Kreisman, Bruce.	PS3611.R443
Krentz, Jayne Ann.	PS3561.R44
Krepps, Robert W., 1919-	PS3521.R527
Kress, Nancy.	PS3561.R46
Kreuter, Katherine E., 1932-	PS3561.R4637
Kreutz, Gregg, 1947-	PS3561.R464
Krich, Rochelle Majer.	PS3561.R477
Krieg, Joyce.	PS3611.R54
Kring, Tim, 1957-	PS3611.R547
Krist, Gary.	PS3561.R565
Kristensen, Tom.	PT8952.21.R575
Kristeva, Julia, 1941-	PQ2671.R547
Kritlow, William.	PS3561.R567
Krizhanovskiĭ, Artur.	none
Kroetsch, Robert, 1927-	PR9199.3.K7
Kroll, Steven.	none
Krone, Chester.	none
Kronenwetter, Michael.	PS3611.R66
Kropp, Lloyd.	PS3561.R6
Krueger, Robert M.	PS3561.R764
Krueger, William Kent.	PS3561.R766
Kruger, Chuck, 1938-	PR6061.R79
Krüger, Hardy, 1928-	PT2671.R725
Kruger, Mary.	PS3561.R775
Kruger, Paul, 1917-	PS3537.E1884
Kruger, Rayne.	PR6061.R794
Kruger, Wolf, 1958-	none
Kubeev, Mikhail.	none
Kublicki, Nicolas M.	PS3611.U27
Kubuitsile, Lauri.	PS3611.U29
Kuhlken, Ken.	PS3561.U36
Kuhn, Krystyna, 1960-	none
Kuhns, William.	PS3561.U43
Kulikova, Galina.	PG3482.8.U446
Kullar, Amarjeet.	none
Kummer, Frederic Arnold, 1873-1943.	PS3521.U65
Kuniczak, W. S., 1930-2000.	PS3561.U5
Kunz, Kathleen.	PS3561.U58

Kunzmann, Richard.	PR6111.U59
Kunzru, Hari, 1969-	PR6111.U68
Kupfer, Fern.	PS3561.U619
Küpper, Heinz, 1930-2005.	PT2671.U36
Kuprii‹a›nov, Sergeĭ.	PG3492.58.U68
Kurata, Phillip, 1946-	PS3611.U73
Kurkov, Andreĭ.	PG3482.8.U6756
Kurland, Michael.	PS3561.U647
Kurumizawa, Kōshi, 1925-	PL855.U745
Kurzweil, Allen.	PS3561.U774
Kuttner, Henry.	PS3521.U87
Kuttner, Paul.	PS3561.U797
Kuźmińska, Małgorzata, 1982-	PG7211.U96
Kuzneski, Chris.	PS3611.U98
Kvavle, Jean P.	PS3611.V38
K'wan.	PS3606.O96
Kwitny, Jonathan.	PS3561.W54
Kyerewaa, Amma.	PR9379.9.K96
Kyle, Duncan.	PR6061.Y4
Kyle, Elisabeth, 1901-	PR6007.U554
Kyle, Sefton—see: Vickers, Roy.	
Kytle, Ray.	PS3561.Y8
La Barre, Harriet.	PS3562.A12
La Bern, Arthur J.	PR6023.A22
La Fountaine, George.	PS3562.A312
La Frenais, Ian.	none
La Plante, Jerry.	none
La Plante, Lynda.	PR6062.A65
La Plante, Richard.	PR6062.A66
La Pointe, Diane.	none
La Tourrette, Jacqueline, 1926-	PS3562.A75895
Labatt, Mary, 1944-	none
Laborde, Jean, 1918-	PQ2672.A2
Labovitz, Trudy, 1954-	PS3562.A2355
Lacefield, Lori.	PS3612.A33
Lacey, Sarah.	PR6062.A29
Lachnit, Carroll.	none
Läckberg, Camilla, 1974-	PT9877.22.A34
Lackey, Mercedes.	PS3562.A246
Lacey, Peter, 1941-	PR6062.A28
Lacy, Ed.	PS3523.A238
LaFavor, Carole, 1948-	PS3562.A27
LaFevers, R. L. (Robin L.)	none
Lafferty, Mur.	PS3612.A3743
Lafferty, Perry Francis.	PS3562.A278
Laffin, John.	none
Laflin, Jack.	none
Laforest, Serge.	PQ2672.A286
LaHaye, Tim F.	PS3562.A315
Lahey, Ed.	PS3612.A435
Laidlaw, Ross.	PR6062.A3585
Laine, Annabel.	PR6062.A359
Laird, Brian Andrew.	PS3562.A354
Laird, Thomas.	PS3562.A364

Lait, Robert.	PR6062.A37
Lake, Deryn.	PR6062.A4853
Lake, Jane.	none
Lake, M. D.	PS3562.A3777
Lake, Paul, 1951-	PS3562.A379
Lake, Peter A.	PS3562.A38
Lakeman, Thomas.	PS3612.A53
Laker, Rosalind.	PR6065.E9
Lakey, Babs, 1942-	PS3612.A54
Lakin, Rita.	PS3612.A5424
Lakritz, Esther.	PS3562.A388
Lalicki, Tom.	none
Lalos, Peter.	PS3562.A418
Lamalle, Cecile.	PS3562.A4185
Lamanda, Al.	PS3612.A5433
Lamanna, Lois.	PS3612.A5434
Lamar, Jake.	PS3562.A4216
Lamb, Antonia.	none
Lamb, Bette Golden.	PS3612.A544
Lamb, Charlotte.	PR6062.A43
Lamb, J. Dayne.	PS3562.A4227
Lamb, J. J.	PS3562.A423
Lamb, John J., 1955-	PS3612.A5457
Lamb, Joyce, 1965-	PS3612.A546
Lamb, Lynton.	PR6062.A45
Lamb, Margaret, 1936-	PS3562.A424
Lamb, Max.	none
Lamb, Robert, 1935-	PS3562.A429
Lambert, Derek, 1929-	PR6062.A47
Lambert, Eric, 1921-1966.	PR9619.3.L35
Lambert, John R., 1952-	PS3612.A54645
Lambert, Lee.	none
Lambert, Mercedes.	PS3562.A454
Lambert, Robert, 1930-	PS3562.A458
Lambirth, F. Edwin.	none
Lambkin, David, 1947-	PR6062.A4814
Lambot, Isobel, 1926-2001.	none
Lamensdorf, Leonard.	PS3562.A4635
Lamont, Stewart, 1947-	none
L'Amour, Louis, 1908-1988.	PS3523.A446
Lamport, Stephen.	none
Lampp, James W.	none
Lancaster, Bill, 1946-	PS3612.A54747
Lancaster, Graham.	PR6062.A486
Lance, Victory, 1927-	PS3562.A4668
Land, Jane.	PS3552.O754
Land, Jon.	PS3562.A469
Land, Myrick, 1922-	PS3562.A47
Landay, William.	PS3612.A5477
Landers, Gunnard.	PS3562.A4755
Landesman, Peter, 1965-	PS3562.A4762
Landgraf, Sherry.	PS3562.A4764
Landis, Jill Marie.	PS3562.A4769
Landolt, Lisa.	PS3612.A54836

Landon, Christopher.	PR6062.A497
Landon, Herman, 1882-1960.	PS3523.A53
Landreth, Marsha.	PS3562.A4774
Landrum, Graham, 1922-	PS3562.A4775
Landry, Dallari.	PS3612.A549
Lane, Andrew.	none
Lane, Andy.	none
Lane, Christopher.	none
Lane, Christopher A.	PS3562.A4842
Lane, Jim R.	PS3562.A484415
Lane, Vicki.	PS3612.A54996
Lanford, Mickey.	none
Lang, Brad.	none
Lang, Jack.	none
Lang, Maria, 1914-	PT9875.L275
Lang, Rocky.	PS3612.A5547
Langan, Mike.	PS3612.A558
Langdon, Gee, 1907-	none
Lange, John, 1942-2008.	PS3553.R48
Lange, Kelly.	PS3562.A48495
Lange, Oliver.	PS3562.A485
Lange, Richard, 1961-	PS3612.A565
Lange, Vladimir.	PS3612.A567
Langfield, Martin, 1962-	PR6112.A546
Langford, Diane.	PR6062.A5326
Langford, Ernest, 1920-	PR9199.3.L323
Langley, Bob.	PR6062.A5328
Langley, Lee, 1927-	PR6062.A535
Langley, Sarah, 1927-	PR6062.A535
Langley-Hawthorne, Clare.	PS3612.A584
Langmueller, Amalie Hedwig.	PS3562.A5124
Langton, Jane, 1922-	PS3562.A515
Langwith, Linda.	PR9199.4.L3595
Lanham, Edwin, 1904-1979.	PS3523.A612
Lanier, Virginia, 1930-2003.	PS3562.A524
Lanigan, Catherine.	PS3562.A53
Lankford, Terrill.	PS3562.A542
Lansbury, Coral.	PR9619.3.L36
Lansdale, Joe R., 1951-	PS3562.A557
Lansdale, Nina.	PS3562.A56
Lanskai⟨a⟩, Ol'ga.	PG3492.6.A57
Lantigua, John.	PS3562.A57
Lanyon, Josh.	PS3612.A588
Lapatine, Kenneth A.	PS3562.A58
Lapierre, Dominique.	PQ2672.A595
LaPierre, Janet.	PS3562.A624
Lapin, Lawrence L.	PS3612.A6437
LaPlante, Alice, 1958-	PS3612.A6438
Larabee, Kim.	PS3562.A667
Larany, Daniel.	PQ2672.A64
Lardo, Vincent.	PS3562.A7213
Largent, R. Karl.	PS3562.A7218
Lariar, Lawrence, 1908-1981.	PS3523.A71237
Larkin, E. L.	PS3562.A7238

Larkin, Patrick.	PS3612.A65
Larkin, Rochelle.	none
Larner, Celia.	PR6062.A69
Larsen, David L.	PS3612.A77
Larsen, Michael, 1961-	PT8176.22.A7155
Larson, Leslie, 1956-	PS3612.A7737
LaRocque, Paula, 1937-	PS3612.A737
LaRosa, Linda J., 1951-	PS3562.A727
Larsen, Ernest, 1946-	PS3562.A733
Larsen, Gaylord, 1932-	PS3562.A734
Larsen, Jodie.	PS3562.A736
Larsen, K. J.	PS3612.A7726
Larsen, Ward.	PS3612.A7734
Larsgaard, Chris.	PS3562.A746
Larson, Bob, 1944-	PS3562.A747
Larson, Charles.	PS3562.A75
Larson, Elyse.	PS3562.A7522235
Larson, Pete.	PS3612.A7745
Larsson, Åsa, 1966-	PT9877.22.A78
Larsson, Stieg, 1954-2004.	PT9876.22.A6933
Lartéguy, Jean, 1920-	PQ2672.A73
LaRue, Frank, 1948-	PR9199.4.L376
Lascelles, Esme.	none
Lash, Vincent.	PS3612.A82
Lash, Jennifer.	PR6062.A743
Lashley, Thomas, 1967-	PS3562.A75247
Lashner, William.	PS3562.A75249
Laski, Marghanita, 1915-1988.	PR6023.A72
Lasky, Kathryn.	PS3561.N485
Lasseter, Don.	none
Lassiter, Adam.	none
Latham, Aaron.	PS3562.A7536
Latham, Brad.	none
Latham, Lorraine.	PS3562.A7544
Lathen, Emma.	PS3562.A755
Lathrop, John.	PS3612.A87
Lathom, Francis, 1774-1832.	PR4878.L175
Latimer, John, 1937-	PR9199.3.L327
Latimer, Jonathan, 1906-1983.	PS3523.A773
Latouche, Harriet.	none
Latour, José, 1940-	PR9240.9.L38
Latt, Mimi Lavenda.	PS3562.A7598
Lauben, Philip.	PS3562.A783
Lauder, Peter, 1947-	PR6062.A778
Lauder, William.	none
Laughlin, Anne, 1955-	PS3612.A94285
Laughner, Rob, 1958-	PS3612.A943
Laumer, Keith, 1925-1993.	PS3562.A84
Launay, André, 1930-	PR6062.A785
Launay, Drew, 1930-	PR6062.A785
Laurel, C. S.	PS3612.A944226
Laurence, Janet.	PR6062.A795
Lauren, Jessica, 1965-	PS3562.A8416
Laurens, Marshall.	none

Lauria, Frank.	PS3562.A8419
Laurie, Hugh, 1959-	PR6062.A8139
Laurie, Victoria.	PS3612.A94423
Laurie-Long, E. (Ernest)	PR6023.O435
Lavender, Will, 1977-	PS3612.A94424
Lavene, Joyce.	PS3562.A8479
Lavin, Audrey A. P. (Audrey Ann Perlman)	PS3612.A9443
Lavrent'eva, Irina.	PG3483.A7932
Lavrov, Valentin.	PG3483.A797
Law, J. Patrick.	PS3562.A859
Law, Janice.	PS3562.A86
Law, Lawrence J.	PS3612.A9329
Lawhead, Steve.	PS3562.A865
Lawler, Jennifer, 1965-	PS3612.A94435
Lawrence, Alfred.	none
Lawrence, Caroline.	none
Lawrence, Cynthia.	PS3562.A9115
Lawrence, David, 1942 Dec. 9-	PR6112.A988
Lawrence, Hilda.	PS3523.A9295
Lawrence, James Duncan, 1918-	none
Lawrence, Lisa, 1970-	PR6112.A989
Lawrence, Lucy.	PS3612.A948
Lawrence, Margaret (Margaret K.)	PS3562.A9133
Lawrence, Margery, 1896-1969.	PR6023.A935
Lawrence, Martha C.	PS3562.A9135
Lawrence, Mary Margaret.	none
Lawrence, Paul Phillip.	none
Lawrence, Paul, 1963-	PR9619.4.L385
Lawrence, Ron.	none
Lawrence, Susannah.	none
Laws, Michael, 1957-	PR9639.3.L365
Laws, Stephen.	PR6062.A933
Lawson, Dorie McCullough.	PS3612.A933
Lawson, Michael, 1948-	PS3612.A934
Lawson, Mike—see: Lawson, Michael, 1948-	
Lawson, Philip.	PS3562.A945
Lawson, Steve.	none
Lawton, Blythe.	PS3562.A9522
Lawton, John, 1949-	PR6062.A938
Laxalt, Robert, 1923-2001.	PS3562.A9525
Lay, Graeme, 1944-	PR9639.3.L37
Laymon, Carl.	PS3562.A9555
Laymon, Richard.	PS3562.A9555
Layton, Clare, 1951-	PR6073.R47
Layton, Edith.	PS3562.A9595
Lazar, Aaron Paul.	PS3612.A97
Lazarus, Mell, 1927-	PS3562.A98
Lazuta, Gene.	none
Le Breton, Auguste, 1913-1999.	PQ2623.E283
Le Carré, John, 1931-	PR6062.E33
Le Fanu, Joseph Sheridan, 1814-1873.	PR4879.L7
Le Grand, Leon, 1940-	none
Le Moult, Dolph,1935-	PS3615.E474
Le Queux, William, 1864-1927.	PR6023.E75

Lea, Timothy.	none
Lea, Tom, 1907-2001.	PS3523.E1142
Leach, Christopher, 1925-	PR6062.E18
Leach, Douglas.	none
Leach, Marilyn.	PS3612.E2128
Leacock, Stephen, 1869-1944.	PR9199.3.L367
Leader, Charles, 1938-	PR6069.M53
Leader, Mary.	PS3562.E18
Leahey, Michael I.	PS3562.E215
Lear, James, 1960-	PR6069.M543
Lear, Peter.	PR6062.O86
Leasor, James.	PR6062.E24
Leather, Edwin.	PR6062.E26
Leather, Stephen.	PR6062.E27
Leather, Sue.	PR6062.E28
Leavenworth, Geoffrey.	PS3612.E24
Leavitt, Alan J.	PS3562.E2616
Leavitt, Caroline.	PS3562.E2617
Leblanc, Maurice, 1864-1941.	PQ2623.E24
LeBor, Adam.	PR6112.E26
Lecale, Errol.	none
Lecard, Marc.	PS3612.E334
LeClaire, Anne D.	PS3562.E2778
Lecomber, Brian.	PR6062.E34
Lederer, William J., 1912-2009.	PS3562.E3
Ledford, Deborah J.	none
Ledwidge, Bernard, 1915-	PR6062.E35
Ledwidge, Michael.	PS3562.E316
Lee, Adrianne.	none
Lee, Amanda, 1967-	PS3620.R4454
Lee, Ann, 1955-	PS3612.E223
Lee, Anthony, 1970-	PS3612.E3425
Lee, Barbara, 1945-	PS3562.E3323
Lee, Bernie.	PS3562.E3326
Lee, Chang-rae.	PS3562.E3347
Lee, Christopher.	none
Lee, Denis.	none
Lee, Don, 1959-	PS3562.E339
Lee, Elsie.	PS3562.E345
Lee, Henry C.	PS3612.E34287
Lee, Gypsy Rose, 1914-1970.	PS3523.E3324
Lee, Jeffrey, 1966-	PR6112.E4
Lee, Joe, 1965-	PS3612.E343
Lee, John, 1931-	PS3562.E3537
Lee, Julianne.	PS3562.E326
Lee, Linda, 1947-	PS3562.E3544
Lee, Marie, M.A.	PS3562.E35444
Lee, Maureen.	PR6062.E385
Lee, Melissa.	none
Lee, Patrick.	PR9369.4.L44
Lee, Patrick, 1976-	PS3612.E2265
Lee, Rachel.	PS3562.E3596
Lee, Rae Ellen, 1945-	PS3612.E348
Lee, Ralph V.	PS3612.E3485

Lee, Stan, 1922-	PS3562.E3648
Lee, Susan.	PS3562.E365
Lee, W. W. (Wendi W.)	PS3562.E3663
Lee, Walt.	none
Lee, Y. S. (Ying S.), 1974-	none
Leech, Audrey.	none
Leeds, Geoffrey.	none
Leek, Margaret, 1922-1985.	PR6073.O63
Leenders, Hiltrud, 1955-	none
Lees, Dan.	PR6062.E418
Lees, Harold P.	none
Leete-Hodge, Lornie.	none
Leever, Jeffrey.	PS3612.E34965
Leffingwell, Albert, 1895-1946.	PS3523.E365
Leffland, Ella.	PS3562.E375
Legaret, Jean.	PQ2623.E3849
Legendre, Thomas.	PR6112.E42
Leggett, B. J. (Bobby Joe), 1938-	PS3612.E352
Lehane, Cornelius.	PS3612.E354
Lehane, Dennis.	PS3562.E426
Lehman, Ernest, 1915-2005.	PS3562.E4283
Lehmann, R. C. (Rudolf Chambers), 1856-1929.	PR4883.L16
Lehmann-Haupt, Christopher.	PS3562.E435
Lehmkuhl, Donald.	PS3562.E437
Lehrer, James.	PS3562.E4419
Lehtolainen, Leena, 1964-	PH355.L376
Leigh, Danny, 1972-	PR6112.E43
Leigh, James, 1937-	PR6062.E445
Leigh, Lora.	PS3612.E357
Leigh, Robert, 1933-	PR6062.E4467
Leigh, Susannah.	none
Leigh, Veronica.	none
Leighton, Marie Connor, d. 1941.	PR6023.E46
Leighton, Tom.	none
Leinster, Murray, 1896-1975.	PS3519.E648
Leitch, Maurice, 1933-	PR6062.E46
Leitz, David.	none
Lejeune, Anthony.	PR6062.E465
Leland, Christopher T.	PS3562.E4637
Lelchuk, Alan.	PS3562.E464
Lelic, Simon.	PR6112.E48
Lellenberg, Jon L.	PS3612.E445
Lem, Stanisław.	PG7158.L39
Lemarchand, Elizabeth.	PR6062.E5
Lemon, Brendan.	PS3612.E47
LeMone, Charles Shea.	none
L'Engle, Madeleine.	PS3523.E55
Lengyel, Péter, 1939-	PH3281.L62
Lennon, F. J., 1964-	PS3612.E5426
Lennon, J. Robert, 1970-	PS3562.E489
Lennox, Joanne.	PR6062.E647
Lennox, Kara.	none
Lennox, Mary, 1944-	PS3612.E55
Lenton, Anthony.	none

Lentricchia, Frank.	PS3562.E4937
Leokum, Leonard.	none
Leon, Donna.	PS3562.E534
Leon, Judith, 1940-	none
Leonard, Constance.	PS3562.E54
Leonard, Elmore, 1925-	PS3562.E55
Leonard, Frank.	PS3562.E555
Leonard, George, 1946-	PS3562.E557
Leonard, Peter A.	PS3612.E5737
Leonard, Phyllis G.	PS3562.E57
Leone, Laura, 1962-	PS3568.E689
Leoni, Giulio.	PQ4912.E665
Leonov, Nikolaĭ.	PG3483.E554
Leopold, Christopher.	PR6062.E727
Leotta, Allison.	PS3612.E59
Leppard, Lois Gladys.	none
Leppart, Jerry, 1945-	PS3562.E6135
Lerner, Edward M.	PS3562.E726
Lerner, Eric.	PS3612.E69
Lerner, Richard A. (Richard Alan), 1938-	none
Leroux, Etienne.	PT6592.22.E7
Leroux, Gaston, 1868-1927.	PQ2623.E6
Leroy, Margaret.	PR6112.E765
Lescroart, John T.	PS3562.E78
Leslie, Aleen.	PS3562.E817
Leslie, John, 1944-	PS3562.E8174
Leslie, Peter, 1922-	none
Leslie-Melville, Betty.	PS3562.E83
Lester, Judy.	PR6112.E78
Lester, Julius.	PS3562.E853
Lester, Mark.	none
Lestienne, Voldemar, 1932-	PQ2672.E823
Lethem, Jonathan.	PS3562.E8544
Leto, Julie Elizabeth.	PS3612.E82885
Letton, Jennette Dowling.	PS3523.E794
Letts, Elizabeth.	PS3612.E88
Leuci, Bob, 1940-	PS3562.E857
Levack, Simon.	PR6112.E886
Levenson, Barbara.	PS3612.E9234
Leventhal, Stan, 1951-	PS3562.E8734
Levi, Peter.	PR6023.E912
Levien, David.	PS3562.E8887
Levin, Daniel, 1975-	PS3612.E92373
Levin, Donna.	PS3562.E88955
Levin, Ira.	PS3523.E7993
Levin, Lee.	PS3562.E88964
Levine, Gail Carson.	PS3562.E8965
Levine, Larry.	none
Levine, Laura, 1943-	PS3612.E924
Levine, Lawrence.	none
Levine, Michael, 1939-	PS3562.E8979
Levine, Paul (Paul J.)	PS3562.E8995
Levine, Peter, 1967-	PS3562.E8998
Levine, Robert.	none

Levinson, Paul.	PS3562.E92165
Levinson, Robert S.	PS3562.E9218
Levitin, Sonia, 1934-	none
Levitina, Nataliï‹a›.	PG3483.E8587
Levitsky, Ronald.	PS3562.E92218
Levon, Fred, 1919-	PS3562.E923
Levous, Devonnia.	PS3612.E9367
Levy, Barbara.	PS3562.E925
Levy, Bob, 1953-	PS3562.E9249
Levy, D. Lawrence.	PS3562.E926
Levy, Elizabeth, 1942-	none
Levy, Harry, 1944-	PS3562.E92717
Levy, Joseph.	none
Lewbart, Greg.	PS3562.E92782
Lewin, Elsa.	none
Lewin, Jackie.	PS3562.E92796
Lewin, Leonard C.	PS3562.E928
Lewin, Michael Z.	PS3562.E929
Lewin, Patricia.	PS3612.E957
Lewis, Andre, 1974-	PS3612.E962
Lewis, Arthur H., 1906-	PS3562.E937
Lewis, C. Jack.	PS3612.E963
Lewis, Canella.	none
Lewis, Catherine, 1956-	PS3562.E9385
Lewis, Colin.	none
Lewis, Craig A., 1955-	none
Lewis, David.	none
Lewis, Deborah.	none
Lewis, Elliott.	none
Lewis, Heather.	PS3562.E9453
Lewis, Jack, 1924-2009.	PS3562.E9468
Lewis, James.	none
Lewis, James Wm.	none
Lewis, June R.—see: Lewis-Jones, June R.	
Lewis, Lange.	PS3503.E97
Lewis, Margo.	none
Lewis, Norman.	PR6062.E948
Lewis, Pam, 1943-	PS3612.E974
Lewis, Peter, 1952-	PS3612.E9745
Lewis, Richard.	none
Lewis, Ronald J.	PS3562.E9734
Lewis, Roy, 1933-	PR6062.E954
Lewis, Roy Harley.	PR6062.E9543
Lewis, Sherry.	none
Lewis, Simon, 1971-	PR6062.E95454
Lewis, Stephen.	PS3562.E9754
Lewis, Stephen, 1942-	PS3562.E9755
Lewis, Susan.	PS3611.I446
Lewis, Susan, 1956-	PR6062.E9546
Lewis, Ted, 1940-1982.	PR6062.E955
Lewis, Terry, 1951-	PS3562.E9765
Lewis, Tom, 1940-	PS3562.E977
Lewis, William.	PS3562.E984
Lewis-Jones, June R.	PR6062.E944

Lewitt, S. N.	none
Lewton, J. V.	none
Ley, Alice Chetwynd.	PR6062.E965
Leyton, Patrick.	none
L'Heureux, Maurice.	none
Li, Bihua.	PL2877.P48
Liang, Diane Wei, 1966-	PS3612.I224
Lichtenberg, Fred.	PS3612.I2465
Lichtman, Charles H., 1955-	PS3562.I322
Liddy, G. Gordon.	PS3562.I34
Lieber, Julia.	PS3612.I33
Lieberman, Herbert H., 1933-	PS3562.I4
Lieberman, Robert.	PS3562.I44
Liebling, Howard.	PS3562.I45
Lienau, R. M. (Richard M.)	PS3562.I4533
Lientz, Gerald.	none
Lier, Stein Morton, 1967-	none
Liesche, Margit.	PS3612.I3355
Liffner, Eva-Marie.	PT9877.22.I34
Lifson, David S.	PS3562.I4538
Liggett, Hunter, 1916-	PS3566.A34
Light, Don.	PS3612.I344
Lilley, Kathryn	PS3612.I4225
Lilley, Tom.	PR6062.I36
Lillie, Helen.	PR6062.I37
Lilliefors, Jim, 1955-	PS3562.I4573
Lim, Rebecca.	none
Lima, Joel.	PS3562.I4624
Lima, Maria Y.	PS3612.I47
Limón, Martin, 1948-	PS3562.I465
Lin, Ed.	PS3562.I4677
Lin, Francie.	PS3612.I497
Linakis, Steven, 1923-	PS3562.I47
Linares, Luisa-María	PQ6621.I33
Lincoln, Natalie Sumner, 1881-1935.	PS3523.I48
Lind, Hailey.	PS3612.I5326
Lindall, Edward, 1915-	PR9619.3.L475
Linden, Catherine.	none
Linder, Mark.	PS3562.I51116
Linderman, Frank Bird, 1869-1938.	PS3523.I535
Lindley, Erica.	PR6062.I466
Lindop, Audrey Erskine, 1920-	PR6062.I47
Lindquist, Donald.	PS3562.I5116
Lindquist, N. J. (Nancy J.)	PS3562.I51166
Lindsay, Douglas, 1964-	none
Lindsay, Frederic.	PR6062.I484
Lindsay, Jeffry P.	PS3562.I51175
Lindsay, Joan Weigall, Lady.	PR9619.3.L49
Lindsay, Kathleen.	none
Lindsay, Paul, 1943-	PS3562.I511915
Lindsay, Tony, 1959-	PS3562.I511922
Lindsey, David L.	PS3562.I51193
Lindsey, Dawn.	PS3562.I51194
Linington, Elizabeth.	PS3562.I515

Link, Charlotte.	PT2672.I515
Link, William.	PS3562.I52
Linn, Edward.	PS3562.I54
Linscott, Gillian.	PR6062.I54
Linsley, Clyde.	PS3562.I5517
Linz, Cathie.	PS3562.I558
Linzee, David, 1952-	PS3562.I56
Linzner, Gordon, 1949-	PS3562.I565
Liparulo, Robert.	PS3612.I63
Lipez, Richard, 1938-	PS3562.I57
Lipinski, Thomas.	PS3562.I574
Lippincott, Beverly.	none
Lippincott, David.	PS3562.I58
Lippman, Laura, 1959-	PS3562.I586
Lipsyte, Marjorie, 1932-	PS3562.I63
Lira, Gonzalo.	PS3562.I68
Lisle, Holly.	PS3562.I775
Liss, David, 1966-	PS3562.I7814
Lister, Michael.	PS3562.I78213
Liston, Robert A.	none
Litman, Viqui.	PS3562.I78246
Litt, Toby, 1968-	PR6062.I827
Littell, Blaine.	PS3562.I7825
Littell, Robert, 1935-	PS3562.I7827
Little, Christine C.	PS3612.I875
Little, Constance.	PS3523.I827
Little, Eddie.	PS3562.I78279
Little, Gwenyth.	none
Littlefield, Sophie.	PS3612.I882
Littlepage, Layne.	PS3562.I786
Littlewood, Ann.	PS3612.I8827
Litvinoff, Emanuel.	PR6023.I7
Litvinoff, Ivy.	PR6023.I73
Litvinova, Anna.	PG3492.6.I88
Litwak, Leo, 1924-	PS3562.I79
Litzinger, Boyd.	PS3562.I795
Liu, Aimee.	PS3562.I797
Liu, Marjorie M.	PS3612.I93
Livesay, Ann, 1923-	PS3562.I856
Livingston, Armstrong, b. 1885.	PS3523.I942
Livingston, Georgette.	PS3562.I933
Livingston, Jack, 1925-	PS3562.I937
Livingston, Joyce.	PS3562.I9435
Livingston, M. Jay.	PS3562.I944
Livingston, Nancy.	PR6062.I915
Livingstone, J. B.	none
Llewellyn, Caroline.	PR9199.3.L568
Llewellyn, John R.	PS3562.L673
Llewellyn, Richard.	PR6023.L47
Llewellyn, Sam, 1948-	PR6062.L39
Llewelyn, Gwyn.	PB2298.L55
Lloyd, A.	none
Lloyd, Elizabeth.	none
Lloyd, MacDonald, 1953-	PS3573.I5326

Lochte, Dick. PS3562.O217
Locke, Attica. PS3612.O247
Locke, Thomas. PS3562.O236
Lockridge, Frances Louise Davis. PS3523.O243
Lockridge, Richard, 1898-1982. PS3523.O245
Lockwood, Ethel. none
Lockwood, Mary, 1934- PS3562.O28
Loder, Vernon, b. 1881. PR6043.A33
Lodge, Marc. PS3562.O32
Loehfelm, Bill. PS3612.O36
Lofts, Norah, 1904-1983. PR6023.O35
Logan, Don. none
Logan, Chuck, 1942- PS3562.O4453
Logan, Jake. PS3562.O446
Logan, Margaret, 1936- PS3562.O4478
Logue, John, 1933- PS3562.O454
Logue, Mary. PS3562.O456
Loh, Frank Chan. PR9619.3.L6167
Loker, Aleck. PS3612.O43
Lombardi, Linda, 1961- PS3612.O44
London, Cait. none
London, Jack, 1876-1916. PS3523.O46
[Z8514.6]
Lonergan, Kenneth. PS3562.O4886
Long, Amelia Reynolds, 1904-1978. PS3523.O462
Long, Christopher E. none
Long, David Ryan. PS3562.O4926
Long, Dustin, 1977- PS3612.O493
Long, Ernest Laurie—see: Laurie-Long, E.
(Ernest)
Long, Frank Belknap, 1903- PS3523.O465
Long, Freda Margaret. PR6062.O512
Long, Jeff. PS3562.O4943
Long, John Arthur. none
Long, Lyda Belknap. none
Long, Lydia Belknap—see: Long, Lyda Belknap.
Long, Manning, 1906- PS3523.O4725
Long, Patrick. none
Longfellow, Ki, 1944- PS3562.O499
Longmate, Norman, 1925- PR6062.O5155
Longrigg, Roger, 1929-2000. PR6062.O516
Longstreet, Roxanne. none
Longstreet, Stephen, 1907-2002. PS3523.O486
Longworth, Gay. PR6112.O54
Longworth, M. L. (Mary Lou), 1963- PR9199.4.L596
Lonsdale, Harry Paul, 1934-2009. PS3560.E36
Loomis, Jon. PS3562.O593
Lopez, Steve. PS3562.O673
Lorac, E. C. R., 1894-1958. PR6035.I9
Loraine, Philip. PR6062.O67
Lord, Diana. none
Lord, Gabrielle. PR9619.3.L63
Lord, Graham, 1943- PR6062.O72
Lord, J. Edward. none

Lord, Shirley.	PR6062.O724
Lordahl, Jo Ann.	none
Lordon, Randye.	PS3562.O7524
Lore, Phillips—see: Smith, Terrence Lore.	
Lorena.	none
Lorens, M. K.	PS3562.O7525
Loring, Ann.	none
Loring, Emilie Baker.	PS3523.O645
Lorne, David.	none
Lorrah, Jean.	PS3562.O767
Lorrimer, Claire.	PR6062.O77
Lory, Robert.	PS3562.O78
Lott, Bret.	PS3562.O784
Lottman, Eileen.	PS3562.O79
Loughran, Rob.	PS3612.O7856
Louis, Joseph.	none
Louis, Mary-Ben,1919-	none
Lourenco, J. A., 1955-	PS3612.O83
Lourey, Jess, 1970-	PS3612.O833
Lourie, Richard, 1940-	PS3562.O833
Love, C. J.	PS3612.O83385
Love, Edmund G.	PS3562.O84
Love, Kathy.	PS3612.O834
Love, William F.	PS3562.O848
Lovegrove, Peter.	none
Lovejoy, William H.	PS3562.O855
Lovelace, Merline.	PS3612.O835
Loveless, Dashiell.	PS3562.O8615
Lovell, Glenville, 1955-	PS3562.O8624
Lovell, Marc.	PR6062.O853
Lovell, Ronald P.	PS3612.O84
Lovesey, Peter.	PR6062.O86
Lovesey, Phil.	none
Lovett, Charles C.	PS3612.O86
Lovett, Sarah (Sarah Poland)	PS3562.O873
Lowden, Desmond.	PR6062.O88
Lowe, Jonathan, 1953-	PS3562.O8816
Lowe, Sheila R.	PS3612.O886
Lowe, Steve.	PS3562.0884
Lowe, Tom, 1952-	PS3562.O88423
Loweecey, Alice.	PS3612.O8865
Lowell, Elizabeth, 1944-	PS3562.O8847
Lowell, J. R.	PS3562.O885
Lowell, Virginia.	PS3612.O888
Lowing, Anne.	PR6062.O92
Lowndes, Marie Belloc, 1868-1947.	PR6023.O95
Lowry, Rich.	PS3612.O93
Luard, Nicholas.	PR6062.U12
Lubar, David.	none
Luber, Philip.	PS3562.U22
Lucarelli, Carlo, 1960-	PQ4872.U255
Lucarotti, John.	none
Lucas, Frances, 1956-	PS3562.U2337
Lucas, J. K., 1916-	PS3566.A34

Lucas, Nick, 1955-   PS3612.U245
Luce, Helen.   PR6062.U16
Luck, John, 1928-   PS3612.U257
Lucke, Margaret.   PS3562.U2547
Luckett, Jonathan.   PS3612.U26
Luckless, John.   PS3562.U255
Ludlum, Robert, 1927-2001.   PS3562.U26
Ludwig, Dale.   none
Ludwig, Elizabeth.   PS3612.U33
Ludwig, Jerry.   PS3562.U29
Ludwig, Ken.   PS3562.U295
Luibhéid, Colm.   PR6112.U36
Luiken, N. M.   PR9199.3.L83
Lukas, Susan Ries.   PS3562.U45
Lukasik, Gail.   PS3612.U385
Luke, Gregg R.   PS3612.U43
Luke, Thomas.   PR6063.A834
Luna, Louisa.   PS3612.U53
Luna, Rachel Nickerson.   none
Lund, James.   PR6062.U47
Lundy, Mike.   PS3562.U58
Lungu, Dan, 1969-   PC840.422.U548
Lupica, Mike.   PS3562.U59
Lupoff, Richard A., 1935-   PS3562.U6
Lupton, Rosamund.   PR6112.U77
Lusby, Jim.   PR6062.U73
Lustbader, Eric.   PS3562.U752
Lustgarten, Edgar, 1907-1978.   PR6023.U73
Luttrell, Wanda.   PS3562.U7885
Lutz, John, 1939-   PS3562.U854
Lutz, Lisa.   PS3612.U897
Lutz, Raymond Clark.   PS3612.U899
Lyall, Francis.   PR6062.Y29
Lyall, Gavin.   PR6062.Y3
Lyday, David Paul.   none
Lydecker, J. J.   PR6062.Y37
Lyle, D. P.   PS3612.Y43
Lymington, John.   PR6062.Y53
Lynch, Frances, 1930-   PR6062.Y58
Lynch, Jack, 1930-2008.   none
Lynch, Lawrence L.   PS3114.V78
Lynch, Lee, 1945-   PS3562.Y426
Lynch, Miriam.   PS3562.Y434
Lynch, Patrick.   PR6062.Y596
Lynde, Stan, 1931-   PS3562.Y439
Lynds, Dennis, 1924-2005.   PS3562.Y44
Lynds, Gayle.   PS3562.Y442
Lynn, Allison.   PS3612.Y544
Lynn, Jack, 1927-   PS3562.Y444
Lynn, Jackie.   PS3612.Y547
Lynn, Margaret, 1915-   PR6052.A83
Lynn, Mary Elizabeth.   PS3562.Y44475
Lynn, Matt—see: Lynn, Matthew.
Lynn, Matthew.   PR6112.Y56

Lynne, James Broom.   PR6062.Y62
Lynxwiler, Christine.   PS3612.Y554
Lyon, Bentley.   PS3562.Y44487
Lyon, Jack M.   PS3612.Y559
Lyon, Mabel Dana, 1897-1982.   PS3523.Y753
Lyons, Andrew.   PS3612.Y57
Lyons, Arthur.   PS3562.Y446
Lyons, Cat.   PS3562.Y4482
Lyons, CJ, 1964-   PS3612.Y573
Lyons, Delphine C.   none
Lyons, Elena, 1928-   PR6056.A49
Lyons, Genevieve.   PR6062.Y627
Lyons, Ivan.   none
Lyons, Kate, 1965-   PR6112.Y66
Lyons, Nan.   PS3562.Y449
Lyons, Richard, 1935-   PS3562.Y44938
Lysaght, Brian.   PS3562.Y4498
Lytton, Edward Bulwer Lytton, Baron, 1803-1873.   PR4900-4948
Maas, Peter, 1929-2001.   PS3563.A2
Maas, Virginia H.   none
Maberry, Jonathan.   PS3613.A19
Mabey, Martha.   PS3563.A2226
Mabry, Richard L.   PS3613.A2
Mac Confhaola, Colm.   PB1399.M1449
Macadam, Heather Dune.   PS3613.A22
MacAlan, Peter.   none
MacAlister, Ian, 1924-   PS3551.L26
MacAlister, V. A.   PS3613.A23
MacAndrew, Richard.   PR6113.A23
Macao, Marshall.   none
Macartney-Filgate, Terence.   PR6063.A1188
MacBain, Bruce.   PS3613.A246
MacBeth, George.   PR6063.A13
MacBride, Stuart.   PR6113.A24
Maccabee, John.   none
MacCargo, J. T.   none
MacColl, Mary-Rose, 1961-   PR9619.3.M23
MacDonald, Ann-Marie, 1958-   PR9199.3.M2985
MacDonald, Donald.   none
Macdonald, Elisabeth, 1926-   PS3563.A2767
MacDonald, Hugh, 1945-   PR9199.3.M2513
MacDonald, Janice E. (Janice Elva), 1959-   PR9199.4.M3228
MacDonald, John D. (John Dann), 1916-1986.   PS3563.A28
                                                          [Z8532.383]
Macdonald, John Ross, 1915-1983.   PS3525.I486
MacDonald, Marianne.   PR6063.A16915
MacDonald, Patricia J.   PS3563.A287
MacDonald, Philip.   PR6025.A2218
Macdonald, Ross, 1915-1983.   PS3525.I486
                                                          [Z8532.386]
MacDonald, William Colt, 1891-1968.   PS3525.A2122
MacDonnell, Julia.   PS3563.A29142
MacDougal, Bonnie.   PS3563.A2917
MacDougall, James K.   PS3563.A2918

MacDougall, Ruth Doan, 1939-	PS3563.A292
MacDowell, Rose.	PS3613.A27147
MacElravy, R. Charles.	PS3613.A2719
MacEnulty, Pat.	PS3613.A272
MacGill-Callahan, Sheila.	PS3563.A29825
MacGowan, Jonathan.	none
MacGrath, Harold, 1871-1932.	PS3525.A2423
MacGregor, Bill.	none
Macgregor, James Murdoch.	PR6063.A234
MacGregor, T. J.	PS3563.A31115
MacHardy, Charles.	PR6063.A235
Machin, Meredith Land.	PS3563.A31155
Macias, Kathi, 1948-	PS3563.I42319
Macidull, John C.	PS3613.A272535
MacInerney, Karen, 1970-	PS3613.A27254
MacInnes, Hamish.	none
MacInnes, Helen, 1907-1985.	PS3525.A24573
Macintyre, Rebbie.	PS3613.A272543
MacIsaac, Frederick John, 1886-1940.	none
MacIvers, Donald.	none
MacIvers, Sarah.	none
Mack, Carol K.	PS3563.A3126
Mack, David, 1969-	PS3613.A272545
MacKay, Alistair McColl.	none
Mackay, Amanda.	PS3563.A31335
MacKay, Scott, 1957-	PR9199.3.M3239
Mackel, Kathryn, 1950-	PS3613.A2734
MacKellar, Sinclair.	none
MacKenzie, Donald, 1918-	PR9199.3.M325
Mackenzie, Ian.	PS3613.A27259
Mackenzie, Jassy.	PR9369.4.M335
MacKenzie, Nigel.	none
Mackenzie-Lamb, Eric.	PS3563.A31356
MacKersey, Ian.	none
Mackesy, Serena.	PR6063.A2438
Mackey, Mary.	PS3563.A3165
Mackie, John, 1935-	none
MacKinnon, Allan.	PR6025.A25465
MacKinnon, Amy.	PS3613.A27346
MacKinnon, Colin.	PS3563.A3176
Mackintosh, Ian.	PR6063.A24635
Mackintosh, May.	PR6063.A2464
Mackle, Elliott J. (Elliot James), 1940-	PS3613.A273
MacLane, Jack, 1941-	PS3553.R497
Maclaren, Angus.	PS3558.A44825
Maclaren, Deanna, 1944-	PR6063.A2473
MacLarty, Jay.	none
Maclay, John.	PS3563.A317972
MacLean, Alistair, 1922-1987.	PR6063.A248
Maclean, Anna.	PS3563.A3169
MacLean, Jane.	PS3563.A317983
MacLean, Julia.	PR9199.3.M3316
MacLean, Katherine.	PS3563.A31799
MacLean, Kenneth D.	PR3563.A23

MacLeish, Roderick, 1926-2006.	PS3563.A3183
MacLeod, Charlotte.	PS3563.A31865
MacLeod, Ken.	PR6063.A2515
MacLeod, Maggie, 1935-	PS3613.A274
MacLeod, Robert, 1928-1999.	PR6061.N6
MacLeod, Ruth.	PS3563.A31873
MacManus, Yvonne.	PS3563.A31885
MacMillan, Ian T.	PS3563.A318955
MacNeal, Susan Elia.	PS3613.A2774
Macnee, Patrick, 1922-	PR6063.A2577
MacNeil, Duncan, 1920-	PR6063.A167
MacNeil, Neil, 1903-1980.	PS3503.A5575
Macomber, Daria.	PS3563.A3235
Macomber, Debbie.	PS3563.A2364
Macomber, Doc.	PS3613.A278
Macomber, James.	PS3563.A3236
Macomber, Robert N., 1953-	PS3613.A28
Macpherson, Colin.	PR9619.3.M217
MacPherson, Malcolm.	PS3563.A3254
Macpherson, Colin.	PR9619.3.M217
MacPherson, Rett.	PS3563.A3257
Macquet, Claire.	PR9369.3.M3344
MacQuigg, Donna.	PS3613.A283
MacRae, Molly.	PS3613.A2833
MacVicar, Angus, 1908-2001.	PR6025.A34
Madden, David, 1933-	PS3563.A339
Madden, Gary, 1967-	PS3613.A28348
Madden, Thomas J. (Thomas James)	PS3563.A33926
Madderom, Gary.	PS3563.A3394
Madison, Bennett.	none
Maddison, Lauren.	PS3563.A33942
Maddock, Stephen—see: Walsh, J. M. (James Morgan), 1897-1952.	
Maddren, Gerry.	PS3563.A33947
Madinger, John.	PS3613.A28445
Madsen, Axel.	PS3563.A343
Madsen, David, 1929-	PS3563.A344
Madsen, Diane Gilbert.	PS3613.A289
Maffini, Mary Jane.	PR9199.4.M3275
Magali, pseud.	PQ2625.A63
Magandaazi, Simon Peter, 1956-	none
Magdalen, I. I.	PR6063.A326
Magee, Doug, 1947-	PS3613.A3425
Magee, James, 1969-	PS3613.A3427
Maggio, Joe.	PS3563.A345
Magnan, Pierre, 1922-	PQ2625.A637
Magnay, William, Sir, 1855-1917.	PR6025.A366
Magnuson, James.	PS3563.A352
Magnuson, Teodore.	PS3563.A3523
Magowan, Ronald.	PR6063.A33
Magruder, Owen, 1931-	PS3563.A35275
Magson, Adrian.	PR6113.A3356
Maguire, Eden.	none
Maguire, Michael, 1945-	PR6063.A332
Maher, Frank J.	none

Maher, Mary.	PS3563.A358
Mahetā, Yaśavanta, 1938-	PK1859.M474
Mahmood, Abdulhameed, 1975-	PR9387.9.M295
Mahon, Annette.	PS3563.A3595
Mahoney, Dan.	PS3563.A364
Mahoney, Gene, 1923-	none
Mai, Denyse.	PQ2673.A35
Maier, Paul L.	PS3563.A382
Maifair, Linda Lee.	none
Mail, Michael, 1959-	PR6113.A34
Mailer, Norman.	PS3525.A4152
Maiman, Jaye, 1957-	PS3563.A38266
Maimane, Arthur, 1932-	PR9369.3.M34
Main, Elizabeth C.	PS3613.A34935
Main, Gregg.	PS3563.A382668
Maines, Bethany.	PS3613.A34964
Mainwaring, Daniel, 1902-1977.	PS3525.A4157
Mainwaring, Marion.	PS3563.A383
Mainwaring, Michael.	none
Mair, Alistair.	PR6063.A347
Mair, George Brown.	PR6063.A3475
Maitland, Barry.	PR9619.3.M2635
Maitland, Karen.	PR6113.A35
Majerus, Janet, 1936-	PS3563.A38763
Major, Clarence.	PS3563.A39
Majzels, Robert, 1950-	PR9199.3.M3456
Makins, Clifford, 1925-	none
Malarkey, Tucker.	PS3563.A424
Malashenko, A. V. (Alekseĭ Vsevolodovich)	PG3483.2.L338
Malcolm, Jahnna N.	none
Malcolm, John, 1936-	PR6063.A362
Malcolm, M. L.	PS3613.A433
Malcolm, Margaret.	PR6063.A363
Malcolmson, David, 1899-1970.	PS3563.A426
Malcolm-Smith, George.	PS3525.A4355
Maleeny, Tim, 1962-	PS3613.A4353
Maley, Alan, 1937-	PR6063.A364
Malfi, Ronald Damien.	PS3613.A4355
Malicki, Maciej.	PG7213.A45
Maling, Arthur.	PS3563.A4313
Mallanson, Todd.	none
Mallary, Amos.	none
Mallery, Susan.	PS3613.A453
Mallet, Jacqueline.	PR6063.A3657
Mallett, Richard.	PR6063.A3658
Mallette, Gloria, 1953-	PS3563.A4315
Malliet, G. M., 1951-	PS3613.A4535
Mallo, Ernesto, 1948-	PQ7798.423.A443
Malloch, Peter, 1909-1975.	PR6007.U535
Mallon, Jim.	PS3563.A43156
Mallory, Drew.	PS3563.A4316
Mallory, Kate.	PS3563.A43166
Mallory, Peter.	none
Mallory, Roosevelt.	none

Malloy, Mary, 1955-	PS3613.A455
Malm, Dorothea.	PS3525.A4568
Malmont, Valerie S.	PS3563.A43184
Malmquist, K. L.	PS3563.A43187
Malone, L. K., 1959-	PS3613.A464
Malone, Michael, 1942-	PS3563.A43244
Maloney, J. J., 1940-	PS3563.A4329
Maloney, Mack.	none
Maloney, Ralph.	PS3563.A433
Maloney, Shane, 1953-	PR9619.3.M2645
Malte, Marcus.	PQ2673.A4337
Maltz, Albert, 1908-1985.	PS3525.A49
Malysheva, Anna.	PG3483.2.L983
Malzberg, Barry N.	PS3563.A434
Mamalis, George.	none
Manchee, William.	PS3563.A43497
Manchester, Ivy.	none
Mancini, Anthony.	PS3563.A4354
Mandé, Elizabeth Erin.	none
Mandel, Steven B.	PS3613.A5295
Mandelkau, Jamie.	none
Mandelman, Avner.	PR9199.3.M34814
Mandelsberg, Rose G.	none
Mander, Christine, 1935-	PR9199.3.M34815
Mandeville, Colin.	PS3563.A4639
Mandeville, D. E.	none
Mandeville, Merivel.	PS3613.A5366
Mandino, Og.	PS3563.A464
Maner, William.	PS3563.A465
Maness, Larry.	PS3563.A4655
Maney, Mabel, 1958-	PS3563.A466
Manfredo, Lou.	PS3613.A5368
Mangat Rai, E. N. (Edward Nirmal), 1915-	PR9499.3.M35
Mangum, James A.	PS3613.A5375
Manicom, David, 1960-	PR9199.3.M3485
Mankell, Henning, 1948-	PT9876.23.A49
Mankiewicz, Don M., 1922-	none
Mankowitz, Wolf.	PR6025.A4755
Manktelow, Bettine.	PR6063.A3736
Manley, Mark.	none
Mann, Abby.	PS3563.A534
Mann, Anthony, 1914-	PR6063.A3737
Mann, Edward Andrew.	PS3563.A5355
Mann, George.	PR6113.A546
Mann, Jack.	PR6043.I9
Mann, Jessica.	PR6063.A374
Mann, Josephine.	none
Mann, Linda, 1959-	PR6113.A55
Mann, Patrick, 1923-2007.	PS3545.A565
Mann, Paul, 1947-	PS3563.A53623
Mann, Peter.	none
Mann, Roderick, 1922-	PR6063.A375
Mann, William J.	PS3563.A53629
Mannel, Beatrix.	none

Manners, Alexandra.	PR6068.U7
Mannin, Ethel, 1900-1984.	PR6025.A477
Manning, James C.	PS3563.A5367
Manning, Jo, 1940-	PS3613.A564
Manning, Mary.	PR6025.A498
Mannion, John B.	none
Manno, Mike, 1949-	PS3613.A568
Manor, Jason.	PS3558.A373
Mansfield, Elizabeth.	none
Manso, Peter.	none
Manson, Cynthia.	none
Mantel, Hilary, 1952-	PR6063.A438
Mantell, Laurie.	PR9639.3.M264
Manthorne, Jackie, 1946-	PR9199.3.M3495
Manthoulēs, Rovēros.	PA5624.A6
Manuel, David.	PS3563.A5747
Manus, Peter.	PS3613.A584
Manville, William H. (William Henry), 1930-	PS3563.A58
Manzi, Warren.	PS3563.A585
Mapes, Creston, 1961-	PS3613.A63
Maples, Jerry, 1939-	PS3613.A66
Mara, Wil.	PS3613.A725
Maracotta, Lindsay.	PS3563.A6225
Marais, Marc.	none
Marasco, Robert.	PS3563.A63
Marberg, Peg.	PS3613.A728
March, Hannah.	PR6063.A617
March, Lindsay.	PS3563.A633
March, William, 1893-1954.	PS3505.A53157 [Z8549.8]
Marchant, Catherine.	PR6053.O525
Marchant, Herbert.	none
Marchant, William, 1923-	PS3525.A584
Marchetta, Melina, 1965-	none
Marchetti, Victor.	PS3563.A635
Marchmont, Arthur William, 1852-1923.	PR6025.A612
Marcinko, Richard.	PS3563.A6362
Marcos, subcomandante.	PQ7298.23.A642
Marcott, James.	none
Marcoux, Alex.	PS3563.A6365
Marcum, Robert.	PS3563.A6368
Marcus, Jerry.	PS3563.A6387
Marcus, Joanna.	PR6051.N4654
Marcus, Morton.	PS3563.A639
Marcuse, Irene, 1953-	PS3563.A6433
Marcy, Jean.	PS3563.A6435
Margolin, Leslie, 1945-	PS3613.A74
Margolin, Phillip.	PS3563.A649
Margolis, Seth Jacob.	PS3563.A652
Margos, J. F.	PS3613.A743
Margoshes, Dave.	PR9199.3.M354
Mariani, Scott.	PR6113.A745
Marías, Javier.	PQ6663.A7218
Marie, Jeanne.	none

Mariel, Anne—see: Anne-Mariel, 1907-	
Marin, A. C., 1921-	PS3553.O64
Marinello, Lorelle.	PS3613.A7482
Mariner, David, 1920-	none
Marinick, Richard, 1951-	PS3613.A7484
Marinina, Aleksandra.	PG3483.2.R535
Marino, James.	none
Mariotte, Jeff.	PS3613.A7523
Maristed, Kai.	PS3563.A6597
Mariz, Linda, 1948-	none
Mark, Alane.	PS3563.A662
Mark, Norman.	PS3613.A7537
Markaris, Petros, 1937-	PA5624.A713
Markham, Q. R.	PS3613.A7542
Markham, Robert, 1922-1995.	PR6001.M6
Marklund, Liza, 1962-	PT9876.23.A653
Markowitz, Jeff.	PS3613.A7544
Marks, Alan.	none
Marks, Bridget.	PS3613.A7545
Marks, Erika.	PS3613.A754525
Marks, John, 1963-	PS3563.A66655
Marks, Lander.	PS3613.A764
Marks, Peter.	PS3563.A667
Marks, Tinker.	PS3613.A7656
Marks, Walter.	PS3563.A669
Markson, David.	PS3563.A67
Markstein, George.	PR6063.A644
Marler, Michael.	none
Marlett, Melba, 1909-	PS3525.A66665
Marlow, Edwina.	PS3558.U323
Marlow, John Robert.	PS3613.A766
Marlow, Terry.	PS3563.A67375
Marlow, Vanessa, 1954-	PS3558.O3954
Marlowe, Ann.	PS3563.A6739
Marlowe, Dan J., 1914-1987.	PS3563.A67395
Marlowe, Derek.	PR6063.A655
Marlowe, Hugh, 1929-	PR6058.I343
Marlowe, Katharine.	PR9199.3.M365
Marlowe, Stephen, 1928-2008.	PS3563.A674
Maron, Margaret.	PS3563.A679
Marquand, John P. (John Phillips), 1893-1960.	PS3525.A6695
Marquis, Max.	PR6063.A6559
Marr, John S.	PS3563.A7113
Marric, J. J.—see: Creasey, John or Butler, William Vivian, 1927-	
Marrin, Minette.	PR6063.A6568
Marriner, Brian.	none
Marriott, Michel.	PS3613.A7693
Mars, Peter.	PS3563.A7135
Marsella, Celeste.	PS3613.A7697
Marsh, Geoffrey, 1912-	PS3563.A7145
Marsh, James J.	PS3563.A715
Marsh, John, 1907-1997.	PR6062.A877
Marsh, Ngaio, 1895-1982.	PR9639.3.M27
Marsh, Patrick—see: Hiscock, Leslie, 1902-	

Marsh, Richard, d. 1915.	PR6025.A645
Marsh, Rob.	PR9369.4.M37
Marsh, Robert W.	none
Marshall, Bruce, 1899-1987.	PR6025.A654
Marshall, Dagmar.	PS3613.A773
Marshall, Evan, 1956-	PS3563.A72236
Marshall, James Vance, 1924-	PR6066.A9
Marshall, Joanne.	PR6068.U7
Marshall, Lovat, 1909-1975.	PR6007.U535
Marshall, Mel, 1911-	PS3525.A7276
Marshall, Michael, 1965 May 3-	PR6069.M5225
Marshall, William Leonard, 1944-	PR9619.3.M275
Marsland, Amy Louise.	PS3563.A7226
Marsoli, Lisa Ann, 1958-	PS3563.A6595
Marsten, Richard, 1926-2005.	PS3515.U585
Marston, Edward.	PR6063.I3175
Mart, Mikhail.	PG3492.72.R78
Martel, John S.	PS3563.A72315
Martell, Charles.	none
Martell, Dominic.	PS3568.E2694
Martens, Arnie.	PS3613.A77774
Martens, Paul—see: Bell, Neil, 1887-1964.	
Mårtenson, Jan, 1933-	PT9876.23.A69
Martin, A. E.	PR9619.3.M2768
Martin, Allana.	PS3563.A72319
Martín, Andreu, 1949-	PQ6663.A74434
Martin, Andrew, 1962-	PR6113.A78
Martin, Ann M., 1955-	none
Martin, Bruce, 1922-	PS3563.A723258
Martin, Dannie M.	PS3563.A723286
Martin, David Lozell, 1946-	PS3563.A72329
Martin, Desmond.	PR9619.3.M278
Martin, Dwight.	PS3563.A7236
Martín, Esteban.	PQ6713.A543
Martin, Hansjörg, 1920-	PT2673.A55
Martin, Ian Kennedy.	PR6063.A715
Martin, J. Malcolm, 1955-	PS3563.A72415
Martin, J. Wallis.	PR6063.A7155
Martin, James E., 1936-	PS3563.A7243
Martin, Kay.	PS3563.A7247
Martin, Lee, 1943-	PS3563.A7249
Martin, Lee, 1955-	PS3563.A724927
Martin, Les, 1934-	none
Martin, Marian, 1923-	PS3563.A72495
Martin, Nancy, 1939-	PS3563.A7266
Martin, Nancy, 1953-	PS3563.A7267
Martin, P. D. (Phillipa Deanne)	PR9619.4.M368
Martin, Robert, 1900-1971.	none
Martin, Robert, 1908-1976.	PS3563.A7278
Martin, Robert Bernard.	none
Martin, Rosemary, 1955-	PS3569.T4524
Martin, Roy, 1939-	PS3563.A7283
Martin, Russ.	PS3563.A7284
Martin, Sharron.	PS3613.A78623

Martin, Sheila.	none
Martin, Stephen Hawley.	PS3563.A72915
Martin, Tom.	PR6113.A787
Martin, Trevor.	none
Martin, Valerie, 1948-	PS3563.A7295
Martin, William, 1950-	PS3563.A7297
Martín Moreno, Francisco, 1946-	PQ7298.23.A7135
Martínez, Al.	PS3563.A7333
Martínez, Guillermo, 1962-	PQ7798.23.A69165
Martínez, Max, 1943-	PS3563.A73344
Martinez, Michele, 1962-	PS3613.A78648
Martinez, S. A.	none
Martinez, Salvador.	none
Martini, Steve, 1946-	PS3563.A73358
Martini, Teri.	none
Martins, Richard.	PS3563.A7345
Martinusen-Coloma, Cindy, 1970-	PS3563.A737
Marton, Dana.	none
Marton, George.	PS3563.A738
Martyn, Don.	none
Martyn, Wyndham, b. 1875.	PR6025.A745
Marvin, Isabel R.	PS3563.A7432
Marx, Arthur, 1921-2011.	PS3525.A773
Marx, Randi.	none
Maryk, Michael, 1935-	PS3563.A76
Mascott, Trina.	PS3563.A782
Masek, Linda Lehmann.	PS3613.A7965
Masello, Robert, 1952-	PS3613.A81925
Masiello, Joseph.	none
Maslov, Valeriĭ.	none
Mason, A. E. W. (Alfred Edward Woodley), 1865-1948.	PR6025.A79
Mason, Alexander.	none
Mason, Anita.	PR6063.A757
Mason, Clifford.	PS3563.A7878
Mason, Colin, 1926-	PR9639.3.M28
Mason, Daniel, 1981-	PR9619.4.M375
Mason, David, 1951-	PR6063.A759
Mason, David V.	none
Mason, F. van Wyck (Francis van Wyck), 1901-1978.	PS3525.A7943
Mason, J. D.	PS3613.A817
Mason, Lee W., 1939-	PS3563.A434
Mason, Michael, 1939-	PS3563.A793
Mason, Paule.	PS3563.A785 [sic]
Mason, Sarah J.	PR6063.A7648
Massey, Brandon, 1973-	PS3613.A8193
Massey, Charlotte.	PR6063.A774
Massey, Ellen Gray.	PS3563.A79964
Massie, Sonja.	PS3563.C3758
Massey, Sujata.	PS3563.A79965
Massie, Allan, 1938-	PR6063.A79
Massie, Chris, b. 1880.	PR6025.A7944
Masson, Richard.	none

Masson, Sophie, 1959-   PR9619.3.M2884
Masterman, J. C. (John Cecil), 1891-1977.   PR6025.A796
Masterman, Walter S. (Walter Sidney), b. 1876.   PR6025.A797
Masters, Anthony, 1940-2003.   PR6063.A83
Masters, Doug.   none
Masters, Hilary.   PS3563.A82
Masters, John, 1914-1983.   PS3525.A8314
Masters, Priscilla.   PR6063.A833
Masterson, Andrew.   PR9619.3.M2895
Masterson, Linda.   none
Masterson, Whit.   PS3563.A835
Masterton, Graham.   PR6063.A834
Mastras, George, 1966-   PS3613.A81994
Masur, Harold Q., 1909-2005.   PS3525.A835
Matchaba, Patrice   PR9390.9.M335
Matera, Lia.   PS3563.A83537
Matetsky, Amanda.   PS3613.A8255
Mather, Arthur R.   PR9619.3.M29
Mather, Berkely.   PR9619.3.M3
Mather, Linda.   PR6063.A845
Mathes, Charles.   PS3563.A83543
Matheson, Don.   PS3563.A83545
Matheson, Richard, 1926-   PS3563.A8355
Mathews, Adrian, 1957-   PR6063.A848
Mathews, Francine.   PS3563.A8357
Mathews, Harry, 1930-   PS3563.A8359
Mathews, Jean Holbrook.   PS3613.A84333
Mathewson, John.   none
Mathewson, Joseph.   none
Mathis, Edward.   PS3563.A8364
Matome, M. G. D.   none
Matranga, Frances Carfi.   none
Matsumoto, Seichō, 1909-1992.   PL856.A8
Matteson, Stefanie.   PS3563.A8393
Matthews, Alex.   PS3563.A83958
Matthews, Andrew, 1948-   none
Matthews, Christopher, 1954-   PR9619.3.M315
Matthews, Clayton.   PS3563.A84
Matthews, Clyde.   PS3563.A842
Matthews, Greg.   PR9619.3.M317
Matthews, Jeanne.   PS3613.A8485
Matthews, Patricia, 1927-2006.   PS3563.A853
Matturro, Claire Hamner, 1954-   PS3613.A87
Maudsley, Jere.   PR9199.3.M398
Maugham, Robin, 1916-1981.   PR6025.A858
Maugham, W. Somerset (William Somerset), 1874- PR6025.A86
1965.

                                                           [Z8555.3]
Mauner, Claudia.   none
Maurensig, Paolo, 1943-   PQ4873.A8947
Maurice, John, 1933-   PR6063.A866
Mawdsley, Gemma.   PR6113.A93
Mawer, Simon.   PR9120.9.M38
Maxes, Anna.   PS3563.A895

Maxfield, Henry S.	PS3563.A896
Maxim, John R.	PS3563.A8965
Maxwell, A. E.	PS3563.A899
Maxwell, Ann, 1944-	PS3562.O8847
Maxwell, Helen K.	PS3563.A9
Maxwell, Jan.	none
Maxwell, John, 1965-	PS3613.A9
Maxwell, Patricia, 1942-	PS3563.A923
Maxwell, Peter, 1940 Aug. 26-	PR6053.A865
Maxwell, Richard.	PS3563.A98
Maxwell, Thomas, 1937-	PS3557.I284
May, Janis Susan, 1946-	PS3563.A9418
May, Lori A.	none
May, Peter, 1951-	PR6063.A884
Maybury, Anne.	PR6025.A943
Mayer, Edward E.	none
Mayer, Martin, 1928-	PS3563.A9525
Mayer, Patricia (Patricia M.)	PS3563.A9535
Mayer, Robert, 1939-	PS3563.A954
Mayersberg, Paul.	PS3563.A9552
Mayes, Frances.	PS3563.A956
Mayfield, Serena.	none
Mayhew, Dianne.	none
Mayhew, Margaret, 1936-	PR6063.A887
Mayhew, Vic.	PS3563.A963
Mayle, Peter.	PR6063.A8875
Maynard, Joyce, 1953-	PS3563.A9638
Maynard, Nan.	PR6063.A889
Maynard, Roy.	PS3563.A96387
Mayne, William, 1928-2010.	none
Mayo, J. K.	PR6063.A925
Mayo, James, 1914-	PR6053.O8
Mayo, Nick.	PS3563.A964
Mayor, Archer.	PS3563.A965
Mayr, Ilsa.	PS3613.A97
Mazel, Henry F.	PS3563.A981176
Mazin, Aleksandr.	PG3483.2.Z49
Mazza, Cris.	PS3563.A988
Mazzaro, Ed.	none
Mbugua, Kahiu.	none
McAfee, John P.	PS3563.C2645
McAfee, Paul K.	none
McAlary, Mike.	PS3563.C2647
McAleer, John J.	PS3563.A2447
McAllester, Melanie, 1962-	PS3563.C266
McAllister, Alister, b. 1877.	PR6025.A12
McAllister, Amanda, 1932-	PS3558.A3232
McAllister, Annie Laurie, 1920-2005.	PS3553.A79555
McAllister, Peter, 1965-	none
McAulay, Alex.	PS3563.C32
McAuley, Paul J.	PR6063.C29
McAuley, Roisin.	PR6113.C32
McAuliffe, Frank, 1926-	none
McBain, Ed, 1926-2005.	PS3515.U585

McBriarty, Douglas, 1918-　　　　　　PS3563.C3336
McBride, Susan, 1964-　　　　　　　　PS3563.C33363
McBurney, Richard W.　　　　　　　　none
McCabe, Cameron—see: Borneman, Ernest, 1915-
McCabe, Eugene, 1930-　　　　　　　　PR6063.A135
McCabe, Pat, 1955-　　　　　　　　　　PR6063.C32
McCabe, Peter, 1945-　　　　　　　　　PS3563.C33373
McCafferty, Barbara Taylor.　　　　　PS3563.C33376
McCafferty, Jeanne.　　　　　　　　　PS3563.C33378
McCaffrey, Joseph A.　　　　　　　　　PS3563.C33382
McCaffrey, K. T.　　　　　　　　　　　PR6063.C325
McCaffrey, Vincent, 1947-　　　　　　PS3613.C3435
McCahery, James R.　　　　　　　　　　PS3563.C33384
McCaig, Donald.　　　　　　　　　　　PS3563.A2555
McCain, Charles.　　　　　　　　　　　PS3613.C344
McCall, Amaleka G.　　　　　　　　　　PS3613.C3447
McCall, Anthony, 1918-　　　　　　　　PS3521.A4347
McCall, Dinah.　　　　　　　　　　　　PS3569.A4565
McCall, Linda Lane.　　　　　　　　　none
McCall, Penny.　　　　　　　　　　　　none
McCall, Thomas.　　　　　　　　　　　PS3563.C3342
McCall, Wendell.　　　　　　　　　　　PS3566.E234
McCall Smith, Alexander, 1948-　　　PR6063.C326
McCammon, Robert R.　　　　　　　　　PS3563.C3345
McCandless, Anthony.　　　　　　　　PR6063.A1576
McCann, Thomas.　　　　　　　　　　　PR6063.A158
McCarry, Charles.　　　　　　　　　　PS3563.C336
McCartan, Dominic.　　　　　　　　　PR6063.C34
McCarthy, Billy.　　　　　　　　　　　PS3613.C3457
McCarthy, Cormac, 1933-　　　　　　　PS3563.C337
McCarthy, Dudley.　　　　　　　　　　none
McCarthy, Edward V., Jr.　　　　　　　PS3563.A2587
McCarthy, Ellen.　　　　　　　　　　　PR6113.C365
McCarthy, Jane E.　　　　　　　　　　none
McCarthy, Keith, 1960-　　　　　　　　PR6113.C367
McCarthy, Kevin, 1968-　　　　　　　　PR6113.C3673
McCarthy, Maureen, 1953-　　　　　　PR9619.3.M31966
McCarthy, Shaun, 1928-2001.　　　　PR6053.O774
McCarthy, Wilson, 1930-　　　　　　　PS3563.A2593
McCartney, P.　　　　　　　　　　　　none
McCarty, Sarah.　　　　　　　　　　　PS3613.C3568
McCarver, Sam.　　　　　　　　　　　　PS3563.C337425
McClafferty, S. K. (Susan Kay)　　　none
McClain, Florence Wagner, 1938-　　PS3563.C3392
McClain-Watson, Teresa, 1960-　　　PS3563.C261185
McClean, J. Sloan.　　　　　　　　　　none
McCleary, Carol.　　　　　　　　　　　PS3613.C35765
McCleave, Annette.　　　　　　　　　PS3613.C35774
McClellan, Janet, 1951-　　　　　　　PS3563.C3413
McClellan, Sharron.　　　　　　　　　none
McClellan, Tierney.　　　　　　　　　none
McClendon, Lise.　　　　　　　　　　　PS3573.E19595
McClintick, Malcolm.　　　　　　　　PS3563.C3415
McClister, Michael.　　　　　　　　　PS3563.C34157

McCloskey, Walter.	PS3563.C34165
McCloud, Susan Evans.	PS3563.A26176
McCloy, Helen.	PS3525.A1587
McClure, Brad.	PS6316.C3588
McClure, Holly.	PS3613.C3589
McClure, James, 1939-2006.	PR9369.3.M394
McClure, Marcia Lynn.	PS3613.C36
McClure, Rusty, 1950-	PS3613.C363
McClurg, Grace, 1964-	none
McColley, Kevin.	PS3563.O34316
McCollum, Thomas C., 1939-	PS3563.C3434
McCombie, J. A. S.	none
McConnell, Frank D., 1942-1999.	PS3563.C3437
McConnell, Malcolm.	PS3563.A2624
McConnell, Vicki P.	PS3563.C344
McConnor, Vincent.	PS3525.A1653
McCormack, Eric P.	PR9199.3.M42378
McCormack, Tom.	none
McCormick, Claire.	PS3563.C3445
McCormick, Jim, 1920-	PS3563.A2645
McCormick, Lois Elizabeth.	none
McCourtney, Lorena.	PS3563.C3449
McCoy, Andrew.	PR9369.3.M396
McCoy, Horace, 1897-1955.	PS3525.A1715
McCoy, Judi.	PS3613.C385
McCoy, Shirlee.	PS3613.C38574
McCreede, Jess.	PS3563.C35263
McCrery, Nigel, 1953-	PR6063.C365
McCrum, Robert.	PR6063.A1658
McCrumb, Sharyn, 1948-	PS3563.C3527
McCulley, Johnston, 1883-1958.	PS3525.A17725
McCulloch, Michael, 1969-	PS3613.C3864494
McCullough, Andrew.	PS3563.A2677
McCullough, Colleen, 1937-	PR9619.3.M32
McCullough, David W.	PS3563.C35293
McCullough, Kae.	none
McCullough, Karen G.	PS3563.C35296
McCurtin, Peter.	none
McCurtin, Peter, 1935-	PS3563.C3532
McCusker, Paul, 1958-	PS3563.C3533
McCutchan, Philip, 1920-	PR6063.A167
McCutcheon, Hugh.	PR6025.A216
McDaniel, David.	none
McDaniels, Abigail.	none
McDermid, Val.	PR6063.C37
McDermott, John, 1919-1977.	PS3563.A274
McDonald, Cherokee Paul.	PS3563.C3559
McDonald, Craig, 1962-	PS3613.C38698
McDonald, Eva.	PR6063.A16794
McDonald, Frank, 1941-	PS3563.A2768
Mcdonald, Gregory, 1937-2008.	PS3563.A278
McDonald, Hugh C.	none
McDonald, Ian, 1960-	PR6063.C38
McDonald, Joe, 1931-	PS3613.C38725

McDonald, Megan.	PS3563.A2864
McDonald, Stephen E.	PS3563.C358365
McDonell, Nick.	PS3613.C388
McDonell, Terry.	PS3563.A29143
McDowall, Iain.	PR6113.C38
McDowell, Josh.	PS3613.C395
McDowell, Michael, 1950-	none
McDowell, Rider.	PS3563.C3594
McDuffie, Susan.	PS3613.C396
McEldowney, Eugene.	PR6063.C396
McElroy, Joseph.	PS3563.A293
McErlean, Sheila.	none
McEuen, Paul.	PS3613.C428
McEvoy, John, 1936-	PS3613.C432
McEvoy, Marjorie.	PR6063.A196
McEwan, Ian.	PR6063.C4
McFadden, Joseph T.	PS3563.C36225
McFadden, Marlene E. (Marlene Elizabeth), 1937-	PR6063.C43
McFadden, T. J.	none
McFadyen, Cody.	PS3613.C438
McFall, Patricia.	PS3563.C36275
McFalls, Dorothy.	PS3613.C4383
McFarland, Nora, 1973-	PS3613.C4395
McFarlane, Ian, 1937-	PR9619.3.M2518
McFarlane, Leslie, 1902-1977.	PR9199.3.M3148
McFather, Nelle.	PS3563.C3633
McFerrin, Linda Watanabe, 1953-	PS3573.A7987
McFetridge, John, 1959-	PR9199.4.M426
McGann, Michael.	none
McGarrity, Mark, 1943-	PS3563.A296
McGarrity, Michael.	PS3563.C36359
McGaughey, Neil.	PS3563.C36372
McGee, James, 1950-	PR6063.C468
McGerr, Patricia.	PS3525.A23276
McGhee, Edward.	none
McGiffin, Janet.	none
McGill, Bernie, 1967-	PR6113.C474
McGill, E. J.	PS3563.C36389
McGill, Gordon, 1943-	PR6063.A2177
McGill, Nancy.	none
McGill, Robert, 1976-	PR9199.4.M427
McGilloway, Brian, 1974-	PR6113.C4755
McGinley, Marjorie M.	PS3563.C36399
McGinley, Patrick, 1937-	PR6063.A21787
McGinty, Sue, 1937-	PS3613.C4835
McGirr, Edmund—see: Giles, Kenneth.	
McGivern, William P.	PS3525.A236
McGlothin, Victor.	PS3613.C484
McGovern, Cammie.	PS3613.C49
McGovern, James I.	PS3563.C3649
McGowan, Kathleen, 1963-	PS3613.C494
McGown, Jill.	PR6063.C477
McGrady, Mike.	none
McGrath, M. J., 1964-	PR6113.C4775

McGrath, Patrick, 1950-   PS3563.C3663
McGraw, Lee.   PS3563.A2997
McGregor, H. R.   PR6063.C488
McGregor, Iona.   PR6063.C49
McGriff, Michelle.   PS3613.C4974
McGrory, Brian.   PS3563.C36814
McGuire, Christine.   PS3563.C36819
McGuire, Patrick O.—see: Mitchell, James, 1926-2002.
McGuire, Paul, 1903-1978.   PR9619.3.M255
McGurk, Slater, 1925-   PS3568.O852
McGuyer, Nadine.   none
McHale, Tom.   PS3563.A3115
McHenry, Paul T., 1952-   PS3563.C36845
McHugh, Frances Y.   PS3563.C3685
McHugh, Paul, 1950-   PS3563.A31163
McIlvanney, Liam.   PR9639.4.M37
McIlvanney, William, 1936-   PR6063.A237
McInerny, Ralph, 1929-2010.   PS3563.A31166
McIntosh, J. T.   PR6063.A234
McIntosh, Kenneth, 1959-   none
McIntosh, Pat.   PR6113.C485
McIntyre, Hope, 1946-   PS3571.P33
McIver, N. J.   PS3563.C373
McKay, Claudia.   PS3563.C3734
McKay, Donald Neal.   PS3613.C545
McKay, Gardner.   PR6063.C54
McKay, Kenneth R.   none
McKay, Lisa.   PS3613.C54517
McKay, Sue.   none
McKemmish, Jan.   PR9619.3.M325
McKenna, Bridget.   none
McKenna, Evelyn, 1899-1986.   PS3519.O712
McKenna, Lindsay, 1946-   PS3563.C37525
McKenna, Shannon.   PS3613.C555
McKenney, Kenneth, 1929-   PR6063.A2429
McKenzie, Alecia, 1960-   PR9265.9.M2735
McKenzie, J. Alexander.   PS3563.A31345
McKenzie, Valerie.   PR9619.3.M326
McKernan, Victoria.   PS3563.C3756
McKevett, G. A.   PS3563.C3758
McKew, Robert.   none
McKibben, Nancy J.   PS3563.C36875
McKillip, Patricia A.   PS3563.C38
McKimmey, James.   PS3563.A317
McKinlay, Jenn.   PS3612.A948
McKinney, Meagan.   PS3563.C38168
McKinney, Michael.   PS3563.C3817
McKinsey, John A.   PS3613.C5646
McKinty, Adrian.   PS3563.C38322
McKinzie, Clinton.   PS3613.C568
McKitterick, Molly, 1951-   PS3563.A31767
McKnight, Carolyn.   PS3563.A31773
McKnight, Gill.   PS3611.C56816
McLachlan, Donald, 1908-1971.   PR6063.A247

McLachlan, Ian, 1938-	PR6063.A2472
McLaren, John, 1951-	none
McLaren, Philip, 1943-	PR9619.3.M3266
McLarty, Ron.	PS3613.C573
McLaughlin, Gerald T.	PS3613.C5753
McLaughlin, Robert, 1925-	PS3563.A31796
McLean, Margaret, 1966-	PS3613.C577
McLean, Matthew.	PS3563.C38439
McLean, Russel D.	PR6113.C545
McLeave, Hugh.	PR6063.A249
McLeish, Dougal.	PS3563.A318
McLendon, James.	PS3563.A3184
McLoughlin, Jane.	PR6063.C573
McLoughlin, Tim, 1959-	PS3613.C5835
McMahon, Franci, 1941-	PS3563.C38557
McMahon, Jennifer.	PS3613.C584
McMahon, Katharine.	PR6063.C5755
McMahon, Neil.	PS3568.H545
McMahon, Thomas Patrick.	PS3563.A31883
McManus, Leslie.	none
McManus, Patrick F.	PS3563.C38625
McMath, Phillip H., 1945-	PS3563.C3865
McMikle, Barbara.	none
McMillan, Ann, 1952-	PS3563.C38657
McMillan, Dorothy, 1932-	none
McMillan, DuBois T.	PS3563.A31895
McMillan, Elsie Mills.	none
McMordie, Taber.	PS3563.A31897
McMullen, Beth.	PS3613.585455
McMullen, Mary, 1920-	PS3563.A31898
McNab, Andy, 1959-	PR6063.C59
McNab, Claire.	PS3563.C3877
McNab, Oliver—see: Frede, Richard.	
McNairy, Mel J.	PS3563.C38825
McNally, Clare.	none
McNally, Terrence.	PS3563.A323
McNamara, Evan.	PS3613.C5858
McNamara, Joseph D.	PS3563.C3883
Mc Namara, Michael M., 1940-	PS3563.A3234
McNamara, Tom, 1944-	PS3563.C38835
McNamee, Eoin, 1961-	PR6063.C63
McNaught, Judith.	PS3563.C3884
McNaughton, Brian.	PS3563.C38843
McNay, Mark, 1965-	PR6113.C57
McNear, Robert, 1930-	none
McNeil, John.	PS3563.A32343
McNeile, H. C. (Herman Cyril), 1888-1937.	PR6025.A317
McNeilly, Wilfred.	PR6052.A37
McPherson, Catriona, 1965-	PR6113.C586
McPherson, Christopher, 1952-	PR9199.3.M42483
McPheters, Mike, 1943-	PS3613.C58745
McQuay, Mike.	none
McQuillan, Karin.	PS3563.C654
McQuinn, Donald E.	PS3563.C66

McRae, Cricket.	PS3613.C58755
McRae, Diana, 1951-	PS3563.C68
McReynolds, Glenna.	PS3563.C75
McShane, Mark, 1930-	PR6062.O853
McShea, Susanna Hofmann.	PS3563.C8
McSparren, Carolyn.	PS3563.C84
McSweeney, Joyelle, 1976-	PS3613.C588
McVean, James.	PR6063.C8
Mead, Richelle.	PS3613.E1275
Mead, Robert Douglas.	PS3563.E168
Mead, Russell, 1947-	none
Mead, Shepherd.	PS3525.E1147
Meade, Amy Patricia, 1972-	PS3613.E128
Meade, Everard.	none
Meade, Glenn, 1957-	PS3563.E16845
Meade, L. T., 1854-1914.	PR4990.M34
Meade, Richard, 1926-1977.	PS3558.A17
Meador, Daniel John.	PS3563.E1687
Meadows, David E.	PS3613.E13
Meadows, Lee E.	PS3563.E1698
Meaney, John.	PR6113.E17
Medawar, Mardi Oakley.	PS3563.E234
Mede, Charlotte.	PR9199.4.M43
Medici, Stephen F.	none
Meehan, Meagan J.	PS3613.E368
Meek, M. R. D.	PR6063.E35
Megahy, Cooper.	none
Meggs, Brown.	PS3563.E34
Mehl, Nancy.	PS3613.E4254
Mehling, Harold.	PS3563.E3437
Mehlum, Jan, 1945-	none
Meier, Leslie.	PS3563.E3455
Meigs, Henry.	PR9515.9.M45
Meiring, Desmond.	PR9381.9.M44
Meisels, Andrew.	PS3563.E37
Meissner, Hans Otto.	PT2625.E314
Meissner, Susan, 1961-	PS3613.E435
Mekavāna, Saroja.	none
Mekuy, Guillermina, 1982-	PQ6713.E447
Melchior, Ib.	PS3563.E435
Meldrum, James.	PR6063.E415
Melheim, Richard Alan.	PS3563.E4418
Melikan, R. A.	PS3613.E4464
Melikan, Rose—see: Melikan, R. A.	
Mello, Sérgio Bandeira de.	PQ9698.423.E45
Mellor, Jodie, 1949-	none
Mellor, Kevin.	PS3613.E44826
Melnick, Alexei.	PS3613.E4488
Mel'nikova, Irina.	PG3492.76.E44
Melo, Patrícia, 1962-	PQ9698.23.E4625
Melton, Patrick.	PS3613.E4655
Melton, William.	PS3563.E448
Meltzer, Brad.	PS3563.E4496
Melville, James.	PR6063.E439

Melville, Jennie.	PR6052.U813
Melville-Ross, Antony.	PR6063.E455
Memory, Ashley.	PS3613.E477
Mendelhall, Kitty.	none
Mendelsohn, Felix, 1906-	PS3563.E48
Mendes, Bob, 1928-	PT6466.23.E46
Méndez, Roberto, 1958-	PQ7390.M458
Mendoza, Eduardo, 1943-	PQ6663.E54
Menegas, Peter.	PS3563.E5
Menkes, John H., 1928-	PS3563.E527
Meno, Joe.	PS3563.E53
Mentink, Dana.	PS3613.E496
Mercer, J. P.	PS3613.E696
Mercer, Judy.	PS3563.E7325
Mercer, Ken, 1962-	PS3613.E7
Meredith, D. E.	PR6113.E74
Meredith, D. R. (Doris R.)	PS3563.E7355
Meredith, F.M.	PS3563.E7366
Meredith, Marilyn.	PS3563.E7366
Meredith, Richard C.	PS3563.E737
Merkel, E. L. (Earl L.)	PS3613.E7565
Merle, Robert, 1908-2004.	PQ2625.E5278
Merlin, Christina.	PR6058.E23
Merlino, Linda.	PS3613.E7568
Merrick, Gordon.	PS3525.E6413
Merritt, Abraham, 1884-1943.	PS3525.E676
Merritt, Don, 1945-	PS3563.E74538
Mertz, Barbara.	PS3563.E747
Mertz, Stephen, 1947-	PS3613.E788
Merullo, Roland.	PS3563.E748
Merz, Jon F.	PS3613.E7885
Mesce, Bill.	PS3563.E74627
Messer, Mona Naomi Anna Hocking—see: Hocking, Anne.	
Messick, Hank.	none
Messmann, Jon.	none
Metcalf, Susan.	none
Methold, Ken, 1931-	PR9619.3.M434
Metikosh, Anne, 1954-	PR9199.4.M474
Mettler, Felix, 1945-	PT2673.E853
Mettler, George.	none
Metzl, Jamie Frederic.	PS3613.E895
Mewshaw, Michael, 1943-	PS3563.E87
Meydan, Lena.	PG3492.76.E93
Meyer, Charles, 1947-	PS3563.E8726
Meyer, Deon.	PT6592.23.E94
Meyer, Jlee.	PS3613.E96
Meyer, Joanne.	PS3613.E97
Meyer, Lawrence, 1941-	PS3563.E875
Meyer, Lynn.	PS3563.E878
Meyer, Nicholas, 1945-	PS3563.E88
Meyer, Philipp, 1974-	PS3613.E976
Meyer, Stephenie, 1973-	PS3613.E979
Meyerding, Jane.	PS3563.E886
Meyers, Annette.	PS3563.E889

Meyers, Kent.	PS3563.E93
Meyers, Maan.	PS3563.E889
Meyers, Manny, 1930-	PS3563.E94
Meyers, Marc A.	PS3613.E985
Meyers, Martin.	none
Meyers, Richard, 1953-	PS3563.E96
Meynell, Laurence, 1899-1989.	PR6025.E93
Mezrich, Ben, 1969-	PS3563.E986
Miall, Robert, 1922-	PR6003.U54
Miano, Mark.	PS3563.I22
Miasha, 1981-	PS3613.I18
Mi‹a›snikov, Viktor.	none
Michael, David J., 1944-	PS3563.I25
Michael, Sean, 1966-	PS3613.I3435
Michaels, Alan.	PS3563.I268
Michaels, Barbara, 1927-	PS3563.E747
Michaels, Bill, 1946-	none
Michaels, Fern.	PS3563.I27
Michaels, Grant.	PS3563.I2715
Michaels, Jan.	none
Michaels, Joanna, 1954-	PS3563.I2718
Michaels, Kasey.	PS3563.I2725
Michaels, Melisa C.	PS3563.I2734
Michaels, Philip, 1950-	none
Michaels, Richard, 1965-	PS3570.E447
Michelson, Bennett.	none
Michener, James A. (James Albert), 1907-1997.	PS3525.I19
Michie, David.	PR6063.I223
Michod, Alec.	PS3613.I346
Mickelbury, Penny, 1948-	PS3563.I3517
Mickelson, Marcia Argueta.	PS3613.I354
Micou, Paul.	PS3563.I354
Middlemass, Jean.	PR5021.M427
Middlemiss, Robert.	none
Middleton, T. J., 1947-	PR6052.I77294
Midgley, John, 1931-	none
Miehe, Ulf, 1940-	PT2673.I3
Miéville, China.	PR6063.I265
Migliore, John.	none
Mignerey, Sharon.	PS3563.I37152
Mignogna, Eduardo, 1940-2006.	PQ7798.23.I33
Mihesuah, Devon A. (Devon Abbott), 1957-	PS3563.I371535
Mikes, George.	PR6025.I37
Mikhaleva, Anna.	PG3483.3.I43344
Mikołajewski, Jarosław, 1960-	PG7172.I38
Mikolowski, Ken.	PS3563.I37156
Mikulski, Barbara.	PS3563.I371564
Milán, Victor.	PS3563.I371568
Milburn, Ellen.	none
Mildon, Marsha, 1946-	PR9199.3.M4565
Miles, Cassie.	PS3563.I3717
Miles, Gareth.	PB2298.M44
Miles, Keith.	PR6063.I3175
Miles, John, 1930-1997.	PS3552.I3

Miles, Richard.   none
Milevskai‹a›, Li‹u›dmila.   PG3483.3.I4477
Millar, Jeff, 1942-   PS3563.I3723
Millar, Kenneth, 1915-1983.   PS3525.I486
Millar, Margaret, 1915-1994.   PS3563.I3725
Millar, Peter.   PR6113.I55
Millar, Sam, 1955-   PR6113.I555
Millard, Joe—see: Millard, Joseph, 1908-A4259
Millard, Joseph, 1908-   none
Millard, Oscar E.   PR6063.I355
Miller, Andrew, 1961-   PR6063.I3564
Miller, Barbara Lynch.   none
Miller, Carlene, 1935-2009.   PS3563.I3763
Miller, David C.   none
Miller, Denis.   PR6063.I358
Miller, Geoffrey, 1945-   PS3563.I3776
Miller, Hugh, 1937-   PR6063.I373
Miller, J. M. T. (Janice M. T.), 1944-   PS3563.I4117
Miller, Joan Drummond.   PS3563.I4129
Miller, John.   PS3613.I53855
Miller, John A., 1946-   PS3563.I4132
Miller, John J.   PS3613.I53857
Miller, John R. (John Ramsey), 1949-   PS3563.I41323
Miller, Jonathan C.   PS3613.I5386
Miller, Judi.   none
Miller, Julie, 1960-   none
Miller, Karen E. Quinones.   PS3563.I41335
Miller, Lanora.   none
Miller, Lauritz, 1927-   PS3563.I4136
Miller, Linda Lael.   PS3563.I41373
Miller, Lynn, 1951-   PS3613.I544
Miller, Martha, 1947-   PS3563.I4158
Miller, Maryann, 1943-   PS3613.I545
Miller, Norman L.   PS3563.I4192
Miller, Raymond.   PS3613.I548
Miller, Rex, 1939-2004.   PS3563.I42
Miller, Ron (Ronald Eugene)   PS3613.I5527
Miller, Russell R., 1928-   PS3613.I5528
Miller, Sherry Ann.   PS3563.I42139
Miller, Stephen E., 1947-   PS3563.I42143
Miller, Susan Cummins, 1949-   PS3613.I555
Miller, Tekla Dennison.   PS3613.I558
Miller, Thos. Kent (Thomas Kent), 1945-   PS3563.I421454
Miller, Vanessa.   PS3613.I5623
Miller, Victor.   none
Miller, Wade.   PS3563.I421475
Millett, Larry, 1947-   PS3563.I42193
Millhiser, Marlys.   PS3563.I4225
Milligan, Spike, 1918-2002.   PR6063.I3777
Millington, Mil.   PR6113.I57
Mills, Arthur, b. 1887.   PR6025.I6245
Mills, Charles, 1950-   PS3563.I422957
Mills, D. F.   none
Mills, Deanie Francis.   PS3563.I422964

Mills, DiAnn.   PS3613.I567
Mills, Gerald W., 1935-   PS3613.I5684
Mills, Jackie.   PR6063.I37782
Mills, James, 1932-   PS3563.I423
Mills, Jenna.   none
Mills, John, 1930-   PR9199.3.M48
Mills, Kyle, 1966-   PS3563.I42322
Mills, Mark, 1963-   PS3613.I569
Mills, Osmington—see: Brooks, Vivian Collin,
1922-
Mills, Robert E.   none
Mills, Sara, 1978-   PS3613.I5698
Mills, Wendy Howell, 1973-   PS3613.I57
Millspaugh, Bert.   PS3613.I5915
Milne, A. A. (Alan Alexander), 1882-1956.   PR6025.I65
Milne, John.   PR6063.I3787
Miloradovic-Weber, Christa, 1952-   PT2673.I44
Miłoszewski, Zygmunt, 1976-   PG7213.I455
Milton, David, 1944-   PS3563.I4477
Milton, David Scott, 1934-   PS3563.I448
Mina, Denise.   PR6063.I457
Minahan, John.   PS3563.I4616
Minard, Dalton.   PS3613.I593
Minchin, Devon George, 1919-   PR9619.3.M5
Minde, Jeff.   PS3613.I595
Miner, Erica.   PS3613.I598
Miner, Valerie.   PS3563.I4647
Minghella, Anthony.   PR6063.I475
Minichino, Camille.   PS3563.I4663
Minick, Michael.   none
Minnick, Wayne C.   PS3563.I4732
Minns, Eric.   PR9220.9.M56
Minshull, Evelyn White.   PS3563.I476
Minter, Alex.   PS3613.I675
Minter, Sharon.   PS3613.I68
Minton, Paula, 1915-1987.   none
Miranda, Ana Maria.   PQ9698.23.I618
Miron, Charles.   none
Mischke, Susanne, 1960-   PT2673.I67
Misercola, Mark.   PS3613.I84
Misra, Jaishree, 1961-   PR9499.3.M54
Mitchard, Jacquelyn.   PS3563.I7358
Mitchelhill, Barbara.   none
Mitchell, Dreda Say.   PR6113.I86
Mitchell, Gladys, 1901-1983.   PR6025.I832
Mitchell, Ian.   none
Mitchell, James, 1926-2002.   PR6063.I793
Mitchell, James C. (James Craig), 1942-   PS3613.I855
Mitchell, John D., 1917-   none
Mitchell, Kay.   PR6063.I815
Mitchell, Kirk.   PS3563.I7675
Mitchell, Michele.   PS3613.I86
Mitchell, Sara, 1949-   PS3563.I823
Mitchell, Todd.   none

Mitchelson, Austin.	PR6063.I84
Mitcheltree, Tom, 1946-	PS3613.I87
Mitford, Bertram, 1855-1914.	PR5021.M8
Mitzner, Adam.	PS3613.I88
Miyabe, Miyuki, 1960-	PL856.I856
Mjåset, Christer, 1973-	PT8952.23.J37
Modan, Rutu.	none
Modesitt, L. E.	PS3563.O264
Moerk, Christian.	PS3613.O34
Moffat, Gwen.	PR6063.O4
Moffatt, James, 1922-	none
Moffitt, Ian.	PR9619.3.M55
Mofina, Rick.	PS3613.O37
Moinot, Pierre.	PQ2625.O244
Molchanov, Andreï.	PG3483.3.O35
Moler, Lee.	PS3563.O396
Monahan, Brent, 1948-	PS3563.O5158
Monahan, George.	none
Monahan, Robert, 1947-	PS3613.O523
Monbrun, Estelle.	PQ2673.O4277
Moncrieff, Seán.	PR6063.O48525
Mondaca, Jimmy, 1965-	PQ8098.423.O53
Mondoloni, Jacques.	PQ2673.O4297
Mones, Nicole.	PS3563.O519
Monette, Paul.	PS3563.O523
Monfredo, Miriam Grace.	PS3563.O5234
Monig, Christopher, 1910-1981.	PS3505.R89224
Monigle, Martha, 1910-	PS3563.O524
Moning, Karen Marie.	PS3613.O527
Monninger, Joseph.	PS3563.O526
Monnow, Peter.	PR6063.O49
Monreal, Sergio J., 1971-	PQ7298.23.O6845
Monro, Gavin.	PR6063.O496
Monroe, Aly.	PR6113.O535
Monroe, Lucy, 1967-	PS3613.O537
Monsarrat, Nicholas, 1910-1979.	PR6025.O36
Monsky, Mark.	PS3563.O534
Monsour, Theresa.	PS3613.O544
Montague, Dan.	PS3563.O5372
Montague, J. J.	none
Montalbán, Manuel Vázquez—see: Vázquez Montalbán, Manuel.	
Montalbano, William D.	PS3563.O5377
Montana, Lynn.	none
Montana, Ron.	none
Montanari, Richard.	PS3563.O5384
Montandon, Pat.	none
Montano, Paulo.	none
Montavon, Jay.	none
Montecino, Marcel.	PS3563.O539
Montefiore, Santa, 1970-	PR6113.O544
Monteilhet, Hubert.	PQ2625.O384
Monteleone, Thomas F.	PS3563.O542
Montero, Rosa.	PQ6663.O554
Montgomerie, James.	none

Montgomery, Lewis B.	none
Montgomery, Michael, 1938-	PR6063.O53
Montgomery, Yvonne.	PS3563.O5458
Montrose, Graham, 1924-	none
Moody, Bill, 1941-	PS3563.O552
Moody, Clifford J., 1934-	PS3563.O5523
Moody, Greg, 1952-	PS3563.O5525
Moody, Mary, 1950-	PR9619.4.M656
Moody, Rick.	PS3563.O5537
Moody, Ron.	PR6063.O574
Moody, Skye Kathleen.	PS3563.O5538
Moody, Susan.	PR6063.O575
Mooney, Chris.	PS3563.O565
Mooney, Ted.	PS3563.O567
Moor, Emily—see: Deming, Richard.	
Moor, Margriet de.	PT5881.23.O578
Moorcock, Michael, 1939-	PR6063.O59
Moorcraft, Paul L.	PR6113.O55
Moore, Alan, 1953-	PR6063.O593
Moore, Andrew.	none
Moore, Arthur.	none
Moore, Barbara, 1934-	PS3563.O57
Moore, Brian, 1921-1999.	PR9199.3.M617
Moore, Clayton, 1927-	PS3558.E487
Moore, Christopher, 1946-	PR9199.3.M618
Moore, Dan Tyler.	none
Moore, Donald Lloyd.	PS3563.O614
Moore, Dorinne.	none
Moore, Graham, 1981-	PR6113.O5566
Moore, Harker.	PS3613.O559
Moore, Jim, 1927-	PS3613.O5626
Moore, Laurie.	PS3613.O564
Moore, Leo.	none
Moore, Maureen.	PR9199.3.M619
Moore, Richard A.	none
Moore, Robin, 1925-2008.	PS3563.O644
Moore, Ruth, 1903-1989.	PS3525.O5666
Moore, Ruth Nulton.	none
Moore, Susanna.	PS3563.O667
Moore, William.	PS3563.O6685
Moore, Y. Blak (Yanier Blak)	PS3613.O569
Moore, Yanier—see: Moore, Y. Blak (Yanier Blak)	
Moorhead, Finola.	PR9619.3.M59
Moorhouse, Frank.	PR9619.3.M6
Mooser, Stephen.	none
Mootoo, Shani.	PR9199.3.M6353
Moquist, Richard.	PS3563.O695
Morales, Pablo.	none
Moran, J. J.	PS3613.O6815
Moran, John, 1954-	PS3613.O6817
Moran, Richard, 1942-	PS3563.O767
Morant, Jean-Marie de, 1945-	PQ2673.O6244
Moray, Helga.	PR6025.O62
More, Meredith, 1937-	PS3563.O7718

Morea, Marianne.	PS3613.O7172
Moreau, Daniel.	none
Morell, Mary, 1945-	PS3563.O773
Morella, Joe.	none
Moreton, Casey.	PS3613.O718
Morgan, Al, 1920-2011.	PS3563.O78
Morgan, Allan.	none
Morgan, Brooke.	PS3613.O727
Morgan, Claire, 1921-1995.	PS3558.I366
Morgan, D. Miller.	PS3563.O826
Morgan, Deborah (Deborah A.)	PS3613.O744
Morgan, Fidelis, 1952-	PR6063.O715
Morgan, Hunter.	none
Morgan, J. M.	none
Morgan, Jason.	none
Morgan, John, 1916-	PS3566.A34
Morgan, John S.	none
Morgan, Kaye.	PS3613.O7454
Morgan, Mary, 1931-	PS3563.O81724
Morgan, Maybeth.	none
Morgan, Murray, 1916-2000.	PS3563.O8714
Morgan, Patrick.	none
Morgan, Philippa.	PR6113.O746
Morgan, Richard K., 1965-	PR6113.O748
Morgan, Robert.	none
Morgan, Speer, 1946-	PS3563.O87149
Morgan, Stanley.	PR6063.O734
Morgan, Ted, 1932-	PS3563.O871495
Morgan, Wesley.	none
Morgan, Wynn L.	none
Morgenroth, Kate.	PS3563.O871497
Morgulas, Jerrold.	PS3563.O87158
Mori, Ei, 1941-	PL856.O67
Moriarty, Jim.	PS3613.O7497
Moriarty, Michael, 1941-	PS3563.O871637
Morice, Anne.	PR6063.O743
Morison, B. J. (Betty Jane), 1924-	PS3563.O87167
Morlan, Diane, 1943-	PS3613.O7547
Morland, Catherine.	none
Morland, Nigel, 1905-1986.	PR6025.O683
Morley, Des.	PR6063.O7443
Morley, Ellen.	none
Morozov, Vladislav, 1960-	none
Morrant, Jean.	PR6113.O755
Morreale, P.	PS3613.O75525
Morrell, David.	PR9199.3.M65
Morris, Alan, 1959-	PS3563.O87395
Morris, Bob, 1950-	PS3613.O75555
Morris, Chris.	PS3563.O87399
Morris, Chris, 1946-	none
Morris, Elizabeth.	none
Morris, Gilbert.	PS3563.O8742
Morris, Goodall Varne.	none
Morris, Ira.	none

Morris, Janet, 1946-	PS3563.O87435
Morris, Jim, 1937-	PS3563.O87436
Morris, John.	PR6063.O75
Morris, M. E., 1926-	PS3563.O87444
Morris, Paula.	PR9639.4.M67
Morris, Roger, 1960-	PR6113.O785
Morris, Sandra A.	PR9199.3.M6522
Morris, T. B. (Thomas Baden), 1900-	PR6025.O754
Morris, Tee.	PS3613.O7758
Morris, Tracy S.	PS3613.O77585
Morris, W. R., 1934-	none
Morrisey, Tom, 1952-	PS3613.O776
Morrison, Arthur, 1863-1945.	PR5089.M7
Morrison, Boyd, 1967-	PS3613.O7774
Morrison, Danny.	PR6063.O7939
Morrison, James W. R.	none
Morrison, Mary B.	PS3563.O87477
Morrissey, J. P.	PS3613.O777
Morrone, Wenda Wardell.	PS3563.O874973
Morrow, Bradford, 1951-	PS3563.O8754
Morrow, Susan.	PS3563.O878
Morse, Carlton E., 1901-	PS3563.O8787
Morse, L. A.	none
Morsi, Pamela.	PS3563.O88135
Morson, Ian.	PR6063.O799
Mortensen, Niels.	none
Mortimer, John, 1923-2009.	PR6025.O7552
Mortimore, Jim.	PS3563.O88176
Mortman, Doris.	PS3563.O8818
Morton, Anthony, 1908-1973.	PR6005.R517
Morton, C. W.	PS3563.O244
Morton, Carson.	PS3613.O77863
Morton, Kate, 1976-	PR9619.4.M74
Morton, Paul.	PS3613.O77867
Morton-Shaw, Christine.	none
Morwood, Carolyn.	PR9619.3.M68
Mosby, Steve.	PR6113.O85
Mosca, Mark.	PS3563.O88385
Mosco, Maisie.	PR6063.O819
Moseley, Margaret.	PS3563.O88388
Moser, Nancy.	PS3563.O88417
Moses, Antoinette.	PR6063.O8194
Mosiman, Billie Sue.	PS3563.O88444
Mosley, Walter.	PS3563.O88456
Moss, Baron.	none
Moss, Jack.	none
Moss, Marissa.	none
Moss, Robert, 1946-	PR6063.O83
Moss, Roger S.	PR6063.O8315
Moss, Rose.	PS3563.O8848
Mostert, Natasha.	PR9369.3.M6284
Mostofi, S.	PS3613.O789
Mounce, David R.	none
Mount, Guy.	PS3563.O8987

Mountain, Fiona.	PR6113.O935
Mountford, B. J.	PS3613.O86
Mouritsen, Laurel.	PS3563.O9215
Mowatt, Ian.	PR6063.O87
Moxley, Joseph Michael.	PS3563.O935
Moya Palencia, Mario.	PQ7298.23.O93
Moyes, Patricia.	PR6063.O9
Moynahan, Jean Ann.	PS3563.O963
Mrazek, Robert J.	PS3563.R39
Mucha, Susan Polonus.	PS3613.U35
Muchamore, Robert.	none
Mugler, Frederick, 1923-	none
Muir, Augustus, 1892-	PR6025.U55
Muir, Dexter, 1908-	PR6013.R718
Muir, Jean.	PS3563.U38
Mũkoma wa Ngũgĩ.	PR9381.9.M778
Muldoon, Paul.	PR6063.U367
Mulisch, Harry, 1927-2010.	PT5860.M85
Mulkeen, Thomas P.	PS3563.U395
Mullally, Frederic.	PR6063.U38
Mullen, Ann.	PS3613.U445
Mullen, Thomas.	PS3613.U447
Muller, Dominique.	PQ2673.U36
Muller, Eddie.	PS3613.U45
Muller, Marcia.	PS3563.U397
Muller, Mary.	none
Muller, Paul, 1924-	PR6063.U39
Mulligan, Andy.	none
Mullin, Arthur, 1917-	PS3563.U3984
Munder, Laura.	PS3563.U453
Mundis, Hester.	PS3563.U454
Mundy, Talbot, 1879-1940.	PR6025.U66
Munnings, Clare.	PS3563.U482
Muñoz Molina, Antonio.	PQ6663.U4795
Munro, Alice.	PR9199.3.M8
Munro, Hugh.	none
Munro, James, 1926-2002.	PR6063.I793
Munsey, Terence.	PR9199.3.M82
Munson, Diane.	PS3613.U693
Munson, Ronald, 1939-	PS3563.U58
Munson, Trevor O.	PS3613.U69366
Murakami, Ryū, 1952-	PL856.U696
Murano, Vincent.	PS3563.U717
Murari, Timeri.	PR9499.3.M85
Murdoch, Anna.	PR9619.3.M73
Murdoch, Graham.	none
Murfi, Lidie.	PS3563.U7254
Murie, Martin.	PS3563.U7262
Murphey, Cecil.	PS3613.U723
Murphy, Brian, 1939 May 25-	PS3563.U7278
Murphy, C. E. (Catie E.)	PS3613.U726
Murphy, Christopher.	PR6063.U729
Murphy, Dallas.	PS3563.U7283
Murphy, Debra.	PS3613.U727

Murphy, Gloria.	PS3563.U7297
Murphy, Haughton.	PS3563.U734
Murphy, James F., 1932-	PS3563.U737
Murphy, John, 1921-	PS3563.U74
Murphy, Ken, 1935-	PR6063.U733
Murphy, Margaret, 1959 Apr. 14-	PR6063.U7337
Murphy, Mary Elizabeth.	none
Murphy, Pat, 1955-	PS3563.U748
Murphy, Robert Franklin.	none
Murphy, Shirley Rousseau.	PS3563.U7619
Murphy, Tom, 1935-	PS3563.U762
Murphy, Warren.	PS3563.U7634
Murphy, Yannick.	PS3563.U7635
Murray, Colin, 1949-	PR6113.U7755
Murray, David Christie, 1847-1907.	PR5101.M45
Murray, Donna Huston.	none
Murray, Edmund P.	PS3563.U766
Murray, Fiona.	none
Murray, Helen.	PS3563.U769
Murray, John, 1923-	PS3563.U77
Murray, Lynne.	PS3563.U7716
Murray, Max, 1901-1956.	PR9619.3.M84
Murray, Paul, 1975-	PR6113.U78
Murray, Stephen.	PR9619.3.M85
Murray, W. H. (William Hutchinson)	PR6063.U78
Murray, William, 1926-2005.	PS3563.U8
Muse, Patricia.	PS3563.U834
Muser, Martin, 1965-	none
Muske-Dukes, Carol, 1945-	PS3563.U837
Mustian, Mark, 1959-	PS3563.U843
Musto, Barry.	PR6063.U87
Myers, Amy, 1938-	PR6063.Y38
Myers, Beverle Graves.	PS3613.Y465
Myers, Bill, 1953-	PS3563.Y36
Myers, Gerald.	PS3613.Y47
Myers, Isabel Briggs.	PS3525.Y427
Myers, Katherine, 1952-	PS3563.Y422
Myers, John L. (John Lee), 1958-	PS3563.Y424
Myers, Mary Ruth.	PS3563.Y44
Myers, Paul.	PR6063.Y47
Myers, Tamar.	PS3563.Y475
Myers, Tim.	PS3613.Y477
Myerson, Julie.	PR6063.Y48
Myette, Michael.	PS3613.Y48
Mykel, A. W.	PS3563.Y49
Myles, Symon.	PR6056.O45
Mynheir, Mark.	PS3613.Y58
Myroup, Ronald Krine, 1960-	PS3563.Y76
Nabb, Magdalen, 1947-2007.	PR6064.A18
Nabokov, Vladimir Vladimirovich, 1899-1977.	PS3527.A15
Nadel, Barbara.	PR6114.A34
Nadelson, Reggie.	PS3564.A287
Naef, Adam.	PS3564.A33
Nagle, Anthony, 1945-	PS3614.A46

Nagornyĭ, Alekseĭ.   PG3484.A38
Nagy, Gloria.   PS3564.A36
Naha, Ed.   none
Nahai, Gina Barkhordar.   PS3552.A6713
Nahum, Lucien.   PR6064.A32
Names, Larry D.   PS3564.A545
Nance, John J.   PS3564.A546
Nance, Kathleen.   none
Nanda, Serena.   PS3614.A579
Napier, Bill.   PR6114.A65
Napier, Mary, 1932-   PR6073.R54
Napier, Melissa.   none
Napier, Robert S.   PS3614.A65
Naramore, Rosemarie.   PS3614.A685
Narcejac, Thomas, 1908-1998.   PQ2627.A675
Nardimon, Dov, 1947-   PJ5055.35.A364
Nasaw, Jonathan Lewis, 1947-   PS3564.A74
Nash, Jay Robert.   PS3564.A823
Nash, N. Richard.   PS3527.A6365
Nash, Simon.   PR6005.H323
Naslund, Sena Jeter.   PS3564.A827
Nason, Michael F.   PS3614.A76
Năstase, Ilie, 1946-   PS3564.A846
Nathan, Micah.   PS3614.A86
Nathan, Paul, 1913-   PS3564.A8493
Nathan, Robert Stuart.   PS3564.A8495
Nathan, Sandy.   PS3614.A865
Nathanson, E. M., 1928-   PS3564.A85
Nathenson, Joseph.   PS3564.A864
Natsuki, Shizuko, 1938-   PL857.A85
Naughton, Edmund.   none
Nava, Michael.   PS3564.A8746
Navarro, Julia, 1953-   PQ6664.A8932
Navratilova, Martina, 1956-   PS3564.A892
Nayes, Alan.   PS3614.A94
Naylor, Helen.   none
Nazel, Joseph.   PS3564.A98
Ndunguru, S. N.   PR9399.9.N38
Neal, Stanley B.   none
Neate, Patrick.   PR6114.E25
Nebrensky, Alex—see: Cooper, Parley J.
Neebel, Richard.   none
Neel, Dan.   PS3564.E2313
Neel, Janet.   PR6064.E417
Neely, Barbara.   PS3564.E244
Neely, Esther Jane.   none
Neely, Richard, 1941-   PS3564.E25
Neff, Heather.   PS3564.E2625
Neff, Jonathan.   PS3614.E37
Neggers, Carla.   PS3564.E2628
Nehrbass, Arthur F.   PS3564.E2642
Nehrbass, Richard, 1943-   PS3564.E2645
Nehring, Radine Trees, 1935-   PS3614.E44
Neiderman, Andrew.   PS3564.E27

Neilan, Sarah.	PR6064.E43
Neill, Robert.	PR6064.E44
Neilson, Andrew, 1946-	PR6064.E456
Neilson, Marguerite.	PR6064.E46
Nekrasova, Ol'ga.	none
Nelscott, Kris.	PS3568.U7
Nelson, Casey.	PS3564.E457
Nelson, D. L., 1942-	PS3614.E4455
Nelson, Jack.	none
Nelson, Jill Elizabeth.	PS3614.E44585
Nelson, Kent, 1943-	PS3564.E467
Nelson, Mark—see: Johnston, Ronald, 1926-	
Nelson, Mildred.	none
Nelson, Peter.	none
Nelson, Rick.	PS3614.E4494
Nelson, Walter Henry.	PS3564.E479
Nemec, David.	PS3564.E4797
Nemere, István.	PH3291.N37
Neri, Kris, 1948-	PS3564.E64
Nesbitt, John D.	PS3564.E76
Nesbø, Jo, 1960-	PT8951.24.E83
Nessen, Ron, 1934-	PS3564.E82
Nesser, Håkan, 1950-	PT9876.24.E76
Nesterenko, I‹U›riĭ, 1972-	PG3492.84.E855
Nesterov, Mikhail (Mikhail Petrovich)	PG3484.E756
Netesova, Él'mira.	PG3484.E77
Netzen, Klaus.	none
Neuharth, Jan.	PS3614.E54
Neuman, Fredric.	PS3564.E846
Neville, Katherine, 1945-	PS3564.E8517
Neville, Margot.	PR9619.3.N452
Neville, Stuart, 1972-	PR6114.E943
Nevins, Francis M.	PS3564.E854
New, Christopher.	PR6064.E847
New, William Sloane.	none
Newberg, Kathleen, 1947-	PS3614.E566
Newcomb, Kerry.	PS3564.E875
Newell, Rosemary.	none
Newland, John.	none
Newman, Bernard, 1897-1968.	PR6027.E914
Newman, Christopher, 1952-	PS3564.E9153
Newman, G. F. (Gordon F.)	PR6064.E925
Newman, Gary.	PR6123.I55
Newman, Kim.	PR6064.E9277
Newman, Robert, 1909-1988.	none
Newman, Robert, 1964-	PR6064.E9293
Newman, Sharan.	PS3564.E926
Newmark, Elle.	PS3614.E668
Newsome, Muriel.	none
Newton, Alistair.	PS3614.E725
Newton, Charlie.	PS3614.E73
Newton, Mike.	none
Newton, W. Douglas (Wilfrid Douglas), 1884-1951.	PR6027.E96
Newton, William, 1923-	none

Neznanskiĭ, Fridrikh.   PG3549.N45
Nichol, James W.   PR9199.3.N49
Nichols, Aeleta.   none
Nichols, Beverley, 1898-1983.   PR6027.I22
Nichols, Fan.   PS3515.A486
Nichols, Judy, 1956-   PS3614.I343
Nichols, Lee.   PS3614.I344
Nichols, Leigh, 1945-   PS3561.O55
Nichols, Peter, 1922-   PR6053.H75
Nichols, Robert, 1944-   PS3564.I27478
Nichols, Sarah.   none
Nicholson, Geoff, 1953-   PR6064.I225
Nicholson, Joy.   PS3564.I2774
Nicholson, Michael, 1937-   PR6064.I228
Nicholson, Peggy.   none
Nicholson, Robin, 1930-   PR9320.9.N5
Nickels, O. Lee.   PS3564.I282
Nickolae, Barbara.   PS3564.I32
Nickolay, Michael.   PS3564.I3315
Nickson, Chris.   PR6114.I34
Nicol, Mike, 1951-   PR9369.3.N54
Nicole, Anya.   PS3614.I336
Nicolaysen, Bruce, 1934-   PS3564.I334
Nicole, Christopher.   PR9320.9.N5
Nicole, Claudette.   none
Nicole, Claudia.   none
Nida, Jodie Larsen.   none
Niederman, Derrick.   PS3564.I343
Nielsen, Helen.   PS3564.I35
Nielsen, Torben, 1918 Apr. 22-   PT8176.24.I36
Nielsen, Wayne F.   PS3614.I36
Niemirski, Arkadiusz, 1962-   PG7214.I37
Niesewand, Peter.   PR6064.I33
Nighbert, David F.   PS3564.I363
Nightingale, Ursula.   none
Nigro, Paul A.   PS3614.I38
Nikitas, Derek.   PS3614.I54
Nile, Dorothea, 1924-1999.   PS3551.V3
Niles, Chris.   PR6064.I44
Nimse, Gordon.   PR6114.I58
Nipper, Clara.   PS3614.I67
Nisbet, Helen C.   none
Nisbet, Hume, 1849-1921?   none
Nisbet, Jim.   PS3564.I7
Nishimura, Kyōtarō, 1930-   PL857.I78
Nishio, Ishin, 1981-   PL873.5.I84
Niven, Larry.   PS3564.I9
Nixon, Alan, 1937-   PR6064.I83
Nixon, Allan.   none
Nixon, Joan Lowery.   none
Niziurski, Edmund.   PG7158.N55
Nizza, Paul.   PS3564.I97
Nnamani, G. C.   PR9387.9.N574
Noble, C. Norman.   PS3614.O24

Noble, Diane, 1945-	PS3563.A3179765
Noble, Kate, 1978-	PS3614.O246
Noël, Atanielle Annyn.	PS3564.O29
Noël, Denise.	PQ2674.O3
Noel, Jeffrey.	none
Noel, Sterling.	none
Noguchi, Thomas T., 1927-	PS3564.O354
Nøkland, Gunlaug, 1957-	PT9802.N63
Nolan, Deborah.	PS3614.O466
Nolan, Frederick W., 1931-	PR6064.O413
Nolan, Madeena Spray.	none
Nolan, Nick.	PS3614.O473
Nolan, William F., 1928-	PS3564.O39
Noll, Ingrid, 1935-	PT2674.O435
Nolta, David Derbin.	PS3614.O48
Nonami, Asa, 1960-	PL857.O494
Nooe, Troy D.	PS3614.O64
Noonan, John, 1953-	PR6114.O56
Noone, Carl.	none
Noone, Edwina, 1924-1999.	PS3551.V3
Noone, John.	PR6064.O49
Nooteboom, Cees, 1933-	PT5881.24.O55
Nordan, Robert.	PS3614.O73
Nordberg, Bette.	PS3564.O553
Nordberg, Nils.	PT8952.24.O74
Norden, Eric.	none
Nordhoff, James.	PS3564.O56
Norham, Gerald.	none
Norman, Barry, 1933-	PR6064.O722
Norman, Elizabeth, 1924-	PS3564.O564
Norman, Frank.	PR6064.O74
Norman, Geoffrey.	PS3564.O5645
Norman, Hilary.	PR6064.O743
Norman, Michael (Michael D.)	PS3614.O763
Norman, Yvonne.	none
Norman-Bellamy, Kendra.	PS3614.O765
Noro, Fred.	none
Norris, Carolyn B.	PS3564.O645
Norris, Kathleen Thompson, 1880-1966.	PS3527.O5
Norst, Joel.	none
North, Anthony, 1945-	PS3561.O55
North, Darian.	PS3557.I25
North, Elizabeth, 1932-	PR6064.O764
North, Gil, 1916-	PR6015.O6824
North, Howard.	PS3564.O74
North, Jessica.	PS3564.O763
North, Oliver.	PS3614.O776
North, Sam.	PR6064.O765
North, Sara.	PS3558.A3232
North, Suzanne, 1945-	PR9199.3.N575
Northrop, John.	PS3614.O779
Norton, Andre.	PS3527.O632
Norton, Michael C.	none
Norton, Olive.	PR6064.O767

Norwood, Elliott.	none
Norwood, Frank.	PS3564.O78
Norwood, Victor George Charles.	PR6064.O79
Nottingham, Poppy.	none
Nova, Craig.	PS3564.O86
Novak, Brenda.	PS3614.O926
Novak, Karen.	PS3564.O893
Novak, Robert, 1935-	none
Nowak, Jacquelyn.	PS3564.O936
Nowlan, Joe, 1954-	PS3614.O966
Noyer, Albert.	PS3614.O975
Noyes, Stanley.	PS3564.O98
Nuelle, Helen.	PS3564.U34
Nuetzel, Charles.	none
Nugent, Andrew.	PR6114.U36
Nugent, James.	none
Nugent, P. M. (P. Michael)	PS3564.U349
Null, Gary.	none
Nunes, Rachel Ann, 1966-	PS3564.U468
Nunn, Kem.	PS3564.U49
Nunn, Malla.	PR9619.4.N86
Nunnally, Tiina, 1952-	PS3564.U53
Nurowska, Maria.	PG7173.U76
Nuttall, Anthony.	none
Nuttall, Jeff.	PR6064.U8
Nwankwo, Arthur Agwuncha, 1942-	PR9387.9.N888
Nykanen, Mark.	PS3564.Y52
Nyquist, Gerd, 1913-	PT8950.N9
Ó Ruairc, Mícheál, 1953-	PB1399.O76
	PR6065.R76
Oakes, Andy, 1952-	PR6115.A37
Oakes, Philip, 1928-	PR6065.A38
Oakroyd, Simon.	none
Oasis, author.	PS3615.A35
Oates, Joyce Carol, 1938-	PS3565.A8
Oberhansly, Curtis.	PS3615.B47
Obiora, Emeka Joseph.	PR9387.9.O276
O'Brian, Patrick, 1914-2000.	PR6029.B55
O'Brien, Charles, 1927-	PS3615.B74
O'Brien, Edna.	PR6065.B7
O'Brien, Fitz James, 1828-1862.	PS2485
O'Brien, Flann, 1911-1966.	PR6029.N56
O'Brien, Kevin, 1955-	PS3565.B714
O'Brien, Lee.	none
O'Brien, Martin.	PR6115.B755
O'Brien, Maureen, 1943-	PR6065.B743
O'Brien, Meg.	PS3565.B718
O'Brien, Patricia.	PS3565.B73
O'Brien, Robert C.	PS3565.B74
O'Brien, Saliee, 1908-	none
O'Brien, Sonia.	PS3615.B78
O'Brine, Manning, 1913-1977.	PR6065.B75
Obrist, Jürg.	none
O'Bryan, Sofi.	none

Obstfeld, Raymond, 1952-	PS3554.U4632
O'Callaghan, Gareth.	PR6065.C34
O'Callaghan, Gary (Gary C.)	PS3565.C32
O'Callaghan, Maxine.	PS3565.C35
O'Carroll, Gerry, 1946-	PR6115.C37
Ocean, T. Lynn.	PS3615.C43
O'Clare, Lorie.	PS3615.C58
O'Connell, Carol, 1947-	PS3565.C497
O'Connell, Catherine, 1955-	PS3565.C5
O'Connell, Jack, 1959-	PS3565.C526
O'Connell, Jennifer.	PS3615.C65
O'Connor, Dermot.	none
O'Connor, Ed.	PR6115.C666
O'Connor, Gemma.	PR6065.C557
O'Connor, J. Regis.	PS3565.O33
O'Connor, Jane.	PS3615.C59
O'Connor, Joseph, 1963-	PR6065.C558
O'Connor, Richard, 1915-1975.	PS3565.C642
O'Connor, Seán.	PB1400.O34
OCork, Shannon.	PS3565.C66
Odell, Terry.	PS3615.D456
Oden, Marilyn Brown.	PS3615.D46
Odgers, Darrel.	none
O'Diear, James, 1945-	PS3565.D45
Odier, Daniel, 1945-	PQ2675.D5
Odom, Mel.	PS3565.D53
O'Donnell, Lillian.	PS3565.D59
O'Donnell, Margaret.	PR6065.D577
O'Donnell, Peter, 1920-2010.	PR6029.D55
O'Donohoe, Nick.	none
O'Donohue, Clare.	PS3615.D665
O'Donovan, Gerard, 1965-	PR6115.D655
Odze, György, 1949-	PH3291.O27
Oelker, Petra, 1947-	PT2409.K66
O'Farrell, Maggie, 1972-	PR6065.F36
O'Farrell, William, 1904-	none
Offord, Lenore Glen, 1905-	PS3529.F42
Offutt, Andrew J.	PS3565.F386
O'Flaherty, Louise.	none
O'Flynn, Catherine.	PR6115.F59
Ogan, George.	none
Ogan, Margaret.	none
Ogilvie, Elisabeth, 1917-2006.	PS3529.G39
Ognall, Leopold Horace.	PR6029.G6
O'Grady, Anne.	PR9619.3.O33
O'Grady, Leslie.	PS3565.G68
O'Grady, Rohan, 1922-	PR9199.3.O343
O'Hagan, Joan.	PR9619.3.O38
O'Halloran, Jack, 1943-	PS3615.H35
O'Hanlon, Ray.	PS3615.H355
O'Hara, Kenneth.	PR6065.H28
O'Hara, Patrick.	PR6065.H3
O'Hehir, Diana, 1929-	PS3565.H4
Ohnemus, Günter, 1946-	PT2675.H54

Ohnet, Georges, 1848-1918.   PQ2378.O3
O'Kane, Leslie.   PS3565.K335
O'Keefe, Bobbie.   PS3615.K43
Okoba, Matthew.   PR9387.9.O37835
Okonowicz, Ed, 1947-   PS3565.K58
Okrant, Mark J.   PS3565.K65
Okun, Lawrence E., 1929-   PS3565.K8
Olbrich, Freny.   PR6065.L35
Olcott, Anthony, 1950-   PS3565.L28
Old Sleuth, 1839?-1898.   PS1784.H24
Olden, Marc.   PS3565.L29
Oldfield, Pamela.   PR6065.L38
Oldham, Robert K.   PS3565.L328
Oldsey, Bernard S. (Bernard Stanley), 1923-2008. PS3565.L35
O'Leary, Ed.   none
Oleksiw, Susan.   PS3565.L42
Olesker, J. Bradford, 1949-   PS3565.L44
Olgin, Howard A., 1939-   PS3565.L45
Olin, Sean.   none
Oliphant, B. J.   none
Olisaeloka, Anozie.   PR9387.9.O39477
Oliver, Andrew (Andrew Thomas)   PS3615.L584
Oliver, Anthony.   PR6065.L47
Oliver, Gloria   PS3615.L5845
Oliver, Maria-Antònia.   PC3942.25.L53
Oliver, Steve, mystery writer.   PS3565.L519
Oliver, Teagan.   PS3615.L588
Olivy, D. J.   PS3565.L54
Olsen, D. B., 1907-1973.   PS3515.I955
Olsen, Gregg.   none
Olsen, Jack.   PS3565.L77
Olsen, Jimmy, 1946-   PS3565.L774
Olsen, Mark Andrew.   PS3615.L73
Olshaker, Mark, 1951-   PS3565.L823
Olson, Donald.   PS3565.L825
Olson, Karen E.   PS3615.L7525
Olson, Neil, 1964-   PS3615.L735
Olson, Toby.   PS3565.L84
O'Malley, Mary Dolling Saunders, Lady—see: Bridge, Ann, 1889-1974.
Omamo, Steven Were.   none
O'Marie, Carol Anne.   PS3565.M347
O'Meara, Megan.   PS3565.M43
O'Nan, Stewart, 1961-   PS3565.N316
Ondaatje, Michael, 1943-   PR9199.3.O5
O'Neal, James, 1960-   PS3602.O76
O'Neil, Russell.   PS3565.N45
O'Neil, Vincent H.   PS3615.N48
O'Neil, Will.   PS3565.N47
O'Neill, Archie.   PS3565.N48
O'Neill, Dorothy P.   PS3565.N488
O'Neill, Edward A.   PS3565.N49
O'Neill, Frank.   PS3565.N495
O'Neill, Gilda.   PR6065.N417
O'Neill, Jack, 1930-   PS3615.N444

O'Neill, Mark R.	PS3615.N446
O'Neill, Shane, 1964-	PR9619.4.O54
O'Neill, Tom, 1961-	PS3615.N46
O'Neill-Barna, Anne.	none
Onugha, Chukwudum.	PR9387.9.O535
Onuzuruike, Eddie.	PR9387.9.O5355
Onyeama, Dillibe, 1951-	PR9387.9.O54
Onyefulu, David Azubike.	PR9387.9.O5445
Ooi, Yang-May.	PR6065.O4
Oosting, Katrina A.	PS3565.O58
Oppegaard, David.	PS3615.P63
Oppel, Kenneth, 1967-	PR9199.3.O67
Oppenheim, E. Phillips (Edward Phillips), 1866-1946.	PR6029.P5
Oppenheimer, Joan L.	PS3565.P66
Opper, Richard Henry, 1952-	PS3615.P65
Oppong, Peggy.	PR9379.9.O76
Oran, Dan.	PS3565.R3
Oran, Daniel, 1965-	PS3565.R32
Orczy, Emmuska Orczy, Baroness, 1865-1947.	PR6029.R25
Orde, A. J.	PS3565.R36
Orde, Lewis.	PS3565.R38
O'Reilly, Bill.	PS3565.R3865
Oren, Michael B., 1955-	PS3615.R46
Orenduff, J. Michael (Jess Michael), 1944-	PS3615.R463
Orenstein, Frank.	PS3565.R39
Orford, Ellen.	none
Orford, Margie.	PR9369.4.O74
Organ, Perry.	PS3565.R45
Orgill, Douglas, 1922-	PR6065.R68
Oriol, Laurence.	PQ2672.O7
Orlando, Carlos.	PQ8520.25.R57
Orlando, Jordan, 1966-	PS3565.R574
Orlemann, Betty.	PS3615.R55
Orloff, Alan, 1960-	PS3615.R557
Ormerod, Jayne.	PS3615.R575
Ormerod, Roger.	PR6065.R688
O'Rourke, Andrew P.	none
O'Rourke, Erin, 1972-	PS3615.R585
O'Rourke, Frank, 1916-1989.	PS3529.R58
O'Rourke, Sally Smith.	PS3615.R587
O'Rourke, Tempest, 1944-	PS3615.R588
Orr, Mary.	PS3529.R66
Ortega, Gregorio, 1948-	PQ7298.25.R78
Ortiz, Orlando.	PQ7298.25.R8
Ortiz, Oscar F., 1959-	PQ7390.O716
Ørum, Poul.	PT8176.25.E7
Orvis, Kenneth.	none
Ōsawa, Arimasa, 1956-	PL858.S29
Osborn, David, 1923-	PS3565.S37
Osborn, John Jay.	PS3565.S38
Osborn, Stephanie.	PS3615.S268
Osborne, Beresford.	none
Osborne, Charles, 1927-	PR6065.S15

Osborne, Denise.	PS3565.S374
Osborne, Dorothy.	none
Osborne, Erin.	none
Osborne, Geoffrey.	none
Osborne, Helena.	PR6065.S17
Osborne, Liz.	PS3611.R34
Osborne, Louise.	none
O'Shaughnessy, Perri.	PS3565.S542
Osier, John, 1938-	PS3565.S55
Osmond, Andrew, 1938-	PR6065.S6 [sic]
Osmond, Andrew, 1967-	PR6065.S6
Ossman, David.	PS3615.S63
Oster, Jerry.	PS3565.S813
Osterman, Helen Macie.	PS3565.S8235
Osterman, Mark, 1935-	PS3565.S824
Ostlere, Gordon—see: Gordon, Richard, 1921-	
Ostozhin, Vladimir, 1953-	none
Ostrander, Isabel, 1883-1924.	PS3529.S75
Ostrander, Kate.	PS3565.S83
Ostrom, Hans A.	PS3565.S86
Ostrovsky, Victor.	PR9510.9.O85
O'Sullivan, James Brendan, 1919-	none
Oszustowicz, Len.	PS3565.S95
O'Toole, G. J. A. (George J. A.), 1936-	PS3565.T6
Ottosyrin, Hanna Irene.	PS3565.T797
Ottum, Bob.	PS3565.T8
Ouředník, Patrik.	PG5039.25.U74
Oursler, Fulton, 1893-1952.	PS3529.U65
Oust, Gail, 1943-	PS3620.U7645
Outland, Orland.	PS3565.U96
Ovalov, Lev, 1905-1997.	PG3476.O89
Overgard, William.	PS3565.V427
Overholser, Stephen.	PS3565.V43
Overholser, Wayne D., 1906-1996.	PS3529.V33
Overson, H. Wayne.	PS3615.V47
Overton, Thomas.	PS3615.V476
Owen, Charlie, 1957-	PR6115.W45
Owen, Dean.	PS3565.W53
Owen, Howard, 1949-	PS3565.W552
Owen, June Duncan.	PR9619.4.O97
Owen, Lauri J.	PS3615.W43
Owen, Llwyd.	PB2299.O96
Owen, Philip, 1903-1989.	PS3531.H442
Owen, Ray.	PR6065.W44
Owen, Richard, 1942-	PS3565.W56
Owens, George, 1950-	PS3565.W566
Owens, Louis.	PS3565.W567
Owens, Michael T., 1975-	PS3615.W47
Owens, Virginia Stem.	PS3565.W576
Ozaki, Milton K.	PS3529
Paar, Angelica.	none
Pace, Eric, 1936-	PS3566.A24
Pace, Tom.	PS3566.A26
Packard, Frank L. (Frank Lucius), 1877-1942.	PS3531.A2154

Packer, Bernard.   PS3566.A316
Packer, Joy Petersen, Lady, 1905-   PR9369.3.P27
Packer, Mez.   PR6116.A32
Packer, Vin, 1927-   PS3561.E643
Padden, Ian.   none
Paddie, Dennis.   PS3616.A3353
Paddock, Jennifer.   PS3616.A3355
Padgett, Abigail.   PS3566.A3197
Padilla, Ignacio, 1968-   PQ7298.26.A285
Padura, Leonardo.   PQ7390.P32
Page, Emma.   PR6066.A29
Page, Jake.   PS3566.A333
Page, Katherine Hall.   PS3566.A334
Page, Martin, 1938-   PR6066.A34
Page, Robert W. (Robert Wesley), 1927-   PS3616.A3376
Page, Spider.   none
Page, Thomas, 1942-   PS3566.A335
Pagel, Tempa.   PS3616.A33765
Pagliarulo, Antonio.   none
Paier, Robert.   PS3566.A339
Paige, Leslie.   none
Paige, Richard, 1945-   PS3561.O55
Paige, Robin.   PS3566.A3396
Pain, Barry, 1864-1928.   PR6031.A25
Paine, Lauran.   PS3566.A34
Pairo, Preston.   PS3563.A3129
Pak, Gary, 1952-   PS3566.A39
Pakeman, Louise, 1936-   PR9619.4.P35
Palahniuk, Chuck.   PS3566.A4554
Palfrey, Evelyn.   PS3566.A4629
Palin, Michael.   PR6066.A42
Paling, Chris.   PR6066.A425
Pall, Ellen, 1952-   PS3566.A463
Palliser, Charles, 1947-   PR6066.A43
Palmer, Catherine, 1956-   PS3566.A495
Palmer, Daniel, 1969-   PS3616.A33883
Palmer, Diana.   PS3566.A513
Palmer, Frank, 1934-   PR6066.A438
Palmer, Joe, 1951-   PS3616.A339
Palmer, Karen, 1961-   PS3566.A526
Palmer, Lilli, 1914-1986.   PT2631.A36
Palmer, Linda.   PS3566.A528
Palmer, Michael, 1942-   PS3566.A539
Palmer, P. K.   none
Palmer, Shirley.   PR6052.R44316
Palmer, Stuart, 1905-1968.   PS3531.A3868
Palmer, Will.   none
Palmer, William J., 1943-   PS3566.A547
Palmtag, Dinah.   none
Palumbo, Dennis, 1951-   PS3566.A5535
Pamuk, Orhan, 1952-   PL248.P34
Panati, Charles, 1943-   PS3566.A558
Pangborn, Edgar, 1909-1976.   PS3566.A56
Panger, Daniel.   PS3566.A57

Panov, Vadim.	PG3492.94.A56
Paoletti, Marc.	PS3616.A54
Paolucci, Anne.	PS3566.A595
Papazoglou, Orania, 1951-	PS3566.A613
Pape, Gordon.	PR9199.3.P33
Pape, Sharon B.	none
Pappano, Marilyn.	PS3566.A618
Paradis, Vincent A.	none
Paranya, P. K.	PS3616.A73
Paredes, Julio, 1957-	PQ8180.26.A69
Parenti, Gina.	PS3616.A743
Paretsky, Sara.	PS3566.A647
Pargeter, Edith, 1913-1995.	PR6031.A49
Paris, Ann.	none
Paris, Matthew, 1938-	PS3566.A66
Park, David, 1953-	PR6066.A577
Park, Jacqueline.	PS3566.A6735
Park, Jordan, 1924-1958.	PS3566.O36
Park, Owen.	none
Park, Yongsoo.	PS3566.A674728
Parke, Daryn.	PS3616.A7438
Parker, Alan Michael, 1961-	PS3566.A674738
Parker, Ann, 1952-	PS3616.A744
Parker, Barbara (Barbara J.)	PS3566.A67475
Parker, Beatrice.	PS3558.U323
Parker, Bob.	none
Parker, Claire.	PS3566.A677
Parker, Gary E.	PS3566.A6784
Parker, I. J. (Ingrid J.)	PS3616.A745
Parker, Judith R.	none
Parker, Lee.	none
Parker, M. M.	PS3566.A68
Parker, Michael, 1941-	PR6066.A648
Parker, Michael, 1959-	PS3566.A683
Parker, Nancy (Nancy A.)	PS3566.A6837
Parker, Norman.	PS3566.A684
Parker, Percy Spurlark.	PS3566.A685
Parker, Ranse.	PS3616.A746
Parker, Richard, 1915-	PR6066.A67
Parker, Robert B., 1932-2010.	PS3566.A686
Parker, Rosa Abbott.	none
Parker, T. Jefferson.	PS3566.A6863
Parker, Una-Mary.	PR6066.A694
Parkes, Roger.	PR6066.A6953
Parkhurst, Carolyn, 1971-	PS3616.A754
Parkhurst, Jane.	none
Parkman, Sydney M. (Sydney Müller), b. 1895.	PR6031.A635
Parks, Brad, 1974-	PS3616.A7553
Parks, Electa Rome.	PS3616.A7555
Parks, Tim.	PR6066.A6957
Parnell, Andrea.	none
Parot, Jean-François.	PQ2676.A7255
Parras, John, 1964-	PS3616.A7655
Parris, S. J., 1974-	PR6113.E77

Parrish, Barney.	none
Parrish, Frank.	PR6062.O516
Parrish, Leslie, 1965-	none
Parrish, P. J.	PS3566.A7567
Parrish, Richard.	PS3566.A757
Parrish, Robin.	PS3616.A7684
Parrish, Stephen, 1958-	PS3616.A7685
Parrott, Gwen.	PB2299.P37
Parry, David, 1941-	PR9199.3.P343
Parry, James, 1943-	PS3566.A76
Parry, Michel.	none
Parry, Owen.	PS3566.E7559
Parshall, Craig, 1950-	PS3616.A77
Parshall, Sandra.	PS3616.A772
Parsons, Julie.	PR6066.A7177
Parsons, Thornton.	PS3616.A784
Partridge, J. J. (John J.)	PS3616.A874
Parvin, Brian.	none
Pârvulescu, Ioana, 1960-	PC840.426.A78
Pascal, Francine.	PS3566.A7727
Pascoe, Jim.	none
Pascual, Javier S., 1956-	PQ7798.426.A85
Pasewicz, Edward.	PG7216.A83
Passarella, John.	none
Passman, Donald S.	PS3566.A774
Pastor, Ben, 1950-	PS3566.A77525
Pate, Alexs D., 1950-	PS3566.A777
Pate, Jeff.	PS3566.A77575
Paton, Allison Cesario.	PS3616.A8678
Paton Walsh, Jill, 1937-	PR6066.A84
Patrick, Jennifer, 1965-	PS3616.A87
Patrick, Q.	PR6033.U43
Patrick, Vincent.	PS3566.A7869
Patten, Brian, 1946-	PR6066.A86
Patterson, Harry, 1929-	PR6058.I343
Patterson, James, 1947-	PS3566.A822
Patterson, John M. (John McCready), 1913-1983.	PS3566.A823
Patterson, Michael S., 1962-	PS3566.A8234
Patterson, Paul E., 1926-	PS3566.A8238
Patterson, Richard North.	PS3566.A8242
Patterson, T. D.	PS3616.A88
Patterson-Z, Tanna, 1955-	PR9199.4.P3819
Patti, Paul.	PS3566.A8248
Pattillo, Beth.	PS3616.A925
Pattillo, James G., 1944-	PS3566.A8249
Pattinson, James, 1915-	PR6066.A877
Pattison, Eliot.	PS3566.A82497
Pattison, Ruth—see: Abbey, Ruth.	
Patton, Cliff.	none
Patton, Jim, 1953-	PS3566.A8256
Paul, Barbara, 1931-	PS3566.A82615
Paul, Celeste.	none
Paul, Charlotte.	PS3531.A8519
Paul, Elliot, 1891-1958.	PS3531.A852

Paul, Jeremy.   PR6066.A882
Paul, Raymond.   PS3566.A8266
Paul, William, 1955-   PR6066.A8837
Paul-Bloxham, Regina.   PR9199.4.P3855
Pauley, Barbara Anne.   PS3566.A828
Paull, D. C.   PS3616.A953
Paull, Jessyca.   none
Paulsen, Gary.   PS3566.A834
Pavlou, Stel.   PR6116.A95
Pavlovskiĭ, Sergeĭ.   none
Pawel, Rebecca, 1977-   PS3616.A957
Pawlik, Tom, 1965-   PS3616.A9573
Paxson, John.   PS3616.A958
Paxton, Bill (William C.)   PS3566.A925
Paxton, Lois.   PR6066.A885
Payes, Rachel Cosgrove.   PS3566.A933
Payn, James, 1830-1898.   PR5150-5158
Payne, Donald Gordon—see: Cameron, Ian, 1924-
Payne, Laurence.   PR6066.A93
Payne, Peggy.   PS3566.A954
Paz Paredes, Lorena.   none
Paz Soldán, Edmundo, 1967-   PQ7820.P39
Paz, Pedro de, 1969-   PQ6716.A92
Peace, David.   PR6066.E116
Peachment, Christopher.   PR6116.E15
Peacock, Caro.   PR6116.E16
Peacock, Justin.   PS3616.E225
Peak, John A.   PS3566.E157
Peale, Cynthia.   PS3576.A74
Pearce, Bob.   PS3616.E24
Pearce, Gerald, 1928-   PR6066.E157
Pearce, Michael, 1933-   PR6066.E166
Pearl, Jack, 1923-   PS3566.E218
Pearl, Matthew.   PS3616.E25
Pearlman, Gilbert.   none
Pearlman, Ruthie.   PS3566.E22
Pears, Iain.   PR6066.E167
Pearsall, Ronald, 1927-2005.   PR6066.E168
Pearson, A. Scott.   PS3616.E2543
Pearson, Ann.   none
Pearson, Edmund Lester, 1880-1937.   PS3531.E2358
Pearson, John, 1930-   PR6066.E2
Pearson, Peter.   PR6066.E225
Pearson, Ridley.   PS3566.E234
Pearson, Ryne Douglas.   PS3566.E2343
Pearson, T. R., 1956-   PS3566.E235
Pearson, William, 1922-   PS3566.E237
Peart, Jane.   PS3566.E238
Peart, Rudolph.   none
Pease, William D.   PS3566.E2425
Peck, Leonard, 1906-   none
Peck, M. Scott (Morgan Scott), 1936-2005.   PS3566.E2524
Peck, Richard E.   PS3566.E253
Peck, Robert Newton.   PS3566.E254

Pederiali, Giuseppe.	PQ4876.E24
Pedersen, Lloyd.	PS3566.E2565
Pedler, John Branfroot Simpson—see:	Torr, Dominic.
Pedneau, Dave.	none
Pedrazas, Allan.	PS3566.E263
Peel, Colin D.	PR6066.E36
Peel, John, 1954-	PS3566.E275
Peeples, Samuel Anthony, 1917-	PS3531.E286
Peffer, Randall S.	PS3616.E35
Pelé, 1940-	PS3566.E35
Pelecanos, George P.	PS3566.E354
Pelham, Howard.	PS3566.E38
Pell, Robert.	none
Pella, Judith.	PS3566.E415
Pelletier, Chantal, 1949-	PQ2676.E424
Pellicane, Patricia.	PS3566.E435
Peltz, Rosemonde S.	PS3566.E44
Pember, Ron.	none
Pemberton, Margaret.	PR6066.E488
Pemberton, Max, Sir, 1863-1950.	PR6031.E4
Pemberton, S. C. (Sharee Cravero)	PS3566.E446
Pembroke, Peter.	none
Pence, James H.	PS3616.E53
Pence, Joanne.	PS3566.E453
Pendarvis, Jack, 1963-	PS3616.E535
Pendergrass, Tess.	PS3566.E457
Pendleton, Don, 1927-1995.	PS3566.E465
Pendleton, Tom.	PS3572.A55
Pendower, Jacques, 1899-1976.	PR6019.A336
Penman, Sharon Kay.	PS3566.E474
Penn, H.	none
Penn, John.	PR6066.E496
Pennac, Daniel.	PQ2676.E525
Pennant-Rea, Rupert.	PR6066.E497
Penney, Stef.	PR6116.E58
Pennington, Winter.	PS3616.E5574
Penny, Louise.	PR9199.4.P464
Penoyre, Mary.	none
Pensoneau, Taylor.	PS3616.E57
Pentecost, Hugh, 1903-1989.	PS3531.H442
Penzler, Otto.	none
Pepper, Andrew, 1969-	PR6116.E66
Perales, Iosu.	PQ6666.E6695
Perdue, Lewis.	PS3566.E69122
Perec, Georges, 1936-1982.	PQ2676.E67
Pereira, Michael, 1928-	PR6066.E63
Perez, Marlene.	none
Pérez-Reverte, Arturo.	PQ6666.E765
Perissinotto, Alessandro, 1964-	PQ4876.E68925
Perkins, Suzetta.	PS3616.E747
Perkins, Wilder.	PS3566.E6914867
Perlman, Rhea.	none
Perona, Tony.	PS3616.E75
Perowne, Barry.	PR6031.E54

Perrault, E. G. (Ernest G.)	PR9199.3.P43
Perrault, Gilles, 1931-	PQ2676.E7
Perret, Geoffrey.	PS3566.E6952
Perriman, Cole.	PS3566.E6943
Perrin, Kayla.	PR9199.3.P434
Perrin, Robert, 1939-	PR6066.E684
Perrone, Joe, 1945-	PS3616.E77
Perry, Anne.	PR6066.E693
Perry, Isaac.	PS3616.E79296
Perry, Kenneth H.	PS3616.E793
Perry, Mark C.	none
Perry, Marta.	PS3616.E7933
Perry, Michelle.	PS3616.E7935
Perry, Patricia, 1934-	none
Perry, Ritchie, 1942-	PR6066.E72
Perry, Robin.	PS3566.E716
Perry, Roland, 1946-	PR9619.3.P376
Perry, Steve.	PS3566.E7168
Perry, Sue.	PS3566.E7169
Perry, Tasmina.	PR6116.E78
Perry, Thomas, 1947-	PS3566.E718
Perry, V. M.	none
Perry, Will.	PS3566.E722
Pershing, Diane.	none
Persico, Joseph E.	PS3566.E727
Persons, Terri, 1958-	PS3616.E797
Pertwee, Roland, 1885-1963.	PR6031.E6
Perutz, Leo, 1882-1957.	PT2631.E5
Pessl, Marisha.	PS3616.E825
Peter, John Desmond.	PR6066.E73
Peters, Bryan, 1924-1966.	PR6057.E54
Peters, Elizabeth, 1927-	PS3563.E747
Peters, Ellis, 1913-1995.	PR6031.A49
Peters, Jordan, 1952-	PS3616.E8423
Peters, L. T.	none
Peters, Ludovic.	PR6052.R42
Peters, Othello.	none
Peters, Ralph, 1952-	PS3566.E7559
Peters, Ron.	none
Peters, Stephanie True, 1965-	none
Peterson, Ann Voss.	none
Peterson, Audrey.	PS3566.E765
Peterson, Bernard.	PS3566.E766
Peterson, Brenda, 1950-	PS3566.E767
Peterson, Doug.	none
Peterson, Jerry A.	PS3616.E84286
Peterson, Jim, 1929-	none
Peterson, Jim, 1948-	PS3566.E7693
Peterson, Kathi Oram.	PS3616.E84289
Peterson, Keith, 1954-	PS3561.L334
Peterson, Larry Len.	PS3616.E84296
Peterson, Margaret, 1883-1933.	none
Peterson, Patrick E.	PS3616.E844
Peterson, Tracie.	PS3566.E7717

Peterson, Will.	none
Peterzén, Elisabet, 1938-	PT9876.26.E74
Petievich, Gerald.	PS3566.E773
Petit, Caroline.	PR9619.4.P47
Petit, Christopher.	PR6066.E7535
Petit, Diane.	PS3566.E774
Petrakis, Harry Mark.	PS3566.E78
Petree, Sheree, 1942-	PS3616.E866
Petrie, Glen.	PR6066.E755
Petrie, Rhona.	PR6053.U79
Petrou, Sophia.	PS3616.E87
Petrov, Dmitriĭ.	PG3485.E679
Petrovich, Aaron.	PS3616.E873
Petrucha, Stefan.	PS3566.E864
Pettit, Mike.	none
Petty, Barbara.	none
Pevel, Pierre, 1968-	PQ2716.E94
Pevny, Wilhelm, 1944-	PT2676.E9
Peyrou, Manuel.	PQ7797.P534
Pfarrer, Chuck.	PS3616.F37
Pfarrer, Donald.	PS3566.F3
Pfefferle, Seth.	none
Pharr, Robert Deane.	PS3566.H33
Phelan, Twist.	PS3616.H44
Phelps, E. Floyd.	PS3616.H446
Philbin, Tom, 1934-	none
Philbrick, W. R. (W. Rodman)	PS3566.H474
Philips, Judson, 1903-1989.	PS3531.H442
Phillifent, John T., 1916-1976.	PR6068.A235
Phillips, Arthur, 1969-	PS3616.H45
Phillips, Carly.	PS3616.H454
Phillips, Christi.	PS3616.H4545
Phillips, Clyde.	PS3566.H4764
Phillips, Clyde B.	none
Phillips, David Atlee.	PS3566.H477
Phillips, Dennis, 1924-	PR6066.H463
Phillips, Edward, 1931-	PR9199.3.P476
Phillips, Gary, 1955-	PS3566.H4783
Phillips, James Atlee, 1915-	none
Phillips, Leon, 1914-1988.	PS3513.E8679
Phillips, Meredith, 1943-	PS3566.H488
Phillips, Michael R., 1946-	PS3566.H492
Phillips, Mike, 1911-	PS3566.H494
Phillips, Mike, 1941-	PR6066.H485
Phillips, Pat.	none
Phillips, R. B., 1943-	PS3552.R2298
Phillips, Scott.	PS3566.H515
Phillips, Sonia.	PS3566.H518
Phillips, Stella.	PR6066.H493
Phillips, Steven, 1947-	PS3566.H52
Phillips, T. J.	PS3566.H523
Phillips, Thomas, 1970-	PS3616.H478
Phillpotts, Eden, 1862-1960.	PR5177
	[Z8684.5]

Philo, Thomas.   PS3566.H55
Philpin, John.   none
Phinney, Barbara.   PS3616.H48
Phoenix, Adrian.   PS3616.H6
Picano, Felice, 1944-   PS3566.I25
Picard, Sam.   none
Picardie, Justine.   PR6116.I33
Piccirilli, Tom.   PS3566.I266
Pici, J. R.   none
Pickard, Nancy.   PS3566.I274
Pickens, Cathy.   PS3616.I27
Picoult, Jodi, 1966-   PS3566.I372
Picton, Bernard.   none
Pieczenik, Steve R.   PS3566.I3813
Pierce, David M.   PR9199.3.P486
Pierce, Jessica.   none
Pierce, Margret.   PS3566.I388
Pierce, Noel, 1907-   PS3531.I412
Piesman, Marissa.   PS3566.I4235
Pifer, Drury L.   PS3566.I43
Pike, Christopher, 1955-   PS3566.I486
Pike, Larry C., 1947-   none
Pike, Robert L., 1912-1981.   PS3556.I79
Pikser, Jeremy.   PS3566.I47
Pilcher, Rosamunde.   PR6066.I38
Pileggi, Nicholas.   none
Pilgrim, David.   PR6003.E3
Pilgrim, Kitty.   PS3616.I446
Pilkington, John, 1948 June 11-   PR6066.I435
Pina, Gabrielle.   PS3616.I53
Pincher, Chapman.   PR6066.I47
Pincus, Elizabeth, 1957-   PS3566.I517
Piñeiro, Claudia, 1960-   PQ7798.426.I56
Pineiro, R. J.   PS3566.I5215
Pines, Paul.   PS3566.I522
Pinget, Robert.   PQ2631.I638
Pinkerton, A. Frank.   none
Pinkerton, Allan, 1819-1884.   PS2590
Pinkston, Tristi.   PS3616.I575
Pinkwater, Daniel Manus, 1941-   PS3566.I526
Pintoff, Stefanie.   PS3616.I58
Pintoro, John.   none
Piper, Evelyn.   PS3531.I76
Piper, H. Beam.   PS3566.I58
Pirie, David, 1946-   PR6116.I74
Pirinçci, Akif.   PT2676.I728
Pirkis, Catherine Louisa, 1839-1910.   PR5185.P57
Pirnie, Amy.   PR6104.A86
Pirrone, D. M.   PS3616.I76
Pistone, Joseph D.   none
Pita, Maria Isabel, 1961-   PS3616.I87
Pitchford, Kenneth.   PS3566.I8
Pitkin, David J.   PS3616.I874
Pitt, Ingrid.   none

Pitt, Roxane.	none
Pittinger, Virginia.	none
Pittman, Joseph.	PS3566.I852
Pitts, Denis.	PS3566.I86
Pizzolatto, Nic, 1975-	PS3616.I99
Plagemann, Bentz, 1913-	PS3566.L25
Plaidy, Jean, 1906-1993.	PR6015.I3
Plakcy, Neil S. (Neil Steven)	PS3616.L35
Plante, Edmund.	none
Plate, Peter.	PS3566.L267
Platova, Viktorii‹a›, 1967-	PG3485.L36
Platt, Charles.	PS3566.L2848
Platt, Kin.	PS3566.L29
Platz, Jonathon.	PR9199.4.P58
Plaza, Elsa, 1950-	PQ7798.426.P39
Player, Robert.	PR6031.L36
Pledger, Derrick R.	none
Ples, Sally, 1947-	none
Plowman, Mary Sharon.	PS3566.L59
Plum, Jennifer—see: Kurland, Michael.	
Plummer, T. Arthur (Thomas Arthur)	none
Plunkett, Susan.	PS3616.L89
Pluti‹a›gin, Vladimir.	none
Poddubnyĭ, Oleg, 1963-	none
Podojil, E. William.	PS3616.O29
Podol'skiĭ, Nal'.	PG3485.2.D577
Podrug, Junius.	PS3566.O325
Poe, Edgar Allan, 1809-1849.	PS2600-2648 [Z8699]
Poe, Robert.	PS3566.O34
Pogorelov, Oleg.	none
Polansky, Daniel.	PS3616.O557
Polansky, Steven, 1949-	PS3566.O43
Polevoi, Lee, 1952-	PS3616.O558
Poli‹a›kova, Tat'i‹a›na.	PG3485.2.L464
Polidoro, J. P.	PS3616.O567
Poling, Charles.	PS3616.O5674
Polisar, Lisa.	PS3616.O5675
Polk, Dora.	PS3566.O476
Pollack, Barry, 1946-	PS3616.O5679
Pollack, Elisabeth, 1921-	PS3566.O4796
Pollack, Pam.	none
Pollack, Rachel, 1945-	PS3566.O4798
Pollak, Richard.	PS3566.O512
Polland, Madeleine A.	PR6066.O38
Pollard, A. O. (Alfred Oliver), b. 1893.	none
Pollard, Tony.	PR6116.O45
Pollero, Rhonda.	PS3616.O5684
Pollitz, Edward A., 1937-	PS3566.O534
Pollock, Daniel, 1944-	PS3566.O5346
Pollock, Donald Ray, 1954-	PS3616.O5694
Pollock, J. C.	PS3566.O5348
Pollock, Robert, 1930-	PR6066.O42
Pollock, Ted.	PS3566.O535

Pomeroy, Julia.	PS3616.O578
Pomidor, Bill.	none
Ponder, Patricia, 1942-	PS3563.A923
Pons, Maurice.	PQ2631.O6443
Ponthier, François.	PQ2631.O6476
Ponti, James.	none
Poole, Sara, 1951-	PS3569.E43
Poole-Carter, R. (Rosemary)	PS3616.O64
Poore, Charles M.	PS3566.O624
Poore, Dawn Aldridge.	none
Pope, Leo.	none
Popescu, Petru, 1944-	PC840.26.O57
	PS3566.O6267
Popplewell, Jack.	PR6031.O625
Portela, Ena Lucía, 1972-	PQ7390.P64
Porter, Anna.	PR9199.3.P624
Porter, Dorothy, 1954-2008.	PR9619.3.P558
Porter, Henry, 1953-	PR6066.O715
Porter, Joyce.	PR6066.O72
Porter, Margaret Evans.	PS3566.O653
Porter, Steven, 1943-	PS3616.O788
Portnoy, Howard N.	PS3566.O664
Portway, Christopher, 1923-	none
Posey, Carl A., 1933-	PS3566.O67
Posner, Richard.	PS3566.O673
Posnick, Paul.	none
Posse, Abel.	PQ7798.26.O78
Post, Don E.	PS3616.O838
Post, Melville Davisson, 1871-1930.	PS3531.O76427
Postgate, Raymond, 1896-1971.	PR6031.O713
Potter, Dan.	PS3566.O696
Potter, Dennis.	PR6066.O77
Potter, Ellen, 1963-	PS3616.O85
Potter, Jeremy.	PR6066.O78
Potter, Jerry Allen.	PS3566.O698
Potter, Patricia, 1940-	PS3566.O718
Pottinger, Stanley.	PS3566.O724
Potts, Jean.	PS3531.O789
Potts, Ron.	none
Potts, Ruth.	none
Potts, Sharon.	PS3616.O8563
Pötzsch, Oliver.	PT2676.O895
Poulson, Christine.	PR6116.O93
Poulson, Clair.	PS3566.O812
Pournelle, Jerry, 1933-	PS3566.O815
Povey, Jeff.	PS3616.O874
Powe, Bruce.	PR9199.3.P65
Powell, Deborah, 1951-	PS3566.O827
Powell, John D.	none
Powell, Michael, 1905-1990.	PR6066.O935
Powell, Richard, 1908-1999.	PS3531.O966
Powell, Talmage.	PS3566.O8345
Powell, V. K.	PS3616.O8828825
Power, Edmund.	PR6116.O954

Power, Jo-Ann.	PS3616.O883
Power, Margo.	PS3566.O83576
Power, Patricia.	PR9199.3
Powers, Charles T.	PS3566.O8368
Powers, Elizabeth, 1944-	PS3566.O837
Powers, James.	PS3566.O838
Powers, Martha.	PS3566.O888
Powers, Tim, 1952-	PS3566.O95
Pownall, David, 1938-	PR6066.O995
Poyer, David.	PS3566.O978
Poyer, Joe.	PS3566.O98
Pozo, Raúl del.	PQ6666.O95
Pozzessere, Heather Graham.	PS3557.R198
Prada, Juan Manuel de, 1970-	PQ6666.R313
Prado, Benjamín, 1961-	PQ6666.R319
Praed, Campbell, Mrs., 1851-1935.	PR9619.2.P7
Prantera, Amanda.	PR6066.R325
Prather, Marilyn.	PS3566.R273
Prather, Richard S.	PS3531.R14
Pratt, Scott.	PS3616.R3845
Pratt, Sheralyn.	PS3616.R3846
Pratt, Theodore, 1901-1969.	PS3531.R248
Preedy, George, 1888-1952.	PR6003.O676
Preisler, Jerome.	none
Preiss, Byron.	none
Preller, James.	none
Presberg, Shirley.	PS3566.R367
Prescott, Casey.	PS3566.R368
Prescott, Jerry.	PS3566.R374
Prescott, Michael.	PS3566.R3743
Press, Lloyd Douglas, 1950-	none
Press, Margaret L.	PS3566.R38
Prest, Thomas Peckett.	PR5189.P95
Preston, Alison, 1949-	PR9199.3.P728
Preston, Douglas J.	PS3566.R3982
Preston, James, 1913-	none
Preston, John.	PS3566.R412
Preston, M. K. (Marcia K.), 1944-	PS3566.R4123
Preston, T.	none
Price, Anthony.	PR6066.R5
Price, Bruce D., 1941-	PS3566.R44
Price, Charlie.	none
Price, John-Allen.	none
Price, Nancy, 1925-	PS3566.R49
Price, Richard, 1941-	PS3566.R543
Price, Richard, 1949-	PS3566.R544
Price, Suzanne.	PS3616.R5276
Priest, Cherie.	PS3616.R537
Priestley, Brian.	none
Priestley, J. B. (John Boynton), 1894-1984.	PR6031.R6 [Z8713.535]
Prince, Peter, 1942-	PR6066.R564
Pringle, Peter.	PS3616.R55
Prior, Allan, 1922-2006.	PR6066.R57

Prior, Lily, 1966-	PS3566.R5767
Pritchard, Stuart, 1921-	PS3566.R582
Pritchett, Ariadne.	none
Prochnau, William W., 1937-	PS3566.R587
Procter, Maurice.	PR6031.R74
Proctor, Kate.	PR6066.R595
Proffitt, Nicholas, 1943-2006.	PS3566.R643
Prone, Terri.	PR6066.R62
Pronin, Barbara.	none
Pronin, Viktor, 1938-	PG3485.3.R642
Pronzini, Bill.	PS3566.R67
Propper, Milton, M (Milton Morris), 1906-	PS3531.R785
Prospero, Ann.	PS3566.R688
Proud, Franklin M., 1920-	PR6066.R625
Prowell, Sandra West.	PS3566.R77
Prucha, Lynette.	PS3566.R8
Pruitt, Robert G.	PS3616.R85
Pryce, Larry.	none
Pryce, Malcolm.	PR6116.R93
Pryce-Jones, David, 1936-	PR6066.R88
Pryor, Hugh.	PR9381.9.P79
Pryor, Josh.	PS3616.R97
Pryor, Larry.	PS3566.R86
Puccetti, Roland.	PS3566.U25
Puchkov, Lev, 1965-	PG3485.3.U24
Puckett, Andrew.	PR6066.U35
Puebla, Javier.	PQ6666.U32
Puerta Martín, Adolfo, 1956-	PQ6716.U27
Pugh, Dianne G.	PS3566.U33
Pugh, Marshall.	PR6066.U4
Puig, Manuel.	PQ7798.26.U4
	PR9300.9.P84
Pujol, Carlos.	PQ6666.U45
Pullinger, Kate.	PR9199.3.P775
Pullman, Philip, 1946-	PR6066.U44
Pulman, Jack.	PR6066.U45
Pulver, Mary Monica.	PS3566.U47
Punshon, E. R. (Ernest Robertson), 1872-1956.	PR6031.U6
Purcell, Deirdre.	PR6066.U64
Purdy, James, 1914-2009.	PS3531.U426
Purser, Ann.	PR6066.U758
Purser, Philip, 1925-	PR6066.U78
Purtell, Joseph.	PS3566.U7
Purvis, James L.	none
Putnam, Sean.	none
Putney, Mary Jo.	PS3566.U83
Putre, John Walter.	PS3566.U86
Puzo, Mario, 1920-1999.	PS3566.U9
Pye, Michael, 1946-	PR6066.Y4
Pykare, Nina.	PS3566.Y48
Pyle, A. M. (Albert M.)	PS3566.Y53
Pyper, Andrew.	PR9199.3.P96
Qiu, Xiaolong, 1953-	PS3553.H537
Quan, Richard.	PS3617.U357

Quarrington, Paul.	PR9199.3.Q34
Quarry, Nick, 1924-	PS3551.L26
Quartermain, James.	PR6067.U3
Quartey, Kwei J.	PS3617.U37
Quarto, James.	PS3567.U22
Queen, Ellery.	PS3533.U4
Queneau, Raymond, 1903-1976.	PQ2633.U43
Quentin, Patrick.	PS3545.H2895
Querry, Ronald B. (Ronald Burns), 1943-	PS3567.U283
Quest, Erica.	PR6067.U347
Quest, Rodney.	PR6067.U35
Quick, Amanda.	PS3561.R44
Quick, W. T.	PS3567.U295
Quigley, Aileen, 1930-	PR6067.U38
Quigley, John, 1925-	PR6067.U4
Quilici, Folco.	PQ4877.U513
Quill, Monica, 1929-2010.	PS3563.A31166
Quilty, Rafe.	PR6067.U47
Quincey, Emma.	PR6069.O38
Quincy, Olivia.	PS3617.U538
Quindlen, Anna.	PS3567.U336
Quinlan, Patrick.	PS3617.U56
Quinn, Derry.	PR6067.U54
Quinn, Erin, 1963-	PS3617.U5635
Quinn, Jake.	none
Quinn, Olga.	none
Quinn, Patrick.	PR6067.U55
Quinn, Patrick, 1957-	PS3567.U3485
Quinn, Peter (Peter A.)	PS3567.U3486
Quinn, Sally.	PS3567.U349
Quinn, Seabury, 1889-1969.	PS3533.U69
Quinn, Sherrill.	PS3617.U837
Quinn, Simon, 1942-	PS3569.M5377
Quinn, Spencer.	PS3617.U584
Quinn, Tara Taylor.	PS3617.U586
Quinn, Terry, 1945-	PS3567.U3543
Quinn, Tom, 1948-	PR9619.3.Q56
Quinnell, A. J.	PS3567.U36
Quintano, Dorothy.	PS3533.U697
Quirina, Fiona.	PS3617.U59
Quirk, Peter James, 1940-	PS3617.U593
Quittner, Joshua.	PS3567.U57
Quogan, Anthony.	PR9199.3.Q66
Qureshi, Mobashar, 1978-	PR9199.4.Q74
Rabb, Jonathan.	PS3568.A215
Rabb, M. E.	PS3618.A32
Rabe, Peter.	PS3568.A233
Rabe, Sheila.	PS3568.A235
Rabinowitz, Max.	none
Rabkin, William, 1959-	PS3618.A325
Rachee.	none
Racina, Thom, 1946-	PS3568.A25
Radano, Gene.	none
Radcliffe, Ann Ward, 1764-1823.	PR5200-5204

Radcliffe, Janette, 1925-1982.	PS3552.R656
Radcliffe, Jocelyn.	none
Radclyffe, 1950-	PS3618.A347
Radford, Edwin, 1891-1973.	none
Radford, John P.	PS3568.A33
Radley, Edward.	none
Radley, Sheila.	PR6068.O846
Radu, Kenneth.	PR9199.3.R238
Radulescu, Domnica, 1961-	PS3618.A358
Rae, Catherine M., 1914-	PS3568.A355
Rae, Hugh C.	PR6068.A25
Raedeke, Christy, 1966-	none
Raef, Laura C.	none
Raffel, Keith, 1951-	PS3618.A375
Rafferty, S. S.	PS3568.A38
Ragen, Naomi.	PS3568.A4118
Ragosta, Millie J.	PS3568.A413
Rahman, Mizanur.	PS3618.A383
Raichev, R. T.	PR6118.A34
Raimes, H. P.	PR6068.A29
Raine, Jerry, 1955-	PR6068.A3135
Raine, Richard, 1923-2006.	PR6069.A94
Raine, William MacLeod, 1871-1954.	PS3535.A385
Rainsford, Trisha.	PR6118.A35
Raleigh, Michael.	PS3568.A4316
Ralph, Anna, 1974-	none
Ralston, Gilbert A., 1912-1999.	PS3568.A435
Ramirez, Melissa Bourbon.	PS3618.A464
Ramm, Carl.	PS3568.A4465
Ramos, Luis Arturo, 1947-	PQ7298.28.A4197
Ramos, Manuel.	PS3568.A4468
Ramos y Sánchez, Raúl.	PS3618.A4765
Ramrus, Al.	PS3568.A448
Ramsay, Diana.	PR3568.A449
Ramsay, Frederick.	PS3618.A477
Ramsay, Jack.	none
Ramsey, Mason L.	PS3568.A4635
Ramthun, Bonnie.	PS3568.A4744
Ramus, David.	PS3568.A4745
Ranbern, James, 1920-	none
Rance, Joseph.	PR6068.A53
Rand, Lou.	PS3568.A4775
Rand, Naomi R., 1954-	PS3568.A478
Randall, Bob, 1937-	PS3568.A489
Randall, Brant.	PS3618.A624
Randall, Florence Engel, 1917-	PS3568.A493
Randall, John D., 1944-	PS3568.A4957
Randall, Rona, 1911-	PR6035.A58
Randell, Christine.	none
Randisi, Robert J.	PS3568.A53
Randle, Kevin D., 1949-	PS3568.A534
Randolphe, Arabella.	none
Rankin, Ian.	PR6068.A57
Rankin, Robert, 1949-	PR6068.A574

Ransley, Peter.	PR6068.A58
Ransom, Christopher.	PS3618.A685
Ransom, Daniel.	PS3557.O759
Ransome, Stephen, 1902-1977.	PS3507.A728
Raphael, Frederic, 1931-	PR6068.A6
Raphael, Lev.	PS3568.A5988
Raphael, Morris.	PS3568.A599
Raphael, Rick.	PS3568.A614
Rardin, Jennifer, 1965-	PS3618.A74
Rash, Ron, 1953-	PS3568.A698
Raskin, Barbara.	PS3568.A69
Raskin, Ellen.	PS3568.A696
Raskin, Jonah, 1942-	PS3568.A713
Rath, Sara.	PS3568.A718
Rathbone, Julian, 1935-2008.	PR6068.A8
Rathbun, Bill.	PS3568.A7195
Rattray, Simon.	PR6039.R518
Rauch, Constance.	PS3568.A788
Rautbord, Sugar.	PS3568.A827
Raven, Francis.	PS3618.A927
Raven, James.	none
Raven, Simon, 1927-2001.	PR6068.A9
Ravenscroft, Anthony, 1958-	PS3618.A93
Ravenswood, Fritzen.	none
RavenWolf, Silver, 1956-	PS3568.A833
Ravin, Neil.	PS3568.A84
Rawle, Graham.	PR6068.A917
Rawles, James Wesley.	PS3568.A8437
Rawlings, Maurice.	PS3568.A8485
Rawlings, Paul.	none
Rawlings, William, 1948-	PS3618.A96
Rawlinson, Peter.	PR6068.A925
Rawls, Philip, 1935-	none
Rawson, Clayton, 1906-1971.	PS3535.A848
Rawson, David, 1963-	PS3568.A86
Ray, Robert J. (Robert Joseph), 1935-	PS3568.A92178
Raybourn, Deanna.	PS3618.A983
Rayfiel, Thomas, 1958-	PS3568.A9257
Raymond, Derek.	PR6068.A946
Raymond, Diana.	PR6068.A947
Raymond, Ernest, 1888-1974.	PR6035.A9
Raymond, Jonathan.	PS3618.A985
Raymond, Patrick.	PR6068.A948
Rayne, Sarah.	PR6118.A55
Rayner, Claire.	PR6068.A949
Rayner, Jay.	PR6068.A9493
Rayner, Richard, 1955-	PS3568.A94
Rayner, William.	PR6068.A95
Raynes, Jean.	PS3568.A95
Reach, James.	PS3535.E12
Read, Cornelia.	PS3618.E22
Read, Piers Paul, 1941-	PR6068.E25
Read, Ray.	none
Reade, Bill.	PR6068.E258

Reade, Hamish, 1936-2008.   none
Reading, Mario.   PR6118.E24
Readus, James-Howard.   none
Ready, Stuart.   PR6035.E244
Reagan, Thomas B.   PS3568.E25
Reah, Danuta, 1949-   PR6068.E275
Reakes, Paul.   PR6068.E28
Reardon, Lisa.   PS3568.E26825
Reasoner, James.   PS3568.E2685
Reaver, Chap.   none
Reaves, Brian.   PS3618.E226
Reaves, Michael.   PS3568.E269
Reaves, Sam, 1954-   PS3568.E2694
Rebeta-Burditt, Joyce.   PS3568.E27
Rebrov, Dmitriĭ.   PG3493.34.E23
Recacoechea S., Juan.   PQ7820.R37
Rector, John.   PS3618.E425
Red Corn, Charles H. (Charles Harold), 1936-   PS3618.E426
Reddoch, Jennifer.   none
Redfern, Elizabeth.   PR6068.E29
Redfern, Jon, 1946-   PR9199.3.R43
Redfield, Malissa.   PS3568.E345
Redgate, John.   PS3561.E425
Redmann, J. M. (Jean M.), 1955-   PS3568.E3617
Redmon, Anne.   PS3568.E362
Redwood, Alec, 1903-   PR6003.A543
Reece, Colleen L.   PS3568.E3646
Reed, Barry C.   PS3568.E36475
Reed, Christine, 1947-   none
Reed, Dana.   none
Reed, David D.   PS3618.E4355
Reed, Eden.   PS3568.E36485
Reed, Harry.   none
Reed, Ishmael, 1938-   PS3568.E365
Reed, J. D., 1940-   PS3568.E366
Reed, John R. (John Roland), 1942-   PS3568.E36646
Reed, Joy.   PS3568.E36647
Reed, Joyce Lasky.   PS3569.H75
Reed, Kit.   PS3568.E367
Reed, Mary.   PS3568.E36768
Reed, Philip (Philip C.)   PS3568.E3693
Reed, Rex.   PS3568.E3694
Reed, Rick R.   PS3568.E3695
Rees, Arthur J. (Arthur John), 1872-1942.   none
Rees, Eloise Rodkey.   none
Rees, Joan, 1927-   PR6068.E38
Rees, Lloyd.   PR6068.E384
Rees, Matt, 1967-   PS3618.E438
Rees, Rod.   PR6118.E57
Reese, John Henry.   PS3568.E43
Reese, Judith.   none
Reese, Ralph.   none
Reese, Sammy.   PS3568.E433
Reeve, Arthur B. (Arthur Benjamin), 1880-1936.   PS3535.E354

Reeves, Ami Elizabeth.	PS3618.E4437
Reeves, John, 1926-	PR9199.3.R425
Reeves, Robert Nicholas.	PS3568.E472
Reeves-Stevens, Judith.	PR9199.3.R428
Regan, Linda, 1959-	PR6118.E584
Regan, Mark.	none
Regester, Seeley—see: Victor, Metta Victoria Fuller, 1831-1885.	
Reginald, R.	PS3568.E4754
Regrut, Brian, 1946-	PS3568.E47614
Rehder, Ben.	PS3618.E45
Rehner, Jan.	PR9199.4.R44
Reich, Christopher, 1961-	PS3568.E476284
Reichlin, Linus, 1957-	PT2678.E3388
Reichs, Kathy.	PS3568.E476345
Reid, Daniel P., 1948-	PS3618.E534
Reid, David, 1976-	PS3618.E5343
Reid, Desmond, 1939-	none
Reid, Elwood.	PS3568.E47637
Reid, James (James W.)	PR6068.E44
Reid, Jamie.	PR6068.E45
Reid, Pamela Carrington, 1956-	PR9639.4.R45
Reid, Philip.	PR6068.E454
Reid, Robert Sims.	PS3568.E4769
Reid, Van.	PS3568.E47697
Reiffel, Leonard.	PS3568.E4795
Reifman, Steve.	PS3618.E5554
Reilly, Helen, 1890-1962.	PS3535.E474
Reilly, Matthew.	PR9619.3.R445
Reinken, Patrick.	PS3568.E494
Reinsmith, Richard, 1930-	none
Reisman, John M.	none
Reisner, Mary.	none
Reiss, Bob.	PS3618.E5726
Reiss, Kathryn.	none
Reit, Seymour.	none
Reiter, B. P., 1945-	PS3568.E525
Relentless Aaron.	PS3618.E57277
Rellas, Dorothy.	none
Relling, William.	PS3568.E554
Reloba, Juan Carlos, 1947-	PQ7389.R43
Remes, Ilkka.	PH356.R46
Rémy, Pierre-Jean, 1937-2010.	PQ2678.E42
Renauld, Ron.	none
Rendell, Ruth, 1930-	PR6068.E63
Renek, Morris.	PS3568.E58
Renn, Chris.	PS3568.E595
Rennert, Maggie.	PS3568.E6
Rennison, Nick, 1955-	PR6118.E597
Reno, Marie R.	PS3568.E65
Rense, Paige.	PS3568.E654
Repp, Gloria, 1941-	none
Resnicow, Herbert.	PS3568.E69
Resnick, Laura, 1962-	PS3568.E689
Resnick, Michael D.	PS3568.E698

Resnick, Mike—see: Resnick, Michael D.
Reston, James, 1941-   PS3568.E75
Reuben, Shelly.   PS3568.E777
Reuland, Rob, 1963-   PS3568.E778
Reuter, Bjarne B.   PT8176.28.E98
Revelle, G. R. (Gerald R.)   PS3618.E88
Revelli, George.   PR6068.E9
Revoyr, Nina, 1969-   PS3568.E7964
Rexford, Dottie.   PS3618.E93
Rey, Pierre, 1930-   PQ2678.E888
Rey, Rainer.   none
Rey Rosa, Rodrigo, 1958-   PQ7499.2.R38
Reybold, Malcolm.   PS3568.E86
Reyburn, Stanley S., 1930-   PS3568.E882
Reynolds, Aaron, 1970-   PS3618.E965
Reynolds, Baillie, Mrs.   PR6035.E73
Reynolds, Bonnie Jones.   PS3568.E887
Reynolds, Catherine.   none
Reynolds, Clay, 1949-   PS3568.E8874
Reynolds,   George   W.   M.   (George   William PR5221.R35
MacArthur), 1814-1879.
Reynolds, Gertrude M. Robins—see: Reynolds, Baillie, Mrs.
Reynolds, Mack.   PS3568.E895
Reynolds, Marjorie, 1944-   PS3568.E8954
Reynolds, William J., 1956-   PS3568.E93
Rhea, Nicholas, 1936-   PR6068.H4
Rhoades, J. D., 1962-   PS3618.H623
Rhoads, Colleen.   PS3553.O2285
Rhode, John, 1884-1964.   PR6037.T778
Rhodes, Evan H.   PS3568.H57
Rhodes, Evie.   PS3618.H6256
Rhodes, Jewell Parker.   PS3568.H63
Rhodes, Richard, 1937-   PS3568.H64
Rhodes, Russell L.   PS3568.H65
Rhodes, Stephen.   PS3568.H66
Rhys, Jean.   PR6035.H96
Ri‹a›binina, Tat'i‹a›na.   none
Ricardo, Jack.   PS3568.I24
Riccardi, Theodore.   PS3618.I27
Riccio, Dolores, 1931-   PS3618.I28
Rice, Anne, 1941-   PS3568.I265
Rice, Christopher, 1979-   PS3568.I2717
Rice, Craig, 1908-1957.   PS3535.I2236
Rice, David, 1934-   PR6068.I1215
Rice, Jeff.   none
Rice, Linda Lightsey, 1950-   PS3568.I288
Rice, Lisa Marie.   PS3618.I2998
Rice, Luanne.   PS3568.I289
Rice, Robert, 1945-   PS3568.I294
Rich, Nicholas.   none
Rich, Virginia.   PS3568.I298
Ri'chard, A. P.   PS3618.I3337
Richard, James L.   none
Richard, Susan—see: Ellis, Julie, 1933-

Richard, T. Dawn.	PS3618.I335
Richards, Ann Vaughan.	PS3618.I34
Richards, Ben, 1964-	PR6068.I2453
Richards, Clay, 1910-1981.	PS3505.R89224
Richards, Curtis.	none
Richards, David Adams.	PR9199.3.R465
Richards, Emilie, 1948-	PS3568.I31526
Richards, Guy, b. 1905.	none
Richards, Judith.	PS3568.I3155
Richards, Kel, 1946-	PR9619.3.R485
Richards, Leslie.	none
Richards, Linda, 1960-	PR9199.4.R5226
Richards, Nat, 1942-	PS3568.I316
Richards, Paul.	none
Richards, Ramona, 1957-	PS3618.I3438
Richards, Tad.	none
Richards, Tony, 1956-	none
Richardson, Carl.	none
Richardson, Doug, 1959-	PS3568.I31743
Richardson, Frank, 1943-	PS3618.I3446
Richardson, H. L., 1927-	PS3568.I3175
Richardson, Kat.	PS3618.I3447
Richardson, Mozelle.	PS3568.I319
Richardson, Robert, 1940-	PR6068.I2467
Richardson, Stephen, 1957-2002.	PR9199.4.R526
Richardson, Tracey, 1964-	PS3568.I3195
Richardson, W. James.	PS3568.I3198
Richer, Lois.	PR9199.4.R53
Richman, Alyson.	PS3568.I3447
Richman, Phyllis C.	PS3568.I3506
Richmond, Donald.	PS3568.I3515
Richmond, Grace, 1907-1997.	PR6073.O635
Richmond, Mary.	none
Richtel, Matt.	PS3618.I36
Rickard, Hannah.	PS3618.I366
Rickard, Jessie Louisa Moore, 1879-	PR6035.I385
Rickards, John.	PS3618.I37
Rickman, Philip.	PR6068.I264
Ricks, Thomas E.	PS3618.I38
Rico, Don.	none
Riddell, J. H., Mrs., 1832-1906.	PR5227.R33
Rider, Anne, 1924-	PR6068.I282
Rider, J. W.	PS3569.T453
Rider, Warrick W.	none
Ridgway, Keith, 1965-	PR6068.I287
Ridley, John, 1965-	PS3568.I3598
Ridout, James W.	PS3568.I35997
Ridpath, Michael.	PR6068.I294
Ridyard, Richard D.	none
Riedel, John.	PS3568.I363
Riefe, Alan.	none
Riefe, Barbara, 1925-	PS3568.I3633
Riehl, Gene.	PS3618.I3924
Rife, Ellouise A.	none

Rifkin, Shepard.	PS3568.I365
Rigbey, Liz.	PS3568.I3667
Rigg, Jennifer, 1939-	PR6068.I336
Riggs, Cynthia.	PS3618.I394
Riggs, John R., 1945-	PS3568.I372
Riggs, Paula Detmer.	PS3618.I398
Rigolosi, Steven A.	PS3618.I43
Riis, David Allen.	none
Riley, Cole, 1950-	PS3618.I53273
Riley, Dick.	PS3568.I3778
Riley, Frank, 1927-	PS3568.I378
Riley, Joe.	none
Riley, Judith Merkle.	PS3568.I3794
Riley, Kelly Ann.	PS3618.I43
Riley, Wilma.	PR9199.3.R517
Rilla, Wolf Peter.	PR6035.I597
Rimington, Stella.	PR6118.I44
Rimmer, Robert H., 1917-	PS3568.I4
Rinehart, Mary Roberts, 1876-1958.	PS3535.I73
Ring, Raymond H.	PS3568.I567
Ringo, John, 1963-	PS3568.I577
Riordan, Rick.	PS3568.I5866
Riphouse, Acascias.	PS3618.I59
Ripley, Ann.	PS3568.I598
Ripley, H. A. (Harold Austin), 1896-	none
Ripley, J. R., 1955-	PS3568.I635
Ripley, Jack—see: Wainwright, John William, 1921-	
Ripley, Mike.	PR6068.I56
Ripley, W. L. (Warren L.)	PS3568.I64
Rippon, Marion.	PR9199.3.R523
Riskin, Boris.	PS3618.I73
Risku, Cillay.	none
Rispin, Karen, 1955-	PR9199.3.R5237
Ritchie, Rita.	none
Ritchie, Simon.	PR9199.3.R524
Ritner, Peter, 1927-	PS3568.I82
Ritter, Margaret.	PS3568.I827
Ritter, Todd.	PS3618.I79
Ritz, David.	PS3568.I828
Riva, John.	PS3568.I8284
Riveaux, James.	PS3618.I84
Rivera, David, Jr.	PS3618.I844
Rivera, E. Allan.	PS3618.I845
Rivera, William L.	PS3618.I85
Rivers, Anne.	PR6068.I93
Rivers, Caryl.	PS3568.I8315
Rivers, Gayle.	PR6068.I94
Rivers, Joan.	PS3618.I858
Rivers, Reggie.	PS3568.I833
Rivett, Edith Caroline, 1894-1958.	PR6035.I9
Rizer, Fran.	PS3618.I93
Rizzolo, S. K.	PS3618.I98
Roach, R. L.	PS3618.O27
Roadarmel, Paul.	PS3568.O16

Roat, Ronald Clair. PS3568.O194
Robards, Karen. PS3568.O196
Robb, B. R., 1958- PS3618.O29
Robb, Candace M. PS3568.O198
Robb, J. D., 1950- PS3568.O243
Robbe-Grillet, Alain, 1922-2008. PQ2635.O117
Robbins, Alan. PS3568.O2227
Robbins, David, 1950- PS3568.O22288
Robbins, David L., 1954- PS3568.O22289
Robbins, Harold, 1916-1997. PS3568.O224
Robbins, Norman. PR6068.O13
Robens, Howard. PR9199.3.R5266
Roberge, Rob. PS3618.O31525
Roberts, Alene. PS3568.O2367
Roberts, Ann, 1964- PS3618.O31545
Roberts, Ann Victoria. PR6068.O1414
Roberts, Barrie, 1939- PR6068.O1415
Roberts, Carey. PS3568.O2375
Roberts, Cefin. PB2299.R63
Roberts, David, 1944- PR6118.O233
Roberts, Doreen, 1934- none
Roberts, Gareth, 1968- PR6068.O143
Roberts, Gillian, 1939- PS3557.R356
Roberts, James Hall, 1927- PS3554.U465
Roberts, James R. PS3618.O31576
Roberts, Jan. PS3568.O2386
Roberts, Jan, 1939- PR6068.O1446
Roberts, Janet Louise, 1925-1982. PS3552.R656
Roberts, John Maddox. PS3568.O23874
Roberts, Julian. none
Roberts, Lee, 1908-1976. PS3563.A7278
Roberts, Les, 1937- PS3568.O23894
Roberts, Liam, 1952- PS3618.O31585
Roberts, Lillian M. none
Roberts, Lora. PS3569.M537635
Roberts, Michele. PR6068.O155
Roberts, Morley, 1857-1942. PR6035.O532
Roberts, Natalie M. PS3603.O4545
Roberts, Nora. PS3568.O243
Roberts, Patricia (Patricia Flora Clementina) PS3568.O246
Roberts, Peggy. none
Roberts, Rinalda—see: Cudlipp, Edythe.
Roberts, Suzanne, 1925- PS3568.O2474
Roberts, Thomas A., 1947- PS3568.O2475
Roberts, Wendy. PR9199.4.R58
Roberts, Willo Davis. PS3568.O2478
Robertson, Brewster Milton, 1929- PS3568.O2479
Robertson, Brian. none
Robertson, C. P. none
Robertson, Charles. none
Robertson, Colin, 1906- PR6035.O539
Robertson, Ellison. PR9199.3.R5314
Robertson, Imogen, 1973- PR6118.O2376
Robertson, Keith, 1914- PS3568.O2493

Robertson, Linda Shirley.	PS3618.O317
Robertson, Michael, 1951-	PS3618.O31726
Robertson, Netta.	none
Robertson, Paul, 1957-	PS3618.O3173
Robeson, Kenneth.	PS3507.E5777
Robin, Liliane, 1925-	PQ2635.O182
Robin-Clerc, Michèle, 1956-	PQ3949.2.C574
Robinett, Stephen.	PS3568.O274
Robins, Madeleine.	PS3568.O2774
Robinson, Abby.	PS3568.O2775
Robinson, Cheryl.	PS3618.O323
Robinson, Cynthia, 1958-	PS3618.O3235
Robinson, Derek, 1932 Apr. 12-	PR6068.O1954
Robinson, Edward L.	PS3568.O288
Robinson, Frank M., 1926-	PS3568.O2888
Robinson, Giovanna.	PS3568.O289124
Robinson, Gregor.	PR9199.3.R5337
Robinson, Howard R., 1939-	PS3618.O326
Robinson, Jeffrey, 1945-	PS3568.O28913
Robinson, Jeremy, 1974-	PS3618.O3268
Robinson, John B., 1968-	PS3618.O327
Robinson, John Laurence.	PS3618.O328
Robinson, Katy, 1977-	PR9639.4.R63
Robinson, Kevin.	PS3568.O2892
Robinson, Kim Stanley.	PS3568.O2893
Robinson, Leah Ruth.	PS3568.O297
Robinson, Leonard Wallace, 1912-1999.	PS3568.O3
Robinson, Lillian S.	PS3568.O312
Robinson, Lynda Suzanne.	PS3568.O31227
Robinson, Patricia, 1923-	PS3568.O3135
Robinson, Patrick, 1939-	PR6068.O1959
Robinson, Peter, 1950-	PR6068.O1964
Robinson, Richard.	none
Robinson, Rick, 1958-	PS3618.O33367
Robinson, Robert, 1927-	PR6068.O197
Robinson, Sondra Till.	PS3568.O3154
Robinson, Spider.	PS3568.O3156
Robitaille, Julie.	PS3568.O3175
Robotham, Michael, 1960-	PR6118.O26
Robski, Oksana.	PG3493.36.B77
Robson, James, 1944 or 5-	PR6068.O23
Robson, Justina.	PR6118.O28
Roby, Adelaide Q.	none
Roby, Kinley E.	PS3618.O3385
Roby, Mary Linn.	PS3568.O319
Rocha, Luís Miguel, 1976-	PQ9318.O34
Roche, Arthur Somers, 1883-1935.	PS3535.O2678
Rochester, George E. (George Ernest)	none
Rock, Judith.	PS3618.O3543
Rock, Phillip, 1927-	PS3568.O33
Rockey, G. L. (Gary L.)	PS3618.O3544
Rockliff, B. J.	PR6068.O27
Rockwell, Patricia Ann.	PS3618.O35448
Rockwood, Harry, 1832-1873.	PS33364.Y46

Rodda, Emily.	none
Roddy, Lee, 1921-	PS3568.O344
Roderus, Frank, 1942-	PS3568.O346
Rodgers, Anne Marie.	PS3573.I5332
Rodi, Robert.	PS3568.O34854
Rodriguez, Abraham, 1961-	PS3568.O34876
Rodriguez, Jerry A.	PS3618.O3583
Rodríguez Bajón, Miguel Angel, 1964-	PQ6668.O3573
Roe, C. F.	PR6068.O328
Roe, Caroline.	PR9199.3.S165
Roe, Graeme.	PR6118.O35
Roeburt, John.	PS3535.O383
Roffman, Jan.	PR6069.U4
Rogan, Barbara.	PS3568.O377
Rogers, Barbara, 1935-	PS3568.O39
Rogers, Chris, 1944-	PS3568.O424
Rogers, David, 1927-	PS3568.O43
Rogers, J. Trumbell.	none
Rogers, James Cass.	PS3618.O464
Rogers, Joel Townsley.	none
Rogers, Patrick F., 1929-	none
Rogers, Ray Mount, 1912-	PS3568.O455
Rogers, Sharon Carter.	PS3618.O468
Rogow, Roberta, 1942-	PS3568.O492
Rogoza, I⟨U⟩riĭ.	PG3485.6.G3874
Rohan, Donald.	PS3568.O495
Rohmer, Richard, 1924-	PR9199.3.R58
Rohmer, Sax, 1883-1959.	PR6045.A37 [Z8949.27]
Rohn, Jennifer L.	PS3618.O486
Roit, Natasha, 1960-	PS3618.O535
Rojas, Carlos, 1928-	PQ6633.O594
Rojas Gómez, Antonio.	PQ8098.28.O374
Roker, Al, 1954-	PS3618.O537
Roland, Betty.	PR9619.3.R615
Roland-James, Patricia.	PS3618.O538
Rold, Marlys, 1943-	PS3618.O54
Rollins, David, 1958-	PR9619.4.R66
Rollins, James, 1961-	PS3568.O5398
Romaine, Dallas.	none
Roman, A. E. (Alex Echevarria)	PS3618.O566
Roman, Eric, 1926-	PS3568.O545
Roman, Howard.	PS3568.O546
Romanes, Julian.	PR6068.O43
Romano, Deane.	PS3568.O547
Romano, Don.	PS3568.O548
Romanovskiĭ, Vladimir Vi⟨a⟩cheslavovich.	PG3485.6.M293
Romberg, Nina, 1955-	none
Rome, Tony.	none
Romov, Anatoliĭ.	PG3485.6.M6
Ronns, Edward, 1916-1975.	PS3501.A79
Ronson, Mark.	none
Rontal, Gene.	PS3568.O577
Rook, Tony.	PR6068.O53

Rooke, Rebecca.	none
Roome, Annette.	PR6068.O54
Rooney, Mickey.	PS3568.O632
Roos, Kelley.	PS3535.O54665
Roosevelt, Elliott, 1910-1990.	PS3535.O549
Roosevelt, James, 1907-1991.	PS3568.O638
Roote, Mike.	none
Rooth, Anne Reed.	PS3568.O67
Roper, Gayle G.	PS3568.O68
Roper, L. V. (Lester Virgil), 1931-	none
Roper, Robert, 1946-	PS3568.O69
Roscoe, Patrick, 1962-	PR9199.3.R587
Roscoe, Theodore.	PS3535.O6423
Rose, Carolyn J.	PS3618.O7829
Rose, Christie, 1949-	PS3618.O783
Rose, Elizabeth.	none
Rose, Geoffrey, 1932-	PR6068.O66
Rose, Heather, 1964-	PR9619.3.R619
Rose, Joel.	PS3568.O7634
Rose, Karen, 1964-	PS3618.O7844
Rose, M. J., 1953-	PS3568.O76386
Rose, Malcolm.	none
Rose, Michael E. (Michael Edward)	PR9199.4.R673
Rose, Patricia.	none
Rosemoor, Patricia.	none
Rosen, Marion.	PS3568.O7687
Rosen, Rob.	PS3618.O831565
Rosen, Dorothy.	PS3568.O7648
Rosen, Leonard J.	PS3618.O83148
Rosen, Norma.	PS3568.O77
Rosen, Richard Dean, 1949-	PS3568.O774
Rosen, Selina.	PS3568.O7746
Rosen, Sidney.	none
Rosenbaum, Ron.	PS3568.O778
Rosenberg, Joel, 1954-2011.	PS3568.O786
Rosenberg, Joel C., 1967-	PS3618.O832
Rosenberg, Nancy Taylor.	PS3568.O7876
Rosenberg, Philip, 1942-	PS3568.O7877
Rosenberg, Robert, 1951-	PS3568.O7878
Rosenberg, Stuart.	PS3568.O7883
Rosenberger, Joseph R.	none
Rosenblum, Robert J.	PS3568.O795
Rosenfeld, Arthur.	PS3568.O812
Rosenfeld, Lulla.	PS3568.O815
Rosenfelt, David.	PS3618.O838
Rosenheim, Andrew.	PR6068.O763
Rosenthal, Erik.	PS3568.O8374
Rosett, Sara.	PS3618.O844
Roslund, Anders, 1961-	PT9877.28.O77
Rosnau, Wendy.	PS3618.O8443
Rosner, Joseph, 1922-	PS3568.O8419
Ross, Adam, 1967-	PS3618.O84515
Ross, Albert.	PS3557.O388
Ross, Angus, 1927-	PR6068.O817

Ross, Ann B.	PS3568.O84198
Ross, Barbara, 1953-	PS3618.O845245
Ross, Barnaby.	PS3533.U4
Ross, Cameron, 1944-	none
Ross, Clarissa, 1912-	PR9199.3.R5996
Ross, Dan, 1912-	PR9199.3.R5996
Ross, Dana, 1912-	PR9199.3.R5996
Ross, Dana Fuller.	PS3513.E8679
Ross, Frank, 1938-	PR6068.O8187
Ross, Hal, 1941-	PR9199.3.R598
Ross, Ian—see: Rossmann, John F.	
Ross, Inez.	PS3568.O843465
Ross, JoAnn.	PS3568.O843485
Ross, Joel N., 1968-	PS3618.O8455
Ross, Jonathan, 1916-	PR6068.O835
Ross, Kate.	PS3568.O843494
Ross, Kathleen.	none
Ross, Marilyn, 1912-	PR9199.3.R5996
Ross, Paul.	none
Ross, Paul B.	none
Ross, Paul S.	
Ross, Philip, 1932-	PS3568.O8439
Ross, Regina—see: Mackintosh, May.	
Ross, Robert, 1942-	PS3568.O8443
Ross, Sam, 1912-	PS3535.O7493
Ross, Sheila.	PR6068.O825
Ross, Sinclair.	PR9199.3.R599
Ross, Veronica, 1946 Jan. 7-	PR9199.3.R5994
Ross, W. E. D. (William Edward Daniel), 1912-	PR9199.3.R5996
Ross, William, 1923-	PS3568.O845
Rossetti, Ana, 1950-	PQ6668.O858
Rossetti, Denise.	PS3618.O8484
Rossi, Bruno, 1935-	none
Rossiter, Elizabeth.	PR6068.O833
Rossiter, John.	PR6068.O835
Rossiter, Phyllis.	PS3568.O8476
Rossmann, John F.	none
Rossner, Judith, 1935-2005.	PS3568.O848
Rossner, Robert.	PS3568.O849
Rostand, Robert, 1937-	PS3558.O636
Rosten, Leo Calvin, 1908-1997.	PS3535.O7577
Rostov, Mara.	PS3568.O8493
Rostov, Stefan, 1958-	none
Rotella, Sebastian.	PS3618.O8555
Rotenberg, David (David Charles)	PR9199.3.R618
Rotenberg, Robert, 1953-	PR9199.4.R6845
Roth, Arthur J., 1925-	PS3568.O852
Roth, Gerhard, 1942 June 24-	PT2678.O796
Roth, Holly.	PS3568.O85413
Roth, Philip.	PS3568.O855
Rothberg, Abraham.	PS3568.O857
Rothblatt, Henry B.	none
Rothenberg, Rebecca.	PS3568.O862
Rother, Caitlin.	none

Rothman, Judith. PR6052.L335
Rothrock, Ken. none
Rothstein, Allan. none
Rothstein, Raphael. none
Rothweiler, Paul R., 1931- PS3568.O869
Rothwell, H. T. PS3568.O87
Rotsstein, Aaron Nathan. PS3568.O874
Roubaud, Jacques. PQ2678.O77
Rouch, James. none
Roudybush, Alexandra. PS3568.O88
Roueché, Berton, 1911-1994. PS3535.O845
Roughan, Howard. PS3568.O883
Round, Jeffrey. PR9199.3.R632
Rouverol, Jean. none
Roversi, Paolo, 1975- PQ4918.O89
Rovin, Jeff. PS3568.O8894
Rowan, Deirdre, 1930- PS3573.I4485
Rowan, Hester. PR6068.O846
Rowan, William, 1927- none
Rowden, Dick. none
Rowe, James N., 1938- PS3568.O93
Rowe, Jennifer, 1948- PR9619.3.R6276
Rowe, John, 1936- PR9619.3.R6277
Rowe, Rosemary. PR6118.O97
Rowe, Sean. PS3618.O8735
Rowland, Della. none
Rowland, Laura Joh. PS3568.O934
Rowland, Peter, 1938- PR6068.O915
Rowlands, Betty. PR6068.O92
Rowlands, C. P. PS3618.O8827
Rowley, Brent, 1954- none
Rowse, Sharon. PR9199.4.R687
Roy, A. E. (Archie E.), 1924- PR6068.O95
Roy, Allyson. PS3618.O8923
Roy, Lori. PS3618.O89265
Roy, Ron, 1940- none
Roy-Bhattacharya, Joydeep. PR9499.3.R596
Royal, Priscilla. PS3618.O893
Royce, Kenneth. PR6068.O98
Royes, Gillian, 1947- PS3618.O92
Royle, Nicholas, 1963- PR6068.O987
Royles, Nigel. PR6068.O99
Rozan, S. J. PS3568.O99
Ruark, Eric B. none
Rubart, James L. PS3618.U2326
Rubel, Marc. PS3568.U18
Ruben, William S. none
Rubenfeld, Jed, 1959- PS3618.U233
Rubens, Bernice. PR6068.U2
Rubens, Robert. none
Rubin, Louis Decimus, 1923- PS3568.U26
Rubin, Ron. PS3568.U285
Rubinstein, Matt, 1974- PR9619.3.R67
Rubinstein, Paul, 1935- none

Rucka, Greg.	PS3568.U2968
Rucker, Stall.	PS3618.U33
Rudd, Colin.	none
Rudner, Rita.	PS3568.U3335
Rudolph, Penny.	PS3618.U347
Rudorff, Raymond.	PR6068.U3
Rudy, Catherine M.	PS3618.U349
Rue, Nancy N.	PS3568.U3595
Ruell, Patrick, 1936-	PR6058.I448
Ruevert, Sigmund.	none
Ruff, Matt.	PS3568.U3615
Ruffin, Gary.	PS3618.U4335
Ruffin, Paul.	PS3568.U362
Ruiz de Aguirre, Alfonso, 1968-	PQ6668.U349
Ruiz Zafón, Carlos, 1964-	PQ6668.U49
Ruiz, Luis Manuel, 1973-	PQ6668.U3238
Rumanes, George N.	PR9115.9.R8
Rundle, Anne.	PR6068.U7
Runyon, Charles W., 1928-	PS3568.U53
Rupérez, Javier.	PQ6668.U75
Ruryk, Jean.	PR9199.3.R79
Rusch, Kristine Kathryn.	PS3568.U7
Rusch, Sheldon.	PS3618.U74
Ruse, Gary Alan, 1946-	PS3568.U72
Ruse, Paul.	none
Rush, Jonathan.	PR6118.U83
Rushford, Patricia H.	PS3568.U7274
Russell, Alan, 1956-	PS3568.U7654
Russell, Andrew Joseph.	PS3568.U7655
Russell, Agnes—see: Short, Agnes.	
Russell, Charles—see: Kelly, Terence, 1920-	
Russell, Charlotte Murray, 1899-	PS3535.U682
Russell, Charlsie.	PS3618.U748
Russell, Craig, 1956-	PR6118.U85
Russell, E. S. (Enid S.)	PS3568.U766
Russell, J. S. (Jay S.), 1961-	PS3568.U76667
Russell, Judith, 1941-	PS3618.U75
Russell, Kirk, 1954-	PS3618.U76
Russell, Leigh.	PR6118.U867
Russell, Martin James, 1934-	PR6068.U86
Russell, Norman.	PR6118.U87
Russell, Ona, 1952-	PS3618.U765
Russell, Randy.	PS3568.U7695
Russell, Ray.	PS3568.U77
Russell, Richard.	none
Russell, Sheldon.	PS3568.U777
Russell, Trista.	PS3618.U7685
Russell, William.	PR5271.R8
Russell, William Clark, 1844-1911.	PR5280-5283
Russinovich, Mark E.	PS3618.U7688
Russo, John, 1939-	PS3568.U8115
Russo, John Alfred, 1929-	PS3618.U774
Rust, Ann O'Connell.	PS3568.U8125
Ruth, Jenifer.	PS3618.U777

Rutherford, Cecile.	none
Rutherford, Douglas, 1915-1988.	PR6025.A1697
Rutherford, Ward.	PR6068.U87
Ruttan, Sandra.	PR9199.4.R89
Ruuth, Marianne.	none
Ruyle, John.	PS3568.U88
Ryan, Alan, 1943-	PS3568.Y26
Ryan, Annelise.	PS3568.Y2614
Ryan, Chris, 1961-	PR6068.Y26
Ryan, Donald.	none
Ryan, Garry, 1953-	PR9199.4.R94
Ryan, Hank Phillippi.	PS3618.Y333
Ryan, J. M., 1919-1977.	PS3563.A274
Ryan, Jenna.	none
Ryan, Jim.	none
Ryan, Marie-Nicole.	PS3618.Y3358
Ryan, Patricia (Patricia Burford)	PS3618.Y34
Ryan, Peter.	none
Ryan, Rob, 1951-	PR6118.Y36
Ryan, Thomas J. (Thomas Joseph), 1942-	PS3568.Y394
Ryan, Will Harrison, 1915-	PS3568.Y396
Ryan, William, 1965-	PR6118.Y37
Ryck, Francis.	PQ2678.Y3
Rydell, Forbes.	PS3556.O67
Ryder, Jonathan, 1927-2001.	PS3562.U26
Ryland, Clive, b. 1892.	none
Rylant, Cynthia.	PS3568.Y55
Ryman, Geoff.	PR6068.Y74
Ryū, Keiichirō, 1923-1989.	PL860.Y79
Ryzhkov, Vladimir (Vladimir Vladimirovich)	PG3493.38.Z48
Sabatini, Rafael, 1875-1950.	PR6037.A2
Saberhagen, Fred, 1930-2007.	PS3569.A215
Sachar, Howard Morley, 1928-	PS3569.A225
Sackett, Jeffrey.	none
Sachitano, Arlene, 1951-	PS3619.A277
Sachs, Harley L.	PS3569.A229
Sachs, Leslie Raymond.	PS3569.A2295
Sadler, Barry, 1940-1989.	PS3569.A24
Sadler, Mark, 1924-2005.	PS3562.Y44
Sadulaev, German.	PG3493.42.D85
Saffron, Robert.	PS3569.A282
Safire, William, 1929-2009.	PS3569.A283
Şagola, Mario J.	PS3569.A365
Sāha, Rameśa.	PK1859.S232
Sain, Leanna.	PS3619.A395
Saint-Bois, Danièle.	PQ2679.A437
Saint-Lambert, Patrick.	PQ2679.A478
Sakey, Marcus.	PS3619.A4
Sakol, Jeannie.	PS3569.A455
Sala, Sharon.	PS3569.A4565
Salcido, Craig.	none
Saldaña, René.	none
Sale, Medora.	PR9199.3.S165
Sale, Richard, 1911-1993.	PS3537.A413

Saleh, Nabil A.	PR9570.L43
Salima, Candace E.	none
Salinger, Pierre.	PS3569.A4595
Salinger, Sharon Singer.	PS3569.A459525
Salinger, Steven D.	PS3569.A459527
Salisbury, Carola, 1924-1986.	PR6052.U9
Salisbury, Harrison E. (Harrison Evans), 1908-1993.	PS3569.A4596
Salisbury, John.	PR6069.A474
Sallis, James, 1944-	PS3569.A462
Salmerón Tristante, Jerónimo, 1969-	PQ6719.A5223
Salmon, Charles Ray.	PS3569.A462157
Salt, Jonathan.	none
Salter, Anna C.	PS3569.A46219
Salvadó, Albert, 1951-	PQ6669.A563
Salvato, Sharon.	PS3569.A46233
Salzberg, Charles, 1946-	PS3619.A443
Salzmann, Cynthia S.	PS3619.A446
Samiloglu, Erin, 1978-	PS3619.A455
Sample, Grace Gray.	PS3619.A4587
Samples, Mack	PS3569.A46644
Sampson, Catherine.	PR6119.A45
Samson, Joan, 1937-	PS3569.A4667
San-Antonio.	PQ2607.A558
Sánchez, Clara.	PQ6669.A6125
Sánchez, Julián, 1966-	PQ6719.A5273
Sanchez, Thomas.	PS3569.A469
Sánchez-Garnica, Paloma.	PQ6719.A549
Sánchez López, Enoc.	PQ8550.429.A555
Sancton, Thomas (Thomas Alexander), 1949-	PS3619.A523
Sand, Margaret.	PS3569.A4694
Sandberg, Berent.	PS3569.A4696
Sandberg, Peter Lars, 1934-	PS3569.A4697
Sanders, David, 1915-	PR6069.A512
Sanders, George, 1906-1972.	PR6069.A5125
Sanders, James, 1911-	none
Sanders, Lauren.	PS3569.A5124
Sanders, Lawrence, 1920-1998.	PS3569.A5125
Sanders, Leonard.	PS3569.A5127
Sanders, Louis.	PQ2719.A53
Sanders, William, 1942-	PS3569.A5139
Sanderson, Jim, 1953-	PS3569.A5146
Sanderson, Mark.	PR6069.A5145
Sanderson, Oren.	PJ5055.4.A535
Sandford, Jane.	none
Sandford, John, 1944 Feb. 23-	PS3569.A516
Sandler, Karen.	PS3619.A54
Sandom, J. G., 1956-	PS3569.A51945
Sandrin, Amy, 1961-	PS3619.A55
Sandroff, Ronni.	PS3569.A5196
Sandstrom, Eve K.	PS3569.A51977
Sandulescu, Jacques.	PS3569.A5198
Sanford, Harry.	none
Sanford, Ursula.	none

Sang, Bob.	PS3569.A5267
Sang, Dusty.	none
Sangalli, Arturo, 1940-	PS3619.A566
Sanghoee, Sanjay.	PS3619.A567
Sangster, Jimmy.	PR6069.A53
Sann, Paul.	PS3569.A54
Sanra, Nancy, 1944-	PS3569.A542
Sansom, C. J.	PR6119.A57
Sansom, Ian.	PR6119.A575
Santangelo, Elena.	PS3569.A5443
Santiago, Soledad.	PS3569.A5455
Santiago, V. J.	none
Santini, Rosemarie.	PS3569.A546
Santis, Pablo de, 1963-	PQ7798.29.A616
Santlofer, Jonathan, 1946-	PS3619.A58
Santogrossi, Stephen.	PS3619.A585
Santopolo, Jill.	none
Santos, José Rodrigues dos, 1964-	PQ9319.A685
Sapergia, Barbara, 1943-	PR9199.3.S225
Saperstein, David.	PS3569.A584
Sapir, Richard.	PS3569.A59
Sarabande, William.	none
Saracen, Justine.	PS3619.A69
Saralegui, Jorge.	none
Sarasin, J. G., b. 1897.	PR6037.A785
Sargeant, Patricia.	PS3619.A734
Sargent, Craig.	none
Sargent, Patricia.	PS3569.A6894
Sariola, Mauri.	PH355.S27
Sarrantonio, Al.	PS3569.A73
Sathre, Vivian.	none
Satterthwait, Walter.	PS3569.A784
Saul, John.	PS3569.A787
Saul, John Ralston, 1947-	PR6069.A78
Saul, Oscar.	PS3537.A87
Saulnier, Beth.	PS3569.A7882
Saum, Karen, 1935-	PS3569.A7887
Saums, Mary.	PS3569.A78875
Saunders, Raymond M., 1949-	PS3569.A7938
Saunders, Susan.	none
Sauter, Eric.	PS3569.A8215
Savage, David—see: Hossent, Harry.	
Savage, Ernest, 1918-	PS3569.A8235
Savage, Jeffrey S., 1963-	PS3619.A83
Savage, Jenny.	PR6069.A936
Savage, Marc.	PS3569.A827
Savage, Michael, 1942-	PS3619.A836
Savage, Richard, 1846-1903.	PS2779.S5
Savage, Thomas.	PS3569.A83
Savage, Tom, 1948-	PS3569.A832
Savage, Wallace.	PS3569.A835
Savarin, Julian Jay.	PR6069.A937
Savi, E. W. (Ethel Winifred), b. 1865.	PR6037.A892
Savile, Steve.	PR6119.A95

Saville, Andrew.   PR6070.A79
Savory, Chester J.   PS3569.A848
Sawkins, Raymond, 1923-2006.   PR6069.A94
Sawn, David.   none
Sawyer, Cheryl, 1947-   PR9639.4.S29
Sawyer, Clyde Lynwood.   PS3573.I9153
Sawyer, Corinne Holt.   PS3569.A864
Sawyer, Diane.   PS3569.A8648
Sawyer, Elliott.   PS3619.A95
Sawyer, Meryl.   PS3569.A866
Sawyer, Robert J.   PR9199.3.S2533
Sawyer, Thomas B.   PS3619.A986
Sax, André.   none
Saxon, Alex, 1943-   PS3566.R67
Saxon, Peter.   none
Saxon, Van, 1927-   PS3558.E487
Saxton, Arthur L.   PS3619.A99
Saxton, Lisa.   PS3569.A927
Sayers, Dorothy L. (Dorothy Leigh), 1893-1957.   PR6037.A95
Saylor, Steven, 1956-   PS3569.A96
Scaduto, Anthony.   PS3569.C24
Scaglia, Franco, 1944-   PQ4879.C264
Scalapino, Leslie.   PS3569.C25
Scanlon, Charles Francis, 1935-   PS3569.C2954
Scanlon, Noel.   PR6069.C33
Scannell, Vernon.   PR6037.C25
Scarborough, Chuck.   PS3569.C32
Scarpaci, Sherry.   PS3619.C27
Scarpetta, Frank, 1935-   none
Scerbanenco, Giorgio, 1911-1969.   PQ4841.C4
Schaab, Susan.   PS3619.C3125
Schaefer, Frank, 1936-   PS3569.C343
Schaffer, Dylan.   PS3619.C315
Schätzing, Frank, 1957-   PT2680.A79
Schaub, Urs, 1951-   PT2720.A83
Schechter, Harold.   PS3569.C4776
Schechter, Peter.   PS3619.C338
Scheen, Kjersti.   none
Schenkel, Andrea Maria.   PT2720.E65
Schenkel, S. E.   PS3569.C48295
Scherf, Margaret.   PS3537.C3214
Schermerhorn, James.   PS3569.C48433
Schickler, David.   PS3569.C4848
Schieber, Phyllis.   PS3569.C48515
Schiefelbein, Michael E.   PS3619.C36
Schier, Norma.   PS3569.C4855
Schiff, Barry J.   PS3569.C486
Schilling, Vivian.   PS3569.C492
Schlaman, Jeffrey D.   PS3619.C415
Schleifer, Gerry.   PR6069.C516
Schlink, Bernhard.   PT2680.L54
Schmidli, Werner, 1939-   PT2680.M47
Schmidt, Carol, 1942-   PS3569.C51544
Schmidt, H. Edward.   PS3619.C4455

Schmidt, Kathrin, 1958-	PT2680.M51154
Schneider, Peter, 1940-	PT2680.N37
Schnurr, William.	none
Schock, T. A.	none
Schoell, William.	none
Schoenecker, Mary Fremont.	PS3619.C4493
Scholder, Henry, 1948-	PS3619.C4535
Scholefield, Alan.	PR9369.3.S3
Scholey, Jean.	PR9399.9.S36
Scholten, Jenny, 1968-	PS3569.C52547
Schonberg, Leonard, 1935-	PS3569.C5258
Schone, Robin.	PS3569.C525415
Schopen, Bernard.	PS3569.C52814
Schorr, Mark.	PS3537.C598
Schow, David J.	PS3569.C5284
Schrader, Esther.	PS3619.C456
Schrader, Leonard.	none
Schraff, Anne E.	none
Schreck, Tom, 1961-	PS3619.C462
Schreiber, Joe, 1969-	PS3619.C4635
Schreiber, Joseph.	PS3569.C529325
Schroeder, Eileen.	PS3569.C5299
Schubert, John D.	none
Schuler, Frank.	none
Schulman, David, 1948-	PS3619.C474
Schulman, Sarah, 1958-	PS3569.C5393
Schultz, Jack.	none
Schulz, Monte.	PS3569.C5543
Schulz, Torsten.	PT2720.U53
Schumacher, Aileen.	PS3569.C5546
Schumacher, Barret.	PS3619.C48
Schuman, Malcolm.	none
Schünemann, Christian, 1968-	PT2720.U54
Schunk, Laurel.	PS3569.C55533
Schupack, Deborah.	PS3619.C483
Schutz, Benjamin M.	PS3569.C5556
Schwandt, Stephen.	PS3569.C5645
Schwartz, Alan.	PS3569.C5648
Schwartz, Gary, 1940-	PT5881.29.C594
Schwartz, Leslie, 1962-	PS3569.C5666
Schwartz, Richard B.	PS3569.C56735
Schwegel, Theresa.	PS3619.C4925
Schweitzer, Gertrude, 1909-	PS3537.C816
Sciascia, Leonardo.	PQ4879.C54
Scoppettone, Sandra.	PS3569.C586
Scortia, Thomas N., 1926-1986.	PS3569.C587
Scott, A. D.	PR9619.4.S35
Scott, Annjeanette.	none
Scott, Antonia.	none
Scott, Barbara A.	none
Scott, Barbara, 1948-	PS3569.C595
Scott, Bill, 1946-	PS3619.C655
Scott, Chris, 1945-	PR9199.3.S32
Scott, Deborah.	none

Scott, Douglas, 1926-   PR6069.C586
Scott, Gavin, 1950-   PR6069.C588
Scott, Genevieve.   none
Scott, Holden.   PS3569.C626
Scott, Jack Denton, 1915-   PS3569.C63
Scott, Jack S., 1922-   PR6069.C589
Scott, J. M. (James Maurice), 1906-1986.   PR6037.C927
Scott, Jefferson.   PS3569.C6356
Scott, Jeffry.   none
Scott, Jeremy.   PR6054.I29
Scott, Joanna, 1960-   PS3569.C636
Scott, Jody.   none
Scott, June Meindl.   PS3569.C64
Scott, Justin.   PS3569.C644
Scott, Kemble, 1962-   PS3619.C673
Scott, Kevin, 1952-   PS3619.C674
Scott, Lena.   PS3619.C676
Scott, Leonard B.   PS3569.C647
Scott, Loraine.   PS3619.C677
Scott, Manda.   PR6069.C593
Scott, Margerie.   PR9199.3.S36
Scott, Martin, 1956-   PR6063.I34
Scott, Melissa.   PS3569.C672
Scott, Michele, 1969-   PS3619.C6824
Scott, Milton.   none
Scott, Phillip.   PR9619.4.S38
Scott, R. T. M. (Reginald Thomas Maitland), b. PR9199.3.S365
1882.
Scott, Robert, 1947-   PS3619.C6835
Scott, Rosie, 1948-   PR9639.3.S39
Scott, Steve.   none
Scott, Trevor.   PS3569.C6787
Scott, Valerie, 1928-   PR6069.C615
Scott, Virgil, 1914-   PS3537.C92937
Scott, Warwick.   PR6039.R518
Scott, Willard.   PS3569.C6896
Scott-Heron, Gil, 1949-2011.   PS3569.C7
Scotter, John.   none
Scotti, R. A.   PS3569.C72
Scottoline, Lisa.   PS3569.C725
Scowcroft, Richard.   PS3537.C954
Sea-Lion.   none
Seale, Anne.   PS3619.E255
Seaman, Donald.   PR6069.E154
Seamark.   PR6037.M2
Seamon, Hollis.   PS3569.E1755
Searle, Don L., 1944-   PS3569.E1765
Searle, Weston.   none
Searles, Hank.   none
Searles, John.   PS3569.E1788
Searles, Margaret.   PS3619.E2558
Searls, Hank, 1922-   PS3569.E18
Sears, Richard.   PS3569.E193
Sears, Ruth McCarthy.   none

Sebag Montefiore, Simon, 1965-	PR6063.O525
Sebastian, Margaret, 1921-	PS3569.E28
Sebastian, Tim.	PR6069.E197
Sebenthall, R. E.	PS3537.E1884
Sécary, Jean de.	PQ2679.E25
Secor, William R.	PS3569.E2868
Sederberg, Arelo.	PS3569.E315
Sedgwick, John, 1954-	PS3569.E3164
Sedley, Kate.	PR6069.E323
Sedov, B. K.	PG3486.E273
See, Lisa.	PS3569.E3334
Seeber, Claire.	PR6119.E43
Seeley, Mabel, 1903-1991.	PS3537.E2826
Seely, Norma.	PS3569.E345
Seewald, Jacqueline.	PS3619.E358
Seffer, Neta.	PS3619.E365
Sefton, Maggie.	PS3619.E37
Segal, Alan F., 1945-	none
Segal, Dan.	none
Segriff, Larry.	PS3619.E4
Segura, Jonathan.	PS3619.E416
Sehler, Tom.	PS3569.E465
Seidman, Robert J.	PS3569.E532
Sela, Owen.	PR9440.9.S4
Selby, Clark.	PS3619.E46
Selby, Hubert.	PS3569.E547
Selig, Elaine Booth.	none
Seligson, Tom.	PS3569.E573
Sellar, Maurice.	none
Sellers, Con.	PS3569.E575
Sellers, Mary.	none
Sellers, Michael, 1941-	PR6069.E3695
Selmark, George, b. 1892.	PR6039.R8
Selwyn, Francis.	PR6069.E382
Semenov, I‹U›lian, 1931-1993.	PG3486.E45
Semprún, Jorge.	PQ2679.E4
Senehi, Rose.	PS3619.E659
Senna, Danzy.	PS3569.E618
Sennett, Frank.	PS3619.E66
Sensel, Joni, 1962-	PS3619.E68
Senuta, Michael.	PS3569.E63
Serafín, David.	PR6069.E6
Serah, Tonne.	PS3619.E735
Seranella, Barbara.	PS3569.E66
Seraphinoff, Michael.	PS3619.E7358
Serbin, Ivan.	PG3486.E6375
Serena, Anthony.	PS3619.E74
Serge, Victor, 1890-1947.	PQ2637.E49
Sergeant, Adeline, 1851-1904.	PR5349.S423
Serling, Robert J.	PS3569.E7
Serling, Rod, 1924-1975.	PS3537.E654
Serova, Marina.	PG3486.E718
Serrian, Michael.	none
Sesto, Genevieve.	PS3569.E766

Setlowe, Richard.	PS3569.E78
Settle, Mary Lee.	PS3569.E84
Seuffert, Muir.	none
Severn, Richard.	none
Severt‹s›ev, Petr.	none
Sevilla, Charles M.	PS3569.E875
Seward, Jack.	PS3569.E88
Sewart, Alan.	PR6069.E718
Sewell, Earl.	PS3619.E97
Sewell, Kitty.	PR6119.E96
Seymour, Gerald.	PR6069.E734
Seymour, Henry, 1931-	none
Seymour, Valerie.	PR6119.E984
Shaber, Sarah R.	PS3569.H226
Shabtai, Sabi H.	PS3569.H23
Shaffer, Anthony, 1926-2001.	PR6069.H258
Shaffer, Louise.	PS3569.H3112
Shagan, Steve.	PS3569.H313
Shah, Diane K.	PS3569.H314
Shakespeare, L. M. (L. Marguerite)	PR6069.H285
Shakhov, Maksim.	PG3487.A56
Shakuntala Devi, 1939-	PR9499.3.S443
Shalvis, Jill.	PS3619.H3534
Shames, Laurence.	PS3569.H328
Shamsie, Kamila, 1973-	PR9540.9.S485
Shane, Jack.	none
Shane, Trevor.	PS3619.H35465
Shannon, Barry.	PS3569.H3345
Shannon, Dell, 1921-1988.	PS3562.I515
Shannon, Doris.	PR9199.3.S49
Shannon, Harry.	PS3619.H355
Shannon, J. R.	PS3619.H3554
Shannon, John, 1943-	PS3569.H3358
Shannon, Ray.	PS3558.A885
Shank, Jenny, 1976-	PS3619.H35469
Shankman, Sarah.	PS3569.H3327
Shapiro, Barbara A., 1951-	PS3569.H3385
Shapiro, Harvey, 1924-	PS3537.H264
Shapiro, Marianne.	PS3619.H35624
Shapiro, Milton J.	none
Sharfeddin, Heather.	PS3619.H35635
Sharkey, Jack.	PS3569.H3427
Sharland, Mike.	PR6069.H336
Sharman, Miriam.	none
Sharman, Nick.	none
Sharmat, Marjorie Weinman.	none
Sharp, Alan.	none
Sharp, Charles Dee.	PS3619.H35644
Sharp, Deborah, 1954-	PS3619.H35645
Sharp, Jolyn.	PS3619.H35647
Sharp, Marilyn.	PS3569.H3434
Sharp, Zoë, 1966-	PR6119.H376
Sharpe, Alice.	PS3569.H34358
Sharpe, Isabel.	PS3619.H356645

Sharratt, Mary, 1964-	PS3569.H3449
Shatner, William.	PS3569.H347
Shattuck, Dora.	none
Shattuck, Shari.	PS3619.H3575
Shavelson, Melville, 1917-2007.	PS3569.H357
Shaw, Caroline.	PR6069.H367
Shaw, Catherine, 1961-	PS3619.H3918
Shaw, David, 1943-	none
Shaw, Howard.	PR6069.H375
Shaw, Irwin, 1913-1984.	PS3537.H384
Shaw, Joseph W., 1944-	PS3619.H3934
Shaw, June.	PS3619.H3936
Shaw, Lou.	PS3569.H3837
Shaw, Matt, 1982-	PR9199.4.S5257
Shaw, Murray.	PS3569.H38423
Shaw, P. B.	PS3569.H38424
Shaw, Robin.	PS3569.H386
Shaw, Simon.	PR6069.H3948
Shaw, Terrence.	PS3569.H38635
Shaw, Terry, 1962-	PS3619.H3946
Shay, Kathryn.	none
Shayne, Maggie.	PS3619.H399
Shchupov, Andreĭ.	PG3487.C572
Shea, Michael.	PR6069.H3949
Shea, Robert.	PS3569.H39125
Shealy, Larry.	none
Sheard, Timothy.	PS3569.H3913
Shearer, Alex.	none
Shearing, Joseph, 1888-1952.	PR6003.O676
Shearston, Trevor.	PR9619.3.S482
Sheckley, Robert, 1928-2005.	PS3569.H392
Shedley, Ethan I.	PS3569.H39214
Sheedy, E. C.—see: Sheedy, Edna, 1939-	
Sheedy, Edna, 1939-	PR9199.3.D373
Sheehan, Aurelie, 1963-	PS3569.H392155
Shefchik, Rick.	PS3619.H4514
Sheil, Timothy Francis, 1948-	PR9619.3.S4835
Sheindlin, Gerald.	none
Shelby, Brit.	PS3569.H39257
Shelby, Jeff.	PS3619.H4523
Shelby, Philip.	PR9199.3.S5117
Sheldon, Jean.	PS3619.H45326
Sheldon, Sidney.	PS3569.H3927
Sheldon, Walter J.	PS3569.H3928
Shellabarger, Samuel, 1888-1954.	PS3537.H64
Shelley, Sidney, 1921-	none
Shellito, Tracey.	PR6119.H46
Shelton, Connie.	PS3569.H393637
Shelton, Paige.	PS3619.H45345
Shelynn, Jack.	none
Shenton, Alan, 1939-	none
Shepard, Karen.	PS3569.H39388
Shepard, Lucius.	PS3569.H3939
Shepard, Sam, 1943-	PS3569.H394

Shepard, Sara, 1977-   PS3619.H4543
Shepherd, John, 1903-1980.   PS3503.A5575
Shepherd, L. P.   none
Shepherd, Lynn, 1964-   PR6119.H465
Shepherd, Michael, 1927-2001.   PS3562.U26
Shepherd, Stella, 1953-   PR6069.H454
Sheppard, Stephen, 1945-   PR6069.H4553
Sherbaniuk, Richard.   PS3569.H3987
Sherburne, James, 1925-   PS3569.H399
Sherer, Michael W.   PS3569.H3993
Sherez, Stav.   PR6119.H47
Sheridan, Anne-Marie.   PR6069.H456
Sheridan, D. S.   PR6069.H4563
Sheridan, James, 1970-   PS3619.H4634
Sherman, Beth.   PS3569.H414
Sherman, Charlotte A., 1932-   PS3569.H43
Sherman, Dan.   PS3569.H416
Sherman, David.   PS3569.H4175
Sherman, David J., 1966-   PS3619.H464
Sherman, Jory.   PS3569.H43
Sherman, Patricia J.   none
Sherman, Robert, 1931-   none
Sherman, Robin.   none
Sherman, Roger.   none
Sherman, Scott, 1962-   PS3619.H4675
Sherman, Steve, 1938-   PS3569.H4337
Sherman, William.   none
Sherriff, R. C. (Robert Cedric), 1896-1975.   PR6037.H513
Sherry, Edna.   PS3537.H812
Sherwood, John, 1913-   PR6037.H517
Sherwood, Peter.   none
Shiel, Lisa A.   PS3619.H53
Shiel, M. P. (Matthew Phipps), 1865-1947.   PR6037.H524
Shields, Jody, 1952-   PS3569.H4836
Shilova, I‹U›lii‹a›.   PG3487.I39
Shimer, R. H. (Ruth H.)   PS3569.H49
Shingler, William G.   none
Shinn, Sharon.   PS3569.H499
Shipway, George, 1908-   PR6069.H5
Shiri‹a›nov, Bai‹a›n.   PG3487.I673
Shitov, Vladimir.   PG3487.I78
Shkli‹a›r, Vasyl'.   PG3949.29.H53
Shlian, Deborah M.   PS3619.H625
Shmurak, Carole B., 1944-   PS3569.H5656
Shobin, David.   PS3569.H567
Shoebridge, Marjorie.   PR6069.H56
Shoemaker, Bill, 1931-2003.   PS3569.H5716
Shoesmith, Kathleen A. (Kathleen Anne), 1938-   none
Sholes, Lynn, 1945-   PS3619.H646
Shone, Anna.   PR9105.9.S55
Shore, Norman.   none
Shore, Valery.   none
Short, Agnes.   PR6069.H629
Short, Christopher, 1913-1978.   PR6069.H6292

Short, Sharon Gwyn.	PS3569.H594
Showalter, Gena.	PS3619.H77
Shreve, Susan Richards.	PS3569.H74
Shriner, Larry.	PS3569.H7415
Shroyer, Frederick B.	PS3569.H744
Shryack, Dennis.	none
Shub, Joyce Lasky—see: Reed, Joyce Lasky.	
Shubin, Seymour.	PS3569.H754
Shuker, R. Carl, 1974-	PR9639.4.S56
Shukman, Henry.	PR6069.H74
Shulman, Irving.	PS3537.H99185
Shulman, Sandra.	PR6069.H745
Shuman, George D., 1952-	PS3619.H86
Shuman, M. K.	PS3569.H779
Shura, Mary Francis, 1923-	PS3553.R226
Shusterman, Neal.	PS3569.H8645
Shute, Jenefer.	PR9369.3.S46
Shute, Nevil, 1899-1960.	PR6027.O54
Sibley, Celestine.	PS3569.I256
Sibley, Patricia.	PR6069.I25
Siciliano, Sam, 1947-	PS3569.I268
Siddons, Anne Rivers.	PS3569.I28
Sidor, Steven.	PS3619.I36
Siegal, Nina, 1969-	PS3619.I37
Siegel, Barry, 1949-	PS3569.I368
Siegel, Benjamin, 1914-	PS3569.I37
Siegel, Jack.	none
Siegel, James.	PS3569.I3747
Siegel, Sheldon (Sheldon M.)	PS3569.I3823
Siegrist, Robert R.	none
Sierra, Germán, 1960-	PQ6669.I345
Sierra i Fabra, Jordi.	PQ6669.I36
Sietecase, Reynaldo, 1961-	PQ7798.29.I325
Sigel, Efrem.	PS3569.I412
Siger, Jeffrey.	PS3619.I45
Sikes, Mary Montague, 1939-	PS3619.I54
Silbersky, Leif.	PT9876.29.I39
Silberstang, Edwin, 1930-	PS3569.I415
Silbert, Leslie.	PS3619.I5435
Siler, Jenny.	PS3569.I42125
Siller, Van.	PS3543.A648
Silsbee, Peter.	none
Silva, Daniel, 1960-	PS3619.I5443
Silva, Linda Kay.	PS3569.I4592
Silva, Lorenzo, 1966-	PQ6669.I3877
Silver, Alfred.	PR9199.3.S51765
Silver, Eve.	none
Silver, Horace.	PR6119.I45
Silver, Jim.	PS3569.I466
Silver, Victoria.	none
Silverman, R. M. (Robert M.)	none
Silverman, Robert S.	none
Silverwood, Roger.	PR6069.I365
Silvestri, Mike, 1957-	PS3619.I553

Silvis, Randall, 1950-	PS3569.I47235
Sim, Alastair.	PR6119.I455
Simart, Hélène.	PQ2679.I45
Simenon, Georges, 1903-1989.	PQ2637.I53
	[Z8819.I47]
Simmel, Johannes Mario.	PT2639.I63
Simmons, Dan.	PS3569.I47292
Simmons, Deborah.	PS3569.I472924
Simmons, Diane, 1948-	PS3619.I5584
Simmons, Geoffrey S.	PS3569.I4732
Simmons, Hal, 1938-	PS3619.I5594
Simmons, John, 1949-	none
Simmons, Larry (Larry W.)	PS3619.I56
Simmons, Mary Kay.	PS3569.I474
Simmons, Michael, 1970-	none
Simmons, Steven.	PS3569.I4768
Simmons, T. M.	PS3619.I5614
Simms, Chris, 1969-	PR6119.I464
Simms, William Gilmore, 1806-1870.	PS2840-2858
Simon, Angela, 1921-	none
Simon, Clea.	PS3619.I5619
Simon, Frank, 1943-	PS3569.I4816
Simon, Jessica, 1964-	PR9199.4.S548
Simon, Leonard, 1937-	PS3569.I4825
Simon, Michael.	PS3569.I4829
Simon, Michael, 1963-	PS3619.I5625
Simon, Roger Lichtenberg.	PS3569.I485
Simon, S. J., d. 1948.	none
Simon, Wilfrid, 1955-	PQ2679.I47285
Simons, Paullina, 1963-	PS3569.I48763
Simons, Roger, pseud.	PR6069.I42
Simonson, Louise.	PS3619.I56296
Simonson, Sheila, 1941-	PS3569.I48766
Simpson, Donna.	PR9199.3.S529
Simpson, Dorothy, 1933-	PR6069.I422
Simpson, George E.	PS3569.I4895
Simpson, Howard R., 1925-	PS3569.I49
Simpson, Inga.	PR9619.4.S565
Simpson, John Worsley, 1944-	PR9199.3.S5295
Simpson, M. E.	none
Simpson, Marcia.	PS3569.I51165
Simpson, Margaret, 1913-	PR6069.I427
Sims, Elizabeth, 1957-	PS3619.I564
Sims, George, 1923-	PR6037.I715
Sims, George Robert, 1847-1922.	PR5452.S4
Sims, Janice.	PS3619.I5648
Sims, L. V.	none
Sinclair, Andrew, 1935-	PR6069.I5
Sinclair, Bennie Lee, 1939-	PS3569.I5198
Sinclair, Dani.	PS3569.I5233
Sinclair, Dennis, 1923-1985.	PR9619.3.B725
Sinclair, Iain, 1943-	PR6069.I525
Sinclair, Linnea, 1954-	PS3619.I5684
Sinclair, Michael.	none

Sinclair, Michael, 1938-2009.	PR6069.H3949
Sinclair, Murray.	PS3569.I525
Sinclair, Olga.	PR6069.I55
Singer, Alan, 1948-	PS3569.I526
Singer, June Flaum.	PS3569.I544
Singer, Loren.	PS3569.I545
Singer, Norman.	PS3569.I55
Singer, Randy (Randy D.)	PS3619.I5725
Singer, Rochelle—see: Singer, Shelley.	
Singer, Sally M., 1930-	PS3569.I57
Singer, Shelley.	PS3569.I565
Singerman, Philip.	PS3569.I5743
Singh, Nalini, 1977-	PR9639.4.S566
Singh, Sonia.	PS3619.I5745
Singleton, James R.	PS3569.I575
Singleton, Linda Joy.	none
Sington, Philip.	PR6119.I54
Siniac, Pierre.	PQ2679.I54
Siodmak, Curt, 1902-2000.	PS3537.I875
Siodmak, Kurt—see: Siodmak, Curt, 1902-2000.	
Sipherd, Ray.	PS3569.I59
Sirias, Silvio.	PS3619.I75
Sisco, Andrea.	PS3619.I79
Sisson, Hal C., 1921-	PR9199.3.S5363
Siverling, Michael.	PS3619.I95
Sjoholm, Barbara, 1950-	PS3573.I45678
Sjöwall, Maj, 1935-	PT9876.29.J63
Skalicky, Scott, 1960-	PS3569.K363
Skeggs, Douglas.	PR6069.K34
Skehan, Everett M.	PS3569.K38
Skibbins, David, 1947-	PS3619.K55
Skile, D. M., 1962-	PG1420.29.K55
Skinner, 1951-	PS3619.K557
Skinner, Ainslie.	PR6069.K48
Skinner, Michael, 1924-	none
Skinner, Quinton, 1968-	PS3619.K565
Skinner, Richard, 1965-	PR6119.K36
Skinner, Robert E., 1948-	PS3569.K528
Skipp, John.	none
Skirrow, Desmond.	PR6069.K54
Sklepowich, Edward.	PS3569.K574
Skoggard, Bruno.	PS3569.K6
Skom, Edith.	PS3569.K65
Skurzynski, Gloria.	none
Škvorecký, Josef.	PR9199.3.S545
	PG5038.S527
Skvort‹s›ov, Valerian Nikolaevich.	PG3488.K835
Skwiot, Rick, 1947-	PS3569.K89
Skye, Christina.	PS3569.K94
Slabber, I. G.	none
Slack, Mandi (Mandi Jean), 1980-	PS3619.L328
Slack, Teresa D., 1964-	PS3619.L33
Slade, Bernard, 1930-	PS3569.L2
Slade, Michael.	PR9199.3.S55115

Sladek, John Thomas.	PS3569.L25
Slama, Carol D.	PS3569.L257
Slate, Caroline.	PS3552.R3777
Slater, Harrison Gradwell.	PS3619.L37
Slater, Ian, 1941-	PR9199.3.S5512
Slater, Nigel, 1944-	PR6069.L334
Slater, Susan, 1942-	PS3569.L265
Slaughter, Karin, 1971-	PS3569.L275
Slavitt, David R., 1935-	PS3569.L3
Slawson, Evan.	none
Slear, Genevieve.	PS3569.L35
Sleator, William.	PS3569.L353
Sleem, Patty, 1948-	PS3569.L356
Sleeman, Susan.	PS3619.L44
Slesar, Henry.	PS3569.L38
Slim, Iceberg—see: Iceberg Slim, 1918-1992.	
Sloan, Bob.	PS3569.L5
Sloan, Sarah.	none
Sloan, Susan R.	PS3569.L57
Sloane, Ben.	none
Sloane, William, 1906-1974.	PS3537.L59
Slovo, Gillian, 1952-	PR6069.L56
Small, Austin J.	PR6037.M2
Smallman, Phyllis.	PR9199.4.S62
Smart, Hawley, 1833-1893.	PR5453.S148
Smeraglia, René.	PS3569.M388
Smiley, Jane.	PS3569.M39
Smiley, Patricia.	PS3619.M49
Smilgis, Martha.	PS3569.M42
Smith, A. C. H. (Anthony Charles H.), 1935-	PR6069.M42
Smith, Alison, 1932-	PS3569.M46
Smith, Anthony Neil.	PS3619.M55226
Smith, April, 1949-	PS3569.M467
Smith, B. J. (Brad J.)	PR9199.3.S55148
Smith, B. K. (B. Karen)	PS3569.M482
Smith, Barbara Burnett.	PS3569.M483
Smith, Bridget A.	PS3569.M5117
Smith, Caesar.	PR6039.R518
Smith, Carl T., 1937-	PS3569.M5127
Smith, Carol, 1938-	PR6069.M4215
Smith, Charles Merrill.	PS3569.M5156
Smith, Charlie, 1947-	PS3569.M5163
Smith, Colin, 1944-	PR6069.M428
Smith, Craig, 1947-	PS3569.M5168
Smith, Craig, 1950-	PS3569.M51678
Smith, D. W.—see: Smith, Dan, 1951-	
Smith, Dan, 1951-	PR6069.M444
Smith, Dave.	none
Smith, David Alexander.	PS3569.M51715
Smith, David, N. (David Nathan)	PS3569.M51718
Smith, Debra White.	PS3569.M5178
Smith, Dennis, 1940-	PS3569.M523
Smith, Derek, 1956 Nov. 3-	PS3619.M58
Smith, Dodie, 1896-1990.	PR6037.M38

Smith, Don, 1909-   none
Smith, Edgar, 1934-   PS3569.M534
Smith, Edward Ernest—see: Lindall, Edward, 1915-
Smith, Evelyn E.   PS3569.M53515
Smith, Florence B.   PS3569.M35165
Smith, Frank, 1927-   PR9199.3.S55155
Smith, Frank E.—see: Craig, Jonathan, 1919-1984.
Smith, Frederick E. (Frederick Escreet), 1922-   PR6069.M482
Smith, Godfrey, 1926-   PR6069.M483
Smith, Gregory Blake.   PS3569.M5356
Smith, Guy N.   none
Smith, Iain Crichton, 1928-1998.   PR6005.R58
Smith, Ian, 1969-   PS3619.M588
Smith, J. C. S.   PS3569.M5374
Smith, J. P., 1949-   PS3569.M53744
Smith, Jack Nickle.   PR6069.M487
Smith, Janet L.   PS3569.M537518
Smith, Jasper.   none
Smith, Jerry, 1952-   PS3569.M53744
Smith, Joan, 1938-   PR9199.3.S55157
Smith, Joan, 1953-   PR6069.M4944
Smith, Joan M.   none
Smith, John, 1943 Oct. 2-   PR6069.M495
Smith, Julie, 1944-   PS3569.M537553
Smith, Justin R.   PS3619.M5888
Smith, Kay Nolte.   PS3569.M537554
Smith, L. Neil.   PS3569.M537555
Smith, Laura.   none
Smith, Lawrence R., 1945-   PS3569.M537575
Smith, Lora R. (Lora Roberts)   PS3569.M537635
Smith, Lou.   PR6069.M52
Smith, Lyndsay, 1963-   PR9199.3.S55163
Smith, Mark, 1935-   PS3569.M53766
Smith, Mark Haskell.   PS3619.M592
Smith, Martin Cruz, 1942-   PS3569.M5377
Smith, Mary-Ann Tirone, 1944-   PS3569.M537736
Smith, Mason, 1936-   PS3569.M5378
Smith, Maureen.   none
Smith, Meta.   PS3619.M5922
Smith, Michael A. (Michael Anthony), 1942 Dec.   PS3569.M53783
15-
Smith, Mitchell, 1935-   PS3569.M537834
Smith, Murray (Charles Maurice)   PR6069.M524
Smith, Nancy Carolyn.   none
Smith, Nancy Taylor.   none
Smith, Naomi Gladish.   PS3619.M5923
Smith, Neville, 1940-   PR6069.M5245
Smith, Nick, 1972-   PR6119.M577
Smith, Peter Moore, 1965-   PS3569.M5379126
Smith, Robert A. (Robert Arthur), 1926-   none
Smith, Robert B. (Robert Barr), 1933-   PS3569.M537927
Smith, Robert Charles, 1938-   PR6069.M53
Smith, Robert F., 1970-   PS3569.M537928
Smith, Robert Kimmel, 1930-   PS3569.M53795

Smith, Roger, 1960-	PR9369.4.S65
Smith, Roland, 1951-	none
Smith, Rosamond, 1938-	PS3565.A8
Smith, Sarah, 1947-	PS3569.M5379758
Smith, Scott, 1965 July 13-	PS3569.M5379759
Smith, Shelley.	PS3569.M537976
Smith, Shelley, 1912-	PR6003.O36
Smith, Sid.	PR6119.M583
Smith, Sinclair.	none
Smith, Steven, 1945-	PR9199.3.S5615
Smith, Surrey.	PR6037.M578
Smith, Susan Arnout.	PS3551.R58
Smith, Sydney, 1912-	PR6069.M554
Smith, Taylor.	PS3569.M537995
Smith, Terrence Lore.	PS3569.M538
Smith, Tom Rob.	PR6119.M586
Smith, Vern E.	PS3569.M5394
Smith, Virginia, 1960-	PS3619.M5956
Smith, Wilbur A.	PR9405.9.S5
Smith-Brown, Fern.	PS3569.M546
Smithies, Richard H. R.	PS3569.M56
Smitten, R. L.—see: Smitten, Richard.	
Smitten, Richard.	PS3569.M585
Smoak, Amanda.	PS3619.M63
Smoke, Stephen L., 1949-	PS3569.M645
Smolens, John.	PS3569.M646
Snell, David, 1942-	PS3569.N35
Snell, Edmund.	PR6037.N38
Snelling, Laurence, 1933-	PS3569.N4
Snellings, John.	none
Snider, Gordon J., 1940-	PS3619.N535
Sniegoski, Thomas E.—see: Sniegoski, Tom.	
Sniegoski, Tom.	PS3619.N537
Snodgress, G. M.	none
Snow, C. P. (Charles Percy), 1905-1980.	PR6037.N58
Snow, Carol, 1965-	PS3619.N66
Snow, Kathleen.	PS3569.N623
Snow, Lyndon.	PR6001.N75
Snowden, Faye.	PS3619.N69
Snyder, Don J.	PS3569.N86
Snyder, Eugene E. (Eugene Edmund)	PS3569.N865
Snyder, Gene.	none
Snyder, Keith, 1966-	PS3569.N892
Snyder, Michael, 1965-	PS3619.N938
Snyder, Zilpha Keatley.	PS3569.N93
Soares, Jô.	PQ9698.29.O177
Sobel, Irwin Philip.	PS3569.O2
Sobol, Donald J., 1924-	PS3537.O159
Sobol, Yehoshu'a.	PJ5054.S627
Sodaro, Craig.	PS3569.O3746
Soderberg, Dale L.	none
Soderquist, Larry D., 1944-2005.	PS3569.O376
Soendker, Sandi.	PS3619.O378
Soesbe, Douglas.	PS3569.O38

Sofer, Barbara.	PS3569.O39
Sohl, Jerry, 1913-2002.	PS3569.O4
Sohmers, Barbara.	PS3569.O433
Sokoloff, Alexandra.	PS3619.O425
Soles, Caro.	PR9199.4.S694
Solnt‹s›eva, Natal'i‹a› (Natal'i‹a› Anatol'evna)	PG3493.48.O43
Solomita, Stephen.	PS3569.O587
Solomon, Annie.	PS3619.O433
Solomon, Brad.	PS3569.O595
Soltis, Andy, 1947-	PS3619.O438
Somer, Mehmet Murat, 1959-	PL248.S557
Somers, Jeff, 1971-	PS3619.O64
Somers, Suzanne—see: Daniels, Dorothy, 1915-	
Somerville, Rowan.	PR6119.O63
Somerville-Large, Peter.	PR6069.O43
Somoza, José Carlos, 1959-	PQ6669.O56
Sondheim, Stephen.	PS3569.O65378
Sonenfeld, Nathan.	PR6069.O48
Songer, C. J.	PS3569.O65393
Soos, Troy, 1957-	PS3569.O665
Soracco, Sin, 1947-	PS3569.O667
Sorensen, Harold F.	PS3569.O6755
Sorrells, Walter.	PS3569.O695
Sotto, Samantha.	PS3619.O87
Soucy, Gaétan, 1958-	PQ3919.2.S655
Soule, Maris.	PS3569.O737
Soup, Cuthbert.	none
Soutar, Andrew, 1879-1941.	PR6037.O83
South, Sheri Cobb.	PS3569.O755
Southby-Tailyour, Ewen.	PR6119.O68
Southcott, Audley.	PR6069.O87
Southey, Roz, 1952-	PR6119.O69
Southin, Gwendolyn.	PR9199.4.S723
Southworth, Emma Dorothy Eliza Nevitte, 1819-1899.	PS2890-2893
Southworth, Louis.	none
Soutter, Andy.	PR6069.O885
Souvestre, Pierre, 1874-1914.	PQ2637.O84
Spain, Peter.	PR6069.P28
Spang, Michael Grundt, 1931-	PT8951.29.P3
Spann, Weldon.	none
Spann Craig, Elizabeth.	PS3619.P343
Spanogle, Joshua.	PS3619.P344
Spark, Muriel.	PR6037.P29
Sparkia, Roy B. (Roy Bernard), 1924-	none
Sparks, Christine.	none
Sparks, D. L.	PS3604.U265
Sparks, Nicholas.	PS3569.P363
Sparling, Joyce B.	PS3569.P364
Speare, Candice.	PS3619.P3735
Spears, Heather, 1934-	PR9199.3.S6314
Speart, Jessica.	PS3619.P4345
Specht, Robert, 1928-	PS3569.P425
Specter, B. J.	none

Spector, Craig.	PS3619.P375
Speicher, Helen Ross.	none
Speight, Bernice, 1918-	PS3569.P4417
Speight, T. W. (Thomas Wilkinson), 1830-1915.	PS2894.S54
Speller, Elizabeth.	PR6119.P39
Spelleri, Robert V., 1949-	PS3619.P45
Spencer, Darrell, 1947-	PS3569.P446
Spencer, John B.	PR6069.P482
Spencer, Jon Michael.	PS3569.P4516
Spencer, Ross H.	PS3569.P454
Spencer, Sally.	PR6069.P483
Spencer-Fleming, Julia.	PS3619.P467
Spetz, Steven N., 1940-	none
Spicer, Bart, 1918-	PS3569.P464
Spicer, David, 1947-	PS3619.P536
Spicer, Dorothy Gladys.	PS3569.P465
Spicer, Jack.	PS3569.P47
Spicer, Michael, 1943-	PR6069.P498
Spiegelman, Peter.	PS3619.P543
Spignesi, Stephen J.	PS3619.P544
Spike, Paul, 1947-	PS3569.P53
Spilken, Aron, 1939-	PS3569.P54
Spillane, Mickey, 1918-2006.	PS3537.P652
Spiller, Robert.	PS3619.P5477
Spindler, Erica, 1957-	PS3569.P5436
Spinnaker, Jackson.	PS3619.P564
Spinnen, Burkhard, 1956-	PT2681.P54
Spinosa, Tony, 1956-	PS3553.O47445
Spinrad, Norman.	PS3569.P55
Spizer, Joyce.	PS3569.P59
Spooner, John D.	PS3569.P6
Spore, Keith.	none
Spouse, Mary.	none
Sprague, Gretchen.	PS3569.P629
Sprague, Joyce Claypool.	none
Spring, Michelle.	PR6069.P73
Spring, Peter, 1951-	PS3619.P75
Springer, Kathryn.	PS3619.P76
Springer, Nancy.	PS3569.P685
Sprinkle, Patricia Houck.	PS3569.P687
Spruill, Steven G.	PS3569.P733
Squerent, Will.	PS3552.R213
Squire, Elizabeth Daniels.	PS3569.Q43
Squire, Robin.	PS3569.Q457
Srinivasan, Krishnan, 1937-	PR9499.3.S76
St. Christopher, Koz, 1958-	PS3619.T45
St. Christopher, Victoria M., 1953-	PS3619.T23
St. Clair, David.	PS3569.A425
St. Clair, Elizabeth.	none
St. Clair, Jeananne.	none
St. Clair, Katherine.	PS3558.U323
St. Clair, Leonard.	PS3569.A43
St. Edmunds, Anne.	PS3569.T1215
St. George, Geoffrey.	PS3569.A452

St. George, Judith, 1931-	PS3569.A4522
St. George, Margaret.	none
St. George, Mark.	PS3569.A4524
St. James, Bernard.	PS3569.A4533
St. James, Dorothy.	PS3619.T245
St. James, Ian.	PR6069.A423
St. John, Barnett.	none
St. John, Billy.	PS3569.T1242
St. John, Cheryl.	PS3569.T12424
St. John, D. W.	PS3569.T12425
St. John, David, 1918-2007.	PS3515.U5425
St. John, Nicole.	PS3560.O3897
St. Martin, Thomas.	none
St. Peter, Sarah, 1955-	PS3569.T1245
Staalesen, Gunnar, 1947-	PT8951.29.T3
Stabenow, Dana.	PS3569.T1249
Stableford, Brian M.	PR6069.T17
Stacey, Lyndon.	PR6119.T335
Stacey, Susannah.	PR6069.T177
Stacey, Tom, 1930-	PR6069.T18
Stackhouse, Bill.	PS3619.T3425
Stacpoole, H. De Vere (Henry De Vere), 1863-1951.	PR6037.T15
Stacy, Ryder.	none
Stacy-Deanne, 1978-	PS3619.T3428
Stade, George.	PS3569.T147
Stadley, Pat.	PS3569.T15
Staeger, Will.	PS3619.T343
Stafford, Caroline.	PS3569.T165
Stagge, Jonathan.	PS3545.H2895
Staggs, Earl.	PS3619.T344
Stahl, Hilda.	PS3569.T312
Stahl, Jerry.	PS3569.T3125
Stahl, Norman.	PS3569.T313
Staley, Deborah Grace.	PS3619.T348
Stall, Mike.	none
Stallsmith, Audrey.	PS3569.T3216
Stallwood, Veronica.	PR6069.T195
Stam, Paul Justin.	none
Stamey, Sara.	PS3619.T362
Stamm, Hugo.	PT2681.T3232
Stamos, Ann.	PS3619.T363
Stamoulis, Mary Lukes.	PS3619.T364
Stand, Marguerite.	PR6069.T25
Stander, Siegfried.	PR9369.3.S77
Standiford, Les.	PS3569.T331528
Standish, Burt L., 1866-1945.	PS3531.A82
Standish, Robert.	PR6013.E668
Stang, JoAnne.	PS3569.T332
Stanley, Diane.	PS3569.T3325
Stanley, George Edward.	none
Stanley, J. B.	PS3619.T3655
Stanley, John.	none
Stanley, Kelli.	PS3619.T3657
Stanley, Michael.	PR9369.4.S715

Stanley, Ray.	none
Stanley, Sandra.	none
Stanley, William, 1919-	PR6069.T293
Stanmeyer, William A., 1934-	PS3569.T33335
Stansberry, Domenic.	PS3569.T3335
Stansfield, Anita, 1961-	PS3569.T33354
Stanton, Cathy.	PS3553.L249
Stanton, Coralie.	none
Stanton, Ken.	none
Stanton, Martin.	none
Stanton, Paul, 1919-1999.	PR6003.E264
Stanwood, Brooks.	PS3569.T3342
Stanwood, Donald A.	PS3569.T3343
Stapley, Michèle.	PS3619.T369
Stapp, Robert.	PS3569.T3355
Star, April.	PS3619.T37
Star, Nancy.	PS3569.T33555
Stark, Lucien.	none
Stark, Michael, 1908-1981.	PS3523.A71237
Stark, Nell.	PS3619.T3737
Stark, Richard, 1933-2008.	PS3573.E9
Starks, Richard.	none
Starling, Boris.	PR6069.T345
Starnes, Richard.	PS3569.T336
Starnone, Domenico, 1943-	PQ4879.T345
Starr, Jason, 1966-	PS3569.T336225
Starrett, Vincent, 1886-1974.	PS3537.T246
Stashower, Daniel.	PS3569.T33635
Staub, Wendy Corsi.	PS3569.T336456
Stead, C. K. (Christian Karlson), 1932-	PR9639.3.S7
Stead, Christina, 1902-1983.	PR9619.3.S75
Stearn, Jess.	PS3569.T338
Stebel, S. L.	PS3569.T33815
Steck, Ursula.	PS3619.T4326
Steed, Neville.	PR6069.T387
Steegmuller, Francis, 1906-1994.	PS3537.T267
Steel, Danielle.	PS3569.T33828
Steel, James.	PR6119.T4415
Steele, Bernadette, 1970-	PS3619.T433
Steele, Curtis.	PS3537.T2687
Steeley, Robert Derek.	none
Steen, Marguerite.	PR6037.T3
Steere, O'Ann.	PS3569.T3388
Stegemoeller, Rudy.	PS3619.T448
Stein, Aaron Marc, 1906-	PS3537.T3184
Stein, Benjamin, 1944-	PS3569.T36
Stein, Garth.	PS3569.T3655
Stein, Gertrude, 1874-1946.	PS3537.T323
Stein, Herbert, 1916-1999.	none
Stein, Michael, 1960-	PS3569.T3726
Stein, Michael Eric, 1953-	PS3619.T476
Stein, Peter, 1932-	none
Stein, Sol.	PS3569.T375
Stein, Triss.	PS3569.T37543

Steinberg, Harriet. none
Steinberg, Richard, 1958- PS3569.T375492
Steiner, Barbara A. none
Steiner, Edward, 1956- PS3619.T47625
Steiner, Peter, 1940- PS3619.T4763
Steiner, Wilfried, 1960- PT2681.T384
Steinhauer, Olen. PS3619.T4764
Steirman, Hy. none
Stella, Charlie. PS3619.T47645
Stepanova, Tat'i‹a›na (Tat'i‹a›na I‹U›r'evna) PG3488.T4768
Stephan, Leslie. PS3569.T3827
Stephen, Martin, 1949- PR6119.T45
Stephens, Casey. none
Stephens, Edward Carl, 1924- PS3569.T384
Stephens, Harold. PS3569.T3844
Stephens, Jeffrey S. PS3619.T47676
Stephens, Ransom, 1961- PS3619.T476768
Stephens, Reed. PS3554.O469
Stephenson, Carol. none
Stephenson, Maureen. none
Stephenson, Neal. PS3569.T3868
Sterling, Bruce. PS3569.T3876
Sterling, Ruth. PS3569.T38797
Sterling, Stewart, b. 1895. PS3545.I662
Sterling, Thomas, 1921- PS3569.T38798
Stern, D. A. (David A.) PS3569.T3884
Stern, Daniel, 1928-2007. PS3569.T3887
Stern, Mark, 1951- PS3569.T3896
Stern, Richard G., 1928- PS3569.T39
Stern, Richard Martin, 1915- PS3569.T394
Stern, Stuart, 1935- PR6068.A25
Sternberg, Cecilia. PR6069.T442
Stevens, Amanda. none
Stevens, Carl, 1952- PS3554.U4632
Stevens, Chevy. PR9199.4.S739
Stevens, Christian D. PS3569.T45114
Stevens, Curtis. none
Stevens, Diane. PS3569.T4512
Stevens, Gus. none
Stevens, Jon. none
Stevens, Lucile Vernon. none
Stevens, Marcus, 1959- PS3619.T49
Stevens, Robert Tyler, 1911-2005. PR6069.T4467
Stevens, Rosemary. PS3569.T4524
Stevens, Serita, 1949- PS3569.T4527
Stevens, Shane. PS3569.T453
Stevens, Taylor. PS3619.T4924
Stevenson, Anne. PR6069.T449
Stevenson, Burton Egbert, 1872-1962. PS3537.T476
Stevenson, D. E. (Dorothy Emily), 1892-1973. PR6037.T458
Stevenson, Florence. PS3569.T455
Stevenson, John. none
Stevenson, Richard, 1938- PS3569.T4567
Stevenson, Robert Louis, 1850-1894. PR5480-5498

Stevermer, C. J.	none
Stevermer, Caroline.	PS3569.T4575
Steward, Barbara.	PS3569.T458
Steward, Carol.	PS3619.T493
Steward, Dwight.	PS3569.T459
Steward, Samuel M.	PS3537.T479
Stewart, Alfred W. (Alfred Walter), 1880-1947.	PR6037.T4627
Stewart, Brenda Robertson.	PS3619.T4936
Stewart, Chris, 1960-	PS3569.T4593
Stewart, Desmond, 1924-1981.	PR6069.T4584
Stewart, Ed.	PS3569.T4599
Stewart, Edward, 1938-1996.	PS3569.T46
Stewart, Fran, 1947-	PS3619.T4938
Stewart, Fred Mustard, 1932-2007.	PS3569.T464
Stewart, Gary.	PS3569.T4644
Stewart, Ian, 1928-	PS3569.T4647
Stewart, Kay L. (Kay Lanette), 1942-	PS3619.T4964
Stewart, Kerry—see: Stewart, Linda, 1937-	
Stewart, Leah, 1973-	PS3569.T465258
Stewart, Linda, 1937-	PS3569.T46527
Stewart, Mariah.	PS3569.T4653
Stewart, Mary, 1916-	PR6069.T46
Stewart, Michael, 1945-	PR6069.T464
Stewart, Mike, 1955-	PS3569.T46544
Stewart, Paul, 1955-	PR6069.T467
Stewart, Ramona, 1922-	PS3569.T468
Stewart, Sam—see: Stewart, Linda, 1937-	
Stiles, Martha Bennett.	PS3569.T47785
Stimson, Robert G.	none
Stine, Hank.	PS3569.T4836
Stine, R. L.	PS3569.T4837
Stinson, David, 1946-	PS3619.T567
Stinson, Jim.	PS3569.T53
Stirling, Emma.	PR6069.T495
Stirling, Jessica.	PR6069.T497
Stirling, S. M.	PS3569.T543
Stitt, Milan.	PS3569.T55
Stivers, Dick.	none
Stock, Jon.	PR6069.T518
Stockbridge, Grant.	PS3531.A2355
Stockbridge, Sara, 1966-	PR6119.T64
Stockley, Grif.	PS3569.T612
Stockwell, Richard.	PR6069.T56
Stoddard, Charles, 1906-	PS3537.T862
Stoddard, Jeffrey Lynn.	PS3619.T6424
Stohlman, Richard.	none
Stoker, Bram, 1847-1912.	PR6037.T617
Stokes, Arthur M.	none
Stokes, Naomi Miller.	PS3569.T6218
Stokes, Robert S.	none
Stokoe, Matthew.	PS3619.T648
Stoltey, Patricia.	PS3619.T6563
Stone, David, 1946-	PR9199.3.S833
Stone, Dulcie M.	PR9619.3.S834

Stone, Eddie.   none
Stone, Elna.   PS3569.T633
Stone, Eric.   PS3569.T6333
Stone, George.   PS3569.T6348
Stone, Hampton, 1906-   PS3537.T3184
Stone, Joel, 1931-   PS3569.T641295
Stone, Jonathan, 1956-   PS3569.T64132
Stone, Katherine, 1949-   PS3569.T64134
Stone, Mark, 1968-   PR9199.4.S7575
Stone, Michael, 1950-   PS3569.T64144
Stone, Nick.   none
Stone, Nick, 1966-   PR6119.T675
Stone, Scott C. S., 1932-   PS3569.T642
Stone, Thomas H., 1936-   none
Stone, Zachary.   PR6056.O45
Storey, Anthony.   PR6069.T63
Storey, Michael, 1941-   PR6069.T664
Storm, Michael.   none
Story, Jack Trevor.   PR6037.T7144
Story, William L.   PS3569.T6554
Stott, Rebecca.   PR6119.T69
Stout, David, 1942-   PS3569.T658
Stout, Rex, 1886-1975.   PS3537.T733
                                                                  [Z8849.34]
Stovall, Jim.   PS3569.T6717
Stovall, Walter.   PS3569.T673
Stowe, James L.   PS3569.T675
Straka, Andy.   PS3619.T733
Straker, J. F. (John Foster)   PR6069.T675
Straley, John, 1953-   PS3569.T687
Strand, Jeff.   PS3619.T736
Strange, John Stephen, b. 1896.   PS3539.I522
Strasser, Todd.   PS3569.T69132
Stratford, Michael, 1920-2005.   PS3553.A79555
Stratton, Chris.   none
Stratton, Ted.   PS3569.T69134
Stratton, Thomas.   none
Straub, Peter, 1943-   PS3569.T6914
Strauss, Larry.   PS3569.T692254
Straw, Tom.   PS3619.T7435
Street, Bradford.   none
Street, Cecil J. C. (Cecil John Charles), 1884-1964. PR6037.T778
Street, Pamela, 1921-   PR6037.T8175
Streib, Dan, 1928-1996.   none
Stribling, T. S. (Thomas Sigismund), 1881-1965.   PS3537.T836
Strick, Wesley.   PS3619.T7466
Strieber, Anne.   PS3619.T7525
Strieber, Whitley.   PS3569.T6955
Striker, Randy.   PS3573.H47473
Stringer, Arthur, 1874-1950.   PS3537.T845
Stroby, Wallace.   PS3619.T755
Strohmeyer, Sarah.   PS3569.T6972
Strong, Charles S. (Charles Stanley), 1906-   PS3537.T862

Strong, L. A. G. (Leonard Alfred George), 1896- PR6037.T845
1958.
Strong, Michael, 1929-   PR6069.T73
Strong, Terence.   PR6069.T743
Strong, Tony.   PS3569.T717
Stross, Charles.   PR6119.T79
Strother, Elsie W., 1912-   PS3569.T7263
Stroud, Carsten, 1946-   PR9199.3.S833
Struecker, Jeff, 1969-   PS3619.T845
Strunk, Frank C.   PS3569.T743
Strunk, O. C.   none
Struthers, Betsy, 1951-   PR9199.3.S8398
Strutton, Bill.   PR9619.3.S86
Stryker, Dev.   PS3569.T767
Stuart, Anne (Anne Kristine)   PS3569.T785
Stuart, Anthony, 1940-   PR6058.A4385
Stuart, Blair.   none
Stuart, Dee.   PS3569.T813
Stuart, Diana.   none
Stuart, Ian—see: MacLean, Alistair, 1922-1987.
Stuart, Ian, 1927-   PR6069.T77
Stuart, Jane.   PS3569.T82
Stuart, John.   none
Stuart, Ruth McEnery, 1856-1917.   PS2960
Stuart, Sebastian.   PS3569.T827
Stuart, Sidney, 1924-1999.   PS3551.V3
Stuart, Vivian.   PR6063.A38
Stubbs, Jean, 1926-   PR6069.T78
Stuckart, Diane A. S.   PS3619.T839
Stucki, Warren J., 1946-   PS3619.T84
Stukas, David.   PS3619.T85
Sturgeon, Theodore.   PS3569.T875
Sturges, P. G.—see: Sturges, Preston, Jr.
Sturges, Preston, Jr.   PS3619.T8643
Sturman, Jennifer.   PS3619.T865
Sturrock, Jeremy.   PR6058.E17
Sturz, James.   PS3619.T87
Stuyck, Karen Hanson.   PS3619.T89
Styles, Showell, 1908-2005.   PR6037.T96
Suarez, Daniel, 1964-   PS3619.U327
Sublett, Jesse.   PS3569.U218
Subond, Valerie.   none
Sugar, Andrew.   none
Sukhov, Evg. (Evgeniĭ)   PG3488.U378
Sullivan, Evelin E., 1947-   PS3569.U3467
Sullivan, Leo L.   PS3619.U436
Sullivan, Lewis W.   none
Sullivan, Mark T.   PS3569.U3482
Sullivan, Michael, 1953-   PS3569.U349
Sullivan, Sean Mei, 1913-   none
Sullivan, Thomas.   PS3569.U3579
Sullivan, Tim.   none
Sullivan, Winona.   PS3569.U3594
Sully, Sue.   PR6069.U326

Sultan, Faye.	PS3569.U3596
Sulzberger, C. L. (Cyrus Leo), 1912-1993.	PS3569.U36
Summer Rain, Mary, 1945-	PS3569.U382
Summerfield, Lin, 1952-	PR6069.U36
Summerton, Margaret.	PR6069.U4
Summers, Courtney.	none
Summers, Dennis, 1928-1999.	PR6052.A7175
Summers, E. W.	PS3569.U389
Summers, Jordan.	none
Summerscales, Rowland.	none
Summy, Barrie.	none
Sumner, Cid Ricketts, 1890-1970.	PS3537.U732
Sumner, Penny.	PS3569.U48
Sumners, Cristina.	PS3619.U46
Sunagel, Lois A.	none
Sundell, Joanne.	PS3619.U557
Sundman, Per Olof, 1922-1992.	PT9876.29.U5
Sundstøl, Vidar, 1963-	PT8952.29.U53
Sundstrand, David.	PS3619.U563
Surbeck, Kally Jo.	PS3619.U567
Surr, T. S. (Thomas Skinner), 1770-1847.	PR5499.S36
Süskind, Patrick.	PT2681.U74
Sussman, Barth Jules.	none
Sussman, Paul.	PS3619.U85
Sussman, Susan.	PS3569.U814
Sutcliffe, Katherine.	PS3569.U817
Suter, Martin, 1948-	PT2681.U79
Sutherland, Grant.	PR9619.4.S88
Sutton, Henry, 1935-	PS3569.L3
Sutton, Jeff.	PS3569.U89
Sutton, Michael (Michael David)	PS3569.U894
Sutton, Phoef.	PS3569.U896
Suvorov, Oleg.	PG3488.U923
Suzanne, Kathleen.	PS3569.U95
Suzuki, Kōji, 1957-	PL861.U92716
Svedelid, Olov, 1932-	PT9876.29.V34
Swacker, Frank W.	PS3619.W34
Swager, Peggy O.	PS3619.W344
Swaim, Don.	PS3569.W218
Swaim, Lawrence.	PS3569.W22
Swain, James.	PS3569.W225
Swan, Gladys, 1934-	PS3569.W247
Swan, John, 1949-	PR9199.3.S933
Swan, Mary, 1953-	PR9199.4.S93
Swan, Phyllis.	none
Swan, Rose.	PR6069.W343
Swan, Thomas.	PR6063.W26
Swann, Francis.	none
Swann, Ingo, 1933-	none
Swanson, Denise.	PS3619.W36
Swanson, Doug J., 1953-	PS3569.W2682
Swanton, Scott.	none
Swarthout, Glendon Fred.	PS3537.W3743
Swarup, Vikas.	PR9499.4.S93

Swazee, Ruth.	none
Swearingen, Ida, 1938-	PS3619.W43
Swee, Karen, 1945-	PS3619.W44
Sweeney, Eamonn, 1968-	PR6069.W368
Sweeney, Leann.	PS3619.W44254
Swerdlow, Joel L.	PS3569.W413
Swierczynski, Duane.	PS3619.W53
Swift, Bryan, 1927-	PS3561.N65
Swift, Graham, 1949-	PR6069.W47
Swift, Sue, 1955-	PS3619.W546
Swift, Virginia.	PS3569.W516
Swigart, Rob.	PS3569.W52
Swindells, Madge.	PR6069.W49
Swindle, Howard, 1945-	PS3569.W536
Swinnerton, Frank, 1884-1982.	PR6037.W85
Swinson, Kiki.	PS3619.W57
Swofford, Anthony.	PS3619.W64
Sykes, Jerry.	PR6119.Y535
Sylvain, Dominique.	PQ2679.Y39
Sylvester, Martin.	PR6069.Y43
Symons, Julian, 1912-1994.	PR6037.Y5
Syvertsen, Ryder.	none
Szanto, George H., 1940-	PR9199.3.S99
Szentiday, Klára, 1933-	PH3382.29.Z465
Szilagyi, Steve.	PS3569.Z48
Szolc, Izabela.	PG7219.Z65
Szulc, Tad.	PS3569.Z8
Szymanski, Therese, 1968-	PS3569.Z94
Szyszkowitz, Gerald.	PT2681.Z9
Tabachnik, Maud.	PQ2680.A17
Tabor, Margaret.	PR6070.A2
Tabori, Paul, 1908-1974.	PR6039.A15
Tabucchi, Antonio, 1943-	PQ4880.A24
Tack, Alfred.	PR6070.A25
Taffrail—see: Dorling, H. Taprell (Henry Taprell), 1883-1968.	
Tafoya, Dennis.	PS3620.A33
Taggart, Donald G. (Donald Gilbert)	PS3570.A3
Taggart, Susan.	PS3570.A32116
Taibo, Paco Ignacio, 1949-	PQ7298.3.A58
Taichert, Pari Noskin, 1958-	PS3620.A35
Taillet, Edmond.	none
Takagi, Akimitsu, 1920-1995.	PL862.A4
Talbot, Hake, 1900-1986.	none
Talbot, Michael, 1953-	PR6070.A36
Talley, Marcia Dutton, 1943-	PS3570.A3995
Tallis, Frank.	PR6120.A44
Tallman, Kristy, 1969-	PS3620.A538
Tallman, Shirley.	PS3620.A54
Talmy, Shel.	none
Talton, Jon.	PS3620.A58
Tan, Amy.	PS3570.A48
Tan, Maureen.	PS3570.A485
Tanenbaum, Barry, 1944-	none
Tanenbaum, Robert.	PS3570.A52

Tanneberg, Ward M.	PS3570.A535
Tanner, Jake.	PS3570.A553
Tanner, Janet.	PR6070.A545
Tanous, Peter J.	PS3570.A56
Tapply, William G.	PS3570.A568
Tar, Sándor, 1941-	PH3351.T349
Taranov, Sergeĭ.	none
Tarmey, Martin.	PR6070.A56
Tarrant, John, 1927-	PR6055.G55
Tarrant, Newell.	PS3620.A77
Tarre, Marcos.	PQ8550.3.A77
Tartt, Donna.	PS3570.A657
Taschdjian, Claire.	PS3570.A694
Tashjian, Janet.	none
Tasker, Peter.	PR6070.A65
Tate, Kelly Anne.	PS3570.A825
Tate, Richard, 1940-2003.	none
Tattersall, Jill.	PR6070.A68
Taube, Lester S., 1920-	PS3570.A87
Tavis, Alec.	PR6070.A75
Tayleur, Karen.	none
Taylor, Alison G.	PR6070.A775
Taylor, Andrew, 1951 Oct. 14-	PR6070.A79
Taylor, Barry, 1938-	PS3570.A92713
Taylor, Bernard, 1934-	PR6070.A884
Taylor, Bonnie.	none
Taylor, Brad, 1965-	PS3620.A9353
Taylor, Caroline, 1943-	PS3620.A9358
Taylor, Chad, 1964-	PR9639.3.T32
Taylor, Charles D.	PS3570.A92723
Taylor, D. J. (David John), 1960-	PR6070.A9118
Taylor, Domini.	PR6062.O516
Taylor, Don.	none
Taylor, Donn.	PS3620.A943
Taylor, Edith.	PS3570.A9284
Taylor, Edward, 1931-	PR6070.A9147
Taylor, Elizabeth Atwood.	PS3570.A9286
Taylor, Fred.	PR9619.3.T318
Taylor, Georgia Elizabeth.	PS3570.A929
Taylor, Gordon, 1943-	PS3570.A9292
Taylor, H. Baldwin.	PS3573.A9
Taylor, Jane.	PR9369.4.T39
Taylor, Jean (Jean M.)	PS3570.A935
Taylor, Joan E.	PR9639.4.T394
Taylor, Kathleen, 1952-	PS3620.A95
Taylor, L. A. (Laurie Aylma), 1939-	PS3570.A943
Taylor, Mary Ann.	none
Taylor, Matt, 1934-	PS3570.A946
Taylor, Mel.	PS3570.A9462
Taylor, Phoebe Atwood, 1909-1976.	PS3539.A9635
Taylor, Robert D.	PS3620.A966
Taylor, Roger, 1938-	none
Taylor, Roger E.	none
Taylor, Sam, 1970-	PR6120.A954

Taylor, Sarah Stewart.	PS3620.A97
Taylor, Timothy L., 1963-	PR9199.4.T39
Taylor, Travis S.	PS3620.A98
Tchaikovsky, Adrian, 1972-	PR6120.C53
Teague, John Jessop—see: Gerard, Morice, 1856-1929.	
Teasley, Lisa, 1962-	PS3620.E43
TeBordo, Christian.	PS3620.E435
Tedder, Lorna.	PS3570.E285
Teel, Jerome, 1967-	PS3620.E4355
Tefs, Wayne, 1947-	PR9199.3.T4
Teilhet, Darwin L., 1904-1964.	PS3539.E245
Teixeira, Bernardo, 1926-2008.	none
Telford, Don.	none
Tell, Dorothy, 1939-	PS3570.E518
Telushkin, Joseph, 1948-	PS3570.E525
Temmey, Bob.	none
Temple, Lou Jane.	PS3570.E535
Temple, Peter, 1946-	PR9619.3.T37
Temple, Richard.	none
Templesmith, Ben, 1978-	none
Templeton, Aline.	PR6070.E49
Templeton, Charles, 1915-2001.	PR9199.3.T42
Tennant, Emma.	PR6070.E52
Tenuto, Jim.	PS3620.E58
Tepper, Sheri S.	PS3570.E673
Tepperman, Emile C.	PS3537.T2687
Teran, Boston.	PS3570.E674
Teresa, Vincent Charles.	PS3570.E675
Terhune, Albert Payson, 1872-1942.	PS3539.E65
Terman, Douglas, 1933-	PS3570.E676
Terpening, Ron, 1946-	PS3570.E6767
Terrall, Robert.	PS3539.E69
Terrell, Bob.	PS3570.E67748
Terrell, Whitney.	PS3570.E692
Terrenoire, David.	PS3620.E76
Terreri, Malinda.	none
Terry, Mark, 1964-	PS3620.E769
Tesh, Jane.	PS3620.E775
Tesler, Nancy.	PS3570.E825
Tessier, Thomas.	PS3570.E84
Tessler, Margaret.	PS3620.E777
Tester, Victoria Edwards, 1964-	PS3620.E78
Teta, Jon A.	none
Tetel, Julie, 1950-	PS3551.N4139
Tevis, Walter S.	PS3570.E95
Teweles, Claude.	none
Tey, Josephine, 1896 or 7-1952.	PR6025.A2547
Thacker, Becky.	PS3620.H326
Thackeray, Alec.	none
Thackeray, Kit.	PR6070.H34
Thackrey, Ted.	none
Thackston, Lawrence.	none
Thall, Michael.	PS3570.H318
Thatcher, Julia, 1927-	PS3552.E54765

Thayer, Cynthia A.   PS3570.H344
Thayer, David, 1947-   PS3570.H3445
Thayer, Donlu D.   PS3570.H345
Thayer, James Stewart.   PS3570.H347
Thayer, Lee, b. 1874.   PS3539.H163
Thayer, Steve.   PS3570.H3477
Thayer, Terri.   PS3620.H393
Thayne, RaeAnne.   PS3570.H363
Thelwell, Michael.   PR9265.9.T5
Themerson, Stefan.   PR6039.H37
                                                            PG7179.H4
Theorin, Johan, 1963-   PT9877.3.H46
Theroux, Marcel, 1968-   PS3570.H395
Theroux, Paul.   PS3570.H4
Thesman, Jean.   none
Thielbar, Melinda.   none
Thiesler, Sabine.   none
Thirkell, Angela, 1890-1961.   PR6039.H43
Thoene, Jake.   PS3570.H465
Thomas, Alan Ernest Wentworth, 1896-   PR6039.H48
Thomas, Basil Home, Sir, 1861-1939.   none
Thomas, Bob, 1922-   PS3570.H562
Thomas, Brenda L., 1957-   PS3620.H625
Thomas, Craig, 1942-2011.   PR6070.H56
Thomas, D.   none
Thomas, David N.   PR6039.H52
Thomas, Dicey, 1943-   PS3570.H562514
Thomas, Donald, 1926-   PR6070.H6
Thomas, Dylan, 1914-1953.   PR6039.H52
Thomas, Edwin, 1977-   PR6120.H644
Thomas, Frank, 1926-   PS3570.H56263
Thomas, Gordon, 1933-   PR6070.H625
Thomas, Herbert, 1957-   PS3570.H5628
Thomas, Jack W. (Jack William), 1930-   none
Thomas, Jessica.   PS3620.H628
Thomas, Jim—see: Reagan, Thomas B.
Thomas, Lee, 1965-   PS3620.H6317
Thomas, Leslie, 1931-   PR6070.H647
Thomas, Michael M.   PS3570.H574
Thomas, Paul, 1951-   PR9639.3.T45
Thomas, Quentin.   PS3570.U5764
Thomas, Ross, 1926-   PS3570.H58
Thomas, Sam.   PS3570.H586
Thomas, Scarlett.   PR6120.H66
Thomas, Suzanne, 1949-   PS3620.H6434
Thomas, Trisha R., 1964-   PS3570.H5917
Thomas, Will, 1958-   PS3620.H644
Thomas-Graham, Pamela.   PS3570.H5923
Thomason, Cynthia.   PS3570.H5925
Thomey, Tedd.   none
Thompson, Alice (Alice Frances Mary)   PR6070.H6578
Thompson, Ann Lorraine.   none
Thompson, Anne Armstrong.   PS3570.H593
Thompson, Arthur Leonard Bell—see: Clifford, Francis.

Thompson, Brian, 1935-	PR6070.H662
Thompson, Carlene.	PS3570.H5964
Thompson, Craig O.	PS3570.H59687
Thompson, Christian.	none
Thompson, E. V. (Ernest Victor), 1931-	PR6070.H6647
Thompson, Estelle.	PR9619.3.T447
Thompson, Gene.	PS3570.H614
Thompson, Harrison R.	none
Thompson, James, 1964-	PS3620.H675
Thompson, Janice A.	PS3620.H6824
Thompson, Jean, 1933-	PS3570.H624
Thompson, Jean, 1950-	PS3570.H625
Thompson, Jim, 1906-1977.	PS3539.H6733
Thompson, John.	PS3620.H6828
Thompson, John M. (John Milliken), 1959-	PS3620.H68325
Thompson, Joyce, 1948-	PS3570.H6414
Thompson, Larry D., 1940-	PS3620.H68345
Thompson, Marlena.	PS3620.H6837
Thompson, Maurice.	PS3620.H6838
Thompson, Mike, ca. 1942-	PS3620.H6839
Thompson, Raymond, 1949-	PS3570.H6433
Thompson, Richard A. (Richard Alvin), 1942-	PS3620.H687
Thompson, Steven L.	PS3570.H6437
Thompson, Victoria (Victoria E.)	PS3570.H6442
Thompson, W. Crawford.	none
Thomsen, Frieda.	none
Thomson, Daisy Hicks.	PR6070.H676
Thomson, David, 1941-	PR6070.H678
Thomson, June.	PR6070.H679
Thomson, Keith, 1965-	PS3620.H745
Thomson, Rupert.	PR6070.H685
Thomson, Maynard F.	PS3570.H646
Thor, Brad.	PS3620.H75
Thor, Raymond.	PS3570.H6475
Thoreau, David.	PS3570.H6477
Thorn, Ronald Scott, 1920-	PR6039.H77
Thornburg, Newton.	PS3570.H649
Thorndike, Russell, b. 1885.	PR6039.H78
Thorne, Guy, 1876-1923.	PR6013.U54
Thorne, Jim.	none
Thorne, Ramsay, 1924-	PS3553.A434
Thornton, Betsy.	PS3570.H6645
Thornton, Francis John.	PS3570.H667
Thornton, L. D.	PS3620.H784
Thornton, Lawrence, 1937-	PS3570.H6678
Thorp, Roderick.	PS3570.H67
Thorpe, Adam, 1956-	PR6070.H696
Thorpe, Edward.	PR6070.H698
Thrasher, L. L. (Linda L.)	PS3570.H6922
Thrasher, Travis, 1971-	PS3570.H6925
Thum, Marcella.	PS3570.H75
Thurlo, Aimée.	PS3570.H82
Thurlo, David.	PS3570.H825
Thurlow, David.	none

Thurston, Carol, 1927-   PS3570.H845
Thynn, Alexander.   PR6070.H95
Tibbetts, Peggy.   PS3570.I165
Tibble, Anne Northgrave.   PR6039.I2
Tidyman, Ernest.   PS3570.I3
Tiedemann, Mark W.   PS3620.I33
Tierney, Ronald.   PS3570.I3325
Tiffin, George.   PR6120.I36
Tiger, John.   PS3573.A35
Tigges, John, 1932-   none
Tiller, Denise Fagerberg.   PS3570.I3524
Tillett, Dorothy Stockbridge—see: Strange, John Stephen, b. 1896.
Tillis, Tracey.   none
Tillman, Lynne.   PS3570.I42
Tilton, Alice, 1909-1976.   PS3539.A9635
Timlin, Mark, 1950-   PR6070.I387
Timperley, Rosemary, 1920-   PR6070.I4
Tindall, Gillian.   PR6070.I45
Tine, Robert.   PS3570.I48
Tippette, Giles.   PS3570.I6
Tippin, G. Lee, 1935-   PS3570.I62
Tisdale, Deborah.   PS3620.I84
Tishy, Cecelia, 1942-   PS3570.I726
Title, Elise.   PS3570.I77
Tobin, Betsy, 1961-   PS3570.O287
Tobin, Brian.   PS3570.O288
Todd, Catherine.   PS3570.O36
Todd, Charles.   PS3570.O37
Todd, Diane K.   none
Todd, Ian.   PR6070.O36
Todd, Marilyn.   PR6070.O37
Todd, Paul—see: Posner, Richard.
Todd, Peter—see: Hamilton, Charles, 1875-1961.
Todd, Ruthven, 1914-1978.   PR6039.O26
Toepfer, Ray Grant.   PS3570.O415
Tofte, Arthur.   PS3570.O424
Togawa, Masako, 1933-   PL862.O3
Tokarczuk, Olga, 1962-   PG7179.O37
Tokson, Elliot H.   none
Tolan, Stephanie S.   PS3570.O42675
Toldson, Achebe, 1973-   PS3620.O326
Toliver, Hal.   PS3570.O42765
Tolkien, Simon, 1959-   PR6120.O44
Toll, Emily.   PS3553.A5295
Toma, David.   none
Tomaso, Carla.   PS3570.O4297
Tomaszewski, Mirosław.   PG7179.O435
Tomerlin, John, 1930-   none
Tomlinson, Gerald, 1933-2006.   PS3570.O458
Tone, Teona.   none
Tonkin, Peter.   PR6070.O498
Tooley, S. D.   PS3570.O543
Toombs, Jane.   PS3570.O55
Toomey, Jeanne, 1921-   PS3570.O56

Tope, Rebecca.	PR6070.O58
Topil'skai‹a›, Elena.	PG3493.5.O65
Topol, Allan.	PS3570.O64
Topol, B. H.	none
Topol, Eduard—see: Topol, Edward, 1938-	
Topol, Edward, 1938-	PG3549.T66
	PS3570.O643
Topor, Tom, 1938-	PS3570.O65
Topping, John A.	none
Topping, Seymour, 1921-	PS3570.O663
Torday, Paul, 1946-	PR6120.O73
Torgov, Morley.	PR9199.3.T613
Toro, Guillermo del, 1964-	PS3620.O5875
Torr, Dominic.	PS3566.E26
Torre, Gerardo de la, 1938-	PQ7298.3.O66
Torres, Edwin.	PS3750.O697
Torres, Steven.	PS3620.O59
Torrey, Michele.	none
Torrez, Everardo.	PS3620.O64
Torrie, Malcolm, 1901-1983.	PR6025.I832
Torrio, Vincente.	none
Tosches, Nick.	PS3570.O74
Tourney, Leonard D.	PS3570.O784
Toussaint, Maggie.	PS3620.O89
Tow, R.	PR9199.4.T69
Tower, Diana, 1930-	none
Townend, Peter, 1935-	PR6070.O89
Townsend, Guy M.	PS3570.O935
Townsend, Larry.	PS3570.O94
Townsend, Lindsay.	PR6070.O8966
Townsend, Sue.	PR6070.O897
Townsend, Tom, 1944-	PS3570.O945
Toyne, Simon.	PR6120.O98
Tracey, Grant.	PR6070.R23
Tracy, Don, 1905-1976.	PS3539.R124
Tracy, Hugh.	PR6070.R27
Tracy, Louis, 1863-1928.	PR6039.R24
Tracy, Margaret.	none
Tracy, P. J.	PS3620.R33
Tracy, Pamela Kaye.	PS3620.R34
Train, Arthur Cheney, 1875-1945.	PS3539.R23
Trainor, J. F.	PS3570.R333
Tramble, Nichelle D.	PS3570.R334
Tranter, Kirsten.	PS9619.4.T73
Tranter, Nigel G.	PR6070.R34
Traugot, Leanore.	none
Traum, Joe.	PS3620.R374
Traver, Robert, 1903-1991.	PS3570.R339
Travis, Gretchen.	PS3570.R35
Travis, John, 1972-	PR6120.R37
Travis, Mark, 1946-	PS3620.R38
Traylor, Ellen Gunderson.	PS3570.R357
Treat, Lawrence, 1903-	PS3539.R3442
Tregillis, Ian.	PS3620.R4446

Tremayne, Peter.   PR6070.R366
Tremblay, Paul.   PS3620.R445
Tremonte, Julia.   none
Trench, Jason.   PR6070.R3665
Trenhaile, John.   PR6070.R367
Trent, Gayle.   PS3620.R4454
Trent, Lawrence.   none
Trent, Lee.   none
Trent, Paul.   PR6039.R435
Trevanian.   PS3570.R44
Trevelyan, Julia.   none
Trevelyan, Robert, 1929-   PR6056.O692
Trevor, Elleston.   PR6039.R518
Trevor, James.   none
Trevor, Leslie—see: Chappell, Helen, 1947-
Trevor, Ralph.   PR6045.I5735
Trevor, William, 1928-   PR6070.R4
Trew, Antony, 1906-   PR9369.3.T7
Trieschman, Charles.   none
Trigoboff, Joseph.   PS3570.R46
Trimble, Louis, 1917-   PS3539.R565
Trimmer, Gerald.   PS3620.R564
Trinchieri, Camilla.   PS3553.R435
Tripp, Ben, 1966-   PS3620.R569
Tripp, Dawn Clifton.   PS3620.R57
Tripp, Miles, 1923-   PR6070.R48
Tripp, Valerie, 1951-   PS3570.R545
Trobaugh, Augusta.   PS3570.R585
Trocchi, Alexander, 1925-1984.   PR6070.R56
Trocheck, Kathy Hogan, 1954-   PS3570.R587
Trolley, Jack.   PS3551.R39
Trollope, Anthony, 1815-1882.   PR5684-6688
                                                    [Z8885.9]
Trollope, Thomas Adolphus, 1810-1892.   PR5699.T4
Tromben, Carlos, 1966-   PQ8098.43.R66
Tronson, Robert.   none
Trott, Susan.   PS3570.R594
Troup, Gary.   PS3620.R68
Troutt, David Dante.   PS3570.R643
Trow, M. J.   PR6070.R598
Troy, Simon.   PR6045.A8143
Troyan, Sasha, 1962-   PS3620.R69
Trudel, Pierre, 1944-   PQ3919.2.T7885
Truluck, Bob (Robert)   PS3570.R817
Truman, Margaret, 1924-2008.   PS3570.R82
Trump, Ivana.   PS3570.R834
Truscott, Lucian K., 1947-   PS3570.R86
Truss, Seldon, b. 1892.   PR6039.R8
Trussoni, Danielle.   PS3620.R93
Tryon, Thomas.   PS3570.R9
Tsiţer, Ķeren.   PJ5055.44.I88
Tsui, David   PS3620.S85
Tsuji, Masaki, 1932-   PL862.S7314
Tucci, James.   PS3620.U28

Tucker, James.	PS3570.U298
Tucker, James, 1929-	PR6070.U23
Tucker, John Bartholomew.	PS3570.U33
Tucker, Kerry.	PS3570.U34
Tucker, Terry Ward, 1947-	PS3570.U359
Tucker, Wilson, 1914-2006.	PS3539.U324
Tullett, J. S. (James Stuart)	none
Tully, Andrew, 1914-1993.	PS3570.U43
Tully, James, 1946-	PR6070.U45
Turaicāmi, Ṭi. Es., b. 1869.	PL4758.9.T774
Turkov, Mark, 1954-	PG3489.U683
Turland, Eileen.	none
Turnbull, Agnes Sligh, 1888-	PS3539.U76
Turnbull, Peter, 1950-	PR6070.U68
Turner, Elaine.	none
Turner, James, 1909-1975.	PR6039.U64
Turner, Jann, 1964-	PR9369.4.T87
Turner, Linda.	none
Turner, Lynn M.	PR9199.3.T837
Turner, Nikki.	PS3620.U7659
Turner, Pearl.	none
Turner, Ray.	none
Turner, Robert, 1915-	PS3570.U73
Turner, W. Price (William Price), 1927-	PR6070.U75
Turow, Scott.	PS3570.U754
Turpin, Allan.	PR6070.U77
Turrill, David A.	PS3570.U756
Tursten, Helene, 1954-	PT9876.3.U55
Turtledove, Harry.	PS3570.U76
Tusset, Pablo, 1965-	PQ6720.U87
Tute, Warren.	PR6070.U79
Tutt, Mervyn C.	none
Tuttle, Gene.	PS3570.U83
Tuttle, Lisa, 1952-	PS3570.U85
Tuttle, W. C. (Wilbur C.), 1883-1969.	PS3539.U988
Tvedt, Chris, 1954-	PT8952.3.V43
Twain, Mark, 1835-1910.	PS1300-1348 [Z8176]
Twedt, Jerry L.	PS3570.W43
Twelve Hawks, John.	PS3620.W45
Twining, James.	PR6120.W56
Tyler, Alison.	PS3570.I77
Tyler, Anne.	PS3570.Y45
Tyler, L. C.	PR6125.Y545
Tyler, Lee, 1929-	PS3570.Y48
Tyler, Stephanie.	PS3620.Y598
Tyler, W. T.	PS3570.Y53
Tynan, Kathleen.	PR6070.Y57
Tyndall, John.	PR6070.Y63 [Z8899]
Tyner, Paul, 1939-	none
Tyre, Nedra.	PS3539.Y68
Tyre, Peg.	PS3570.Y58
Tyrer, Walter.	PR6070.Y78

Valentine, Deborah P., 1948-   PS3572.A389
Valentinetti, Joseph.   PS3572.A397
Valentino, Amanda.   none
Valenzuela, Luisa, 1938-   PQ7798.32.A48
Vali, Ali.   PS3622.A47
Vali‹a›ev, Sergeĭ.   PG3489.3.A3949
Valin, Jonathan.   PS3572.A4125
Vallance, Douglas.   none
Vallone, Ralph.   PS3572.A4132
Valley, Mel.   none
Vallvey, Angela, 1964-   PQ6672.A573
Valtos, William M.   PS3572.A4135
Van Adler, T. C.   PS3572.A4136
Van Arman, Derek.   PS3572.A4137
Van Ash, Cay.   PR6072.A55
Van Atta, Winfred.   PS3572.A416
Van de Wetering, Janwillem, 1931-2008.   PS3572.A4292
Van der Zee, John.   PS3572.A429
Van Deventer, Emma Murdoch—see: Lynch, Lawrence L.
Van Dine, S. S.   PS3545.R846
Van Draanen, Wendelin.   none
Van Dyke, Annette Joy.   PS3572.A4298
Van Dyke, Henry, 1928-   PS3572.A43
Van Gieson, Judith.   none
Van Gieson, Judith, 1941-   PS3572.A42224
Van Greenaway, Peter, 1929-   PR6072.A65
Van Gulik, Robert—see: Gulik, Robert Hans van, 1910-1967.
Van Hazinga, Cynthia.   none
Van Heerden, Etienne, 1954-   PT6592.32.A5235
Van Heugten, Antoinette.   PS3622.A585493
Van Hook, Beverly Hennen.   PS3572.A444
Van Horne, Hollie.   PS3572.A4224
Van Itallie, Jean Claude, 1936-   PS3572.A45
Van Meter, David A.   PS3572.A42265
Van Orsdell, John.   PS3572.A496
Van Patten, Vincent.   PS3622.A5856
Van Rjndt, Philippe, 1950-   PR9199.3.V36
Van Rooy, Michael, 1968-   PR9199.4.V3656
Van Rooyen, P. H. (Piet H.)   PT6592.32.A573
Van Siller, Hilda.   PS3543.A648
Van Slyke, Helen, 1919-1979.   PS3572.A54
Van Tol, Alex, 1973-   none
Van Valkenburgh, Norman J. (Norman James), PS3572.A5445
1930-
Van Wormer, Laura, 1955-   PS3572.A42285
Van Zandt, Edmund—see: Pendleton, Tom.
Van Zyl, P. R.   PR9369.3.V35
Vance, Charles C.   none
Vance, Ethel, 1891-1991.   PS3537.T667
Vance, Jack, 1916-   PS3572.A424
Vance, John Holbrook—see: Vance, Jack, 1916-
Vance, Lee.   PS3622.A58595
Vance, Louis Joseph, 1879-1933.   PS3543.A453
Vance, Steve, 1952-   PS3572.A4245

Vandagriff, G. G.   PS3572.A427
Vanderberry, Robert.   none
Vanderbes, Jennifer.   PS3622.A59
Vandergriff, Aola, 1920-1989.   none
Vanneman, Alan.   PS3622.A67
Vardamis, Frances D. (Frances Diem)   PS3622.A733
Vardre, Leslie—see: Davies, L. P. (Leslie Purnell)
Varesi, Valerio, 1959-   PQ4922.A7
Vargas Llosa, Mario, 1936-   PQ8498.32.A65
Vargas, Fred.   PQ2682.A725
Varley, Declan, 1965-   PR6072.A794
Varley, John, 1947 Aug. 9-   PS3572.A724
Vasile, Nick.   PS3572.A83
Vasilikos, Vasilēs, 1934-   PA5633.A46
Vasquez, Ian, 1966-   PS3622.A828
Vasquez, Richard.   PS3572.A85
Vassilikos, Vassilis—see: Vasilikos, Vasilēs, 1934-
Vaughan, Gary, 1946-   none
Vaughan, Julian.   none
Vaughan, Matthew.   PR6072.A9
Vaughan, Ralph.   PS3572.A898
Vaughan, Robert, 1937-   PS3572.A93
Vaughn, Dennis.   PS3622.A9476
Vaughn, Evelyn.   none
Vayinshṭoḳ, Ya'ir.   PJ5055.12.R3815
Vaz de Soto, José María.   PQ6672.A86
Vázquez-Figueroa, Alberto.   PQ6672.A9
Vázquez Montalbán, Manuel.   PQ6672.A92
Vázquez Rial, Horacio, 1947-   PQ6672.A94
Veiga, José J.   PQ9697.V292
Veley, Charles, 1943-   PS3572.E4
Vellekoop, Holly Fox.   PS3622.E55
Venables, Hubert.   PS3572.E46
Ventura, Michael.   PS3572.E5
Venters, Archie.   none
Veraldi, Attilio, 1925-   PQ4882.E63
Veraldi, Gabriel, 1926-   PQ2643.E46
Verbinina, Valerii‹a›.   PG3493.74.E7
Verdon, John.   PS3622.E736
Vergara, Francisco, 1958-   PQ8098.32.E74
Verhoef, Esther.   PT5882.32.E745
Veríssimo, Luís Fernando, 1936-   PQ9698.32.E73
Vermandel, Janet Gregory.   PS3572.E7
Vermillion, Mary.   PS3622.E746
Verne, Jules, 1828-1905.   PQ2469
Verner, Gerald.   none
Vernier, Patricia.   none
Vernon, Bill, 1941-   PS3622.E748
Vernon, Kay R.   PS3572.E763
Vernon, Marjorie.   none
Vertrees, Beverly.   PR6072.E8
Véry, Pierre, 1900-1960.   PQ2643.E65
Vesnina, Tiana.   PG3493.74.E8
Vetrova, Marii‹a›.   PG3489.3.E864

Vicary, Jean.	none
Vicary, Tim, 1949-	PR6072.I315
Vicas, Victor.	PQ2682.I243
Vickers, Ralph.	none
Vickers, Roy.	PR6043.I183
Victor, Daniel D.	PS3572.I265
Victor, Gary, 1958-	PQ3949.2.V455
Victor, Marilyn.	PS3622.I286
Victor, Metta Victoria Fuller, 1831-1885.	PS3129.V58
Victor, Roger.	PS3572.I275
Victor, Sam, 1926-	PS3558.E78
Vida, Nina.	PS3572.I29
Vidal, Gore, 1925-	PS3543.I26
Vidal, Harriette.	none
Viehl, Lynn, 1961-	none
Viel, Tanguy.	PQ2682.I316
Vierci, Pablo, 1950-	PQ8520.32.I36
Viét' Linh.	PL4378.9.V489
Viets, Elaine, 1950-	PS3572.I325
Vignant, Jean Francois.	PQ2682.I33
Viguié, Debbie.	PS3622.I485
Vil'chyns'kyĭ, Oleksandr, 1963-	PG3949.32.I43
Villar, Domingo.	PQ9469.3.V56
Villatoro, Marcos McPeek.	PS3572.I386
Villiers, Margot.	none
Vincent, Claire.	none
Vincent, E. Duke.	PS3622.I527
Vincent, Lawrence M.	PS3572.I486
Vincenzi, Penny.	PR6072.I525
Vincenzo, Geno.	none
Vine, Barbara, 1930-	PR6068.E63
Vine, Mary.	PS3622.I54
Vinter, Michael.	none
Violett, Ellen.	PS3572.I587
Vipond, Don.	PR9199.3.V5
Vitoux, Frédéric.	PQ2682.I79
Vittachi, Nury, 1958-	PR9450.9.V58
Vitti, James A.	PS3572.I82
Vittle, Arwel.	PB2298.V58
Vivian, Evelyn Charles.	PR6043.I9
Vivian, Robert, 1967-	PS3572.I875
Vlodavet‹s›, Leonid.	PG3489.3.L63
Vogel, Donald S., 1917-	PS3572.O292
Vogt, Esther Loewen.	PS3572.O3
Vogt, M. Diane, 1952-	PS3572.O32
Voldeng, Karl E. (Karl Edward), 1905-	none
Volgin, Igor' (Igor' Valentinovich)	PG3489.4.L4143
Volkov, Fedor.	PG3489.4.L422
Volkov, Oleksiĭ.	PG3949.32.O42
Vollmer, Kathy.	PS3622.O643
Voloshin, I‹U›riĭ.	PG3489.4.L658
Volpi Escalante, Jorge, 1968-	PQ7298.32.O47
von Block, B. W. (Bela William), 1922-	PS3572.O42
Von Cannon, Sybil.	none

Von Elsner, Don, 1909-   PS3572.O44
Von Hoffman, Nicholas.   PS3572.O46
Von Horváth, Ödön—see: Horváth, Ödön von, 1901-1938.
Vonnegut, Laureen.   PS3622.O676
Vonnegut, Norb.   PS3622.O678
Vorhaus, John.   PS3622.O745
Voronin, Andreï.   PG3489.4.R639
Voronina, Marina.   none
Voront‹s›ova, Marina.   PG3493.76.R658
Vose, Kenneth E.   none
Voss Bark, Conrad.   PR6072.O8
Vowell, David.   none
Vries, Anke de, 1936-   none
Vukcevich, Ray.   PS3572.U85
Waddell, Dan.   PR6123.A325
Waddell, Martin.   PR6073.A25
Wade, Bob, 1920-   PS3573.A3
Wade, Brent, 1959-   PS3573.A313
Wade, Don.   PS3623.A34
Wade, Henry, 1887-1969.   PR6001.U3
Wade, Jennifer—see: Wehen, Joy De Weese.
Wade, Jonathan.   PR6073.A29
Wadley, Margot.   PS3573.A338
Wadsworth, Amy Maida, 1970-   PS3623.A35
Wager, Walter H.   PS3573.A35
Waggoner, Bill.   PS3573.A355
Waggoner, Jack.   PS3623.A3534
Wagner, Elaine.   PS3573.A383
Wagner, Erica, 1967-   PS3573.A3836
Wagner, Jan Costin, 1972-   PT2685.A44442
Wagner, Karl Edward.   PS3573.A38638
Wagner, Sharon.   PS3573.A387
Wagner, Stanley.   PS3573.A3873
Wahlöö, Per, 1926-1975.   PT9876.33.A35
Wainscott, Tina.   PS3573.A4122
Wainwright, John William, 1921-   PR6073.A354
Wait, Lea.   PS3623.A42
Waite, Urban.   PS3623.A35656
Waiwaiole, Lono.   PS3623.A425
Wakefield, Hannah.   PR6063.A3738
Wakefield, Maureen E.   none
Wakling, Christopher, 1970-   PR6123.A38
Wald, Malvin.   none
Walden, Ron.   PS3573.A42127
Waldman, Ayelet.   PS3573.A42124
Waldman, Frank; 1919-   PS3545.A4337
Waldron, Ann.   PS3573.A4226
Waldron, Simon.   none
Waleis, Raúl, 1845-1911.   PQ7797.V27
Wales, Susan.   PS3623.A3585
Walker, Blair S.   PS3573.A42516
Walker, Carolyn.   none
Walker, David Harry, 1911-   PR9199.3.W33
Walker, David J., 1939-   PS3573.A4253313

Walker, Gerald, 1928-	none
Walker, Gertrude.	none
Walker, Irma, 1921-	PS3573.A4253327
Walker, James, 1948-	PS3573.A425334
Walker, Jan.	PS3573.A425335
Walker, Mark.	PS3573.A42535
Walker, Martin, 1947-	PR6073.A413
Walker, Mary Willis.	PS3573.A425354
Walker, Max.	none
Walker, Paul, 1942-	none
Walker, Persia.	PS3623.A438
Walker, Peter Lancaster.	none
Walker, Peter N. (Peter Norman), 1936-	PR6068.H4
Walker, Robert W. (Robert Wayne), 1948-	PS3573.A425385
Walker, Sue, 1960-	PR6123.A45
Walker, T. Mike, 1937-	PS3573.A4254
Walker, Thomas P.—see: Page, Thomas, 1942-	
Walker, Walter.	PS3573.A425417
Walkowski, Paul J. (Paul Joseph), 1945-	PS3573.A42548
Wall, Alan.	PR6073.A415
Wall, Carolyn D.	PS3623.A35963
Wall, David Cooper.	PS3573.A42554
Wall, Judith Henry.	PS3573.A42556
Wall, Kathryn R.	PS3623.A4424
Wall, Michael (Michael Alan)	PR9639.3.W25
Wall, P. S. (Paula S.), 1954-	PS3623.A4427
Wall, William.	none
Wall, William, 1955-	PR6073.A418
Wallace, Amy, 1970-	PS3623.A35974
Wallace, David Rains, 1945-	PS3573.A42564
Wallace, Edgar, 1875-1932.	PR6045.A327
	[Z8947.46]
Wallace, George, 1950-	PS3623.A443
Wallace, Ian, 1912-	PS3573.A4258
Wallace, Irving, 1916-1990.	PS3573.A426
Wallace, Marilyn.	PS3573.A4266
Wallace, Pat, 1929-	none
Wallace, Patricia—see: Wallace, Pat, 1929-	
Wallace, Patricia (Patricia Wallace Estrada)	PS3573.A42698
Wallace, Robert, 1938-	PR9619.3.W285
Wallace, Tom (Fred Thomas Wallace), 1946-	PS3623.A4439
Wallen, Jacqueline.	PS3623.A36
Waller, Leslie, 1923-2007.	PS3545.A565
Waller, Robert James, 1939-	PS3573.A4347
Walling, R. A. J. (Robert Alfred John), 1869-1949.	PR6045.A3375
Wallingford, Lee.	PS3573.A438
Wallmann, Jeffrey M., 1941-	PS3573.A4395
Wallner, Michael, 1958-	PT2685.A4742
Walpole, Hugh, Sir, 1884-1941.	PR6045.A34
Walpow, Nathan.	PS3573.A4478
Walsh, J. M. (James Morgan), 1897-1952.	PR9619.3.W29
Walsh, Marcie.	PS3563.A43244
Walsh, Michael, 1949-	PS3573.A472242
Walsh, Ray, 1949-	PR9144.9.W34

Walsh, Thomas, 1908-1984.	PS3545.A592
Waltch, Lilla M.	PS3573.A47227
Walter, Elizabeth (Elizabeth Margaret)	PR6073.A4285
Walter, Jess, 1965-	PS3573.A4722834
Walters, Anna Lee, 1946-	PS3573.A47228
Walters, Linda.	PS3623.A4483
Walters, Mike, 1960-	PR6123.A474
Walters, Minette.	PR6073.A444
Walters, Shelly—see: Sheldon, Walter J.	
Waltner-Toews, David, 1948-	PR9199.3.W353
Walton, Alan Hull.	PR6073.A446
Walton, David, 1975-	PS3623.A454
Walton, Jo.	PR6073.A448
Walton, Marion, 1928-	none
Walton, Todd.	PS3573.A474
Waltzer, Jim, 1950-	PS3623.A368
Walz, Audrey.	PS3545.A6422
Wambaugh, Joseph.	PS3573.A475
Wan, Michelle.	PS3623.A456
Wang, Shuo, 1958-	PL2919.S55
Warburton, Carole Thayne, 1957-	PS3620.H395
Warby, Marjorie.	none
Ward, Dewey, 1921-	none
Ward, Donald, 1936-	PS3573.A728
Ward, Edmund, 1928-	PR6073.A72
Ward, Elizabeth C.	PS3573.A7314
Ward, Gregory.	PR9199.3.W359
Ward, I. E. (Irene Ellen)	none
Ward, Robert, 1943-	PS3573.A735
Warden, Florence, 1857-1929.	PR4821.J3
Warden, Gertrude.	PR6045.A42
Warden, Mike.	none
Wardman, Gordon.	PR6073.A72235
Ware, Ciji.	PS3573.A7435
Warfield, Gallatin.	PS3573.A753
Warga, Wayne.	PS3573.A755
Warne, Philip S.	PS3149.W58
Warner, Douglas.	PR6073.A723
Warner, Gertrude Chandler, 1890-1979.	PS3545.A738
Warner, Jack.	PS3623.A863
Warner, Mignon.	PR6073.A7275
Warner, Penny.	PS3573.A7659
Warner, Peter, 1942-	PS3573.A767
Warner-Cohen, Kimberly.	PS3623.A8642
Warren, Barbara, 1934-	PS3623.A8644
Warren, Bill, 1943-	none
Warren, Doug.	none
Warren, George, 1934-	PS3573.A773
Warren, Nancy, 1959-	PR9199.4.W3665
Warren, Patricia.	none
Warren, Paulette.	none
Warren, Robert Penn, 1905-1989.	PS3545.A748 [Z8949.73]
Warren, Samuel, 1807-1877.	PR5730-5734

Warren, Susan May, 1966-	PS3623.A865
Warrier, Shashi, 1959-	PR9499.3.W37
Warsh, Sylvia Maultash.	PR9199.4.W37
Warthen, Ron.	none
Warwaruk, Larry, 1943-	PR9199.3.W367
Warwick, John, 1937-	none
Washburn, James.	PS3573.A7867
Washburn, L. J.	PS3573.A787
Washburn, Livia J.—see: Washburn, L. J.	
Washburn, Mark.	PS3573.A788
Washburn, Stan.	PS3573.A789
Washington, Jesse John, 1969-	PS3623.A8675
Wasserman, George.	PS3623.A8679
Wassermann, Jack.	none
Wassom, Warren, 1944-	PS3623.A868
Waterhouse, Jane.	PS3573.A812
Waters—see: Russell, William.	
Waters, T. A.	PS3573.A82
Waters, T. J.	PS3623.A8692
Watkins, Graham, 1944-	PS3573.A839
Watkins, Gwen C.	PS3623.A869439
Watkins, Ivor.	none
Watkins, Leslie.	PR6073.A84
Watkins, Paul, 1964-	PS3573.A844
Watkins, Ron, 1930-	none
Watkins, Ronald J.	none
Watson, Clarissa.	PS3573.A848
Watson, Colin.	PR6073.A86
Watson, Geoffrey, 1942-	PR6073.A862
Watson, I. K., 1947-	PR6073.A8626
Watson, Jack.	PR9390.9.W3
Watson, James L.	none
Watson, Larry, 1947-	PS3573.A853
Watson, Lawrence—see: Watson, Larry, 1947-	
Watson, Marjorie.	PR6073.A874
Watson, Patrick, 1929-	PR9199.3.W376
Watson, Robert, 1947-	PR6073.A8757
Watson, Sterling.	PS3573.A858
Watson, Will W.	PS3623.A874
Watt, Alan, 1965-	PR9199.3.W3796
Watts, John, 1937-	none
Watts, Leslie Elizabeth, 1961-	PR9199.3.W385
Watts, Timothy, 1957-	PS3573.A88
Waugh, Alec, 1898-1981.	PR6045.A95
Waugh, Harriet, 1944-	PR6073.A916
Waugh, Hillary.	PS3573.A9
Waugh, Teresa.	PR6073.A919
Way, Camilla.	PR6123.A93
Way, Isabel Stewart.	none
Way, John H.	none
Way, Peter.	PR6073.A93
Wayman, Vivienne.	PR6073.A935
Waynar, Chris.	none
Wayne, Joanna.	none

Wayne, Richard. PS3623.A97
Weatherby, William J. PR6073.E13
Weathers, Brenda, 1936- PS3573.E147
Weaver, Graham. PR6073.E143
Weaver, Mary Cesario, 1946- PS3623.E385
Weaver, Michael, 1929- PS3573.E1788
Webb, Betty. PS3623.E39
Webb, Cynthia. PS3573.E1952
Webb, Debra. none
Webb, Don. PS3573.E1953
Webb, Forrest, 1929- PR6056.O692
Webb, Jack, 1916- PS3573.E19543
Webb, James H. PS3573.E1955
Webb, Jean Francis. PS3545.E322
Webb, Jonathan, 1950- PR9199.3.W394
Webb, Martha G. PS3573.E196
Webb, Michael, 1954- none
Webb, Peggy. PS3573.E1985
Webb, Sharon. PS3573.E212
Webb, Victoria, 1935-2005. PS3573.E199
Webber, Heather S. PS3623.E393
Weber, A. A. PS3573.E216
Weber, Janice. PS3573.E218
Weber, Joe, 1945- PS3573.E219
Weber, R. H. (Richard H.) PS3623.E395
Webster, Elizabeth, 1918- PR6073.E2312
Webster, Ernest. none
Webster, F. A. M. (Frederick Annesley Michael), none
b. 1886.
Webster, Henry Kitchell, 1875-1932. PS3545.E362
Webster, Jason, 1970- PS3623.E39645
Webster, Josh. none
Webster, Noah, 1928-1999. PR6061.N6
Weeden, Curt, 1942- PS3623.E416
Weedmark, David. PR9199.4.W4344
Weeks, Dolores. PS3573.E325
Weeks, J. C.—see: Weeks, Jan.
Weeks, Jan. PS3573.E327
Wees, Frances Shelley, 1902- PR6045.E43
Wefer, Fred L. PS3573.E363
Wehen, Joy De Weese. PS3573.E37
Wehrenberg, Charles. PS3573.E3815
Weidman, Jerome, 1913- PS3545.E449
Weikart, Jim. PS3573.E38369
Weil, Barry PR6073.E26
Weil, Jerry. PS3573.E3838
Weill, Gus. PS3573.E388
Wein, Jacqueline. PS3573.E3913
Wein, Len. none
Weinberg, Florence Byham. PS3623.E4324
Weinberg, Gerald M. PS3573.E3917
Weinberger, Caspar W. PS3623.E437
Weiner, Ellis. PS3573.E39323
Weiner, Eric. none

Weiner, Jack B., 1929-	PS3573.E3934
Weiner, Jennifer.	PS3573.E3935
Weinman, Irving, 1937-	PS3573.E3963
Weinstein, Sol.	PS3573.E397
Weir, Charlene.	PS3573.E39744
Weir, Theresa, 1954-	PS3573.E3976
Weisberg, Joseph.	PS3623.E45
Weisman, John.	PS3573.E399
Weismiller, Edward Ronald, 1915-	PS3545.E473
Weiss, Ben.	PS3623.E4326
Weiss, David, 1909-2002.	PS3573.E415
Weiss, Ellen, 1949-	none
Weiss, Jan Merete.	PS3623.E4553
Weiss, Melford S.	none
Weiss, Mike, 1942-	PS3573.E4162
Weiss, Steve (Steven J.)	PS3573.E4166
Weissberger, Ruth E.	PS3623.E459
Weissman, Jerry.	none
Welch, Denis.	PR9639.3.W42
Welch, Donald, 1958-	PS3623.E4623
Welch, Pat, 1957-	PS3573.E4543
Welch, Suzy.	PS3573.E9249
Welcome, John, 1914-2010.	PR6073.E373
Weldon, David J.	none
Weldon, Phaedra.	PS3623.E4647
Welk, Mary.	PS3573.E45655
Well, Chris, 1966-	PS3623.E4657
Wellard, James, 1909-1987.	PR6045.E525
Wellen, Edward.	PS3573.E4566
Welles, Orson, 1915-1985.	PS3545.E522
Welles, Elizabeth.	none
Welles, Patricia.	PS3573.E46
Wellman, Mac.	PS3573.E468
Wellman, Wade.	PS3573.E47
Wells, Anna Mary.	none
Wells, Carolyn, d. 1942.	PS3545.E533
Wells, Dan, 1977-	PS3623.E4688
Wells, Elaine F.	none
Wells, John, 1944-	PS3573.E4916
Wells, Lee.	PS3573.E4925
Wells, Lee E., 1907-1982.	PS3545.E5425
Wells, Melinda.	PS3623.E4765
Wells, Robison E.	PS3623.E478
Wells, Shirley, 1955-	PR6123.E44
Wells, Tobias, 1923-	PS3556.O67
Wells, William K.	none
Wellsley, Julie.	none
Welsh, Irvine.	PR6073.E47
Welsh, Ken, 1941-	PR6073.E48
Welsh, Louise.	PR6123.E47
Wendelboe, C. M.	PS3623.E53
Wender, Theodora, 1934-2003.	none
Wendorf, Patricia.	PR6073.E49
Wentworth, Patricia.	PR6045.E66

Werlin, Marvin.	PS3573.E67
Wernick, Saul, 1921-	none
Werry, Richard R.	PS3545.E8254
Wesley, Carolyn.	PS3573.E814
Wesley, Mary, 1912-2002.	PR6073.E753
Wesley, Valerie Wilson.	PS3573.E8148
Wessel, John, 1952-	PS3573.E8149
Wesson, Marianne.	PS3573.E81498
West, Cameron, 1955-	PS3623.E83
West, Charles, 1927-	PR6073.E7624
West, Charles (Charles Leon)	PS3573.E8158
West, Christopher, 1954-	PR6073.E76245
West, Don.	PS3545.E8279
West, Elliot.	PS3573.E817
West, Eugenia Lovett, 1923-	PS3573.E818
West, Mark, 1943-	PS3573.E8243
West, Michael Lee.	PS3573.E8244
West, Morris, 1916-1999.	PR9619.3.W4
West, Owen, 1945-	PS3561.O55
West, Owen, 1969-	PS3623.E845
West, Pamela Elizabeth.	PS3573.E8246
West, Paul, 1930-	PS3573.E8247
West, Richard F.	none
West, Tracey, 1965-	PS3623.E847
Westall, Sheila.	none
Westall, William, 1835-1903.	PR5779.W19
Westbrook, Kate, 1966-	PR6123.E865
Westbrook, Robert.	PS3573.E827
Westerfeld, Scott.	PS3573.E854
Westerly, Daniel.	none
Westermann, John, 1952-	PS3573.E856
Westerson, Jeri.	PS3623.E8478
Westfall, Patricia Tichenor.	PS3573.E865
Westheimer, David.	PS3573.E88
Westlake, Donald E.	PS3573.E9
Westlake, Michael.	PR6073.E773
Westminster, Aynn.	none
Weston, Carolyn.	PS3573.E92
Weston, John, 1932-	PS3573.E924
Westover, Steve, 1974-	PS3623.E876
Wetherell, June.	PS3545.E917
Wetterhahn, Ralph, 1942-	PS3623.E89
Weverka, Robert.	PS3573.E96
Wexler, Charlene.	PS3623.E93
Wexler, Warren.	none
Whaley, Barton.	none
Whalley, Peter, 1946-	PR6073.H35
Wharton, Althea.	none
Whatley, Tom V., 1940-	PS3573.H33
Wheat, Carolyn.	PS3573.H35
Wheatley, Dennis, 1897-1977.	PR6045.H127
	[Z8969.28]
Wheeler, Gordon.	PS3573.H432
Wheeler, Keith.	PS3545.H294

Wheeler, Leslie, 1945-	PS3623.H44
Wheeler, Paul, 1934-	PR6073.H399
Wheeler, Richard S.	PS3573.H4345
Wheeler, Thomas.	PS3623.H45
Whelan, Hilary.	PR6073.H433
Whelchel, Sandy.	PS3623.H46
Whelton, Clark.	none
Whicker, Mike.	PS3623.H524
Whipple, Dan.	PS3623.H53
Whishaw, Frederick.	PR6045.H1536
Whisman, Dale.	PS3623.H56
Whitaker, Arthur, 1882-1949.	PR6045.H1546
Whitaker, Leo.	PS3573.H445
Whitbeck, William C.	PS3623.H5637
Whitby, Sharon.	PR6052.L335
Whitcomb, Christopher, 1959-	PS3623.H564
White, Alan, 1924-	PR6073.H49
White, Alicen.	none
White, Anne, 1928-	PS3623.H57
White, Charlotte, 1944-	PS3573.H4572
White, Dave, 1979-	PS3623.H5727
White, David Fairbank, 1951-	PS3573.H458
White, Don (Donal L.)	PS3573.H459
White, Elizabeth, 1957-	PS3623.H574
White, Ellen Emerson.	PS3573.H4635
White, Ethel Lina.	PR6045.H1565
White, Franklin.	PS3573.H468
White, Fred M. (Fred Merrick), b. 1859.	PR6045.H15653
White, Gillian, 1945-	PR6073.H4925
White, Grace Miller.	PS3545.H523
White, James Dillon—see: White, Stanley, 1913-	
White, James P. (James Patrick), 1940-	PS3573.H4727
White, Jenny B. (Jenny Barbara), 1953-	PS3623.H5763
White, Jon Ewbank Manchip, 1924-	PR6073.H499
White, Karen (Karen S.)	PS3623.H5776
White, Kate, 1950-	PS3623.H578
White, Kimberley, 1966-	PS3623.H57855
White, Linda J., 1949-	PS3623.H5786
White, Lionel.	PS3573.H4738
White, Loreth Anne.	PR9199.4.W4726
White, Michael C.	PS3573.H47447
White, Ned.	PS3573.H4745
White, Osmar.	PR9639.3.W47
White, Pat (Patricia Mae)	none
White, Randy Wayne.	PS3573.H47473
White, Reginald James.	PR6073.H52
White, Robin A.	PS3573.H47476
White, Stanley, 1913-	PR6045.H196
White, Stephen, 1951-	PS3573.H47477
White, Stewart Edward, 1873-1946.	PS3545.H6
White, Terence De Vere.	PR6073.H53
White, Teri.	PS3573.H47495
White, Thomas, 1956-	PS3623.H5794
White, Tzvi.	none

Whitechurch, Victor L. (Victor Lorenzo), 1868-1933.   PR6045.H227

Whited, Charles.   none
Whitehead, Barbara.   PR6073.H543
Whitehouse, Cynthia C.   PS3623.H5845
Whitelaw, David.   PR6045.H24
Whiteley, L. S.   PS3573.H4874
Whitfield, Raoul.   PS3545.H656
Whiting, Charles, 1926-2007.   PR6073.H6
Whitlatch, John.   none
Whitlow, Robert, 1954-   PS3573.H49837
Whitman, Charles, 1916-   PR6073.H64
Whitmee, Jeanne.   PR6073.H65
Whitmore, Ken.   PR6073.H652
Whitnell, Barbara.   PR6073.H653
Whitney, Alec, 1924-   PR6073.H49
Whitney, Phyllis A., 1903-2008.   PS3545.H8363
Whitney, Polly.   PS3573.H5337
Whitney, Steven.   PS3573.H535
Whitten, Les, 1928-   PS3573.H566
Whittier, Aris.   PS3623.H58716
Whittingham, Richard, 1939-2005.   PS3573.H567
Whittington, Harry, 1915-1989.   PS3545.H896
Whitworth, Bill.   none
Whorton, James, 1967-   PS3623.H6
Wibberley, Leonard, 1915-1983.   PS3573.I2
Wick, Carter—see: Wilcox, Collin.
Wickert, Gary L., 1957-   PS3573.I2525
Widdemer, Margaret.   PS3545.I175
Wiehe, Fred, 1955-   PS3573.I343
Wiehl, Lis W.   PS3623.I382
Wieselberg, Helen.   PS3573.I376
Wigglesworth, Gayle.   PS3623.I42
Wignall, Kevin.   PR6123.I36
Wikarski, Nancy S., 1954-   PS3623.I48
Wilber, Rick, 1948-   PS3573.I38796
Wilbon, Mary.   PS3623.I525
Wilcken, Hugo, 1964-   PR9619.4.W55
Wilcox, Collin.   PS3573.I395
Wilcox, Ronald.   none
Wilcox, Stephen F.   PS3573.I419
Wilden, Theodore, 1936-   PR9115.9.W5
Wilder, Robert, 1901-1974.   PS3545.I343
Wildwind, Sharon Grant.   PR9199.4.W542
Wiles, Domini.   PR6073.I4159
Wiles, Frank.   none
Wiles, Patricia.   none
Wiley, Edward.   none
Wiley, Hugh, 1884-1968.   PS3545.I3587
Wiley, Michael, 1961-   PS3623.I5433
Wiley, Richard.   PS3573.I433
Wilgus, Nick.   PS3623.I5435
Wilhelm, Kate.   PS3573.I434
Wilhite, George.   PS3623.I5445

Wilk, Max.   PS3545.I365
Wilkerson, Carolyn.   PS3623.I5455
Wilkins, Barbara.   PS3573.I4413
Wilkins, Judd Rice, 1920-   PS3623.I548
Wilkinson, Sandra.   PS3573.I44255
Wilkshire, Nick, 1968-   PR9199.4.W543
Willcocks, Roger.   PR6123.I543
Willeford, Charles Ray, 1919-   PS3545.I464
Willett, Herman R.   PS3623.I5558
Willett, Jincy.   PS3573.I4455
Willey, Gordon R. (Gordon Randolph), 1913-2002. PS3573.I44723
Williams, Alan, 1935-   PR6073.I4258
Williams, Amanda Kyle, 1957-   PS3573.I447425
Williams, Ann M., 1937-   PS3573.I447427
Williams, Arthur, 1930-1997.   PS3552.I3
Williams, Ben Ames, 1889-1953.   PS3545.I5115
Williams, Billy Dee, 1937-   PS3573.I4475
Williams, Brad.   PS3573.I4476
Williams, Charles, 1909-1975.   PS3573.I448
Williams, Darren, 1967-   PR9619.3.W55
Williams, David, 1926-   PR6073.I42583
Williams, David, 1939 July 3-   PS3573.I44843
Williams, Gee.   PR6073.I42588
Williams, Gerard.   PR6123.I55
Williams, Gordon M., 1934-   PR6073.I426
Williams, H. R.   PS3623.I5567
Williams, Jay, 1914-1978.   PS3545.I528455
Williams, Jean.   PR6073.I43215
Williams, Jeanne, 1930-   PS3573.I44933
Williams, John, 1961-   PR6073.I43217
Williams, John Ellis.   PR6073.I4322
Williams, John Hartley.   PR6073.I43223
Williams, Katie, 1978-   none
Williams, Kay, 1933-   PS3623.I55827
Williams, Lawrence, 1915-   PS3573.I4497
Williams, Lynn, 1924-   PS3515.A262
Williams, Mary, 1903-   PR6073.I4323
Williams, Matthew, 1963-   PS3623.I55868
Williams, Michael, 1962-   PR9369.3.W544
Williams, Mona Goodwyn, 1906-   PS3545.I533525
Williams, Neil.   none
Williams, Nigel, 1948-   PR6073.I4327
Williams, Philip C., 1952-   none
Williams, Philip Lee.   PS3573.I45535
Williams, Raymond.   PR6073.I4329
Williams, Robert Leonard, 1932-   none
Williams, Rose, 1912-   PR9199.3.R5996
Williams, Ruth.   none
Williams, Sean, 1967-   PR9619.3.W5667
Williams, T. Jeff.   none
Williams, Tennessee, 1911-1983.   PS3545.I5365
                                                        [Z8976.424]

Williams, Thomas, 1926-   PS3573.I456
Williams, Timothy.   PR6073.I43295

Williams, Valentine, 1883-1946.	PR6045.I5464
Williams, Walter Jon.	PS3573.I456213
Williams, Wynn.	none
Williamson, A. M. (Alice Muriel), 1869-1933.	PS3319.W7
Williamson, Audrey, 1913-	PR6073.I43325
Williamson, Bob.	PS3623.I567
Williamson, C. N. (Charles Norris), 1859-1920.	PR5834.W6
Williamson, Chet.	PS3573.I456238
Williamson, J. N. (Jerry N.)	PS3573.I456277
Williamson, John (John Lutz)	PS3623.I568
Williamson, Moncrieff.	PR9199.3.W493
Williamson, Penelope.	PS3573.I456288
Williamson, Penn.	PS3573.I456288
Williamson, Sherman.	PR6073.I43342
Williamson, Tony, 1932-	PR6073.I43344
Williamz, M. J.	PS3623.I5737
Willig, Lauren.	PS3623.I575
Willingham, Bill.	PS3573.I45649
Willis, Anthony Armstrong—see: Armstrong, Anthony, 1897-1976.	
Willis, Maud—see: Lottman, Eileen.	
Willis, Ted.	PR6045.I567
Willock, Ruth, 1904-	PS3545.I578
Wills, Cecil Melville, 1891-	PR6045.I57
Wills, Garry, 1934-	PS3573.I45658
Willsdon, Andrew.	none
Wilmot, James Reginald, 1897-	PR6045.I5735
Wilson, A. N., 1950-	PR6073.I439
Wilson, Barbara—see: Sjoholm, Barbara, 1950-	
Wilson, Barbara Jaye.	PS3573.I45679
Wilson, Charles, 1939-	PS3573.I45684
Wilson, Colin, 1931-	PR6073.I44
	[Z8976.487]
Wilson, Daniel H. (Daniel Howard), 1978-	PS3623.I57796
Wilson, David.	none
Wilson, David L.	none
Wilson, David Niall.	PS3573.I456885
Wilson, Debbie, 1956-	PS3623.I578
Wilson, Derek, 1935-	PR6073.I463
Wilson, Dolores J.	PS3623.I5784
Wilson, Elizabeth, 1936-	PR6123.I5657
Wilson, Eric (Eric P.)	PS3623.I583
Wilson, F. Paul (Francis Paul)	PS3573.I45695
Wilson, G. M. (Gertrude Mary)	PR6073.I465
Wilson, Gahan.	PS3573.I4569538
Wilson, Gar.	PS3558.O76
Wilson, Garrett, 1932-	PR9199.3.W49845
Wilson, Gary D. (Gary Dean)	PS3623.I584
Wilson, Jacqueline.	PR6073.I46737
Wilson, Jeanne, 1920-	PR9265.9.W53
Wilson, John, 1937-	PR6073.I46785
Wilson, John Morgan, 1945-	PS3573.I456974
Wilson, Joyce.	none
Wilson, Judson.	none
Wilson, Karen Ann.	none

Wilson, L.A., 1942-	none
Wilson, Laura, 1964-	PR6073.I4716
Wilson, Mary—see: Roby, Mary Linn.	
Wilson, Mary Anne.	none
Wilson, R. McNair (Robert McNair), 1882-1963.	PR6045.I626
Wilson, Robert, 1957-	PR6073.I474
Wilson, Robert Charles, 1951-	PS3573.I4663
Wilson, Robin Scott.	PS3573.I4664
Wilson, Robley.	PS3573.I4665
Wilson, Sloan, 1920-2003.	PS3573.I475
Wilson, Steve, 1943-	PR6073.I4752
Wilson, T. E. (Trevor Edward)	PR9639.3.W56
Wilson, T. R. (Timothy R.)	PR6073.I4753
Wilson, Tom.	none
Wilson, William, 1935-	PS3573.I476
Wiltse, David.	PS3573.I478
Wiltz, Chris.	PS3573.I4783
Wimberley, Darryl.	PS3573.I47844
Winch, Arden.	PR6073.I4755
Winchell, Prentice, b. 1895.	PS3545.I662
Winchester, David F., 1946-	PS3573.I4795
Winchester, Jack.	PR6073.I4759
Winchester, Stanley.	PR6073.I48
Wind, Ruth	PS3573.I485
Windle, Jeanette.	PS3573.I5172
Windsor, Patricia.	PS3573.I52
Winegardner, Mark, 1961-	PS3573.I528
Wingard, Alan.	none
Wingate, Anne.	PS3573.I5316
Wingate, John, 1920-	PR6073.I53
Wingate, William.	PR9369.3.W55
Wingfield, Andrew, 1966-	PS3623.I6625
Wingfield, R. D.	none
Wings, Mary.	PS3573.I53213
Winkler, Anthony C.	PS3573.I53218
Winkowski, Mary Ann.	PS3623.I6627
Winn, Craig.	PS3623.I663
Winnington, Alan.	none
Winslow, Don, 1953-	PS3573.I5326
Winslow, Emily (Emily Carroll)	PS3623.I6643
Winslow, Pauline Glen.	PR6073.I553
Winsor, Diana.	PR6073.I554
Winsor, George McLeod.	PR6045.I723
Winsor, Roy.	none
Winspear, Jacqueline, 1955-	PR6123.I575
Winstead, Rebecca Noyes.	none
Winston, Daoma, 1922-	PS3545.I7612
Winston, Lois.	PS3623.I666
Winston, Peter.	none
Winter, Abigail—see: Schere, Monroe.	
Winter, James R.	PS3623.I669
Winters, Angela.	PS3573.I5387
Winters, J. C.—see: Cross, Gilbert B.	
Winters, Jill.	PS3623.I675

Winters, Jon—see: Cross, Gilbert B.
Winterton, Wayne (Wayne Allen), 1938-   PS3623.I684
Wintner, Robert.   PS3573.I63
Winward, Walter.   PR6073.I58
Wiprud, Brian M.   PS3623.I73
Wisdom, Linda Randall.   PS3573.I774
Wise, Ardath.   PS3573.I78
Wise, Arthur, 1923-   PR6073.I75
Wise, David.   PS3573.I785
Wise, Joe, 1939-   PS3573.I787
Wise, Leonard.   PS3573.I79
Wise, Robert L.   PS3573.I797
Wise, William, 1923-   PS3573.I842
Wiseman, Richard.   PR6073.I766
Wiseman, Thomas.   PR6073.I77
Wiser, H. Fred.   PS3573.I85
Wishart, David, 1952-   PR6073.I776
Wishart, Nan.   none
Wishman, Seymour.   PS3573.I874
Wishnia, K. J. A.   PS3573.I875
Wisler, Alice J.   PS3623.I846
Wissmann, Ruth H.   PS3573.I88
Witten, Barbara Yager.   PS3573.I918
Witten, Matthew.   PS3573.I919
Wittich, Justine.   PS3573.I925
Witting, Clifford.   PR6045.I95
Wittman, George.   PS3573.I94
Wlaschin, Ken.   none
Wodehouse, P. G. (Pelham Grenville), 1881-1975.   PR6045.O53
Wohl, Burton.   PS3573.O38
Wohl, James P.   PS3573.O39
Wolf, Gary K.   PS3573.O483
Wolf, Joan.   PS3573.O486
Wolf, Joyce.   none
Wolf, Klaus-Peter, 1954-   PT2685.O3633
Wolf, Sarah.   PS3573.O489
Wolfe, Aaron, 1945-   PS3561.O55
Wolfe, Carson.   PS3573.O496
Wolfe, Gene.   PS3573.O52
Wolfe, Inger Ash.   PR9199.4.W65
Wolfe, John.   none.
Wolfe, Jonathan.   none
Wolfe, Linda, 1935-   PS3573.O523
Wolfe, Liz.   PS3623.O553
Wolfe, Michael, 1917-   PS3573.O525
Wolfe, Susan, 1950-   PS3573.O5256
Wolff, B. M. (Bernadette. M.)   PS3623.O557
Wolff, Benjamin.   none
Wolff, Geoffrey, 1937-   PS3573.O53
Wolff, Maritta, 1918-2002.   PS3545.O346
Wolfman, Marv.   PS3573.O56136
Wolfson, Murray.   PS3573.O5617
Wolfson, Vi.   PS3573.O5619
Wolk, George.   PS3573.O565

Wollaston, John G., 1936-	PR9619.4.W65
Wolman, David.	none
Wolstencroft, David.	PR6123.O47
Wolzien, Valerie.	PS3573.O574
Womack, Steven.	PS3573.O576
Wood, Andrew, 1890-1967.	none
Wood, Barbara, 1947-	PS3573.O5877
Wood, Bari, 1936-	PS3573.O588
Wood, Christopher, 1935-	PR6073.O576
Wood, Deborah.	none
Wood, Graham R., 1945-	PR6123.O525
Wood, H. F. (H. Freeman)	PR5842.W92
Wood, Henry, Mrs., 1814-1887.	PR5842.W8
Wood, James, 1918-	PR6073.O58
Wood, Lynn M.	PS3623.O635
Wood, N. Lee.	PR6073.O613
Wood, Samuel Andrew—see: Wood, Andrew, 1890-1967.	
Wood, Simon, 1968-	PS3623.O643
Wood, Ted.	PR9199.3.W57
Wood, Tom, 1978-	PR6073.O6149
Wood, William P.	PS3573.O599
Woodford, Jack, 1894-1971.	PS3545.O765
Woodhouse, Martin, 1932-	PR6073.O616
Woodley, Richard.	PS3573.O626
Woodman, Michael.	none
Woodrell, Daniel.	PS3573.O6263
Woods, Brett F.	PS3623.O675
Woods, John C. (John Charles), 1950-	PS3573.O6315
Woods, Paula L.	PS3573.O6414
Woods, Sara, pseud.	PR6073.O63
Woods, Sherryl.	PS3573.O6418
Woods, Stockton, 1932-	PS3556.O739
Woods, Stuart.	PS3573.O642
Woods, Teri.	PS3573.O6427
Woodthorpe, Michael.	PS3623.O68
Woodworth, Deborah.	PS3573.O64533
Woodworth, Stephen, 1967-	PS3623.O696
Wooley, John.	PS3573.O6457
Wooley, Marilyn.	PS3573.O6458
Woolf, Douglas, 1922-	PS3573.O646
Woolfolk, William.	PS3573.O65
Woolrich, Cornell, 1903-1968.	PS3515.O6455
Worboys, Anne.	PR6073.O667
Work, James C.	PS3573.O6925
Worley, Rob M.	none
Wormser, Richard, 1908-1977.	PS3545.O88
Worsley, T. C. (Thomas Cuthbert), 1907-	PR6045.O78
Worth, Jim, 1947-	PS3623.O774
Worth, Lenora.	PS3573.O6965
Worts, George F. (George Frank), b. 1892.	PS3545.O97
Wozencraft, Kim.	PS3573.O98
Wren, M. K.	PS3573.R43
Wren, Percival Christopher, 1885-1941.	PR6045.R35
	[Z8985.7]

Wright, Alec.   none
Wright, Betty Ren.   none
Wright, Edward.   PS3623.R535
Wright, Eric, 1929-   PR9199.3.W66
Wright, Glover.   PR6073.R488
Wright, Jen.   PS3623.R5395
Wright, Jim, 1950-   PS3573.R53665
Wright, Joseph E.   none
Wright, L. R.—see: Wright, Laurali, 1939-
Wright, Laurali, 1939-   PR9199.3.W68
Wright, Laurie Robeson.   none
Wright, Nancy Means.   PS3573.R5373
Wright, Nina, 1964-   PS3623.R56
Wright, Richard, 1908-1960.   PS3545.R815
                                                       [Z8986.323]

Wright, Richard Bruce, 1937-   PR9199.3.W7
Wright, Sally S.   PS3573.R5398
Wright, Sue Owens.   PS3623.R565
Wright, T. M., 1947-   PS3573.R544
Wright, Wade, 1933-2008.   none
Wright, Wilbur.   PR6073.R58
Wu Ming 1.   PQ4923.U6
Wuamett, Victor.   PS3573.U38
Wulffson, Don L.   none
Wuori, G. K.   PS3573.U57
Wuorio, Eva-Lis, 1918-   PS3573.U6
Würth, Petra, 1956-   none
Wyatt, Dee.   PR6073.Y32
Wyka, Frank.   PS3573.Y484
Wyle, Dirk, 1945-   PS3573.Y4854
Wyler, Allen R.   PS3623.Y625
Wyler, Elizabeth, 1950-   PS3623.Y628
Wylie, Philip, 1902-1971.   PS3545.Y46
Wyllie, John, 1914-   PR6073.Y58
Wylly, Sabrina, 1952-   PS3573.Y55
Wyman, D. M., 1950-   PR9199.4.W96
Wynd, Oswald, 1913-   PR6073.Y65
Wynn, Patricia.   PS3573.Y6217
Wynn, Perry.   PS3623.Y65
Wynn Jones, Hazel.   PR6073.Y68
Wynne, Anthony, 1882-1963   PR6045.I626
Wynne, Barry.   none
Wynne, Marcus.   PS3623.Y66
Wynne-Jones, Tim.   PR9199.3.W95
Wyrick, E. L.   PS3573.Y68
Yablonsky, Yabo.   none
Yaeger, Carl H.   none
Yaffe, James, 1927-   PS3547.A16
Yager, Fred, 1946-   PS3575.A29
Yan, Geling.   PS3625.A673
                                                       PL2925.K55

Yancey, Richard.   PS3625.A675
Yanover, Yori.   PS3625.A686
Yapalater, Karin.   PS3625.A69

Yarborough, Charlotte.	PS3575.A68
Yarbro, Chelsea Quinn, 1942-	PS3575.A7
Yardley, James.	PR6075.A7
Yariv, Fran Pokras.	none
Yarrow, Arnold.	none
Yarrow, Joyce.	PS3625.A7385
Yaşar Kemel, 1922-	PL248.Y275
Yates, Alan, 1923-1985.	PR6052.R5893
Yates, Alex, 1982-	PS3625.A74
Yates, Brock W.	PS3575.A76
Yates, Dan, 1934-	PS3575.A763
Yates, Dornford, 1885-1960.	PR6047.A73
Yates, Edmund Hodgson, 1831-1894.	PR5899.Y3
Ybarra, Ricardo Means.	PS3575.B37
Yeager, Dorian.	PS3575.E363
Yeates, J. Lanier.	PS3625.E17
Yellin, Tamar.	PR6125.E45
Yerby, Frank, 1916-1991.	PS3547.E65
Yessayan, Raffi.	PS3625.E87
Yorgason, Blaine M., 1942-	PS3575.O57
York, Andrew, 1930-	PR9320.9.N5
York, Carol Beach.	none
York, Clifford.	PS3625.O744
York, Elizabeth, 1927-	PR6063.A359
York, Helen.	PS3575.O6
York, Jeremy, 1908-1973.	PR6005.R517
York, Kieran, 1943-	PS3575.O63
York, Rebecca.	PS3575.O6326
York, Sheila.	PS3625.O755
York, Vickie.	none
Yorke, Margaret.	PR6075.O7
Yorkey, Mike.	PS3625.O757
Yoshe.	PS3625.O758
Yost, Elwy.	PR9199.4.Y665
Youmans, Claire, 1952-	PS3575.O67
Young, Al, 1939-	PS3575.O683
Young, Brittany, 1952-	PS3575.O684
Young, Carter Travis.	PS3575.O7
Young, Collier.	PS3575.O75
Young, David, 1946-	PR9199.3.Y58
Young, Douglas H.	PR9199.3.Y583
Young, E. L.	none
Young, Ernest A., 1832-1873.	PS3364.Y46
Young, Felicity, 1960-	PR9199.4.Y674
Young, Francis Brett, 1884-1954.	PR6047.O47
Young, Karen.	PS3575.O7975
Young, Marsha.	none
Young, Nicole, 1967-	PS3625.O968
Young, Paul H. (Paul Henry), 1950-	none
Young, Phyllis Brett.	PR9199.3.Y66
Young, Scott, 1918-2005.	PR9199.3.Y68
Young, Thomas W., 1962-	PS3625.O97335
Young, William P.	PR9199.4.Y696
Younger, Jack.	none

Younkins, Susan Wilson.	PS3575.O875
Yourcenar, Marguerite.	PQ2649.O8
Yrsa Sigurðardóttir.	PT7513.Y77
Yu, Chuansong.	none
Yuill, P. B.	PR6075.U4
Yurick, Sol, 1925-	PS3575.U7
Yvonne, Alisha.	PS3625.V66
Zach, Cheryl.	none
Zacharatou, Sonia.	PA5638.36.A22
Zachary, Hugh.	PS3576.A23
Zackel, Fred.	PS3576.A27
Zagat, Arthur Leo, 1896-1949.	none
Zager, Muriel Kagan, 1933-	PS3576.A288
Zahn, Timothy.	PS3576.A33
Zake, S. Joshua L.	PR9402.9.Z3
Zandri, Vincent.	PS3576.A52
Zanger, Molleen, 1948-	PS3576.A53
Zangwill, Israel, 1864-1926.	PR5920-5924
Zannos, Susan.	PS3576.A55
Zapel, Arthur L. (Arthur Lewis), 1922-	PS3626.A64
Zaremba, Eve.	PR9199.3.Z36
Zaroulis, N. L.	PS3576.A74
Zarubina, Irina.	none
Zavala, Ann.	PS3576.A88
Zawadsky, Pat.	none
Zawadsky, Patience—see: Zawadsky, Pat.	
Zebrun, Gary.	PS3626.E24
Zec, Donald.	PR6076.E25
Zeh, Juli, 1974-	PT2688.E28
Zehel, Wendell.	PS3576.E366
Zeiger, Henry A.	PS3576.E38
Zelazny, Roger.	PS3576.E43
Zelik, Raul, 1968-	PT2688.E3875
Zelinsky, Mary.	PS3626.E36
Zellnik, Miriam.	PS3626.E39
Zelman, Anita.	PS3576.E447
Zeltserman, Dave, 1959-	PS3626.E396
Zelvin, Elizabeth.	PS3576.E48
Zeman, Angela.	PS3626.E43
Zeman, David.	PS3626.E44
Zencey, Eric.	PS3576.E535
Zeno, pseud.	PR6076.E5
Zerries, A. J.	PS3626.E77
Zhagel', Ivan.	PG3490.H24
Zhitkov, Andreï.	none
Zhukov, Vi‹a›cheslav, 1957-	PG3493.96.H86
Zhukova-Gladkova, Marii‹a›.	PG3490.H8117
Ziemann, Hans Heinrich, 1944-	PT2688.I367
Zietlow, E. R., 1932-	PR9199.3.Z54
Zigal, Thomas.	PS3576.I38
Zilinsky, Ursula.	PS3576.I46
Zimler, Richard.	PS3576.I464
Zimmer, Michael, 1955-	PS3576.I467
Zimmerman, Bruce.	PS3576.I48

Zimmerman, R. D. (Robert Dingwall)	PS3576.I5118
Zindel, Paul.	PS3576.I518
Ziran, Goland.	PS3576.I57
Zito, Chuck.	PS3626.I86
Zlatkin, Lev.	none
Znamenskai‹a›, Elena.	PG3490.N26
Zochert, Donald.	PS3576.O23
Zodrow, John Rester.	none
Zollinger, Norman.	PS3576.O45
Zouroudi, Anne.	PR6126.O97
Zschokke, Magdalena, 1950-	PS3576.S75
Zubro, Mark Richard.	PS3576.U225
Zuckerman, Albert.	PS3576.U23
Zuiker, Anthony E., 1968-	PS3626.U35
Zukowski, Sharon.	PS3576.U44
Zumwalt, Eva.	PS3576.U5
Zuravleff, Mary Kay.	PS3576.U54
Zurdo, David.	PQ6726.U73
Zverev, Sergeĭ.	PG3490.V43
Zvi‹a›gint‹s›ev, Aleksandr.	PG3490.V55

4-1. MOTION PICTURE MAIN ENTRIES AND CLASSIFICATION NUMBERS
INTRODUCTION

Books about individual motion pictures, or motion picture screenplays themselves, are classed in PN1997, and, for films released beginning in 2001, PN1997.2. Each film receives a unique cutter number derived from the first letter of the title; a second cutter for main entry completes the classification for a particular book. The subject heading for each film is the motion picture title plus the appellation (Motion picture); these may be subdivided further as required. Films produced at different dates with the same title (remakes, for example) are identified by adding dates to the appellation.

4-2. MYSTERY MOTION PICTURES AND CLASSIFICATION NUMBERS

PN1997 (Motion Pictures Released Through 2000)

.A23—A bout de souffle (Motion picture)
.A255—Absolute power (Motion picture)
.A32255—Alien nation (Motion picture)
.A345—Anatomy of a murder (Motion picture)
.A78—Asphalt jungle (Motion picture)
.B2455—Bandits (Motion picture)
.B273—Batman (Motion picture)
.B316—Batman & Robin (Motion picture)
.B3443—Batman beyond (Motion picture)
.B443—Big heat (Motion picture)
.B4447—Big sleep (Motion picture)
.B445—Big steal (Motion picture)
.B475—Birds (Motion picture)
.B596—Blade runner (Motion picture)
.B673—Blood simple ((Motion picture)
.B678—Blue Dahlia (Motion picture)
.B6783—Blue velvet (Motion picture)
.B6797—Bonnie and Clyde (Motion picture)
    Breathless—see: A bout de souffle
.B792—Bugsy (Motion picture)

.C18—Cabinet der Dr. Caligari (Motion picture)
    Cabinet of Dr. Caligari—see: Cabinet der Dr. Caligari
.C352—Casablanca (Motion picture)
.C46447—Chinatown (Motion picture)
.D3136—Dark knight (Motion picture)
.D373—Dead man (Motion picture)
.D43—Death proof (Motion picture)
.D4593—Diamonds are forever (Motion picture)
.D493—Dick Tracy (Motion picture)
.D55—Dr. Jekyll and Mr. Hyde (Motion picture)
.D6553—Double indemnity (Motion picture)
.F3456—Fargo (Motion picture)
.F348—Fatal attraction (Motion picture)
.F48—Fish called Wanda (Motion picture)
.F578—Force of evil (Motion picture)
.F7466—From dusk till dawn (Motion picture)
.F7473—From Russia with love (Motion picture)
.G4434—Get Carter (Motion picture)
.G56833—Godfather (Motion picture)
.G56863—Goldfinger (Motion picture)
.G596—GoodFellas (Motion picture)
.G6927—Green mile (Motion picture)
.G85—Gun crazy (Motion picture)
.H485—High sierra (Motion picture)
.H616—Homicide (Motion picture)
.H7115—House of games (Motion picture)
.I13—I am a fugitive from a chain gang (Motion picture)
.I95—I went down (Motion picture)
.J25—Jackie Brown (Motion picture)
.K4367—Kind hearts and coronets (Motion picture)
.K6838—Krays (Motion picture)
.L115—L.A. confidential (Motion picture)
.L3473—Laura (Motion picture)
.L589—Little Caesar (Motion picture)
.L5953—Live and let die (Motion picture)

.L735—Lost highway (Motion picture)
.M123—M (Motion picture)
.M256743—Maltese falcon (Motion picture)
.M2635—Marnie (Motion picture)
.M4344—Memento (Motion picture)
.M4353—Men in black (Motion picture)
.N324—Naked city (Motion picture)
.N335—Natural born killers (Motion picture)
.N5213—Night of the hunter (Motion picture)
.N5373—North by northwest (Motion picture)
.O1863—Odd man out (Motion picture)
.O423—On Her Majesty's Secret Service (Motion picture)
.O9—Outland (Motion picture)
.P5243—Play it again, Sam (Motion picture)
.P768—Procès (Motion picture)
.P79—Psycho (Motion picture)
.P797—Public enemy (Motion picture)
.P86—Pulp fiction (Motion picture)
.R353—Rear window (Motion picture)
.R363—Rebecca (Motion picture)
.R48—Reservoir dogs (Motion picture)
.R675—Rope (Motion picture)
.S195—Scarface (Motion picture)
.S3836—Shadow of a doubt (Motion picture)
.S433—Shawshank redemption (Motion picture)
.S4717—Sherlock Jr. (Motion picture)
.S546—Sling blade (Motion picture)
.S548—Smillas fornemmelse for sne (Motion picture)
    Smilla's sense of snow—see: Smillas fornemmelse for sne
.S6145—Snatch (Motion picture)
.S615—Snow falling on cedars (Motion picture)
.T29—Talented Mr. Ripley (Motion picture)
.T349—Taxi driver (Motion picture)
.T42873—Third man (Motion picture)
.T428735—39 steps (Motion picture)

.T6353—Touch of evil (Motion picture)
.T657—Traffic (Motion picture)
.T67—Treasure of the Sierra Madre (Motion picture)
    Trial—see: Procès
.U68—Usual suspects (Motion picture)
.V479—Vertigo (Motion picture)
.W5335—White heat (Motion picture)
.Y53—You only live twice (Motion picture)
.Z3—Zabriskie Point (Motion picture)

PN1997.2 (Motion Pictures Released After 2000)

.A685—Atonement (Motion picture)
.B33—Bad lieutenant (Motion picture)
.B38—Batman begins (Motion picture)
.B86—Burn after reading (Motion picture)
.C3745—Casino Royale (Motion picture)
.C38—Catch me if you can (Motion picture)
.C47—Chicago (Motion picture)
.C665—Constant gardener (Motion picture)
.G36—Gangs of New York (Motion picture)
.G75—Grindhouse (Motion picture)
.K54—Kill Bill (Motion picture)
.M36—Man who wasn't there (Motion picture)
.M66—Mulholland Drive (Motion picture)
.Q37—Quantum of solace (Motion picture)
.R43—Red dragon (Motion picture)
.S57—Sin City (Motion picture)
.S64—Snakes on a plane (Motion picture)
.S94—Sweeney Todd (Motion picture)
.V24—V for vendetta (Motion picture)

5-1. RADIO PROGRAM MAIN ENTRIES AND CLASSIFICATION NUMBERS

INTRODUCTION

Books about specific radio programs are classed in PN1991.77. Each program receives a unique subject cutter derived from the first letter of the show's title; a second cutter for main entry completes the classification for particular books. The subject heading for each show is its name plus the appellation (Radio program).

5-2. MYSTERY RADIO PROGRAMS AND CLASSIFICATION NUMBERS

PN1991.77

.C43—CBS radio mystery theater (Radio program)
.E8—Escape (Radio program)
.G74—Green hornet (Radio program)
.M7—Mr. Keen, tracer of lost persons (Radio program)
.S97—Suspense (Radio program)

6-1. TELEVISION PROGRAM MAIN ENTRIES AND CLASSIFICATION NUMBERS

INTRODUCTION

Books about specific television programs are classed in PN1992.77. Each program receives a unique subject cutter derived from the first letter of the show's title; a second cutter for main entry completes the classification for particular books. The subject heading for each show is its name plus the appellation (Television program).

6-2. MYSTERY
TELEVISION PROGRAMS
AND CLASSIFICATION
NUMBERS

PN1992.77

.A215—24 (Television program)
.A28—Adventures of Sherlock Holmes (Television program)
.A479—Alfred Hitchcock presents (Television program)
.A923—Avengers (Television program)
.B343—Batman, the animated series (Television program)
.B352—Batman beyond (Television program)
.B383—Baywatch (Television program)
.B5925—Bones (Television program)
.B84—Buffy, the vampire slayer (Television program)
.C24—Cagny and Lacey (Television program)
.C46—Charlie's angels (Television program)
.C54—Closer (Television program)
.C583—Columbo (Television program)
.C698—Cracker (Television program)
.C75—CSI, crime scene investigation (Television program)
.D343—Dark shadows (Television program : 1966-1971)
.D345—Dark shadows (Television program : 1991)
.D495—Dexter (Television program)
.D6277—Dollhouse (Television program)
.F79—Fugitive (Television program)

.G4773—Get Smart (Television program)
.G553—Girl from U.N.C.L.E. (Television program)
.H346—Hardy boys (Television program)
.H62—Homicide--life on the street (Television program)
.H622—Honey West (Television program)
.I24—I led 3 lives (Television program)
.I27—I spy (Television program)
.I56—Inspector Morse (Television program)
.J87—Justice League (Television program)
.L395—Law & order (Television program)
.L3955—Law and order (Television program : Great Britain)
.L396—Law & order: Special Victims Unit (Television program)
.M2653—Man from U.N.C.L.E. (Television program)
.M525—Miami vice (Television program)
.M535—Midsomer murders (Television program)
.M574—Mission impossible (Television program)
.M595—Monk (Television program)
.M854—Murder, she wrote (Television program)
.M95—Mystery! (Television program)
.N55—Nikita (Television program)
.N96—NYPD blue (Television program)
.P4—Perry Mason (Television program)
.P67—Prime suspect (Television program)
.P7—Prisoner (Television program)
.R483—Return of the Man from U.N.C.L.E. (Television program)
.R553—Rockford files (Television program)
.S272—Saint (Television program)
    Secret agent (Television program)—see: Danger man
.S4—Danger man (Television program)
.S476—Shield (Television program)
.S66—Sopranos (Television program)
.T564—Thriller (Television program)
.T88—Twin Peaks (Television program)
.U58—Untouchables (Television program)
.V47—Veronica Mars (Television program)

.W53—Wire (Television program)

7-1. COMIC STRIP MAIN ENTRIES AND CLASSIFICATION NUMBERS

INTRODUCTION

Comic books, strips, etc., are classified into PN6728, cuttered by the first letter of the title, and cuttered again by main entry of the book. The subject heading is the name of the comic plus the appellation (Comic strip).

7-2. MYSTERY COMIC STRIPS AND CLASSIFICATION NUMBERS

PN1992.77

.A14—100 bullets (Comic strip)
.A2—Abie the agent (Comic strip)
.A35—Agent 13, the midnight avenger (Comic strip)
.A9—Avengers (Comic strip)
.B358—Batgirl (Comic strip)
.B36—Batman (Comic strip)
.C39—Catwoman (Comic strip)
.D47—Destroyer (Comic strip)
.D53—Dick Tracy (Comic strip)
.D564—Doc Savage (Comic strip)
.G26—Gangland (Comic strip)
.G65—Gotham Central (Comic strip)
.G654—Gotham City sirens (Comic strip)
.H56—Hitman: ace of killers (Comic strip)
.M359—Manhunter (Comic strip)
.R576—Robin (Comic strip)
.R583—Robocop (Comic strip)
.S34—Scene of the crime (Comic strip)
.S39—Secret agent X-9 (Comic strip)
.S68—Spy vs. spy (Comic strip)

ABOUT THE AUTHORS

EVA SORRELL is an Assistant Librarian at California State University, San Bernardino, where she works as the Principal Cataloger. She has a B.A. in Psychology from the University of California Riverside and an M.L.I.S. from the University of California Los Angeles. This is her first book. She lives in Highland, CA with her husband and two young daughters.

MICHAEL BURGESS served as a librarian at California State University, San Bernardino, for forty years, during the latter part of which he oversaw the Collection Development and Technical Services departments, and acted as Chief Cataloger. He currently works as a full-time professional writer and editor; his fiction titles are published under his pen name, Robert Reginald. You can find him at his website:

www.millefleurs.tv